Sixty Years of Scholarship:

The Department of Medical Education at the University of Illinois at Chicago College of Medicine (1959-2019)

Managing Editors
Yoon Soo Park
Alan Schwartz

Associate Editors
Michael Blackie
Jorge Girotti
Ilene Harris
Kristi Kirschner
Rachel Yudkowsky

Contributors
Georges Bordage
Raymond Curry
Marcia Edison
Laura Hirshfield
Timothy Murphy
Pilar Ortega
Christine Park
Janet Riddle
Leslie Sandlow
Sandra Sufian
Ara Tekian
Annette Valenta
Sandra Yingling

Commemorating the 60th Anniversary 1959 – 2019

MEDICAL EDUCATION COLLEGE OF MEDICINE

ISBN 978-0-578-22248-6

Published by the University of Illinois at Chicago Department of Medical Education
808 South Wood Street, Floor 9
Chicago, Illinois 60612
United States of America

All Rights Reserved

Original material in this book is © 2019 to the authors.

Reprinted material in this book is used by permission of the copyright holders. A complete list of copyright holders for each reprinted article can be found at the end of the book.

No part of the material protected by these copyright notices may be reproduced or utilized in any form or by any means, electronic or mechanical, including photocopy, recording, or by any information storage and retrieval system, without written permission from the copyright owner.

Contents

This book commemorates the 60th anniversary of the founding of the Department of Medical Education (DME) at the University of Illinois College of Medicine, one of the first offices of medical education and the longest continuously operating department of medical education in the world.

The 50th anniversary book, *Moving Medical Education Forward* (2009), details the Department's history and contains tributes to DME's eminent founders, George Miller and Christine McGuire, in addition to selections from their scholarship. It also contained articles selected by DME faculty.

In this 60th anniversary book, *Sixty Years of Scholarship* (2019), DME proudly continues the tradition by publishing selected articles from current DME faculty members who are helping move the field forward. Articles published in this book were selected by DME faculty to represent major aspects of their work; in many cases, these articles were co-authored with other DME faculty, adjunct faculty, learners, and alumni.

ACKNOWLEDGMENTS	v
FOREWORD	
Michael Amiridis, Chancellor, University of Illinois at Chicago	vii
Mark Rosenblatt, Executive Dean, University of Illinois College of Medicine	ix
INTRODUCTION	
Alan Schwartz, Interim Head, Department of Medical Education	1
PART I: Policy and Standards for the Health Professions Workforce	
Overview by Ilene Harris	5
Raymond Curry: Policy issues related to educating the future Israeli medical workforce: an international perspective. *Israel Journal of Health Policy Research*.	9
Marcia Edison: Implementing a STEMI system of care in urban Bangalore: rationale and study design for heart rescue India. *Contemporary Clinical Trials Communication*.	25
Ilene Harris (with DME coauthors Carol Kamin and Ara Tekian): The impact of accreditation on medical schools' processes. *Medical Education*.	31
Janet Riddle: Lessons from practice. *International Journal of Health Education*.	41

Alan Schwartz: Medical education practice-based research networks: facilitating collaborative research. *Medical Teacher.*   45

Annette Valenta: AMIA 2017 core competencies for applied health informatics education at the master's degree level. *Journal of Informatics in Health and Biomedicine.*   57

PART II: Advances in Assessment

Overview by Rachel Yudkowsky   69

Georges Bordage: The key-features approach to assess clinical decisions: validity evidence to date. *Advances in Health Sciences Education.*   71

Yoon Soo Park (with DME coauthors Janet Riddle and Ara Tekian): Validity evidence of resident competency ratings and the identification of problem residents. *Medical Education.*   103

Leslie Sandlow (with DME coauthors Steven Downing and Rachel Yudkowsky): Developing an institution-based assessment of resident communication and interpersonal skills. *Academic Medicine.*   113

Rachel Yudkowsky (with DME coauthors Janet Riddle and Georges Bordage): A hypothesis-driven physical examination learning and assessment procedure for medical students: initial validity evidence. *Medical Education.*   121

PART III: Selection Processes, Access, and Retention

Overview by Jorge Girotti   133

Jorge Girotti (with DME coauthor Joanna Michel): The urban medicine program: developing physician–leaders to serve underserved urban communities. *Academic Medicine.*   135

Pilar Ortega: Spanish language concordance in U.S. medical care: a multifaceted challenge and call to action. *Academic Medicine.*   145

Ara Tekian: A longitudinal study of the characteristics and performances of medical students and graduates from the Arab countries. *BMC Medical Education.*   151

Sandra Yingling (with DME coauthors Yoon Soo Park, Raymond Curry, and Jorge Girotti): Beyond cognitive measures: empirical evidence supporting holistic medical school admissions practices and professional identity formation. *MedEdPublish.*   159

PART IV: Bias Issues

Overview by Michael Blackie   171

Michael Blackie: Narrative intersectionality in caring for marginalized or disadvantaged patients: thinking beyond categories in medical education and care. *Academic Medicine.*   173

Laura Hirshfield (with DME coauthors Rachel Yudkowsky and Yoon Soo Park): Pre-medical majors in the humanities and social sciences: impact on communication skills and specialty choice. *Medical Education*. 179

Christine Park: Training induces cognitive bias: the case of a simulation-based emergency airway curriculum. *Simulation in Healthcare*. 189

PART V: Accommodation and Ethics

Overview by Kristi Kirschner 199

Kristi Kirschner (with DME coauthor Raymond Curry): Leading practices and future directions for technical standards in medical education. *Academic Medicine*. 201

Timothy Murphy: The ethics of helping transgender men and women have children. *Perspectives in Biology and Medicine*. 209

Sandra Sufian: Engaging in productive conversation: writing histories of medicine and disability in the Middle East and North Africa. *International Journal of Middle East Studies*. 225

Notes on DME Contributors 229

Past and Present DME 237

Faculty Citations and Credits 239

Acknowledgments

The Department of Medical Education is grateful for the support from Michael Amiridis, Mark Rosenblatt, and John Norcini. We also appreciate the editorial and production support from Rebecca Fiala.

Foreword

Michael Amiridis
Chancellor
University of Illinois at Chicago

At the University of Illinois at Chicago, the value of education advanced through scholarship and practice has been the cornerstone of our mission.

Our Department of Medical Education (DME) in the College of Medicine is a national and international leader – standing at the forefront of the science and implementation of health professions education, medical social sciences, and health humanities. DME was founded 60 years ago by pioneers and visionaries who knew the significance of medical education and has had a transformative impact across the world for six decades. This 60th anniversary gives us an opportunity to celebrate their success, and also to chart our course for many more decades to come.

At UIC, the international reputation of DME is a strength of our community and a legacy that we are obligated to honor and continue. In this regard, I am grateful to the faculty, staff, and students of the Department for their cutting-edge contributions to medical education with the ultimate goal of improving care of patients.

In the ensuing sections, I welcome readers to appreciate this impressive volume that celebrates the scholarship and contributions of DME. I am confident that we will thrive into many more decades of excellence through unparalleled vision, leadership, and teamwork that ignites the UIC spirit and impact throughout the world.

Foreword

Mark Rosenblatt
Executive Dean
University of Illinois College of Medicine

The Department of Medical Education (DME) at the University of Illinois – College of Medicine at Chicago has been setting standards for departments of medical education and health professions education research worldwide. The College of Medicine is proud of DME's achievements and the many historic milestones it has contributed to the field. Since its founding by George Miller and Christine McGuire in 1959, DME has been at the forefront of leadership and scholarship. It has most certainly been a vital and vibrant com-ponent of the UIC College of Medicine, most recently with its contribution to the College of Medicine's curricular transformation. DME's influence and work have extended beyond Chicago to urban and rural areas throughout the world.

On behalf of the College of Medicine, I extend my heartfelt congratulations to DME on

Introduction

Alan Schwartz
The Michael Reese Endowed Professor of Medical Education
Interim Head
Department of Medical Education
University of Illinois at Chicago

In the ten years since the publication of *Moving Medical Education Forward*, the 50th anniversary collection of scholarship from the faculty of the UIC Department of Medical Education, both the Department and the College of Medicine have met new challenges with vigor. There is much to celebrate, and this new collection again represents only a fraction of the scholarly output of the Department, as it seeks to advance the study and practice of education in the health professions.

The earlier volume began with an excerpt from *A History of the Department of Medical Education (DME) at the University of Illinois College of Medicine (UIC)* by then-faculty members Carol Kamin and Steven Downing. It traced the origins of DME—the longest continuously-operating Department of Medical Education in the world—from its establishment as the Office of Research in Medical Education (ORME) in 1959 by George Miller, Lawrence Fisher, and Christine McGuire. ORME set the model for medical education units through its tripartite mission, as Kamin and Downing[1] describe:

> At ORME, George Miller had a grand plan: First, he would work to improve medical education at his home institution; second, he would conduct research to help convince skeptical basic scientists and clinicians about the value-added by professional educators; and third, he would educate health care professionals to influence others. (p. 15)

These missions, and many of the historical events chronicled by Kamin and Downing in the transition from ORME to the Center for Educational Development (CED, 1970) to the Department of Medical Education (1987) have parallels in the current period.

Improving medical education locally: The UIC College of Medicine began a major curricular transformation in 2016, headed by Senior Associate Dean (and DME faculty member) Raymond Curry. Under the leadership of DME Head Ilene Harris, DME faculty members have been broadly and actively engaged in supporting the design and implementation of the new curriculum, in areas ranging from assessment to instruction to remediation. Health humanities and professionalism have been scholarly areas for the Department since the 1980's. Today, faculty members Timothy Murphy (philosophy), Sandra Sufian (history), Kristi Kirschner (ethics), Michael Blackie (literature), Laura Hirshfield (sociology), and Sandra Yingling (psychology) form the core of not only the Department's humanities and professionalism scholarship but also the College's curriculum for health humanities and professional identity formation. UIC's Hispanic Center of Excellence, one of DME's constituent units and represented in this volume by Jorge Girotti and Pilar Ortega, engaged in a variety of educational and research projects to enhance and support a pipeline for Hispanic physicians-in-training; in 2019, UIC trained more Hispanic physicians than any other U.S. medical school.

Education research: During the 1970's, DME (as CED) was instrumental in the formation of the Division I (Education in the Professions) of the American Educational Research Association (AERA). Today, DME faculty member Yoon Soo Park serves as the AERA Vice President for the Division, a position that other DME faculty members including Christine McGuire, William McGaghie, Ilene Harris, and Ara Tekian have also held (see Tekian and Harris's 2011 booklet *Coming of Age: Developing a Community of Educators in the Professions* for a full history of the Division).[2] Ilene Harris's tenure as Head from 2008-2019 was marked by an exceptional level of scholarly productivity, with thousands of presentations and publications by faculty and many prestigious grants, including several federally funded R01 and R01-equivalent grants and the National Board of Medical Examiners' Edward J. Stemmler Medical Education Fund Grant, which DME faculty members have received more often than any those of any other unit: 2018 (Laura Hirshfield, PI); 2014 (Matthew Lineberry, PI); 2009 (Rachel Yudkowsky, PI); 2007 (Alan Schwartz, PI); 2004 (Rachel Yudkowsky, PI); 2001 (Alan Schwartz, PI); and 1998 (Alan Schwartz, PI).

Developing educational leaders and scholars: In 1976, the Master of Health Professions Education (MHPE) degree, which had previously been awarded by the University of Illinois College of Education, became ORME's own graduate program. The MHPE remains a cornerstone of DME's educational programs, developing health professions faculty as leaders in their institutions and organizations and scholars contributing to the field. The Department also continues to have a strong international presence, thanks to the tireless effort of Director of International Programs Ara Tekian, with short- and long-term visiting fellows sojourning at DME and DME faculty providing expertise to newly created medical schools and other health professions units around the world. Since the 50th anniversary volume, DME has also assumed responsibility for UIC's Patient Safety Leadership programs, including the Master of Patient Safety Leadership (MPSL). As this book goes to press, under the leadership of DME faculty member Annette Valenta, the MPSL became one of the first four programs in the field to receive certification from the Commission on Accreditation of Healthcare Management Education. Finally, in 2010, DME began a new graduate program, a PhD in curriculum studies with a concentration in health professions education—as fate would have it, in collaboration with the UIC College of Education.

Since the publication of history in the 50th anniversary volume, Professors Kamin and Downing have both left DME, and there have been several other notable transitions. Department Head Leslie Sandlow retired in 2008, and Ilene Harris assumed the Headship, stepping down in 2019. Through their efforts, DME received its first Endowed Professorship in Medical Education, supported by the Michael Reese Research and Education Foundation, a descendent of the storied Michael Reese Hospital. Yoon Soo Park became Associate Head in 2019, when Alan Schwartz, the previous Associate Head, assumed the Interim Head position. Rachel Yudkowsky transitioned from Director of the Dr. Allan

L. and Mary L. Graham Clinical Performance Center (GCPC) and currently serves as Director of Graduate Studies. Christine Park was recruited jointly by DME and the Department of Anesthesiology as the new GCPC Director. Long-time faculty member Georges Bordage retired and was named Professor Emeritus in 2018. In addition, both Jorge Girotti, Director of the Hispanic Center of Excellence, and Annette Valenta, Director of Patient Safety Leadership Programs, retired in 2019. New Directors will soon join the Department to continue developing these important programs.

Miller's original mission continues to resonate at DME, as the innovations of the past ten years inform the study and practice of health professions education in the years to come.

References

1. Kamin C, Downing S. From: A History of the Department of Medical Education (DME) at the University of Illinois College of Medicine (UIC): Contributions to Moving the Field Forward. In: Schwartz A, editor. *Moving the Field Forward: Scholarship from the Department of Medical Education at the University of Illinois at Chicago.* Chicago: The University of Illinois at Chicago Department of Medical Education; 2009. p. 15-18.
2. Tekian A, Harris I, editors. *Coming of Age: Developing a Community of Educators in the Professions.* [New Orleans]: American Educational Research Association Division I; 2011. P. 74.

Part I: Policy Standards for the Health Professions Workforce

Overview

Ilene Harris
Professor, Department of Medical Education

In this section, we include papers that address policies and standards for various areas of the health professions workforce, such as education of the Israeli medical workforce; implementing a STEMI (ST-elevation myocardial infarction) system of care in urban Bangalore, India; the impact of accreditation on medical schools' quality-improvement processes; lessons learned about faculty development and the role of faculty developers; the role of medical education practice-based research networks in facilitating collaborative research; and core competencies for applied health informatics education at the master's degree level.

In their paper, "Policy issues related to educating the future Israeli medical workforce: An international perspective", Curry and colleagues indicate that a 2014 external review of medical schools in Israel identified policy issues of importance to the nation's health, including planning for a workforce that could meet the needs of Israel's population as well as enhancing coordination and efficiency of medical education across the continuum of education, while also addressing the financing of medical education. Israel's needs for primary care clinicians are increasing, due to growth and aging of the population and to the increasing prevalence of patients' chronic conditions at all ages. Curry et al indicate that the preclinical and clinical phases of Israeli undergraduate medical education are conducted in separate "silos" that are not well coordinated. In response, they proposed that the content of basic science education be made relevant to clinical medicine and research; that clinical experiences begin early in medical school and be as hands-on as possible; and that medical students and residents should acquire and demonstrate specific competencies. With the shift of medical care from hospitals to ambulatory settings, it is important to develop ambulatory teaching and learning environments. In Israel, integration of basic science and clinical education, development of earlier, more hands-on clinical experiences, and increased ambulatory and community-based medical education, will require new funding and partnerships between universities and the nation's health care delivery system.

In their paper, "Implementing a STEMI system of care in urban Bangalore: rationale and study design for heart rescue India", Edison, Prabhakar and Vanden Hoek, and their colleagues, indicate that a system of care, designed to measure and improve process measures, such as symptom recognition, emergency response, and hospital care, has the potential to reduce mortality and improve quality of life for patients with ST-elevation myocardial infarction (STEMI). The purpose of their paper is to document the methods and rationale for implementation and impact measurement of the Heart Rescue India project on STEMI morbidity and mortality in Bangalore.

In, "The impact of accreditation on medical schools' processes", Blouin, Tekian, Kamin, and Harris describe a study to evaluate the impact of accreditation, using an innovative marker: the processes implemented at medical schools as a result of accreditation. In this qualitative study, conducted in 2015-2016, we conducted interviews and focus groups discussions with college of medicine deans, undergraduate medical education deans, and faculty leaders at 13 of 17 Canadian medical schools to elicit perspectives about processes influenced by accreditation. The method of constant comparative analysis associated with grounded theory was used to generate themes of such processes, as well as themes of negative consequences. Nine themes representing processes reported as a result of accreditation were identified, related to: (i) governance, (ii) data collection and analysis, (iii) monitoring, (iv) documentation, (v) creation and revision of policies and procedures for continuous quality improvement, (vi) continuous quality improvement, (vii) faculty members' engagement, (viii) academic accountability, and (ix) curriculum reforms. Themes representing negative consequences of accreditation included: (i) costs, (ii) staff and faculty members' morale and feelings, (iii) school reputation, and (iv) standards. The identified processes, given their nature, appear likely to be associated with improvement of quality in medical education. These results help to justify the costs associated with accreditation.

In her paper, "Lessons from practice", Riddle describes lessons learned from serving as director and facilitator of a teaching scholars program at the University of Illinois at Chicago College of Medicine. She describes three lessons. First, faculty development is what participants choose to pursue to improve their teaching capabilities. Second, the improvement of teaching that is possible is influenced by participants' values, beliefs, and norms. Third, clinical teachers are seeking a community of like-minded colleagues.

In their paper, "Medical education practice-based research networks: facilitating collaborative research", Schwartz, Young, and Hicks, for APPD-LEARN, focus on the role of medical education practice-based research networks in facilitating collaborative research. Overall, research networks formalize multisite collaborations by establishing infrastructures that enable network members to participate in research, propose studies, and use study data to move the field forward. In this paper, the authors provide a definition of medical education practice-based research networks, a description of networks in existence in July 2014, and a case study of the emergence of one such network, the Association of Pediatric Program Directors Longitudinal Educational Assessment Research Network (APPD-LEARN). They searched for networks through a review of peer-reviewed literature and the worldwide web. They identified 15 research networks in medical schools founded since 2002, with membership ranging from 8 to 120 programs. Most networks of this kind focus on graduate medical education in primary care or emergency medicine specialties. The authors provide four recommendations for further development of medical education research networks: increasing faculty development, obtaining central resources, studying networks themselves, and developing networks of networks.

In their white paper, "AMIA 2017 core competencies for applied health informatics education at the master's degree level", Valenta and colleagues describe core competencies for applied health informatics at the master's degree level, as formulated by various committees of the American Medical Informatics Association (AMIA). This paper presents foundational domains of health informatics competencies, with examples of key aspects of competencies intended for curriculum development and accreditation quality assessment for graduate education in applied health informatics. Through a deliberative process, the AMIA Accreditation Committee (AAC) refined the work of a task force of the Health Informative Accreditation Council (HIAC), by establishing 10 foundational domains, with accompanying example statements of knowledge, skills, and attitudes that are components of competencies by which graduates from applied health informatics programs can be assessed at graduation. The AAC developed the domains for application across all the sub-disciplines represented by AMIA, ranging from translational bioinformatics to clinical and public health informatics, and spanning the spectrum from molecular to population levels of health and biomedicine. The authors indicate that this document will be periodically updated as part of the responsibility of the AAC, through continued study, education, and surveys of market trends.

INTEGRATIVE ARTICLE

Open Access

Policy issues related to educating the future Israeli medical workforce: an international perspective

Stephen C. Schoenbaum[1*], Peter Crome[2], Raymond H. Curry[3], Elliot S. Gershon[4], Shimon M. Glick[5], David R. Katz[6], Ora Paltiel[7] and Jo Shapiro[8]

Abstract

A 2014 external review of medical schools in Israel identified several issues of importance to the nation's health. This paper focuses on three inter-related policy-relevant topics: planning the physician and healthcare workforce to meet the needs of Israel's population in the 21st century; enhancing the coordination and efficiency of medical education across the continuum of education and training; and the financing of medical education. All three involve both education and health care delivery.

The physician workforce is aging and will need to be replenished. Several physician specialties have been in short supply, and some are being addressed through incentive programs. Israel's needs for primary care clinicians are increasing due to growth and aging of the population and to the increasing prevalence of chronic conditions at all ages. Attention to the structure and content of both undergraduate and graduate medical education and to aligning incentives will be required to address current and projected workforce shortage areas. Effective workforce planning depends upon data that can inform the development of appropriate policies and on recognition of the time lag between developing such policies and seeing the results of their implementation.

The preclinical and clinical phases of Israeli undergraduate medical education (medical school), the mandatory rotating internship (stáge), and graduate medical education (residency) are conducted as separate "silos" and not well coordinated. The content of basic science education should be relevant to clinical medicine and research. It should stimulate inquiry, scholarship, and lifelong learning. Clinical exposures should begin early and be as hands-on as possible. Medical students and residents should acquire specific competencies. With an increasing shift of medical care from hospitals to ambulatory settings, development of ambulatory teachers and learning environments is increasingly important. Objectives such as these will require development of new policies.

Undergraduate medical education (UME) in Israel is financed primarily through universities, and they receive funds through VATAT, an education-related entity. The integration of basic science and clinical education, development of earlier, more hands-on clinical experiences, and increased ambulatory and community-based medical education will demand new funding and operating partnerships between the universities and the health care delivery system. Additional financing policies will be needed to ensure the appropriate infrastructure and support for both educators and learners. If Israel develops collaborations between various government agencies such as the Ministries of Education, Health, and Finance, the universities, hospitals, and the sick funds (HMOs), it should be able to address successfully the challenges of the 21st century for the health professions and meet its population's needs.

Keywords: Medical education, Physician workforce planning, Health professions workforce planning, Financing medical education

---

* Correspondence: scs@scs-health.com
The views expressed in this manuscript are those of the authors and not necessarily of the authors' institutions, the Israeli Council for Higher Education, or its staff.
[1]Josiah Macy Jr. Foundation, 44 East 64th Street, New York, NY, USA
Full list of author information is available at the end of the article

© 2015 Schoenbaum et al. **Open Access** This article is distributed under the terms of the Creative Commons Attribution 4.0 International License (http://creativecommons.org/licenses/by/4.0), which permits unrestricted use, distribution, and reproduction in any medium, provided you give appropriate credit to the original author(s) and the source, provide a link to the Creative Commons license, and indicate if changes were made. The Creative Commons Public Domain Dedication waiver (http://creativecommons.org/publicdomain/zero/1.0/) applies to the data made available in this article, unless otherwise stated.

Introduction

The principal objective of medical education throughout the world is preparation of a competent workforce of highly skilled physicians who are prepared to handle the challenges they will encounter daily and are capable of responding to the changes in medical practice that inevitably will arise during their working careers.

The capacity of any nation to meet the health care needs of its population depends upon the specific policies and infrastructure that govern the education, postgraduate training, and support of its health care workforce, including physicians and other health care professionals. Since it takes at least 10 – 14 years to educate and train physicians, depending upon their specialty, development of a suitable national physician workforce requires a lot of forward thinking and coordination of resources. Unfortunately, most national governments manage education, health care, and other social services necessary to promote health through a variety of different agencies or ministries without any overarching coordinated workforce strategy or plan. Israel is no exception.

The authors of this paper were members of an *ad hoc* external committee appointed by the Israeli Council for Higher Education (CHE; Hebrew acronym = MALAG) to perform a review in 2014 of Israel's four accredited medical schools. The committee's General Report to the CHE has many recommendations related to a wide spectrum of school-specific, education-specific, and broad national policy issues.[1]

The committee, in writing this paper, recognizes that the Israeli health care system and medical education system have developed against a background of warfare and generations of high immigration. This has resulted in Israel's having a very large number of physicians coming from varied medical educational backgrounds, a large increase in the population to be served by the health system, and great diversity of the population. The committee members were struck by the fact that Israeli medicine had so rapidly reached an advanced stage, and that there were many similarities between the critical issues faced in Israel and those in the United Kingdom (U.K.) and the United States (U.S.), countries with much longer histories of development of their health care and education systems.

In the U.K., U.S., and Israel, there are issues involving the development and financing of the physician workforce. Three key issues are: workforce planning; enhancing the coordination and efficiency of medical education across the continuum of education and training; and the continual need to examine the financing of all the stages of medical education and training so that they best support development and deployment of the needed workforce. In Israel, these issues extend well beyond the purview of the CHE, the agency that commissioned our review of medical schools and formal reports. The collaborative solutions necessary to achieve more efficient and effective production of the Israeli physician workforce will need to involve a varied group of stakeholders including several government, public, and private entities. Given the small size of the country, the intimacy of the academic and practice environment, and the degree to which both the educational and health care systems are supported by government funding, the committee sees great opportunity to attain even better results in planning and developing Israel's national physician workforce.

Methodologic basis of this report

In 2014, a committee of eight senior physicians, who have all had wide experience in medical education and collectively have had extensive experience in areas such as clinical care, research, and management, was assembled by the CHE to perform a periodic review of the four older, accredited medical schools in Israel: Ben-Gurion University, Hebrew University Hadassah, Tel Aviv University, and the Technion. Reviews of these schools had occurred in 2000 and 2007. This, however, was the first review committee whose chair was not Israeli and whose membership consisted primarily of non-Israeli physicians. The eight person committee included four from the U.S., two from the U.K., and two from Israel. Although not part of the original charge to the committee, four members also made a brief advisory visit to the new Bar-Ilan medical school in the Galilee. All school visits took place between mid-February and early June, 2014.

In preparation for the committee's reviews, each of the medical schools produced an extensive self-evaluation report. The CHE specifies the format the schools are to use for the self-evaluation reports [1] and for the site visits. The required general categories of reporting are similar to those of the Liaison Committee on Medical Education (LCME) in the U.S. and cover the institutional setting, the teaching program (s) for an MD degree, admission of and services for students, faculty, and educational resources. The CHE also requires information on research, the self-evaluation process, and implementation of previous recommendations.

The LCME's standards for accreditation and reaccreditation of medical schools in the U.S. are explicit [2]. There is a detailed data collection instrument for the review survey [3], and the format of the survey reports is specified in detail [4]. Ultimately it is possible for the LCME to evaluate whether a school has "met" or "not met" each standard, and those determinations guide accreditation and re-accreditation decisions and remedial actions. In the U.K., the body responsible for accreditation and review of medical schools, the General Medical Council (GMC), also has an explicit set of outcomes and standards for UME that guides reviews and decisions [5]. The CHE does have a 12 page general set of standards for medical education in Israel and a general format for the review committee's report.[2] The CHE format for the school's self-evaluation report, however, is more loosely structured than the analogous LCME and GMC reports, particularly in expectations for the schools' data collection and reporting. Moreover the CHE does not specifically reaccredit a medical school, but reviews and votes upon the reports of the *ad hoc* committee. Accepted reports with their recommendations then serve as the basis for follow-up with the schools.

The members of the committee read the self-evaluation reports in advance of their meetings and then spent approximately one work week on each school's review, including a day of preparation, a three-day site visit, and a day developing an initial report including observations and recommendations. The site visits consisted of meetings with administration, faculty, and students with each school being allowed by the CHE to decide who the committee should meet within each category and what it should see. Additional writing and editing of the reports for each school was done remotely. The reports were submitted to the CHE which, in turn, distributed them to each school for reaction and response before they were presented to the Council.

The committee, informed by the reviews of each school and by the extensive prior experience of each committee member, also identified a large number of general, or national, issues that comprised the basis for the committee's General Report to the CHE. The general issues included: the organization and conduct of the medical study programs across the country; institutional policies and practices among the medical schools' parent universities; the health system in Israel and its interaction with the process of medical education; and a variety of other considerations of national importance.

This paper, written for a policy-making audience, has a section devoted to each of the three key issues mentioned above: workforce planning; enhancing the coordination and efficiency of medical education across the continuum of education and training; and financing medical education. Each section opens by referring to a table listing pertinent knowledge and observations of the committee.

Issues and commentary
Workforce planning

National planning and management of the physician workforce is "an important subset of overall health workforce planning and management, which contributes to a country's having an effective and efficient health care system." Nonetheless, it is "a multifaceted, difficult, and even controversial activity" [6]. Table 1 lists a number of the committee's findings and observations that relate to workforce planning.

Table 1 Observations and Knowledge Related to Workforce Planning

- Israel knows it has shortages of physicians in certain specialties.
- Israel knows it has shortages of nurses.
- The OECD has stated that the strength of the Israeli health system is its primary care infrastructure, has predicted a growing shortage of primary care physicians, and has challenged the educational system to address this.
- Unlike the U.S., Israel does not have a cadre of nurse practitioners to help substitute for physicians.
- Medical schools are geographically distributed through the country.
- To address both a shortage of physicians and distribution of practitioners, there is a new medical school in the periphery.
- There now are financial incentives in Israel for physicians in certain specialties to train and practice in the periphery.
- The Israeli government has been urging all the medical schools to increase their class size.
- The four older medical schools seem to set their own priorities for the types of physicians they produce.
- Other than having developed plans to increase class size, a process that is well underway, none of the four older medical schools gave a clear indication it was contributing to a detailed national workforce plan.
- All Israeli medical schools have MD-PhD programs and emphasize their interest in producing physician scientists and in attracting more medical students into those programs.
  - PhD's, including MD-PhD's are usually advised to take a postdoctoral fellowship abroad if they want to return to Israel in a faculty position.
  - There appear to be no guarantees that there will be faculty positions for all who complete MD-PhD programs and do postdoctoral fellowships.

Planning a national workforce for the future requires having good information on the current composition of the physician workforce and its dynamics, e.g., age distribution, regional distribution, entrants to the profession each year, emigration of physicians from the country, retirements, etc. It requires knowing how adequately the existing physician workforce meets current population needs; and it requires projection of future population needs. The process also requires an understanding of how the workforce might be supplied and whether there are alternatives to physician services.

In the U.K. the GMC maintains a register that records specialty, including primary care. Recently the GMC has introduced a re-registration process termed "revalidation".[3] Although the impact of this on planning of the future U.K. health care workforce is as yet unknown, the committee believes that the absence of physician re-registration information in Israel impedes its having as good information about its current physician workforce and activity as it would need, and could have, for a more robust workforce planning process.

Depending upon the way it crafts its policies, a country can vary the degree to which it educates its own physicians or imports them after they have studied medicine in other countries. In the U.S., U.K., and Israel, a significant percentage of practicing physicians have gone to medical school abroad. In the U.S. and U.K., approximately 25 % of practicing physicians have received their medical degree from schools in other countries. All physicians in the U.S., irrespective of where they went to medical school must pass the U.S. Medical Licensing Examination (USMLE) in order to apply for medical licenses. In addition, in order to apply for a medical license in the U.S., all international medical graduates must complete graduate medical education (residency) within the U.S., even if they already have undertaken graduate medical education in another country. In the U.S. approximately 20 % of international medical graduates, or five % of all U.S. practicing physicians, are Americans who studied abroad.

In Israel, data on newly licensed physicians show that in the years since 1995, over 50 % each year have studied medicine abroad [7]. But, whereas in the 1990s most of Israel's newly licensed international medical graduates were immigrants, now they are predominantly Israelis. In 2013, of 960 newly licensed physicians for whom country of origin and country of their UME were known, 14 % were immigrants, 43 % were Israelis who studied abroad, and only 43 % were graduates of Israeli medical schools. That was despite the fact that the number who were graduates of Israeli medical schools had already increased from approximately 300 per year in the years prior to 2008 to 400 per year by 2012 and 2013.

In the U.K., where most physicians and other health care workers either are employed by the NHS (National Health Service), or receive most of their revenue from it, there have been attempts at central planning of the physician workforce. In 2012, the Higher Education Funding Council for England (HEFCE) and the U.K. Department of Health published a review of medical and dental school intakes that included a review of what had happened following the third report of the Medical Workforce Standing Advisory Committee in 1997, and on this basis made recommendations for the next several years [8, 9]. In contrast to the U.S., the U.K. has a significantly larger primary care physician supply. Indeed general practitioners (GP's) are the backbone of the British NHS and in recent years have been well compensated.

At the present time, both Israel and the U.S. are attempting to increase the number of physicians who receive a medical degree from schools within the country. In the U.S., although there were no new medical schools between 1986 and 2001, as a result of a projected physician shortage, and without a government mandate, 17 new schools granting the MD degree have opened since 2002. Combined with increases in class size in some older medical schools, overall enrollment is projected to increase by 30 % from 2002 to 2017 [10]. The U.S. now has 141 accredited medical (MD-granting) schools and 30 accredited osteopathic medical schools. There are 38 schools in various stages of development.

In the U.K., several new medical schools and programs have opened in recent years including some that offer post-baccalaureate four-year programs. There are now 33 medical schools in the U.K. including nine that have opened since 2000.

In Israel, the government requested substantial increases in the size of the undergraduate student body in the medical schools and has fostered the development of the new Bar-Ilan medical school [11]. As noted above, the previously existing schools have responded to the government's request, and there has been an increase in the number of newly licensed graduates from Israeli medical schools [7]. Further increases are desired by the government and are planned by the schools. However, to handle the increased numbers of students, each of the schools has been concerned about the availability of clinical facilities for teaching, especially in hospitals. The schools also are concerned about having sufficient funds to meet a variety of needs associated with having larger numbers of students.

Across all three countries, despite increased numbers of medical students in existing and new schools, there are short supplies of various medical and surgical specialists, e.g., psychiatry and neurology in the U.S., emergency medicine in the U.K., and fields such as anesthesia, neonatology, and intensive care in Israel. In all three countries, there are growing shortages of primary care physicians, and we shall focus on that issue here.

The U.S. is known to have a higher ratio of specialists to primary care physicians than other developed countries and is widely believed to have a shortage of primary care physicians. Yet, data from the U.S. demonstrate that a locally higher primary care supply and a locally lower ratio of specialists to primary care physicians are associated with lower age-adjusted mortality and mortality from specific causes such as heart disease and cancer [12]. This has been a driver of efforts to increase the primary care supply.

The 2012 OECD report on health care quality in Israel [13] credited Israel "for shaping a strong primary health care system." It said, "At a time when all OECD countries are grappling with more patients living with a chronic disease, Israel's organization of primary health care services is geared towards supporting people who will live longer with more frequent health concerns". It went on to state: "Israel's ability to deliver health outcomes that are amongst the best in the OECD, despite spending less on health than most OECD countries, is attributable not only to a younger and healthier population, but also to the strengths of its primary care system."

The OECD report also noted a paradox - that one of the major factors helping to ensure the adequacy of the Israeli primary care workforce in recent decades is now a factor placing the future physician supply in jeopardy, particularly in the periphery. Many physicians in Israel, including many of the family physicians, entered in the wave of immigration from the former Soviet Union in the early 1990s and many are now beginning to retire. The entire physician workforce in Israel has been aging [14], and this is particularly the case in primary care [15]. In short, Israel, with an increasing prevalence of persons who have chronic conditions [16] as well as a growing and aging population, needs to make a concerted effort just to maintain, not to mention enhance, its primary care workforce [13, 15]. It will have to address the fact that a significant number of the immigrant physicians arrived after medical school. Accordingly, their replacement is likely to require further expansion and refocusing of undergraduate medical education (UME) and graduate medical education (GME) resources.

The external committee saw very little emphasis on undergraduate ambulatory and community-based medical education among the schools it visited, with the exception of Ben-Gurion University. Even there, as at the other medical schools, exposure to family medicine consists of a several week block in the sixth year, which is late for influencing specialty choices. In a survey of sixth-year students in Israeli schools at Hebrew University Hadassah School of Medicine and Ben-Gurion University, only 25 % felt that family medicine was an "interesting and challenging specialty"; and this was lower than for specialties currently considered to be in short supply in Israel, e.g., anesthesiology (43 %) and general surgery (62 %) [17].

Although review of the mandatory rotating internship (*stáge*) was not part of the official charge to the committee, our understanding is that it allows the option of electing, but does not mandate, a family medicine rotation. In 2011, Afek et al. recommended significant changes in graduate medical education [18]. They observed, "The practice of medicine has changed in the last decade. Physicians no longer work largely solo but are part of interdisciplinary medical teams, and patient cases are more complex, as they suffer from multiple diseases. ... There is also a shortage of physicians in Israel, as the number of new immigrant physicians has decreased over the last decade. Other medical professions and infrastructures are also lacking, including nurses, acute care hospital beds, intensive care beds and more." To address these issues, they proposed "cancelling the internship" and dividing the residency program into two stages: "Two years in general medicine, surgery, or pediatrics, and the second part in subspecialties such as pediatric surgery, neurology, gastroenterology, cardiology and others. An option to continue residency in general medicine, pediatrics, or surgery will also be possible and must be encouraged." If family medicine is added to the choices along with general medicine, general pediatrics, and general surgery, then restructuring GME along these lines could possibly be one way of increasing the supply of physicians in generalist fields.

The supply of all physicians, specialists and primary care, is relatively less in the periphery of Israel than in the center of the country [19], and the supply of specialists in the periphery has been even relatively lower than the supply of primary care physicians. There now are financial incentives to encourage taking residencies in the periphery and to practice in distressed specialty fields; but family medicine, despite the OECD Report, is not yet characterized as being a distressed specialty.

Any discussion of national workforce planning issues and primary care workforce supply should consider the potential contributions of non-physician clinicians. In the U.S. in 2010, there were approximately 209,000 practicing primary care physicians [20] out of a total of 850,000 licensed physicians [21]. In addition, there were 56,000 practicing primary care nurse practitioners and 30,000 practicing primary care physician assistants [22]. These non-physician clinicians add significantly to the supply of primary care services and mitigate the U.S. shortage of primary care physicians. Also, in the U.S., nurse practitioners, nurse anesthetists, other specialized nurses, and physician assistants take on roles that used to be performed primarily or exclusively by physicians. We do understand that Israel has a severe shortage of nurses, and only very recently, in the face of union opposition, has begun to develop advanced practice nursing.

In the U.S., the Patient Protection and Affordable Care Act (2010) includes several provisions that are expected to increase the supply of primary care physicians. These include increased reimbursement for primary care services, new slots for primary care residents, and expanded low-interest student loan programs for persons choosing a primary care field [23]. In the U.K. where there is currently a 9 % shortfall in the annual number of primary care physicians needed to maintain the present service, there is concern about recruitment of new primary care physicians. A task force established by Health Education England, a semi-independent governmental advisory body, and the Department of Health has made recommendations for achieving the needed number [24].

Thus, the current and growing primary care workforce supply shortage in Israel is not unique; but it does raise several national policy issues that directly or indirectly affect medical study programs. Though no one thing is in itself sufficient to solve the problem, there are several possibilities for making primary care more attractive and for enhancing the supply of primary care services. Undergraduate medical students need to encounter the subject early in their education; and they need exposure to enthusiastic role models, particularly ones who have been developed to be excellent teachers. In general, there needs to be increased emphasis on ambulatory and community-based medical education including during the internship (*stáge*) year. Financial incentives play a role, but there is also a need to invest in supportive infrastructure. In parallel, there should be an assessment of national primary care needs and the degree to which they are being met by physicians or can be met by other health professionals.

A comprehensive approach to developing the workforce of health professionals that Israel needs for the future and addressing existing and looming shortages will require the interaction and collaboration of multiple stakeholders, including government ministries and agencies. There will need to be clarity at the highest levels of government about who has the lead for the key pieces such as understanding the supply of, and demand for, the health professional workforce, setting policies that support development and retention of health professionals, and aligning the financing of health professions education and health care delivery.

Enhancing the coordination and efficiency of medical education across the continuum of physician education and training

It is important to consider how best to coordinate the several phases of education and training of a physician to meet workforce needs as effectively and efficiently as possible. The series of phases is often referred to as the continuum, trajectory, or arc of medical education. Relevant committee findings and observations are shown in Table 2.

Over 100 years ago, the Carnegie Foundation for the Advancement of Teaching published a book-length report by Abraham Flexner on medical education in the United States and Canada. It is known widely as "The Flexner Report" [25]; and it changed the nature of medical education in the U.S., Canada, and many other countries. It standardized the format into pre-clinical and clinical years and placed an emphasis on scientific knowledge as a basis for modern medicine and medical education. The idea that medical education should be grounded in relevant science and evidence is now taken as a given. But, over the years, it has become apparent that what was regarded as science at that time – biological and physical science - is a necessary but not sufficient basis for developing effective physicians.

In 2010, in commemoration of the 100th anniversary of the Flexner Report, the Carnegie Foundation published a book outlining the need for and steps to achieve "the next level of excellence" in medical education [26]. Importantly, the scope of the book includes not just medical school, or UME, but also residency, or GME. The authors of the 2010 report wrote, "There is a need to motivate continuous learning and improvement across the whole arc of medical training. Those who teach medical students and residents must choose whether to continue in the direction established over a hundred years ago or take a fundamentally different course, guided by contemporary innovation and new understanding about how people learn." The recommendations of the 2010 report do not reject the need for a strong science base, but rather are built on an understanding of the shortcomings of 20th century medical education efforts in an environment that is changing and expanding.

In the past, the education of medical students in basic science was mostly detached from its clinical applicability. Basic science courses were taught as separate subjects by highly accomplished, but clinically unsophisticated scientists; and learning in the clinical settings was often not informed by rapidly advancing knowledge in the basic sciences. Underrepresented in the curriculum were relevant aspects of social sciences - such as psychology, sociology and anthropology; statistical analysis and population-based thinking; and communication, human interrelationships, and principles of team management. Clinical experiences used to occur after the completion of the science courses and took place almost exclusively in hospitals; but today, more and more clinical care is being delivered in ambulatory settings including the patient's home. The past also emphasized acquiring, usually by rote learning, a large body of information on which the physician could depend. Today, with recognition that the rate of development of new knowledge keeps growing rapidly and with new tools such as the internet that can provide the latest information, it is even more essential than in the past that learners be prepared to acquire the knowledge they need, as they need it.

The 2010 Carnegie report took into account existing efforts to address these issues and built upon them. Its recommendations, addressed primarily to the U.S., include:

- Standardize learning outcomes and assess competencies over time.
- Strengthen connections between formal and experiential knowledge across the continuum of medical education.
- Incorporate more clinical experiences earlier in medical school.
- Provide more opportunities for knowledge-building later in medical school and throughout residency.
- Promote learners' ability to work collaboratively with other health professionals, such as medical assistants, nurses, pharmacists, physical therapists and social workers.

Table 2 Observations and Knowledge Related to Enhancing the Coordination and Efficiency of Medical Education across the Continuum of Physician Education and Training

- Successful applicants to medical schools in Israel must have top scores on the matriculation examinations given to all high school students.
- In addition, all medical schools in Israel also base their selection on an assessment of the applicant's humanistic qualities.
- The standard education of Israeli physicians consists of: three preclinical years; three clinical years; a one-year rotating internship (stáge) that must be completed before the MD degree is granted; and four or more years of residency, depending upon the specialty.
    - There also are relatively new four-year, undergraduate medical teaching programs for persons who already have a bachelors or advanced degree in the sciences.
- The course of study and training for an Israeli student who chooses to go into a primary care field such as family medicine or pediatrics, is at least as long as in the U.S.
    - By comparison, the U.S. student who has four years of college, has about three of those to pursue academic interests other than those required for medical school admission; whereas, the curriculum for the Israeli student is fully prescribed.
- In most Israeli schools there has been little integration of the basic sciences and clinical knowledge.
    - Students voiced strong complaints about the lack of relevance of what they were taught in the basic sciences to their future careers.
- The majority of undergraduate teaching, especially in the preclinical basic science curricula, is lecture-based.
    - On average, attendance at lectures is poor.
    - Faculty members report that Israeli medical students want to be "spoon-fed." Students report that they would prefer more interactive teaching.
- Almost all evaluation is done by multiple-choice question (MCQ) examinations.
    - Faculty report that given the numbers of students they must evaluate, they have no alternative to MCQs.
- Responsibility for the continuum/trajectory of physician education is divided.
    - Responsibility for undergraduate curricula rests within the universities.
    - Responsibility for the rotating internship (stáge) rests with the collective group of medical school deans, the Deans Forum, and the Israel Medical Association.
    - Responsibility for residency programs rests with the Israel Medical Association.
- The CHE performs a periodic external review of the undergraduate teaching programs.
    - This is not coordinated or integrated with review of the rotating internship (stáge), or review of graduate medical education programs.
- Israeli medical schools do not have an explicit set of competencies to guide curriculum development.
- Individual courses and clerkships in Israeli medical schools generally do not have specific learning objectives to form the basis for student and faculty accountability.
- The majority of clinical education in Israel has been in hospital settings.
    - Increasingly health care delivery is occurring in ambulatory settings.

Table 2 Observations and Knowledge Related to Enhancing the Coordination and Efficiency of Medical Education across the Continuum of Physician Education and Training *(Continued)*

- All medical schools report scarcity of hospital resources for teaching, especially as class sizes are increasing in response to government requests.
- Ambulatory medical education is occurring increasingly in the U.S. and U.K.
- Ambulatory education requires facilities suitable for teaching and learning, faculty development, and appropriate incentives to engage the faculty.
- The committee did observe teaching of undergraduate medical students in two clinics jointly developed by Clalit and Ben-Gurion University.

- Interprofessional education (IPE) is important for preparing learners to practice effectively in teams.
    - IPE is occurring in most schools in the U.S. and U.K.
    - IPE is occurring at only one university in Israel.
- Promotions for clinical faculty are generally based on research criteria similar to those for pre-clinical faculty.
    - Teaching ability, though considered in promotions, is not a deciding criterion.
    - Many students have a job while in medical school; and it is common for students to leave their clinical clerkships in mid-afternoon in order to work.

- Support learners' responsibility for quality of care, team performance and their own learning while providing skilled supervision.
- Make professional formation an explicit area of focus in medical education through strategies such as formal instruction in ethics and reflective practice, exploration of the role of the physician-citizen and establishment of more supportive learning environments.
- Cultivate a spirit of inquiry and improvement in learners and in health care teams; this spirit supports both innovations in daily practice that translate into better service to patients, system improvements and improved patient outcomes as well as the development of larger research agendas, new discoveries, and knowledge building.
- Be more intentional about selection, development and support of teachers and medical educators.

In its review, our committee observed that the original Flexnerian model had been incorporated into Israeli medical education, but the recommendations of the new 2010 Carnegie Report that are being adopted in the U.S. and U.K. had yet to be introduced.

The external committee found that in most of the Israeli schools there remains a sharp separation between pre-clinical and clinical education. These two components of UME are regarded as separate "silos". The committee learned that the schools, despite some specific positive efforts, generally have not organized their preclinical education to establish clearly that the material being taught in the basic sciences is relevant to clinical medicine. Furthermore, at some of the schools, basic scientists with junior faculty appointments reported being called on to teach subjects that they do not feel qualified to teach.

The predominant methods used for pre-clinical teaching in Israel do not promote engagement of medical students. Faculty consider lectures to be an efficient way for a limited number of teachers to handle a large and increasing number of students; and almost all the preclinical teaching consists of frontal lectures. In a few instances, case studies and problem-solving were being incorporated into courses. This approach was associated with both student and educator enthusiasm. It was, however, the exception.

In other countries, such as the U.S. and U.K., an increasing percentage of preclinical studies have been, or are being, converted to active learning vs. traditional lectures. Nara, et al., who visited 35 medical schools in 12 countries around the world, addressed this subject in a 2011 report [27]: "Formally, the knowledge of medicine has been taught by teachers through lectures in a large theater. Students have learned mainly medical practice by observation at the outpatients' clinic and ward. Although these education methods play important roles even at present, most medical schools have recently introduced new education methods to promote clinical training for medical students. Students get a large amount of recent medical knowledge by tutorial system such as problem-based learning and team-based learning. For this purpose, an e-learning system has been developed in most medical schools."

Nara and his colleagues also observed that "Integrated courses [combining] basic medicine and clinical medicine have been introduced in many medical schools in the world. For example, students simultaneously learn basic bacteriology and clinical infectious disease at the same lecture or tutorial." In the U.S. and U.K. there are some very interesting efforts to introduce learning experiences in clinical settings early in the course of study [28] and to evaluate the effects of early clinical experiences [29].

In their site visits to medical schools around the world, Nara et al. noted that clinical education involves having "students belong to the medical team as staff and do medical practice under the supervision of attendants." They further observed that "this clinical clerkship system is most advanced in the U.S. and Canada [27]."

The committee's understanding was that in Israel meaningful clinical experiences and clinical engagement generally began late in UME. There appeared to be many more small group lecture sessions in the clinical clerkships and relatively fewer direct clinical experiences than in the U.S. and U.K. While some of the part-time work that many Israeli students engage in can provide clinical experiences, such jobs are not uniformly available. The jobs that are available are not routinely and purposefully integrated with their curriculum and monitored appropriately. Furthermore, in the clinical years, we were told that it was common for Israeli students to leave their organized clinical placements in mid-afternoon for their jobs. This limits the degree that students could participate in the continuing clinical care of patients and be considered, as students are in the U.S., members of the clinical team caring for a specific set of patients.

It is very important to note the emphasis throughout the 2010 Carnegie Report recommendations on the entire continuum, arc, or trajectory of medical education from selection and matriculation of students to development of competent and professional physicians. This emphasis is aimed at developing a suitable cadre of physicians more effectively and efficiently. To do so, it is essential to coordinate across the settings of medical education and clinical care, to build competence in a stepwise fashion, and to ensure that essential competencies such as professionalism and capacity for lifelong learning are emphasized at all times in all settings.

In other countries there is a growing emphasis on ambulatory and community-based medical education. In Israel, the enlarging undergraduate class sizes in response to government requests have led to great concerns by the medical schools about limited clinical resources for teaching. Certainly there are limited hospital resources, but Israeli medical schools appear to over-emphasize the need for hospital-based clinical education and under-emphasize ambulatory and community-based education.

Our findings raise several policy-relevant issues:

Even though teaching is a requirement for appointments and promotions in Israeli faculties of medicine, the primary criterion is scholarship as defined by publications in scientific and medical journals, not by teaching or clinical program innovations. This contrasts with a trend to broaden the definition of scholarship in U.S. medical schools. Even highly reputed research universities such as Harvard University and the University of Chicago have developed a more inclusive definition of scholarship.[4] At Harvard, an area of excellence is chosen by each faculty member. Those who seek promotion in the teaching and educational leadership area must demonstrate a progressively broader reputation for leadership – ranging from local to regional to national and international – as well as scholarship. Scholarship may include: "publication of original research, reviews, and chapters; educational material in print or other media such as syllabi, curricula, web-based training modules and courses; and/or, educational methods, policy statements, and assessment tools developed".

Although there have been resemblances between the situations in the U.K. and Israel, the U.K. situation is evolving. In the U.K., teaching and education domains have been introduced recently into the regulatory framework related to promotions, and can be incorporated into the documentation required for re-registration.[5] Tackling the question of how to handle and reconcile tensions between clinical service needs, education and training requirements, and innovation and research, remains an issue that is critical to the future of academic medicine [30]. If Israeli clinical teachers had appropriate incentives to assume teaching responsibilities not only in clinical settings but also in the earliest phases of medical education, it would then be possible to integrate better the current pre-clinical and clinical phases of education of Israeli physicians.

There is an opportunity to establish national policies and practices that could lead to more efficient and effective medical teaching using currently available technologies and approaches. For example, the committee felt that lectures on the same subjects need not be given separately at each of the medical schools or at each of the teaching hospitals. To the extent that oral didactic materials are needed, the most capable teachers could deliver polished lectures that could be recorded and accessed electronically by students at each school. The presentations could be updated periodically. A central resource could be established to do the recording, editing, and maintenance of such material. Online availability of uniformly excellent oral and written didactic material would enable teaching to occur in "flipped classroom" settings[6] or other forms of active learning.[7]

An important reason for fostering more active learning in Israeli medical education is stimulating a sense of inquiry and problem solving. Both of these are essential for life-long learning. Lectures are not as effective as active learning methods in stimulating inquiry in the students [31]. To make the transition from lecturing to active learning, especially with large classes, there will need to be extensive faculty development in each of the schools. Central resources could be developed to support faculty development across the country. The new national organization for persons interested in medical education could facilitate improvements in educational practices and scholarship if it is appropriately supported.[8] This new central resource might also be useful in developing a national set of competencies that could guide curriculum development in each of the medical schools as is now occurring in the U.S. [32].

Promoting active learning will not only enable physicians to benefit their patients as new knowledge is accumulated during their years of practice, but also may stimulate more Israeli medical students, residents, and physicians to engage in all forms of research and inquiry. Lectures have been shown not to be the most effective way to foster a spirit of inquiry, and they are out-of-step with traditional graduate study, with its emphasis on individual inquiry and small-group seminars. Each medical school stated the desire to develop more MD-PhDs. That is more likely to occur if the entire educational process of medical students stimulates more inquiry. Similarly, medical students are more likely to develop lifelong learning skills if their teaching program, starting at the earliest stage, consistently stimulates inquiry.

Simulation provides an opportunity for learners to develop competence in both cognitive and technical skills, and the ability to work in teams in an environment that is safe for them and for patients. In the U.S., in pre-licensure nursing education, a ten-center collaborative study has shown that simulation can replace as much as 25–50 % of clinical hours [33]. Indeed, simulation centers are nearly universal in U.S. and U.K. academic medical centers; and almost all medical students in the U.S. have multiple experiences involving simulation [34]. The Israel Center for Medical Simulation (MSR) based at Sheba Hospital is internationally recognized for its excellence. It has programs for physicians including the national mandatory interns' workshop, and the national board examinations in anesthesia and emergency medicine. Its activities provide a model for having a centralized UME resource. MSR and the Simultech Center at Meir Hospital are used to some extent in medical student teaching and faculty development at Tel Aviv University, but otherwise there is little utilization of clinical simulation in UME in Israel.

The development of ambulatory and community-based teaching should be central to coordination across the trajectory of medical education. This partly involves creating appropriate incentives for faculty in ambulatory and community-based settings and faculty development programs. It also requires developing the physical facilities so that they are appropriate for both efficient clinical care and effective teaching. The committee did observe teaching of undergraduate medical students in two clinics that have been developed jointly by Clalit Health Services and Ben-Gurion University; and these clinics demonstrate the possibility of collaborative development of ambulatory medical educational facilities in Israel.

Yet another issue is whether Israel can move from time-based to competence-based curricula. Currently, students entering medicine spend three preclinical years, three clinical years, one internship year, and at least four years of residency depending upon the specialty. This is a time-based curriculum. In contrast, a competence-based curriculum would specify levels of competence, or milestones, for each of several competencies that a physician was expected to gain but allow the time in which the learner acquired the competencies to vary [35, 36]. A competence-based approach opens new possibilities since learners will acquire basic competencies or reach successively higher levels of competence at different rates. At least in theory, the time a learner spends in each phase of the education and training process can be variable – longer or shorter than the currently allotted time. Israel already allows flexibility in the start date for internship (*stáge*) that may facilitate its moving to a competence-based curriculum in which the time for UME varies with the learner's ability to acquire necessary competencies. Also, with a competence-based curriculum it becomes possible to guarantee to the population that each physician who emerges from a training program meets high standards of competence. And, even if the duration of the study program remains fixed, a competence-based curriculum should permit learners who reach acceptable levels of a competence before the allotted time is up either to acquire mastery in that area or to work on acquiring additional areas of competence.

The external committee was asked to look only at UME. In the U.K., the importance of the continuum of development of a physician from entry as an undergraduate through internship and residency into the career-long phase of continuing professional development has been recognized very recently in a decision that the GMC, a regulatory body, should be responsible for evaluating and monitoring all the phases [37]. The external committee believes that a national review from such a perspective in Israel could provide valuable lessons and lead to more effective and efficient development and maintenance of a competent physician workforce. The individual components of the review need not all be the responsibility of one committee; but oversight of the review components and their coordination could be handled by one group. If the individual component reviews were highly structured, the coordinating group could synthesize them readily.

Financing of medical education

Financing of medical education generally involves a number of policy considerations and decisions. These relate in part to whether medical education is considered a public good; in part to the fact that the various stages in the education and training of a physician that need coordination might have different financing mechanisms; and in part to the fact that the education and professional preparation of physicians and other health professionals occurs in clinical settings as well as in traditional educational institutions. This contrasts with the education of most other professionals, scientists, and scholars. Not surprisingly, different countries take different approaches to these issues.

In the U.S., UME occurs in several types of medical schools including private medical schools with high tuitions, state medical schools with somewhat lower tuitions, and one military medical school, the Uniformed Services University of the Health Sciences, where tuition is waived in consideration for several years' military service. Students in all civilian medical schools are eligible for a variety of loans and some need-based scholarships. A large percentage of graduating medical students have acquired a significant amount of debt due to loans during both their college and medical school years [38]. During the GME years, residents receive a salary. It is lower than it might be if one were simply paying for the medical services delivered by the residents since there is not just service but also an educational component. A significant amount of the funding to academic health centers (AHCs) to support their residency programs comes from the U.S. federal government through the Medicare program. The complex and controversial financing of GME through the national Medicare program that is the major payer for the health care of older Americans raises difficult questions about the specific residency programs supported, the adequacy of support, and the sources of support [39, 40].

Higher education funding in both the U.K. and Israel derives primarily from two sources: a central funding organization that gets its money from the government; and student tuitions. In the U.K., HEFCE funds undergraduate medical and dental training jointly with the NHS. HEFCE support consists of a grant that is part of the annual funding allocations to each university. It is calculated on the basis of the number of medical and dental students in each medical and dental school; and those numbers are determined by a target for each school.[9]

In addition, students may be eligible initially for student loans and later for scholarships to help support tuition fees. In the first four years of the standard five-year UME curriculum, students can apply to a government organization, Student Finance England.[10] From year five, tuition fees can be paid by the NHS Student Bursary Scheme, a scholarship program. Students can apply for a means-tested NHS scholarship "to cover maintenance costs and a reduced maintenance loan from Student Finance England."[11] There is also the possibility that students who apply will receive a small non-means-tested scholarship award.

The committee's findings and observations with respect to financing of medical education in Israel are shown in Table 3. The principal funding stream for UME in Israel is determined by VATAT, the planning and budget committee of the CHE. VATAT is affiliated with the Ministry of Education; and it distributes the funds for higher education to the universities. In turn, the universities are then responsible for distributing the funds to their various faculties. This component of the overall financing of medical education in Israel at the level of the university is structurally similar to that in the U.K. However, as noted above, in the U.K. there is shared funding of the award to the university from the usual source of funding for higher education (HEFCE) and the NHS, the major funder and provider of health care delivery services.

Israeli universities do charge tuition, and the tuition has been rising. Annual tuition fees in Israeli medical schools (approximately 14,000 shekels = 3,650 dollars) are higher than in Europe (approximately 500 Euros = 560 dollars). In the U.K., annual tuition is higher than elsewhere in Europe (9,000 pounds = 14,100 dollars); but tuition in both Israel and the U.K. is much lower than in U.S. medical schools which average over 31,000 dollars at public universities and over 53,000 dollars at private universities. Students in the U.S. have school responsibilities that do not permit significant paid work; and they do accumulate very large levels of debt by the time they graduate medical school. In 2014, 84 % of graduating U.S. medical students had debts reflecting their college and medical school expenses; and the average indebtedness for those students with debt was 180,000 dollars [41]. Israel, however, unlike the U.S., many European countries, and the U.K., does not have significant student-loan programs [42]. Israeli students report that tuition charges and living expenses are major reasons for their needing to take part-time jobs during the course of UME despite financial support from their parents.

In Israel a university faculty appointment carries monetary benefits such as sabbaticals and travel funds. In consequence, a faculty appointment represents a financial commitment for the universities. The basic science faculty members are all employed by the universities and accordingly receive university appointments. Young faculty members are expected to do research and teaching. Assuming the university has chosen persons whose research is productive, those faculty members will be promoted within the university as their careers develop. In effect, all that has been built into the VATAT funding formula for the university. In contrast, the clinical teachers are employed by the health system, not generally by the university. Physicians, unlike PhDs, generally do not get salary support for doing research; but in order to be eligible for university appointments and promotions they still are expected by the universities to have done and published research. Thus, they have to do research during uncompensated time, often nights and weekends. And, were the universities to have a more inclusive definition of scholarship that allowed many more clinical teachers to be eligible for appointments and promotions (see above), then the universities would have to make a financial commitment to a group of people they currently do not support. The funds would need to come either from universities themselves or from funds allocated to the delivery system. In either case, there currently are no funds from either source; and the majority of clinical teachers in Israel do not have a university appointment. This is a disincentive to clinicians engaging in medical school teaching during the pre-clinical years or increasing their teaching commitments in the clinical years.

There are financial implications to providing more ambulatory-based clinical education. Teaching undergraduates and even residents in the early years of GME

Table 3 Observations and Knowledge Related to Financing of Medical Education

- The government of Israel supports higher education, including medical education and other health professions education, through a separate entity called VATAT.
- Funding goes directly to universities and colleges. Even though it is based upon the educational programs of those institutions, the distribution of it within the institutions is a local responsibility.
- In the first decade of the 21st century there was a cutback in funding
    - In the second decade, there has been restoration of some of the funds.
    - Each medical school expressed concern about the number of faculty positions for which it had funding, particularly basic science faculty.
- Three Israeli medical schools have four-year English language programs for non-Israelis with prior baccalaureate degrees that have high tuitions.
    - These programs share faculty with the Hebrew language programs.
    - English-language programs produce significant revenue for the university.
- Schools have understandable concerns that development of ambulatory medical education will require significant financial resources that do not currently exist.
- Promotions for clinical faculty are generally based on research criteria (see Table 2).
    - The majority of clinical teachers do not have any university appointment.
- Academic promotions to senior faculty positions in Israeli universities carry financial benefits including supported sabbatical time and supported meeting travel.
    - Most clinical teachers work for the health system.
    - Universities are expected to fund the benefits associated with academic promotions.
- Students reported needing to work while in medical school to gain necessary income to support family obligations or the high cost of living in some areas.
- The support for the PhD component of MD-PhD programs tends to be short (2–4 years).
    - It is difficult to take on an important and challenging research project when supported research time is short.

in ambulatory settings is known to reduce the clinical productivity of the faculty during the time when they are teaching. Only in the later years of GME do residents usually have the capability of contributing to overall clinical productivity. Thus, if clinicians working in the ambulatory sector who are being paid almost exclusively to be clinically productive are to become more involved in clinical teaching, there will need to be a source of financial support for that teaching. An increase in ambulatory and community-based teaching also involves the need for capital funds. It will require upgrading facilities so that there is space for learners and for related teaching activities. Both this capital expense and the benefits it could provide should be considered against the costs and benefits of expanding hospital facilities and hospital-based clinical teaching.

In light of VATAT's current practice of only providing funding to each individual university, developing and sustaining central resources that can be shared by all the medical schools requires all of the educational institutions to agree jointly to equitable funding for each resource. An alternative would be to supplement the current arrangement with a central source of funding for shared resources and developing a process for planning and allocating funds to the highest priorities.

MD-PhD programs are important for developing physician researchers. Though there is some variation, in the majority of Israeli medical schools a student enrolled in an MD-PhD program can receive funding for doing research for only a relatively short period. It has been as short as two years, although three is more common, and sometimes it is possible to extend to four years. In the U.S., support for the research of MD-PhD students is generally four years and can be longer, particularly if the trainee and his/her mentor obtain grant support from one of several sources including pre-doctoral fellowships from the National Institutes of Health.[12] The committee believes that an expectation of a shorter period of dedicated funding for research can lead to the PhD projects of MD-PhD students being less ambitious than they should be to develop a highly competent investigator and to projects that would be less ambitious than for other doctoral candidates. Also, in Israel, the dual degree student who cannot complete the work in the dedicated research time must continue to spend considerable time on his/her research while attempting to gain clinical experience. This is suboptimal for developing a highly competent MD and PhD. Addressing it would require having sufficient sources of funds for the PhD portion of MD-PhD programs.

Three medical schools (Ben-Gurion University, the Technion, and Tel Aviv University) have four-year English language medical study programs. These programs provide the universities with substantial tuition revenue that complements VATAT funding. With the government's desire that the Hebrew-language medical school class sizes increase to accommodate national needs, the nation's hospital resources for teaching are overburdened. Were the English language programs either to be reduced or eliminated to free up some of the hospital teaching resources, there would be a need for alternate funding sources to replace present tuition revenues. Hebrew University, though it does not have an English language program, appears to face a similar clinical resource strain. It has 60 students per year in the military medicine (Tzameret) program, funded by the military, and the smallest number of affiliated hospital beds per medical student [43].

An important first step for Israel would to understand that medical education raises the many financing issues above. A next step would be to establish a collaborative process to address them. It is likely that the process would involve several relevant government ministries and agencies, with input from educational institutions, the sick funds (HMOs), and health care delivery organizations. The distribution of funds for teaching between the universities and the clinical facilities with which they are affiliated seems to have been a contentious issue in the past [43], and will need to be addressed further going forward.

Additional discussion and conclusions

We believe that Israel needs to reform its medical education system to meet the needs of its population for the 21st century. It will be essential to determine workforce needs and examine the capacity of Israel's medical schools and health care delivery system to develop the number of physicians the country needs. They must be developed effectively and efficiently across the entire trajectory of education and training. Israel's primary care workforce needs to be augmented in order to sustain the successes recently praised by the OECD [13]; and at the same time Israel must produce appropriate numbers and types of competent clinical specialists. Physician-researchers, physician-managers, and public health physicians are all necessary too, and they add value to the nation. Different universities may, due to their particular strengths, produce more of one type of physician than the others, e.g., MD-PhDs; but in a small country no university should be allowed to decide unilaterally to produce a preponderance of one type of physician. This follows both from an obligation to meet national needs and from the fact that the major source of funding is governmental.

Likely reforms within UME include: adopting interactive learning methods and competence-based education; providing earlier exposure to clinical medicine and more hands-on experiences; increasing significantly the use of ambulatory and community-based clinical facilities for teaching; and ensuring that all physicians will have excellent life-long learning skills to cope with the pace of change that is occurring in medicine and is expected to continue.

We definitely believe that Israel can develop an excellent and efficient mechanism for educating the physicians it needs. Israel has the advantage of having a small number of medical schools and a limited number of clinical facilities that will require coordination. It also has the potential advantage of government being the major source of funds both for education and clinical care. Yet, Israel will need to bring into balance the traditional values of higher education institutions and health care delivery organizations. Universities are legitimately concerned about academic freedom and the importance of scholarship. Clinical facilities are legitimately concerned about providing excellent care to their patients. Each type of institution also has legitimate concerns about financial solvency, a pre-requisite for achieving its major mission. Since both the universities and health care delivery system are currently feeling substantial financial pressures, ensuring that the sources of funds to ensure development of the workforce that Israel needs are adequate will require a collaborative effort involving the institutions and their current and potential funders.

We know that Israel was able to prepare an excellent cadre of physicians for the needs of the 20th century. If Israel does develop collaborations between various government agencies such as the Ministries of Education, Health, and Finance, the universities, hospitals, and the sick funds (HMOs), it should be able to address successfully the challenges of the 21st century for the health professions and meet its population's needs.

Endnotes

[1] The external committee submitted its General Report to the CHE on August 19, 2014. It was discussed by a subcommittee of the Council on December 16, 2014, and accepted by the Council on February 10, 2015, marking a formal end of the *ad hoc* committee.

[2] These documents were supplied to the committee, but are not posted on the CHE web site.

[3] See: www.gmc-uk.org/doctors/revalidation.asp

[4] As examples see the criteria for promotion at Harvard Medical School and the University of Chicago Pritzker School of Medicine: Harvard - facultypromotions.hms.harvard.edu/promotions.pdf; Chicago - https://webshare.uchicago.edu/users/vvv1/Public/Pathways_pdf.pdf

[5] www.gmc-uk.org/doctors/revalidation.asp

[6] "Flipped classroom is a form of blended learning in which students learn content online by watching video lectures, usually at home, and homework is done in class with teachers and students discussing questions and solving problems. Teacher interaction with students is more personalized - guidance instead of lecturing." See: http://en.wikipedia.org/wiki/Flipped_classroom

[7] There are a variety of sources of information on active learning. For instance, see: web.calstatela.edu/dept/chem/chem2/Active/ for definitions, techniques, and references on active learning.

[8] The new organization, called HEALER, had its first national meeting in September, 2014.

[9] See: http://www.hefce.ac.uk/lt/Healthcare/hefcerole/

[10] See: https://www.gov.uk/student-finance/overview

[11] See: www.nhscareers.nhs.uk/explore-by-career/doctors/training-to-become-a-doctor/undergraduate-medical-education/financial-support-for-students-on-degree-courses-in-medicine/

[12] See: https://www.aamc.org/students/research/mdphd/financial_md-phd/

Competing interests

All eight authors were members of the *ad hoc* external committee appointed by the CHE to perform a review in 2014 of Israel's four accredited medical schools. The six members of the committee who were non-Israelis reviewed all four schools. SG and OP are members of the faculty of an Israeli medical school and OP is related to a faculty member with an administrative role at a second school. Therefore, OP was not part of the review of two schools and SG was not part of the review of one school due to potential conflict of interest. They did not participate in the *ad hoc* committee's reports to CHE about those specific schools. However, although SG and OP did not participate in 1-2 individual school reviews, no author had a competing interest in the development of this manuscript concerning national issues affecting medical education in Israel.

Authors' contribution

All members of the *ad hoc* committee contributed to the group's General Report to the CHE and to the discussions that formed the basis for this paper about national issues affecting medical education. Although SCS took the lead in drafting the manuscript and its revisions, all of the committee members made substantial substantive contributions to the manuscript and its revisions.

Authors' information

Peter Crome MD PhD DSc FRCP FFPM is Professor Emeritus at Keele University, an Honorary Professor at University College London and Honorary Consultant at Royal Free Hospital. A geriatrician, internist and clinical pharmacologist he has served as Head of the Medical School at Keele and President of the British Geriatrics Society. He presently serves as Chair of the National Audit of Dementia in General Hospitals and as a member of a NICE (National Institute for Health Care Excellence) Technology Appraisal Committee. He is co-editor of Substance Use in Older People (Wiley, 2015).
Raymond H. Curry, MD, FACP is senior associate dean for educational affairs at the University of Illinois College of Medicine, and clinical professor of medicine and medical education at the University of Illinois at Chicago. He previously served as vice dean for education at Northwestern University Feinberg School of Medicine (1998–2014). Dr. Curry has served as an accreditation survey team member for the Liaison Committee on Medical Education for over twenty years. He has also been a consultant on curriculum development and accreditation issues for medical schools in Germany and Mexico as well as for several schools in the United States.
Elliot S. Gershon, MD is Foundations Fund Professor of Psychiatry and Human Genetics and a member of the degree-granting Committee on Neurobiology, University of Chicago, where he formerly was Chairman, Department of Psychiatry (1998–2003). He also is Chairman of the National Institute for Psychobiology in Israel (since 2003). From 1984–1998 he was Chief of the Clinical Neurogenetics Branch of the National Institute of Mental Health (U.S.), and his major research interests continue to be in genetics

and genomics of the human brain, and in genetics of major mental disorders and of newly developed phenotypic classifications for mental disorders.

Shimon M. Glick, MD was a founding member of the Faculty of Medicine at Ben Gurion University of the Negev and is professor of medicine (emeritus-active). He is a former Dean of the Faculty of Health Sciences, Ben Gurion University of the Negev and Director of the Moshe Prywes Center of Medical Education. He also was formerly Ombudsman for Israel's National Health Service.

David R. Katz MB, ChB, PhD, FRCPath is Emeritus Professor of Immunopathology at University College London (UCL); chairs U.K. General Medical Council Medical Practitioners Tribunal Service Fitness to Practice Panels; edits the International Journal of Experimental Pathology; and is Deputy Chair of the British Medical Association Medical Academic Staff Committee. His basic research interest is in antigen presentation. He has led medical educational initiatives interfacing between laboratory and clinic, and contributed to clinical and research ethics programs. He chairs the Jewish Medical Association (U.K.).

Ora Paltiel MDCM, MSc, FRCPC is Full Professor, Faculty of Medicine, Hebrew University Hadassah Medical School and Professor of Epidemiology and Director of the International MPH Program, Braun School of Public Health and Community Medicine. She is Senior Physician, Department of Hematology, Hadassah Hospital, Director of the Center for Research in Clinical Epidemiology, and Director of the Masters in Clinical Epidemiology Program. She is also a member of the Directorate of the National Program for Quality Indicators in Community Healthcare.

Stephen C. Schoenbaum, MD, MPH, is Special Advisor to the President of the Josiah Macy Jr. Foundation, a grant-making organization that supports innovations in health professions education in the U.S. He has had extensive experience as a clinician, epidemiologist, manager, and educator. He is a lecturer in population health at Harvard Medical School, adjunct professor of healthcare leadership at Brown University, and an honorary fellow of the Royal College of Physicians (London). He also is a longtime member and current chairman of the International Academic Review Committee of the Joyce and Irving Goldman Medical School at Ben-Gurion University.

Jo Shapiro, MD is the founder and director of the Center for Professionalism and Peer Support and Chief of the Division of Otolaryngology in the Department of Surgery at the Brigham and Women's Hospital and Associate Professor of Otolaryngology at Harvard Medical School. She is Visiting Professor and Advisor for Mbarara University of Science and Technology in Uganda, and Honorary Professor of Professional Behavior and Peer Support at the University Medical Center Groningen in the Netherlands. She also serves on the Ethics and Professionalism Committee of the American Board of Medical Specialties.

Acknowledgements
The external committee submitted its General Report to the CHE on August 19, 2014. It was discussed by a subcommittee of the Council on December 16, 2014, and accepted by the Council on February 10, 2015, marking a formal end of the *ad hoc* committee.

Author details
[1]Josiah Macy Jr. Foundation, 44 East 64th Street, New York, NY, USA. [2]University College London, Gower St, London WC1E 6BT, United Kingdom. [3]University of Illinois College of Medicine, 1853 West Polk Street, Chicago IL 60612, USA. [4]Department of Psychiatry and Behavioral Neuroscience University of Chicago Medicine, 5841 S. Maryland Ave., MC 3077, Rm M344A, Chicago, Illinois 60637, USA. [5]Faculty of Health Sciences, Ben-Gurion University of the Negev, Beer Sheva 8410501, Israel. [6]University College London, Gower St, London WC1E 6BT, United Kingdom. [7]Faculty of Medicine Hebrew University Hadassah School of Medicine, Braun School of Public Health and Community Medicine, Ein Kerem Campus, Jerusalem, Israel. [8]Division of Otolaryngology Department of Surgery, Brigham and Women's Hospital, 45 Francis St, Boston, MA 02115, USA.

Received: 24 January 2015 Accepted: 23 June 2015

References
1. Council for Higher Education, The Quality Assessment and Assurance Division. "The Self-Evaluation Process: Recommendations and Guidelines." July 2012. Available at: che.org.il/wp-content/uploads/2012/04/Recommendations-and-Guidelines-July-20123.pdf
2. Liaison Committee on Medical Education. Functions and Structure of a Medical School: Standards for Accreditation of Medical Education Programs Leading to the M.D. Degree. June 2013. 28 pp. Available at: www.lcme.org/publications.htm
3. Liaison Committee on Medical Education. Data Collection Instrument (DCI). Available at: www.lcme.org/survey-connect-dci-download.htm#14-15
4. Liaison Committee on Medical Education. Survey Report Guide: For full and limited LCME and CACMS survey visits conducted in the 2013–2014 academic year. Available at: www.lcme.org/publications.htm
5. General Medical Council. Tomorrow's Doctors: Outcomes and standards for undergraduate medical education. September 2009. 104pp. Available at: ww.gmcuk.org/education/undergraduate/tomorrows_doctors.asp
6. Schoenbaum SC. Planning and managing the physician workforce. Isr J Health Policy Res. 2012;1(1):14. doi:10.1186/2045-4015-1-14. Available at: www.ijhpr.org/content/pdf/2045-4015-1-14.pdf.
7. Haklai Z. The Workforce in the Health Professions –2013. Jerusalem: Israel Ministry of Health; 2014. 205pp. [Hebrew].
8. Department of Health and the Higher Education Funding Council for England: The Health and Education National Strategic Exchange (HENSE): Review of Medical and Dental School Intakes in England. December, 2012. Available at: https://www.gov.uk/government/uploads/system/uploads/attachment_data/file/213236/medical-and-dental-school-intakes.pdf
9. Medical Workforce Standing Advisory Committee: Third Report. Planning the Physician Workforce. December, 1997. Available at: www.nhshistory.net/mwfsac3.pdf
10. Association of American Medical Colleges. More Students Going to Medical School Than Ever Before. News Release, October 29, 2014. Available for reading at: https://www.aamc.org/newsroom/newsreleases/411636/10282014.html
11. Reis S, Borkan JM, Weingarten M. The Current State of Basic Medical Education in Israel: Implications for a New Medical School. Med Teach. 2009;31:984–9.
12. Starfield B, Shi L, Grover A, Macinko J. The Effects of Specialist Supply on Populations' Health: Assessing the Evidence. Health Affairs. 2005 Jan-Jun;Suppl Web Exclusives:W5-97-W5-107 doi: 10.1377/hlthaff.w5.97 Available at: content.healthaffairs.org/content/early/2005/03/15/hlthaff.w5.97.full.pdf+html
13. Organization for Economic Cooperation and Development (OECD): OECD Reviews of Health Care Quality: Israel 2012: Raising standards. OECD Publishing, 2012. 172 pp. Available for reading at: www.keepeek.com/Digital-Asset-Management/oecd/social-issues-migration-health/oecd-reviews-of-health-care-quality-israel-2012_9789264029941-en#page1
14. Chernichovsky D, Regev E. Financing and work force issues in Israel's healthcare system. Taub Center for Social Policy Studies in Israel. Policy Paper No. 2014.17. Available at: taubcenter.org.il/wp-content/files_mf/financingandworkforceissuesinisraelshealthcaresystem2014english70.pdf
15. Report of the Advisory Committee for Strengthening the Public Health System. Jerusalem: 2014, 370pp. Available at: www.health.gov.il/PublicationsFiles/publichealth2014.pdf [Hebrew]
16. Arbelle JE, Chodick G, Goldstein A, Porath A. Multiple chronic disorders – health care system's modern challenge in the Maccabi Health Care System. Isr J Health Policy Res. 2014;3:29. doi:10.1186/2045-4015-3-29. eCollection 2014.
17. Weissman C, Tandeter H, Zisk-Rony RY, Weiss YG, Elchalal U, Avidan A, et al. Israeli medical students' perceptions of six key medical specialties. Isr J Health Policy Res. 2013;2(1):19. doi:10.1186/2045-4015-2-19.
18. Afek A, Toker A, Berlovitz Y, Shamiss A. The approach to the physician shortage in Israel Harefuah. 2011 Mar;150(3):212–5, 306. [Hebrew]
19. Israeli Medical Association. Inadequate healthcare and general inequity in the periphery. Section of chapter 4, The Physician Shortage in Israel, May 2011. Available at: www.ima.org.il/ENG/ViewCategory.aspx?CategoryId=6177
20. Agency for Healthcare Research and Quality (AHRQ). The Number of Practicing Primary Care Physicians in the United States. Publication # 12-P001-2-EF Available at: www.ahrq.gov/research/findings/factsheets/primary/pcwork1/index.html
21. Young A, Chaudhry HJ, Rhyne J, Dugan M. A Census of Actively Licensed Physicians in the United States, 2010. J Medical Regulation. 2011;96(4):10–20. Available at: https://www.nationalahec.org/pdfs/FSMBPhysicianCensus.pdf.
22. Agency for Healthcare Research and Quality (AHRQ). The Number of Nurse Practitioners and Physician Assistants Practicing Primary Care in the United

States. Publication # 12-P001-3-EF Available at: www.ahrq.gov/research/findings/factsheets/primary/pcwork2/
23. American Academy of Family Physicians: Primary Care in the Affordable Care Act. Available at: www.aafp.org/dam/AAFP/documents/advocacy/coverage/aca/ES-PrimaryCareACA-061311.pdf
24. GP Taskforce Final Report. Securing the Future GP Workforce. March: Delivering the Mandate on GP Expansion; 2014. 63pp Available at: http://hee.nhs.uk/wp-content/uploads/sites/321/2014/07/GP-Taskforce-report.pdf.
25. Flexner, Abraham (1910), Medical Education in the United States and Canada: A Report to the Carnegie Foundation for the Advancement of Teaching, Bulletin No. 4, New York City: The Carnegie Foundation for the Advancement of Teaching, Available at: archive.carnegiefoundation.org/pdfs/elibrary/Carnegie_Flexner_Report.pdf
26. Cooke M, Irby DM, O'Brien BC. Educating Physicians: A Call for Reform of Medical School and Residency. San Francisco: Jossey-Bass; 2010. 320pp. ISBN 978-0470457979.
27. Nara N, Suzuki T, Tohda S. The Current Medical Education System in the World. Review J Med Dent Sci. 2011;58:79–83. Available at: lib.tmd.ac.jp/jmd/5802/07_Nara.pdf.
28. Curry RH. Meaningful Roles for Medical Students in the Provision of Longitudinal Patient Care. JAMA. 2014;312(22):2335–6.
29. Littlewood S, Ypinazar V, Margolis SA, Scherpbier A, Spencer J, Dornan T. Early practical experience and the social responsiveness of clinical education: systematic review. BMJ. 2005;331:387–91. Available at: https://www.aamc.org/download/130610/data/early_clinical_experiences_bmj.pdf.pdf.
30. Katz D. Is there a threat to academic medicine? A forward look to 2048. British J Hospital Medicine. 2015;76(3):124–5.
31. Bligh DA. What's the Use of Lectures? Intellect Books. Eastbourne: Anthony Rowe, Ltd; 1998. 317pp.
32. Association of American Medical Colleges. Core Entrustable Professional Activities for Entering Residency: Faculty and Learners' Guide. 2014. Available at: https://members.aamc.org/eweb/DynamicPage.aspx?Action=Add&ObjectKeyFrom=1A83491A-9853-4C87-86A4-F7D95601C2E2&WebCode=PubDetailAdd&DoNotSave=yes&ParentObject=CentralizedOrderEntry&ParentDataObject=Invoice%20Detail&ivd_formkey=69202792-63d7-4ba2-bf4e-a0da41270555&ivd_prc_prd_key=E3229B10-BFE7-4B35-89E7-512BBB01AE3B
33. Hayden JK, Smiley RA, Alexander M, Kardong-Edgren S, Jeffries PR. The NCSBN National Simulation Study: A Longitudinal, Randomized, Controlled Study Replacing Clinical Hours with Simulation in Prelicensure Nursing Education. J Nursing Regulation. 2014;5(2):S1–S64. Available at: https://www.ncsbn.org/685.htm.
34. Association of American Medical Colleges. Medical simulation in medical education: results of an AAMC survey. 2011. Available at: https://www.aamc.org/download/259760/data
35. Englander R, Cameron T, Ballard AJ, Dodge J, Bull J, Aschenbrener CA. Toward a common taxonomy of competency domains for the health professions and competencies for physicians. Acad Med. 2013;88(8):1088–94. doi:10.1097/ACM.0b013e31829a3b2b.
36. Nasca TJ, Philibert I, Brigham T, Flynn TC. The next GME accreditation system–rationale and benefits. N Engl J Med. 2012;366(11):1051–6. doi:10.1056/NEJMsr1200117. Epub 2012 Feb 22.
37. General Medical Council. GMC Education Strategy 2011–2013. Shaping the future of medical education and training. 2010. 22 pp. Available at: www.gmc-uk.org/Education_Strategy_2011_2013.pdf_36672939.pdf
38. Youngclaus J, Fresne JA. Physician Education Debt and the Cost to Attend Medical School, 2012 Update. February, 2013; Association of American Medical Colleges. 16 pp. Available at: https://www.aamc.org/download/328322/data/statedebtreport.pdf
39. Health Affairs. Health Policy Brief: Graduate Medical Education. A debate continues over the size and scope of federal subsidies to support residency training of the nation's physicians. August 31, 2012. 4 pp. Available at: www.healthaffairs.org/healthpolicybriefs/brief.php?brief_id = 75
40. Institute of Medicine of the National Academies. Graduate Medical Education That Meets the Nation's Health Needs. 2014; National Academies Press. 209 pp. Available at: http://www.nap.edu/download.php?record_id = 18754
41. Association of American Medical Colleges (AAMC). Medical Student Education: Debt, Costs, and Loan Repayment Fact Card. October 2014. Available at: https://www.aamc.org/download/152968/data/debtfactcard.pdf
42. Skop Y. "University tuition higher in Israel than almost all of Europe, study finds." Haaretz, Oct. 22, 2013. Available at: www.haaretz.com/news/israel/.premium-1.553821
43. Glazer K, Israeli A, Katz O. Financial arrangements between universities and Israeli hospitals: Current situation, failures and recommendations. February 2012, National Institute for Health Policy Research. 63 pp. Available in Hebrew at: www.israelhpr.org.il/e/107/&SearchClean = 1.

Contemporary Clinical Trials Communications

journal homepage: www.elsevier.com/locate/conctc

Implementing a STEMI system of care in urban Bangalore: Rationale and Study Design for heart rescue India

Aruna Ramesh[a], Kenneth A. LaBresh[b],*, Rhea Begeman[c], Bentley Bobrow[d], Teri Campbell[c], Nayanjeet Chaudhury[e], Marcia Edison[c], Timothy B. Erickson[f], John D. Manning[g], Bellur S. Prabhakar[c], Pavitra Kotini-Shah[c], Naresh Shetty[b], Pamela A. Williams[b], Terry Vanden Hoek[c]

[a] M.S. Ramiah Medical College, MSR Nagar, MSRIT Post Bengalaru 56004, India
[b] RTI International, Research Triangle Park, NC, USA, 3040 Cornwallis Rd Research Triangle Park, NC 27709, USA
[c] University of Illinois at Chicago Department of Emergency Medicine and Center for Global Health, 1940 Taylor M/C 584, Chicago, IL, USA
[d] University of Arizona Department of Emergency Medicine, 1609 N. Warren Ave., Room 118, PO Box 245057, Tucson, AZ 85724-5057, USA
[e] Medtronic Philanthropy, Delhi, India
[f] Brigham and Woman's Hospital, Harvard Medical School, Harvard Humanitarian Initiative, 75 Francis St, Boston, MA 02115 USA
[g] Carolinas HealthCare System, Charlotte, NC, USA

ARTICLE INFO

Keywords:
STEMI
Quality improvement
Angioplasty
Thrombolysis

ABSTRACT

Background: A system of care designed to measure and improve process measures such as symptom recognition, emergency response, and hospital care has the potential to reduce mortality and improve quality of life for patients with ST-elevation myocardial infarction (STEMI).

Objective: To document the methodology and rationale for the implementation and impact measurement of the Heart Rescue India project on STEMI morbidity and mortality in Bangalore, India.

Study Design: A hub and spoke STEMI system of care comprised of two interventional, hub hospitals and five spoke hospitals will build and deploy a dedicated emergency response and transport system covering a 10 Km. radius area of Bangalore, India. High risk patients will receive a dedicated emergency response number to call for symptoms of heart attack. A dedicated operations center will use geo-tracking strategies to optimize response times including first responder motor scooter transport, equipped with ECG machines to transmit ECG's for immediate interpretation and optimal triage. At the same time, a dedicated ambulance will be deployed for transport of appropriate STEMI patients to a hub hospital while non-STEMI patients will be transported to spoke hospitals. To enhance patient recognition and initiation of therapy, school children will be trained in basic CPR and signs and symptom of chest pain. Hub hospitals will refine their emergency department and cardiac catheterization laboratory protocols using continuous quality improvement techniques to minimize treatment delays. Prior to hospital discharge, secondary prevention measures will be initiated to enhance long-term patient outcomes.

1. Introduction

Cardiovascular disease (CVD) is now the leading cause of morbidity and mortality worldwide [1]. In India, CVD is the leading cause of death, approaching 4–5 million deaths annually; a rate that has doubled over the past two decades. By 2020, 2.6 million Indians are predicted to die due to coronary artery disease (CAD), which constitutes 54% of all CVD deaths [2]. In addition, by 2020, nearly 60% of patients with cardiovascular disease worldwide will be of Indian descent as Indians have a higher genetic predisposition for and earlier risk of CVDs than other global ethnicities [3,4].

The increase in acute ST-elevation myocardial infarction (STEMI and mortality in India is an expanding public health problem. The Heart Rescue India Project addresses this by using a system of care improvement approach shown to improve outcomes in other CVD conditions [5–7]. This approach includes enhancing patient recognition and

* Corresponding author. 61 Skyline Dr., Hinsdale, MA 01235. USA.
E-mail addresses: arunacr2@gmail.com (A. Ramesh), klabesh@rti.org (K.A. LaBresh), Bentley.Bobrow@azdhs.gov (B. Bobrow), nayanjeet.chaudhury@medtronic.com (N. Chaudhury), marciae@uic.edu (M. Edison), timothyberickson@gmail.com (T.B. Erickson), john.d.manning@gmail.com (J.D. Manning), bprabhak@uic.edu (B.S. Prabhakar), pkotini@gmail.com (P. Kotini-Shah), pamwilliams@rti.org (P.A. Williams), tvh@uic.edu (T. Vanden Hoek).

https://doi.org/10.1016/j.conctc.2018.04.002
Received 5 January 2018; Received in revised form 29 March 2018; Accepted 4 April 2018
Available online 05 April 2018
2451-8654/ © 2018 Published by Elsevier Inc. This is an open access article under the CC BY-NC-ND license (http://creativecommons.org/licenses/BY-NC-ND/4.0/).

timely response to symptoms, improving acute treatment, and initiating secondary prevention therapies prior to hospital discharge. In this context, prehospital delay remains a major hurdle in the institution of early reperfusion therapy, which is crucial in salvaging 'at-risk' myocardium and reducing adverse cardiovascular events following STEMI and has not been well addressed in prior studies [8]. Low public awareness, inadequate emergency transportation infrastructure, and the lack of a coordinated Emergency Medical Services (EMS) system are major contributors to problem [9]. Despite efforts aimed at reducing the prehospital time and treatment delay, a considerable proportion of patients with STEMI present late and receive delayed or no reperfusion therapy. Prehospital delay in India is also associated with difficulty in arranging financial means to cover medical costs, place of symptom onset, symptom interpretation, and mode of transportation [10].

Primary percutaneous coronary intervention (PCI) is the current standard of care for acute ST elevation myocardial infarction. Although most of the data on primary PCI in acute STEMI is from western countries, a recent study describes the outcomes of primary PCI for acute STEMI at a tertiary care center in Northern India [11]. Primary PCI was associated with high success rate, low mortality in non-shock patients, and low complication rates.

The goal of HRI is to adapt tested strategies of working systems of care from the United States to build a replicable sustainable model of STEMI care in a defined 10 km radius geographical area in Bangalore, India. This project aims to demonstrate improved outcome in patients diagnosed with STEMI through a multi hospital integrated Hub & Spoke model of STEMI care. This will be accomplished by creating a novel, dedicated prehospital emergency response program which includes prehospital diagnosis and transport to appropriate hospitals capable of providing timely revascularization, and post-acute treatment preventive care to improve patient outcomes and reduce the likelihood of STEMI recurrence (Table 1).

Table 1
Critical elements for prehospital response to STEMI and related cardiac arrest.

1. Hub and Spoke model of care with a pharmacoinvasive strategy using a tiered response system with first responder motor scooters complemented ambulance response for stabilization and transport.
2. Registration process to identify at-risk patients with the use of hospital help desks and a school program to reach potential patients via their children.
3. Initialization of secondary prevention prior to discharge with primary care provider CME programs to enhance continued prevention therapies and behavior change with opportunities for continued engagement of these high risk and post MI patients through texting, calls, and community events.
4. Electronic data collection and process communication via a unique online system for coordination of emergency response, and data collection and continuous feedback to monitor and improve STEMI care.
5. Coordinated emergency response, equipment and personnel from both private and government systems used in a coordinated system.

2. Methods

2.1. Professional engagement

A professional advisory group has been constituted to share expertise and experience in formulating process recommendations for the conduct of Heart Rescue India (HRI) program, provide ongoing feedback on the conduct of HRI and serve as a vehicle to inform policy makers and the cardiology community in India about the progress and findings from the program. The advisory group is composed of prominent cardiologists, cardiac surgeons, and emergency room physicians from across India involved in both private and government healthcare facilities. In addition, there are representatives from health and family welfare, the government of Karnataka Community Services Groups, Road Transport Department, secondary high school principals, Civil Defense, Home Guards, Red Cross Society, and other non-governmental organizations.

2.2. Patient engagement

Help desks in each of the hub and spoke hospitals will be used to screen, identify, and engage patients at risk for CVD in the HRI catchment area communities, educate them on the signs and symptoms of acute CVD. Help desk staff will teach patients how to access the HRI system of care and motivate them to call the toll-free emergency phone number when they or someone they witness is experiencing symptoms of STEMI. The focus will be on high-risk patients because the information will be more personally relevant and engaging for them since they are more likely to develop heart attack symptoms.

Knowing that simply raising awareness does not necessarily lead to behavior change [12–14], the HRI Program will incorporate formative research (e.g., focus groups) with patients into the development of our education strategies. Patients in the catchment area face several barriers beyond lack of awareness that may prevent behavior change (i.e., calling the toll-free number), such as lack of confidence in emergency medical service response time or the quality of care, and fears about financial burdens that emergency medical services and medical treatment might mean for the family. Formative research will help us develop a better understanding of what educational message(s) and modalities who will motivate them, what influences them, and how they like to receive information, and learn more about the context surrounding patient response to symptom onset so that we can develop more effective messages which can lead to reduction in delays in seeking treatment.

2.3. Engaging school children

One important lesson learned during the implementation of HRI was the impact that children can have in helping their parents recognize the need for cardiac care. As a result, Heart Rescue India (HRI) includes school children in its plans for community engagement by forming a task force of local physicians, teachers and principals. Goals for the program include education to identify CVD risk factors, recognize signs and symptoms of acute CVD and understand when and how to call for help. Students will also be trained in cardiopulmonary resuscitation (CPR) and the use of an automatic external defibrillator (AED). After completing the program, they will be asked to educate their parents by bringing the emergency phone number home, and encourage their parents to enroll in the HRI system and call the HRI emergency phone number if they develop heart attack symptoms.

2.4. Prehospital response

As noted above, delay in treatment of STEMI is a major contributor to morbidity and mortality [15]. Though several factors contribute to prehospital delay, two critical factors are patient's delay in seeking help and transportation delay. In the HRI catchment area, we will increase awareness of heart attack symptoms by organizing community educational outreach events In addition, we will reach higher risk patients through the use of "help desks", manned by volunteers, at the two hub and seven spoke hospitals involved in this project. These high-risk patients, identified through simple World Health Organization (WHO) cardiovascular risk score screenings, will be targeted for continued text messaging and other communication vehicles to reinforce our messaging over time, since heart attack symptoms may develop over the months and years following their initial educational opportunities.

To reduce prehospital delays in the heavy traffic of Bangalore, Motor scooters will be used to transport a first responder nurse or paramedic who will assess and stabilize the patient, perform and transmit an ECG to the MS Ramaiah command center. If there is evidence of STEMI, the cardiac catheterization laboratory personnel will be activated at the nearest available hub hospital. At the same time an ambulance will be dispatched to transport the patient to the hospital for urgent PCI.

Since out of hospital cardiac arrest (OHCA) may occur in patients with STEMI, an organized and coordinated resuscitation program will be part of our STEMI emergency response. The Resuscitation Academies (RA) concept revolves around the motto 'measure and improve' and utilizes hands-on experiential learning for health care providers across the continuum of care. This includes emergency call takers, prehospital providers as well as receiving health care teams at the hospital to train and function as a system. The HRI program will follow the American Heart Association (AHA) recommendations for chain of survival, beginning with the initiation of the call from family members. Early recognition of a cardiac event and immediate initiation of emergency care, including the dispatch of prehospital providers and clear directions to the family regarding compression only CPR, has been demonstrated to double or triple neurologically intact survival [16].

The RA, during its annual continuing medical education programs and training events will follow the American Heart Association (AHA) recommendations and will also include didactic education on the pathophysiology of STEMI, how it differs from sudden cardiac arrest (SCA), and explain Standard of Care treatments for both. The RA will also demonstrate the care priorities and elements associated with High-Performance CPR. Quality CPR training is a means to improve survival from cardiac arrest and for this project, raise awareness about STEMI recognition and emergency care. CPR that is performed in accordance with standard guidelines, minimizing breaks in compressions, allowing full chest recoil, with adequate compression depth, and with adequate compression rate can increase survival from cardiac arrest [17].

2.5. Hospitals

HRI is a complex project reaching across the continuum of acute care for STEMI. The project has engaged two hub hospitals that are percutaneous coronary intervention (PCI) capable and strategically located within a 10 Km radius of each other in the northwest region of Bangalore with a catchment area population of about 400,000. Within this area are five participating spoke hospitals which will provide emergency and general care, including thrombolysis, but do not have invasive cardiology facilities. This group of seven hospitals have agreed to work together as a coordinated network to provide appropriate emergency services for chest pain patients with ECG evidence of STEMI. They will be linked together by a prehospital control system utilizing a central control center coordinating first responder motor scooters with ECG capability to facilitate triage to the appropriate network hospital. Patients with evidence of STEMI as identified by first responders will be transported directly to a hub hospital, if available. There are also five spoke hospitals within the catchment area to provide care for identified patients without evidence of STEMI and for STEMI patients provide thrombolytic therapy as part of a pharmacoinvasive strategy when catheterization facilities are not available. In addition HRI will interface with the only public hospital which provides PCI which is the south of Bangalore. Because of more prolonged transport times, we will use a pharmacoinvasive strategy when STEMI patients request transfer. The relationship of the hub and spoke hospitals is indicated in Table 2. A recent trial of a hub-and spoke model for STEMI patients in Tamil Nadu, India has demonstrated an increase of the use of PCI for STEMI in a more rural setting [18]. We seek to apply this approach to urban Bangalore.

Table 2
Hub & spoke hospitals, with distance to hub hospital.

Hub	Spoke
M S Ramaiah Memorial Hospital	1. People Tree Hospital 5.8 km
	2. Aveksha Hospital-8.3 km
	3. Santhosh Hospital-7.7 km
Hub	**Spoke**
Suguna Hospital	1. Ananya Hospital-2.2 km
	2. Sreenivasa Hospital-3.8 km

2.6. Reperfusion strategies

The most critical component of STEMI care is to quickly recognize the presence of STEMI and activate the emergency response system. HRI will develop and use a dedicated emergency response system with a dedicated toll free emergency number to call for patients experiencing symptoms of a possible myocardial infarction (MI). Patients at high risk of MI, identified by the help desks at each of the hub and spoke hospitals, will receive educational messages as reminders of the symptoms of MI and the importance of calling the emergency number.

Toll free calls will be received by the 24 h helpline/dispatch center located at MS Ramaiah Memorial Hospital (RMH) through a dedicated toll free number staffed by trained professionals who will identify the geographical location of the call and activate the nearest the HRI spoke hospital to attend to the patient. The nearest spoke hospital will send a nurse/EMT on a motor scooter equipped with an emergency kit. On arrival to the location, the first responder will record symptoms, vitals, perform ECG and dispatch the same to the central server of the Ramaiah control center. At the same time, an Advanced Cardiac Life Support (ACLS) ambulance will also be dispatched to the scene, but will usually arrive after the scooter and initial assessment has been completed. The heart code personnel (Emergency/Cardiology) at RMH will interpret the ECG when received in the control center; if the patient is found to have a STEMI and is a candidate for PCI, he/she will be transferred the nearest available hub hospital and the catheterization laboratory will be activated to receive the patient. If the patient requests transfer to Sri Jayadeva Institute government hospital, which may result from patient financial concerns, a pharmacoinvasive strategy will be employed with the PCI done at Jayadeva Hospital. If the ECG is found to be inconclusive, the patient will be asked to be taken to the nearest spoke hospital (if stable) or to the hub hospital (if unstable) for further evaluation and management.

2.7. Secondary prevention

The project will initiate secondary prevention interventions including medical therapy and lifestyle change recommendations prior to hospital discharge as listed as measures 15–20 in Table 3 Quality Measures. This is designed to increase the post hospital adherence to these recommendations as demonstrated in multiple observational studies [16].

2.8. Process improvement strategies

A critical element of Heart Rescue India will be the ability to document and improve care that is based on evidence-based clinical guidelines. Tools and processes to support data collection and the use of these data, as well as the necessary system and cultural changes needed to utilize the data, are critically dependent on a framework of continuous improvement and sharing of best practices. Standardized protocols are a key first step. Much of STEMI care is time dependent and thus relies on efficient care delivery strategies. As noted above, a new system of prehospital care using a pre-notification strategy will facilitate triage and, for STEMI, activation of the catheterization laboratory team prior to the patient's arrival.

Didactic presentations, regular team sharing meetings for all of the involved hospital staff and prehospital responders will be strategies employed to accelerate the rate of improvement [17,18]. Health care staff will be trained to conduct improvement cycles to change existing systems and will be provided with a mechanism to learn from each other to determine what works best. Since hospital environments have their own, unique characteristics, staff will be taught key methods to adapt and customize these ideas. Treatment teams will collectively develop, in conjunction with project leadership, effective evidence-based protocols which will be shared and standardized across the HRI network for prehospital and hospital STEMI care. Prehospital,

Table 3
Quality measures heart rescue India.

Prehospital
1. Number of calls to central call center/month (rolling total to track usage)
2. Time from MI symptom (chest pain, dyspnea, nausea, diaphoresis, dizziness, syncope) onset to call placed to the center
   a. Numerator: number of calls with time ≤ 60 min
   b. Denominator: number of calls reporting symptoms listed above
   c. Mean time and range for all calls per month
3. Time from initial call placed to center to nurse motorcycle arrival
   a. Numerator: number of arrivals ≤ 15 min from call center call
   b. Denominator: number of calls
   c. Mean time and range for all calls per month
4. Time from initial call placed to call center and first ECG
   a. Numerator: Number of patients who call within 30 min
   b. Denominator: Number of patients who have a first ECG done by first responder
5. Time from first responder ECG diagnosis of STEMI to hospital arrival
   a. Numerator: STEMI prehospital setting diagnosis to Hub hospital ambulance arrival within 30 min
   b. Denominator: number of patient with STEMI diagnosis in prehospital setting transported to Hub hospital by ambulance

Hospital
6. Percent STEMI patients arriving at the hospital by ambulance
   a. Numerator: Number of patients with STEMI who arrive by ambulance
   b. Denominator: All STEMI patients who arrive at the hospital
7. STEMI patients with cardiac arrest in prehospital setting and survival to hospital
   a. Numerator: Number of cardiac arrest patients with STEMI diagnosed in prehospital setting surviving to hospital arrival
   b. Denominator: All cardiac arrest patients with STEMI diagnosed in prehospital setting
8. Time from first medical contact to reperfusion
   a. Numerator: Number of STEMI patients who receive PCI or thrombolysis within 3 h from initial call placed to call center
   b. Denominator: Number of patient with STEMI receiving PCI/thrombolysis
9. Door to needle time
   a. Numerator: Number of patients with STEMI who arrive by ambulance and door to needle time < 30 min
   b. Denominator: All patient arriving by ambulance, with STEMI receiving thrombolytic agents in the ED
10. Door to needle time walk-in
    a. Numerator: Number of patients with STEMI who do not arrive by ambulance with door to needle time < 60 min
    b. Denominator: All patients not arriving by ambulance with STEMI receiving thrombolytic agents in the ED
11. Door to balloon time
    a. Numerator: Number of STEMI patients who with door to balloon time ≤ 60 min
    b. Denominator: All STEMI patients receiving PCI on hospital arrival
12. Door to balloon time walk-in
    a. Numerator: Number of STEMI patients who do not arrive by ambulance with door to balloon time ≤ 90 min
    b. Denominator: All STEMI patients not arriving by ambulance, receiving PCI on hospital arrival
13. Percent STEMI patients receiving reperfusion
    a. Numerator: Number of STEMI patients who receive reperfusion
    b. Denominator: All STEMI patients not transferred out of network[a]
14. Survival to hospital discharge (in-hospital mortality)
    a. Numerator: All STEMI patients surviving until hospital discharge not transfer out of network
    b. Denominator: All STEMI patients not transferred out of network[a]
15. Adverse events (heart failure, stroke, bleeding requiring transfusion)
    a. Numerator: All STEMI patients discharge without adverse events
    b. Denominator: All STEMI patients admitted to the hospital
16. Beta blocker
    a. Numerator: All STEMI patients discharged with a beta blocker
    b. Denominator: All STEMI patients discharged without contraindications to beta blockers
17. Angiotensin converting enzyme/angiotensin receptor blockers (ACE/ARB)
    a. Numerator: All STEMI patients discharged with ACE/ARB
    b. Denominator: All STEMI patients discharged without contraindications to ACE/ARB
18. Aspirin (ASA)
    a. Numerator: All STEMI patients discharged with ASA
    b. Denominator: All STEMI patients discharged without contraindications to ASA
19. Statins
    a. Numerator: All STEMI patients discharged with a statin
    b. Denominator: All STEMI patients discharged without contraindications to statins
20. Smoking cessation counseling

Table 3 (continued)

a. Numerator: All STEMI patients who report tobacco use discharged with smoking cessation counseling
b. Denominator: All STEMI patients discharged who report tobacco use
21. Follow-up appointment
    a. Numerator: All STEMI patient discharged who have a follow-up appointment (Family practitioner, cardiologist, or general practitioner)
    b. Denominator: All STEMI patients discharged to home

[a] Network is defined as any Hub, Spoke hospital within the Heart Rescue India list of participating hospitals.

emergency room and catheterization laboratory teams will find the most effective way to move patients through the system for the right treatment at the right time by adapting key strategies from other programs around the world and from each other. Finally, post intervention care will include the initiation of secondary prevention treatments prior to hospital discharge for all STEMI patients [19]. Bringing together resources and expertise to actively support quality improvement programs from the seven diverse hospitals and the prehospital coordinated response system will play a key role in reaching our shared goal of providing the right care for every STEMI patient every time.

2.9. Data collection and measures

Data collection will be largely automated by electronic interfacing with existing hospital systems. Included in the design are customized mobile applications (apps) to enable collection of care processes in real time and to support execution of the processes of care throughout the flow of STEMI patients through the acute response system.

The sequence of events for the response to STEMI patients is illustrated in Fig. 1. The workflow is supported by mobile applications and PC software to be installed and used during the HRI program:

- **Dispatch Phone** - a single phone capable of displaying the incoming caller's phone number.
- **Dispatch App** - a single Windows PC app that will gather patient information and help relay the information and location to the ambulance app (bike and ambulance).
- **Ambulance App** - This app will share information from the Dispatch to track the patient.
- **HRI Ambulance and Hospital App** - This will gather ECG and other vitals, to the remote doctors for STEMI diagnosis.
- **Doctor App** - This app - to be used by Doctors - will share information from the Dispatch to track the patient arrival in the Emergency Department/Coronary Care Unit (ED/CCU), and to capture timestamped events.
- **Patient App** - a single Windows PC software tool that will help gather all patient data elements within the scope of HRI project. This PC software would be used in ED, CCU, Catheterization lab, etc.

Quality measures for HRI have been adapted from STEMI processes of care for prior projects in the United States and India as previously noted. Table 3 lists the measures for prehospital and hospital care of STEMI patients to evaluate the effectiveness of HRI. In addition to the acute care measures, we will also initiate measures of secondary prevention started in the hospital prior to discharge that have been adapted from the American Heart Association's Get with the Guidelines project in the United States, China, and Brazil [20].

2.10. Statistical analysis

Based on the findings of India STEMI studies and our own experience, sample size calculations for the present study will give us the ability to detect decreases in the fraction of STEMI patients who delay over 2 h by at least 7.5% for time from symptom onset to reperfusion

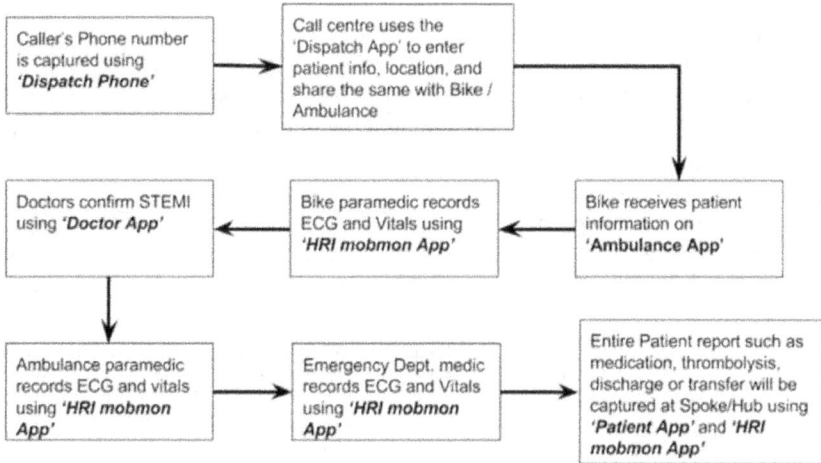

Fig. 1. Workflow of the HRI project.

and at least a 7% reduction in patients with delayed door to reperfusion with 80% power and a 95% confidence level. Our roll out of data collection, targeted at-risk population education, expansion of pre-hospital care and monthly data reports starting in May 2018, will likely require 16 months to demonstrate effect. This time will allow for data collection from at least 300 patients in the initial 3 months of launch to establish a baseline. All analyses will be performed using SAS (SAS Institute, Research Triangle, NC). Data are presented as proportions. For the other HRI measures, changes in compliance rates for the measured outcomes over the study period were assessed using the Fisher exact test, with the Bonferroni method of Holm for multiple comparisons. All P values are 2-sided, with $P \leq 0.05$ considered statistically significant. The baseline period is defined as the time period in which the projects initial 300 records are submitted. Progress over the study period will be further assessed at each calendar quarter subsequent to baseline. When missing data elements are present for a specific measure, that patient was excluded for analysis for the measure. At least 1200 additional STEMI patients seen over the course of the next 12 months will allow for measurement of effect of ongoing quality improvement efforts and further expansion of pre-hospital care.

3. Discussion

3.1. Expected outcomes

HRI will develop and test a model for high quality, timely treatment of STEMI patients in a densely populated urban area of a large city in Southern India. Project success will depend on reaching patients at risk of MI and motivating them and their family to call for help when symptoms occur. The issues of traffic congestion will be addressed by using motor scooters for first responders equipped with ECG transmission capability. It is expected that using ECG transmission to confirm STEMI for catheterization laboratory pre-notification will reduce delays on arrival to the hospital.

A sophisticated data entry and coordination system will substantially automate data collection, including the use of timestamps to accurately determine critical time delays that will be addressed with our structural and quality improvement strategies. In addition, the location of scooters and ambulances will be tracked in the central control center to optimize their availability as needed. Finally, secondary prevention therapies will be initiated in the hospitals, prior to hospital discharge to enhance adherence and reduce recurrent events [21,22].

3.2. Sustainability planning

For any interventional strategy or process improvement to be long lasting, the program will need to be sustained. A sustainability program will need trained personnel who will undergo periodic training and retraining, ongoing process improvement and financial support. Programs are already in place to ensure ongoing personnel training and continuous process improvement. To continue and sustain these activities beyond the 5-year funding from the Medtronic Foundation, HRI will need to identify new sources of funding. There are several sources of funding including support from the Local, State and Central Governments, individual donations and Corporate Social Responsibility (CSR) mandated funds.

We anticipate considerable in-kind support from the local Government by allowing public employees such as police, paramedics, firefighters, home guard, and members of other publicly supported volunteer organizations to undergo training, and provide First Aid and Cardiopulmonary resuscitation (CPR) in the community when the need arises. We anticipate that the State Government will expand their skills development program to include paramedic training required to function effectively as First Responders during medical emergency. The State Government of Karnataka already has such programs, which cover the cost of providing training. The Central Government has several schemes for skills development that will provide financial support to the trainees to cover the cost of transportation to the training site, and boarding and lodging while they undergo training. Heart Rescue India leaders will apply for these funds to ensure continuity of the program. Toward this goal, The State of Karnataka has designated Heart Rescue India as its technical partner.

HRI will create a Development Office that will solicit grants from various National and International funding agencies, charitable foundations, and nonprofit organizations. We also expect this office to launch fund-raising programs to seek donations from individuals and smaller business entities.

The Companies Act 2013, first update in nearly 50 years, passed by the Indian Parliament has a "2%" clause. The 2% clause requires companies to set up a CSR board consisting of at least three directors with one of them being independent. The board is required to ensure that the company spends at least 2% of net profits it earned during the preceding 3 years. This rule applies to companies with a net worth of Indian Rupees (Rs). 5 billion or more, annual turnover or net profit of at least Rs. 10 billion or Rs. 50 million respectively. It is estimated that over 8000 companies will need to spend approximately Rs. 150

annually on CSR. Although there will be considerable demand for the CSR funds from over 3 million NGOs already operating in India, Heart Rescue India is confident that it can draw support from various corporations within the State of Karnataka because the act stipulates that companies "shall give preference to the local area and areas around where it operates." Moreover, the HRI program is independently monitored by a program management team from the Research Triangle Institute (RTI), and the needs and outcome assessments are conducted independently by the Institute for Health Metrics and Evaluation (IHME). These arrangements ensure a high degree of transparency and will also ensure that the impact of the study will be evaluated objectively.

4. Conclusion

HRI is a complex, multi-facet program designed to integrate and optimize existing resources with improved strategies and systems to deliver definitive interventions for patients with STEMI in a defined urban area of Bangalore. The program will draw on practice guidelines, successful improvement strategies and outcome measures of STEMI systems of care in the United States and India to minimize the time from first medical contact to revascularization. This program will focus on ways to reduce the delay time from symptom onset to activating the prehospital emergency response, including training first responders to effectively treat associated cardiac arrest. HRI will support system improvement to reduce time to revascularization and provide improved post PCI care in the hospital, recognizing that initiation of secondary prevention measures will further improve quality of life and reduce recurrence [23,24].

Funding source

Medtronic Philanthropy provided input on site selection and the selection of ST elevation myocardial infarction as the primary focus of this initiative, but did not participate in the design of the study or data collection.

References

[1] A. Kalra, D.L. Bhatt, S. Rajagopalan, et al., Overview of coronary heart disease risk initiatives in South asia, Curr Atheroscler Rep 19 (2017) 25, http://dx.doi.org/10.1007/s11883-017-0662-1.

[2] C.D. Mathers, D. Loncar, Projections of global mortality and burden of disease from 2002 to 2030, PLoS Med. 3 (2006), http://dx.doi.org/10.1371/journal.pmed.0030442 e442.

[3] D. Kohn, Getting to the heart of the matter in India, Lancet 372 (2008) 523–524 https://www.ncbi.nlm.nih.gov/pubmed/18711800.

[4] H.S. Rissam, S. Kishore, N. Trehan, Coronary artery disease in young Indians—the missing link, J. Indian Acad. Clin. Med. 2 (2001) 128–131 http://medind.nic.in/jac/t01/i3/jact01i3p128.pdf.

[5] S.V. Diepen, S. Girotra, B.S. Abella, L.B. Becker, B.J. Bobrow, P.S. Chan, C. Fahrenbruch, C.B. Granger, J.G. Jollis, B. McNally, L. White, D. Yannopoulos, T.D. Rea, Multistate 5-year initiative to improve care for out-of-hospital cardiac arrest: primary results from the HeartRescue project, J Am Heart Assoc 6 (2017), http://dx.doi.org/10.1161/JAHA.117.005716 e005716.

[6] L.H. Schwamm, G.C. Fonarow, M.J. Reeves, W. Pan, M.R. Frankel, E.E. Smith, A.G. Ellrodt, C.P. Cannon, L. Liang, E.D. Peterson, K.A. LaBresh, Get with the Guidelines–Stroke is associated with sustained improvement in care for patients hospitalized with acute stroke or TIA, Circulation 119 (1) (2009) 107–115.

[7] G. Nichol, T.P. Aufderheide, B. Eigel, R.W. Neumar, G. Lurie, V.J. Bufalino, C.W. Callaway, V. Menon, R.R. Bass, B.S. Abella, M. Sayre, C.M. Dougherty, E.M. Racht, M.E. Kleinman, R.E. O'Connor, J.P. Reilly, E.W. Ossmann, E. Peterson, Regional systems of care for out-of-hospital cardiac arrest: a policy statement from the american heart association, Circulation 121 (2010) 709–729, http://dx.doi.org/10.1161/CIR.0b013e3181cdb7db.

[8] A. Khan, M. Phadke, Y.Y. Lokhandwala, et al., A study of prehospital delay patterns in acute myocardial infarction in an urban tertiary care Institute in Mumbai, J Assoc Physicians India 65 (2017) 24–27 https://www.ncbi.nlm.nih.gov/pubmed/28598044.

[9] L. George, L. Ramamoorthy, S. Satheesh, et al., Prehospital delay and time to reperfusion therapy in ST elevation myocardial infarction, J Emerg Trauma Shock 10 (2017) 64–69, http://dx.doi.org/10.4103/0974-2700.201580.

[10] G. Dubey, S.K. Verma, V.K. Bahl, Primary percutaneous coronary intervention for acute ST elevation myocardial infarction: outcomes and determinants of outcomes: a tertiary care center study from North India, Indian Heart J. 69 (2017) 294–298, http://dx.doi.org/10.1016/j.ihj.2016.11.322.

[11] A. Mathew, J. Abdullakutty, P. Sebastian, et al., Population access to reperfusion services for ST-segment elevation myocardial infarction in Kerala, India. Indian Heart J 69 (2017) S51–S56, http://dx.doi.org/10.1016/j.ihj.2017.02.014.

[12] I. Ajzen, M. Fishbein, Understanding Attitudes and Predicting Social Behaviour, Prentice-Hall, 1980, http://www.citeulike.org/group/38/article/235626.

[13] A. Christiano, A. Neimand, Stop raising awareness already, Stanford Soc. Innovat. Rev. 15 (2017) 34–41.

[14] J.T. Cacioppo, R.E. Petty, C.F. Kao, et al., Central and peripheral routes to persuasion: an individual difference perspective, J. Pers. Soc. Psychol. 51 (1986) 1032 http://psycnet.apa.org/fulltext/1987-07221-001.html.

[15] J.-R. Wu, D.K. Moser, B. Riegel, et al., Impact of prehospital delay in treatment seeking on in-hospital complications after acute myocardial infarction, J. Cardiovasc. Nurs. 26 (2011) 184–193, http://dx.doi.org/10.1097/JCN.0b013e3181efea66.

[16] B.J. Bobrow, D.W. Spaite, T.F. Vadeboncoeur, et al., Implementation of a regional telephone cardiopulmonary resuscitation program and outcomes after out-of-hospital cardiac arrest, JAMA Cardiol 1 (2016) 294–302, http://dx.doi.org/10.1001/jamacardio.2016.0251.

[17] P.A. Meaney, B.J. Bobrow, M.E. Mancini, et al., Cardiopulmonary resuscitation quality: [corrected] improving cardiac resuscitation outcomes both inside and outside the hospital: a consensus statement from the American Heart Association, Circulation 128 (2013) 417–435, http://dx.doi.org/10.1161/CIR.0b013e31829d8654.

[18] T. Alexander, A.S. Mullasari, G. Joseph, et al., A system of care for patients with ST-segment elevation myocardial infarction in India: the Tamil Nadu-ST-segment elevation myocardial infarction program, JAMA Cardiol 2 (2017) 498–505, http://dx.doi.org/10.1001/jamacardio.2016.5977.

[19] P.-F. Keller, S. Carballo, D. Carballo, Present and future of secondary prevention after an acute coronary syndrome, EPMA J. 2 (2011) 371–379, http://dx.doi.org/10.1007/s13167-011-0129-3.

[20] D.M. Berwick, The science of improvement, J. Am. Med. Assoc. 299 (2008) 1182–1184, http://dx.doi.org/10.1001/jama.299.10.1182.

[21] K.A. LaBresh, Using 'get with the guidelines' to prevent recurrent cardiovascular disease, Curr. Treat. Options Cardiovasc. Med. 7 (2005) 287–292 https://www.ncbi.nlm.nih.gov/pubmed/16004859.

[22] J.G. Jollis, H.R. Al-Khalidi, M.L. Roettig, et al., Regional systems of care demonstration project: american heart association mission: lifeline STEMI systems accelerator, Circulation 134 (2016) 365–374, http://dx.doi.org/10.1161/CIRCULATIONAHA.115.019474.

[23] K.A. LaBresh, G.C. Fonarow, S.C. Smith Jr.et al., Improved treatment of hospitalized coronary artery disease patients with the get with the guidelines program, Crit. Pathw. Cardiol. 6 (2007) 98–105, http://dx.doi.org/10.1097/HPC.0b013e31812da7ed.

[24] C.D. Bushnell, D.M. Olson, X. Zhao, et al., Secondary preventive medication persistence and adherence 1 year after stroke, Neurology 77 (2011) 1182–1190, http://dx.doi.org/10.1212/WNL.0b013e31822f0423.

The impact of accreditation on medical schools' processes

Danielle Blouin,[1] Ara Tekian,[2] Carol Kamin[2] & Ilene B Harris[2]

OBJECTIVES Increased emphasis is being placed worldwide on accreditation of undergraduate medical education programmes, and costs of participation in accreditation continue to rise. The primary purposes of accreditation are to ensure the quality of medical education and to promote quality improvement. Student performance data as indicators of the impact of accreditation have important limitations. The purpose of this study was to evaluate the impact of accreditation using an innovative marker: the processes implemented at medical schools as a result of accreditation. This conceptual model suggests that accreditation drives medical schools to implement and strengthen processes that support quality in medical education.

METHODS In this qualitative study, conducted in 2015–2016, interviews and focus group discussions with deans, undergraduate medical education deans and faculty leaders at 13 of the 17 Canadian medical schools were used to elicit perspectives about processes influenced by accreditation; the method of constant comparative analysis associated with grounded theory was used to generate themes of processes. Perceived negative consequences of accreditation on medical education programmes were also explored.

RESULTS Nine themes representing processes reported as resulting from accreditation were identified. These processes related to: (i) governance, (ii) data collection and analysis, (iii) monitoring, (iv) documentation, (v) creation and revision of policies and procedures, (vi) continuous quality improvement, (vii) faculty members' engagement, (viii) academic accountability and (ix) curriculum reforms. Themes representing negative consequences of accreditation included (i) costs, (ii) staff and faculty members' morale and feelings, (iii) school reputation and (iv) standards. The identified processes, given their nature, appear likely to be associated with improvement of quality in medical education. These results help justify the costs associated with accreditation.

CONCLUSIONS This study uses an innovative marker, medical schools' processes, to evaluate the impact of accreditation. Results provide evidence that accreditation-related activities steer medical education programmes towards establishment of processes likely to be associated with improved quality in medical education.

Medical Education 2018: 52: 182–191
doi: 10.1111/medu.13461

[1]Department of Emergency Medicine, Queen's University, Kingston, Ontario, Canada
[2]Department of Medical Education, University of Illinois, Chicago, Illinois, USA

Correspondence: Danielle Blouin, Department of Emergency Medicine, Queen's University, 76 Stuart Street, Kingston, Ontario, Canada K7L 2V7. Tel: 613 549 6666 (ext. 3530); E-mail: blouind@queensu.ca

INTRODUCTION

Accreditation of medical schools in Canada and the USA consists of on-site peer reviews of medical education programmes, conducted on an 8-year cycle and managed by the Committee on Accreditation of Canadian Medical Schools (CACMS) and the Liaison Committee on Medical Education (LCME).[1,2] Schools being visited start preparing for accreditation about 2 years before the actual site visit. The documents that need to be submitted to the accreditation body comprise: (i) an extensive database consisting of a school's responses related to each accreditation standard and element; (ii) the evidence supporting the school's responses; (iii) student satisfaction data from a survey conducted by medical students regarding several aspects of their programme; (iv) results from graduation questionnaires, a national questionnaire completed annually by graduating medical students when exiting programmes and (v) a school's self-study with regards to each standard and element, which is a reflection of where the school perceives itself to be in relation to the standards and elements and, if needed, what it plans to do to achieve compliance.

The costs associated with accreditation processes in the health sector are significant.[3,4] For undergraduate medical education (UME) programmes, the costs of completing the required self-study were estimated in the USA to be $219 542 in 1998 ($327 074 in 2017 dollars).[5] In 2016, the overall costs of accreditation at four Canadian medical schools ranged between $373 363 and $1 065 864 (US dollars) over the 2-year preparation period and including the site visit.[6]

The primary purposes of accreditation are to ensure the quality of medical education and to promote quality improvement, with the ultimate goal of providing optimal patient care. As both national and global emphases placed on accreditation of UME programmes and costs of participation in accreditation processes continue to increase, an evaluation of the impacts of accreditation is necessary.

Direct linkages between accreditation and the quality of education are difficult to establish.[7–11] Identifying valid markers of effectiveness across medical schools and countries is challenging.[12] Student performances in national examinations are flawed indicators of the impact of accreditation on the quality of medical education.[13] In Canada and in the USA, all medical schools are accredited, preventing within-countries comparisons of graduates' performance in national examinations from accredited and non-accredited programmes.[9] Comparisons of the performance of North-American graduates with that of graduates from other countries in the same exams are difficult; several confounding factors are likely to contribute to the differences in performance, such as the quality of applicants, schools' entry requirements, available resources, and differences in health care systems used for clinical training.[12] In spite of these challenges, positive associations have generally been found between schools' accreditation status and graduates' performance in national exams.[12,14]

Studies comparing in-residency performance of graduates from USA and international schools show conflicting results; more information is needed about the accreditation status of the international schools studied to allow definitive interpretation of the results.[15–17] In addition, graduates of international schools sometimes have years of clinical practice before they join a USA residency programme.

The challenges associated with the use of student performance data as measures of the impact of accreditation on the quality of medical education programmes suggest the need for identification of new markers. The continuous quality improvement orientation of medical education programmes has been proposed as a potential marker of the impact of accreditation.[13] The current study uses medical schools' processes as indicators. What processes are implemented or influenced by accreditation at medical schools? The conceptual model grounding this study suggests that accreditation drives medical schools to develop, implement and strengthen processes that reflect best practices of continuous quality improvement (CQI). These practices contribute to the development of a CQI culture within medical education programmes that supports ongoing assessment and improvement of the quality of medical education.[13,18] This conceptual model guided the design of the study but not the data analysis (i.e. the themes identified in the current study emerged from the data and were not selected *a priori* based on published CQI best practices).

The purpose of this study was to evaluate the impact of accreditation on the processes put in place by medical schools as a result of, and in relation to, accreditation processes. Perceived negative consequences of accreditation for medical education programmes were also explored.

METHODS

The study was conducted from March 2015 to March 2016. There are 17 medical schools in Canada; all are public medical schools, three are Francophone. Sixteen of the 17 schools were invited to participate in the study; one school was excluded, as the study would have significantly interfered with its planned accreditation activities. The principal investigator (PI) of this study is also the Secretary for the CACMS, the accreditation body for Canadian medical schools. Care was taken to ensure that the study was conducted after schools' accreditation visits and after accreditation decisions were communicated to schools.

This is a qualitative study using interviews and focus group discussions, and the constant comparative method of analysis associated with the grounded theory approach, to generate themes of processes influenced by accreditation.[19,20]

Instruments

Interviews and focus groups were conducted, in English or in French, as chosen by participants, to identify the processes put in place at their schools in relation to accreditation. Appendix S1 (available online) presents the framing questions.

The interview and focus group protocol was piloted for clarity, flow and duration. Each in-person or telephone interview took a maximum of 60 minutes. Focus group discussions lasted 90 minutes and were held face to face. When interested individuals' schedules precluded their participation in focus group discussions, individual interviews were offered and conducted.

All interviews and focus group discussions were audio-recorded and transcribed. To ensure anonymity, participants were only identified by numbers (Speaker 1, etc.) on the transcripts. All focus group participants consented to maintain confidentiality regarding other participants' responses and were notified that the PI could not guarantee that participants would maintain confidentiality. Participants were provided with the interview or discussion transcript to allow them to make changes to clarify their thoughts, if necessary, and to confirm their approval of the use of the data in the analysis.

Participants

Individual interviews were conducted with the dean, undergraduate medical education (UME) dean (or equivalent) and interim review coordinator (faculty member responsible for accreditation) at each participating medical school.

Focus groups were conducted, whenever possible, at each school, with faculty members with UME leadership responsibilities (course or phase directors, student affairs leader, etc.). These individuals are extensively involved in accreditation and medical schools' processes.

Recruitment of participants

The dean of each school was contacted directly by the PI, via e-mail, to ensure his or her approval for the school to participate in the study. Once approval was received, the dean, UME dean and the interim review coordinator were invited by the PI via e-mail to participate in individual interviews.

Sampling was required to invite faculty members with leadership responsibility in UME programmes to participate in focus groups. In order for these individuals not to feel undue pressure from the PI to participate in the study, invitations were sent from the UME office at each school. Interested leaders replied directly to the PI; the UME office did not know who actually participated in the study and the PI did not know who was invited.

Data collection

The PI conducted the interviews and facilitated the focus group discussions. Given the small number of participants in each focus group, the assistance of an additional facilitator was not required. Careful consideration was given to the potential biases introduced by having the CACMS Secretary conduct the interviews and focus groups. The small community of medical education in Canada, where there are only 17 medical schools, means that deans and other education leaders have regular professional interactions with the PI. It was felt that these individuals would actually be more receptive to being interviewed by an individual most knowledgeable about accreditation and engaged in accreditation in a formal role, than by an unknown research assistant. The PI's expertise in accreditation could facilitate probing to obtain richer data. The recruitment information letter specified that the study was not conducted by the PI in her role as CACMS Secretary, and stated that results would not be shared with CACMS members or other secretariat members. The consent form indicated that participants did not have to respond to any question they might find objectionable and this was also stated at the beginning of interviews and focus groups. Interviews with a research assistant were offered to those who would have preferred them; all participants declined the offer.

Ethical approval was obtained from the Queen's University Health Sciences and Affiliated Teaching Hospitals Research Ethics Board, from the Office for the Protection of Research Subjects at the University of Illinois at Chicago, and from the institutional research ethics board affiliated with each participating institution.

Data analysis

The method of open, emergent coding was used for the data analysis.[21] The PI developed the initial coding scheme from inductive analysis of the transcripts of interviews and focus group discussions.[19] Themes consisted of substantive ideas (as judged by the PI) expressed in several separate data sources; although no *a priori* number of sources was set as a cut-off, all themes were formulated from data from at least five sources and from at least two medical education programmes. Two coders (DB and CK) coded the data to ensure that the coding scheme appropriately represented all ideas and to ensure the trustworthiness of the coding; no additional codes were formulated from the second coder analysis and the initial coding scheme remained unchanged. The unit of coding was phrases and sentences. The emphasis was on capturing all themes, as well as agreement between coders. Coding disagreements were resolved by the PI, based on review of the transcripts, definitions of codes, and codes assigned by the two coders.

Data interpretation

The impact of accreditation on medical schools' processes was evaluated based on the themes that were formulated in the qualitative analysis of individual and focus group interviews.

RESULTS

Schools' participation

Of the 16 schools invited to participate, one did not reply, one declined and one asked to postpone its participation by a few months (outside of the study period). Two of the non-participating schools were English speaking, one was French speaking. One participating school had a 3-year curriculum; all other participating schools had a 4-year curriculum. Non-participating schools did not differ from participating schools, in particular with regards to class size or location. The remaining 13 (82%) medical schools contributed to the study to a variable extent. Individual interviews were conducted with 13 medical school deans, 11 UME deans and 10 interim review coordinators (this position was vacant at three schools). Twenty-nine (29) faculty members with leadership positions, from nine schools, participated in focus group discussions or individual interviews. Scheduling logistics prevented the conduct of focus groups at four schools; interested individuals at those schools participated in individual interviews. Focus groups varied in size from two to seven members. All 13 schools were fully accredited at the time of the study; none was on warning or given an unspecified accreditation term.

Overall results

Nine themes were formulated that define key UME processes in which process change was attributed to the impact of accreditation. Four themes captured the reported negative consequences of accreditation for medical education programmes and staff. Together these demonstrate the cost–benefit tensions inherent in accreditation systems.

Impact of accreditation on medical schools processes

The nine themes representing the impact of accreditation on processes related to:
(i) governance, (ii) data collection and analysis, (iii) monitoring systems, (iv) documentation, (v) creation and revision of policies and procedures, (vi) continuous quality assurance and improvement, (vii) faculty members' engagement, (viii) academic accountability and (xi) curriculum reforms (Table 1). Frequently, curricular modifications were implemented as a result of disappointing accreditation decisions, such as programmes previously being placed on warning or probation.

Table 1 Impact of accreditation on medical schools' processes

Process	Quote
Governance	'Someone who's overseeing things at the medical school level so that it's not just me making changes with a colleague but there's some oversight so that someone can see the whole big picture, and I think that's a change that's come about.' (Programme J, Participant #3)
Data collection and analysis	'We've got a very good computer program so now everything is linking into where does this match with accreditation.' (Programme C, Participant #3)
Monitoring systems	'There's a structure now in place to ensure the centralisation and monitoring of the evaluation of all educational activities within the programme.' (Programme H, Participant #2)
Documentation	'We haven't had the paper trail and our programme is growing now. It's getting larger and I think we've seen that we do need the paper trail in many cases.' (Programme C, Participant #2)
Creation and revision of policies and procedures	'What's good also with accreditation is that it encourages the formalising of the various components. What I mean is the drafting of policies, to ensure we have clear policies for specific situations, all the policies that our deans and programmes prepare.' (Programme I, Participant #1)
Continuous quality assurance and quality improvement	'First of all, we have a fulltime manager of accreditation. I would say a third of our time at curriculum committee, clerkship committee, also at our deans' council, … is kind of trying to figure out how to meet accreditation standards where we're deficient or warning people or re-tweaking our processes in order to keep up with the standards.' (Programme K, Participant #2)
Engagement	'It's not just reporting, but it's getting people who care about something together on a regular basis to discuss that.' (Programme C, Participant #2)
Academic accountability	'We're totally restructuring the way we engage and pay doctors to do academic work.' (Programme G, Participant #1)
Curriculum reforms	'My impression is a lot of the change that was made was around curriculum management and renewal as well. The curriculum was totally revamped in those couple of years. The urgent need to change the curriculum was really because of accreditation.' (Programme B, Participant #1)

The theme pertaining to the impacts of accreditation on programme governance included the greatest number of comments. Examples included: clarifying committees' terms of reference and lines of reporting; developing systems as distinguished from relying on single individuals to accomplish tasks; improving programme oversight of the various curricular components and at distributed sites of instruction; enhancing communication within the programme and also with external partners, for example with postgraduate programmes; and hiring of individuals with special expertise, such as financial counsellors and other staff in support of student services. Examples of comments included:

We've put in place more structure around our committees and subcommittees that oversee and manage the curriculum. As part of that, I think those committees have greater clarity around what their role is. There's been improved communication between the committees. (Programme C, Participant #6)

We've really improved our communication coming out of the MD program via a newsletter because we felt that this is a way to communicate the accreditation standards, communicate what we are doing to be compliant and also to reach the broader faculty and so we are also improving communication via emails and web pages and any other way we can to reach people. (Programme J, Participant #2)

The improvement, and in many cases the outright development, of robust data collection systems, along with the necessary investment in human resources and infrastructure, was the second most frequently discussed impact of accreditation. Data collection systems were required to perform curricular mapping in a more effective and efficient way. A respondent commented:

> I mentioned earlier the curricular mapping tool that we just bought. This is a huge expense for the School of Medicine and I think it's a good thing. If it hadn't been for accreditation, I am not sure we would have had the support of the university to buy this resource. (Programme I, Participant #1)

The establishment of systems to monitor specific aspects of the curriculum, as required by accreditation (e.g. timely delivery of feedback and summative grades), to facilitate ongoing compliance with accreditation standards, was also mentioned as an impact. As a respondent commented,

> We needed to be more data driven and we needed this individual who could help us do that and develop dashboards for real time monitoring. That was key. (Programme J, Participant #2)

Accreditation often led to better documentation and to the adoption or revision of policies and formalisation of procedures at the medical education programme level and contributed to better documentation of programmes' policies and procedures. Respondents commented:

> We haven't had the paper trail and our programme is growing now. It's getting larger and I think we've seen that we do need the paper trail in many cases. (Programme C, Participant #2)

> What's good also with accreditation is that it encourages the formalising of the various components. What I mean is the drafting of policies, to ensure we have clear policies for specific situations, all the policies that our deans and programmes prepare. (Programme I, Participant #1)

In several cases, the accreditation process triggered a complete overhaul of the curriculum, perceived as the best way to resolve issues identified at previous accreditation visits, and in some other cases, accreditation led to a restructuring of the funding model for academic faculty members. For example, a respondent commented:

> There were a lot of changes that came out of that accreditation cycle in [year]. We switched to active learning, we started to take harassment more seriously, we started to take resident teacher training more seriously. There were lots of different things we did. A lot of curricular transformation. (Programme J, Participant #4)

Accreditation fosters faculty members' engagement in the affairs of medical education programmes and promotes academic accountability. Respondents commented:

> It's not just reporting, but it's getting people who care about something together on a regular basis to discuss that. (Programme C, Participant #2)

> We're totally restructuring the way we engage and pay doctors to do academic work. (Programme G, Participant #1)

Finally, faculty members at several UME programmes perceived accreditation as a continuous quality improvement process to which permanent staff and resources had been devoted. For example, a respondent commented:

> My [next] point is probably the most important one and we recognised that we needed to maintain continuous quality improvement of the MD programme. This has really percolated through all our committees. (Programme J, Participant #2)

Perceived negative consequences of accreditation

Four themes captured the reported negative consequences of accreditation on medical education programmes and staff. The themes related to: (i) costs, (ii) feelings and morale of faculty members and staff, (iii) school reputation and (iv) standards (i.e. negative consequences on innovation related to accreditation standards). The 'Costs' theme comprised the greatest number of comments and included human and financial resources, as well as opportunity costs. Respondents commented:

> It's actually an impediment or an imposition and a costly one at that but that actually distracts from the real activities of the organisation, medical education or whatever it might be. (Programme D, Participant #1)

> When you start spending huge amounts of time and money that seems to increase every cycle, I think that's part of the problem, is standards appear to be increasing if not ultimately, certainly in the amount of work it takes to satisfy the standard. The workload increases, the costs increase and it's very hard to tie back the bang for the buck, certainly at specific standards and

maybe for the whole process. (Programme K, Participant #1)

Accreditation takes an important toll on faculty members and staff, can lead to low morale and accreditation burnout, and be divisive. Respondents commented:

> A lot of engagement has been lost, that means a lot of people feel disempowered and disenfranchised, that means a lot of people have left medical education and left the medical school and will not come back, and it means that a lot of relationships have been damaged. (Programme J, Participant 4)

> It was incredibly stressful for a lot of people. (Programme C, Focus Group Speaker #3)

Performance on accreditation might affect a school's reputation. One respondent commented:

> The system is oriented towards having the potential to disrupt the reputation of a school, to have a profound impact on its ability to fundraise, a profound effect on maybe the quality of students that subsequently try to get into the medical school. (Programme A, Participant #2)

Finally, accreditation standards are perceived by some as discouraging innovations and creating work without bringing clear value. Respondents commented:

> To a certain degree it thwarts innovation, because we have to follow these rules and we have to get these rules straight or else we're afraid of suffering a fate that we don't want, and so we can't invest the time that we would want and maybe just be very creative and innovative and the things maybe don't work out, but at least we can try, because that's the fun part of our job. (Programme F, Participant 2)

> The negative has to do with the lack of rationale underlying certain questions in the data collection instrument, so that it's perceived as useless and time-consuming. (Programme G, Participant #3)

DISCUSSION

To our knowledge, this is the first study assessing the impact of accreditation on medical schools' processes. As distinguished from student outcomes, this indicator is directly linked to accreditation, and offers a broad and innovative perspective on the impact of accreditation. The Canadian accreditation system (CACMS) is essentially identical to the USA system (LCME); results of this study can be generalised to non-Canadian LCME-accredited schools and to schools accredited by systems inspired by the LCME.

In this study, nine themes were formulated indicating medical schools' processes impacted by accreditation. Establishing systems, as distinguished from relying on individuals' idiosyncratic efforts, requires hiring personnel, either faculty members or administrative staff or both. Accreditation pushes leaders of medical education programmes to consider the credentials needed for committee membership, rather than simply including interested faculty members. It compels education programme leaders to clarify committees' reporting lines and to ensure that the core curriculum committee has central oversight of the work of the sub-committees. An additional impact related to governance is improved communication lines among programme committees and between undergraduate medical education programmes and their aligned counterparts, such as postgraduate programmes. Data collection and monitoring processes are enhanced, often through hiring of information technology specialists and the purchase of electronic platforms. Systematic mapping of the curriculum and assessment strategies, tracking of faculty members' appointments and monitoring of clinical encounters by medical students are all impacts of accreditation. Accreditation drives the creation and implementation of several procedures and policies, or in some cases, simply the better documentation and dissemination of existing ones. Finally, accreditation activities encourage leaders of medical education programmes to develop a continuous quality improvement (CQI) approach, with ongoing internal reviews of programme performance indicators.

It is well accepted that accreditation drives curricular changes in UME programmes.[22,23] The gathering of data and the preparation of documents in anticipation of the site visit provide for identification of potential problems and implementation of strategies for improvement.[24] Modifications of existing accreditation standards, development of new ones, or increased rigour in their application by accreditation committees, force medical schools to adjust their UME programmes.[22]

The current study provides evidence that accreditation also drives the implementation and strengthening of a number of medical schools' processes and specifically identifies the particular processes influenced by accreditation.

Current accreditation standards from the CACMS and from the LCME explicitly request establishment of specific processes, such as central oversight and monitoring of the education programme[25,26]; a direct link between accreditation and the presence of these specific processes was expected. The perception of study participants that these processes were in place as a result of accreditation, suggests that without accreditation, these processes might not exist at several of the schools.

The linkage between medical schools' processes and the desired outcome of accreditation, a quality education for medical students, is difficult to assess when quality medical education is evaluated primarily by students' performance in national exams. Students may perform well in examinations independent of the quality of their programmes. By their nature, the identified processes (governance, data collection, monitoring, etc.) appear inseparable from the quality of medical education. The results of this study thus substantiate the conceptual model that accreditation drives medical schools to develop, implement and strengthen processes that support quality in medical education programmes. The presence of systems for a programme's own evaluation and improvement, on an iterative basis, in anticipation of and in response to accreditation, not only contributes to maintaining and enhancing the quality of medical education but also serves as an indicator of programme quality. Ongoing evaluation would help lower the cost of accreditation as timely identification of issues and their correction would continuously take place, rather than being addressed in the months preceding an accreditation visit, curbing the surge of activities and the associated cost typically observed.

Participants shared many concerns about negative aspects of accreditation, in particular the demands on financial and human resources, the lost opportunities as a result of the redirection of financial resources to accreditation, and the potential impact on the morale of faculty members and staff. Open expression of participants' dissatisfaction with the current accreditation system mitigates the concerns that using the CACMS Secretary as the interviewer had positively biased participants' responses.

Future studies should be carried out to explore the relationship between the processes identified in this study, related to accreditation, and the processes recognised as best practices in organisational quality management.[27,28]

Limitations

The study results provide a snapshot in time of the processes implemented as a result of accreditation at Canadian medical schools. Repeated studies are required to evaluate the sustainability and evolution of these processes at each school.

That the PI was also the Secretary to CACMS might be seen as potentially preventing fair and genuine responses from participants; hence the need to triangulate data from multiple sources within a school and across schools. The rationale for specifically choosing the Secretary to the CACMS to conduct the interviews and focus group was explained earlier in this paper. The commonality between responses from multiple sources, within schools and across schools, and participants' sharing of their negative experiences with accreditation, however, suggest that responses were not biased to provide positive perspectives.

All medical education programmes that participated in the study were in good accreditation standing. Perspectives on the impact of accreditation might have been different had the accreditation status of Canadian programmes been different.

CONCLUSIONS

This study uses an innovative marker, medical schools' processes, to evaluate the impact of accreditation. Results provide evidence that accreditation-related activities steer medical education programmes towards the establishment of many processes, namely those related to governance, academic accountability, data collection and analysis, monitoring, documentation, and the creation and revision of policies. It also contributes to CQI and faculty members' engagement in the medical education programme. In some cases, it triggers a complete overhaul of the curriculum and of the academic accountability scheme. Although a direct link between the implementation or strengthening of medical schools' processes and the improvement of the quality of medical education is difficult to ascertain, the identified processes, given their nature, appear inseparable from the quality and effectiveness of medical education programmes. Counterbalancing the impact on schools' processes, several negative consequences of accreditation for medical education programmes have been identified.

Contributors: DB designed the study; acquired, analysed and interpreted data; drafted and revised the manuscript. IBH participated in the design of the study; interpreted data; revised the manuscript. CK participated in the design of the study; analysed and interpreted data; revised the manuscript. AT participated in the design of the study; revised the manuscript. All authors approved the version being submitted; and agreed to be accountable for all aspects of the work in ensuring that questions related to the accuracy or integrity of any part of the work are appropriately investigated and resolved.
Acknowledgements: None.
Funding: None.
Conflicts of interest: DB serves as Secretary to the Committee on Accreditation of Canadian Medical Schools, which is the accrediting body for Canadian medical schools. Her role is clearly indicated in the paper, and steps to mitigate her influence on the interpretation are presented in the paper. In addition, the paper presents participants' negative views on accreditation to counter the possible argument that participants felt uncomfortable disclosing negative perspectives about accreditation.
Ethical approval: Ethical approval was obtained from the Queen's University Health Sciences and Affiliated Teaching Hospitals Research Ethics Board, from the Office for the Protection of Research Subjects at the University of Illinois at Chicago, and from the institutional research ethics board affiliated with each participating institution.

REFERENCES

1 Committee on Accreditation of Canadian Medical Schools. *CACMS Rules of Procedures.* 2016. Available from https://cacms-cafmc.ca/sites/default/files/documents/CACMS_Rules_of_Procedure_July 2016.pdf. Accessed 10 March 2017.
2 Liaison Committee on Medical Education. *LCME Rules of Procedure.* 2016. Available from http://lcme.org/publications/. Accessed 10 March 2017.
3 Mays GP. *Can accreditation work in public health? Lessons from other service industries.* NJ: University of Arkansas for Medical Sciences 2004.
4 Greenfield D, Braithwaite J. Health sector accreditation research: a systematic review. *Int J Qual Health Care* 2008;**20** (3):172–83.
5 Simpson DE, Golden DL, Rehm JM, Kochar MS, Simons KB. The costs versus the perceived benefits of an LCME institutional self-study. *Acad Med* 1998; **73** (9):1009–12.
6 AFMC Senior Administrators Committee. *Personal communication with D. Blouin,* April 4, 2016.
7 van Zanten M, Norcini JJ, Boulet JR, Simon F. Overview of accreditation of undergraduate medical education programmes worldwide. *Med Educ* 2008; **42** (9):930–7.
8 Cueto JJ, Burch VC, Adnan NAM *et al.* Accreditation of undergraduate medical training programs: practices in nine developing countries as compared with the United States. *Educ Health (Abingdon)* 2006;**19** (2):207–22.
9 Boulet J, van Zanten M. Ensuring high-quality patient care: the role of accreditation, licensure, specialty certification and revalidation in medicine. *Med Educ* 2014;**48** (1):75–86.
10 Davis DJ, Ringsted C. Accreditation of undergraduate and graduate medical education: how do the standards contribute to quality? *Adv Health Sci Educ Theory Pract* 2006;**11**:305–13.
11 Al Alwan I. Is accreditation a true reflection of quality? *Med Educ* 2012;**46** (6):542–4.
12 van Zanten M, McKinley D, Durante Montiel I, Pijano CV. Medical education accreditation in Mexico and the Philippines: impact on student outcomes. *Med Educ* 2012;**46** (6):586–92.
13 Blouin D, Tekian A. Accreditation of medical education programs: moving from student outcomes to continuous quality improvement measures. *Acad Med.* Forthcoming 2017; DOI: 10.1097/ACM.0000000000001835.
14 van Zanten M, Boulet JR. The association between medical education accreditation and examination performance of internationally educated physicians seeking certification in the United States. *Qual High Educ* 2013;**19** (3):283–99.
15 Blonski J, Rahm S. The relationship of residency performance to match status and US versus international graduate status. *Fam Med* 2003;**35** (2): 100–4.
16 Kwakwa F, Biester TW, Ritchie W, Jonasson O. Career pathways of graduates of general surgery residency programs: an analysis of graduates from 1983 to 1990. *J Am Coll Surg* 2002;**194** (1):48–53.
17 Garibaldi RA, Subhiyah R, Moore ME, Waxman H. The in-training examination in internal medicine: an analysis of resident performance over time. *Ann Intern Med* 2002;**137** (6):505–10.
18 Huggan PJ, Samarasekara DD, Archuleta S, Khoo SM, Sim JHJ, Ooi SBS. The successful, rapid transition to a new model of graduate medical education in Singapore. *Acad Med* 2012;**87** (9):1268–73.
19 Miles MB, Huberman AM. *Qualitative data analysis: an expanded sourcebook,* 2nd edn. Thousand Oaks: Sage Publications 1994.
20 Corbin JM, Strauss AL. *Basics of qualitative research: Techniques and procedures for developing grounded theory,* 4th edn. Thousand Oaks, California: Sage 2015.

21 Moghaddam A. Coding issues in grounded theory. *Issues Educ Res* 2006;**16** (1):52–66.
22 Kassebaum DG, Cutler ER, Eaglen RH. The influence of accreditation on educational change in U.S. medical schools. *Acad Med* 1997;**72** (12):1127–33.
23 Leinster S. Role of accrediting bodies in providing education leadership in medical education. *J Health Spec* 2014;**2** (4):132–5.
24 Chandran L, Fleit HB, Shroyer AL. Academic medicine change management: the power of the liaison committee on medical education accreditation process. *Acad Med* 2013;**88** (9):1225–31.
25 Committee on Accreditation of Canadian Medical Schools. *CACMS accreditation standards.* 2017. Available from https://cacms-cafmc.ca/sites/default/files/documents/CACMS_Standards_and_Elements_-_AY_2017-18.pdf. Accessed 10 March 2017.
26 Liaison Committee on Medical Education. *Functions and Structure of a Medical School.* 2016. Available from http://lcme.org/publications/. Accessed 27 March 2017.
27 Brandrud AS, Schreiner A, Hjortdahl P, Helljesen GS, Nyen B, Nelson EC. Three success factors for continual improvement in healthcare: an analysis of the reports of improvement team members. *BMJ Qual Saf* 2011;**20** (3):251–9.
28 Rubenstein L, Khodyakov D, Hempel S, Danz M, Salem-Schatz S, Foy R, O'Neill S, Dalal S, Shekelle P. How can we recognize continuous quality improvement? *Int J Qual Health Care* 2014;**26** (1):6–15.

SUPPORTING INFORMATION

Additional Supporting Information may be found in the online version of this article:

Appendix S1. Questions for interviews and focus groups.

Received 27 March 2017; editorial comments to author 1 June 2017, 10 July 2017; accepted for publication 14 August 2017

Lessons from practice

Janet M. Riddle

Department of Medical Education, University of Illinois at Chicago College of Medicine. Chicago, Illinois, United States of America.
ORCID ID: 0000-0002-8630-9927. jriddle@uic.edu

For the last fifteen years I have been the director and primary facilitator of a longitudinal teaching scholars program. In that time, I have worked with 158 clinical teachers and educators at the University of Illinois-Chicago College of Medicine, and affiliated community sites. I would like to share some of the lessons I have learned about the practice of faculty development and what it means to be a faculty developer. Let me begin by describing our longitudinal program, the Scholars for Teaching Excellence Faculty Fellowship. Each year I recruit a cohort of health professions faculty who are interesting in improving their skills in instruction and curriculum development. We meet for one afternoon a week for almost eight months. During that time we read about, discuss, and reflect on teaching in classroom and clinical contexts. Participants in the program also observe highly regarded teachers. Each of the teaching scholars develops and implements plans to improve his or her teaching. Many also begin to develop new *curricula* and educational programs. I would like to reflect on my experiences to chart my own deepening awareness of what it means to be a faculty developer.

The Scholars for Teaching Excellence is a faculty development community or "teaching commons". As described by O'Sullivan and Irby[1] this faculty development community is composed of the participants in the program, the facilitator or faculty developer, and the faculty development program activities. The teaching commons is situated within the workplace community where clinical faculty care for patients, teach, conduct research, and provide service to the community. The participants, the facilitator, and the faculty development program connect the faculty development community with the workplace community. Both of these communities exist within the larger institutional context and culture. Within the faculty development community the facilitator and the participants learn with and from each other. The activities or *curriculum* of the teaching scholars program allow participants to learn about teaching and reflect on their capabilities and skills. Our activities also afford opportunities to understand the influence of the institutional culture on our teaching and educational work.

Lesson #1 - Faculty development is what participants choose to pursue to improve their capabilities

The participants in our teaching scholars program must apply for the fellowship, although no one is turned away after completing the application process. Participants join the fellowship for their own personal reasons and sometimes at the request of their department heads. Important factors in choosing to apply to the program include prior experiences of teaching, perceptions about current teaching capabilities, and the desire to be connected to a group of likeminded clinical teachers. Steinert reminds us that faculty development is "all activities health professionals pursue to improve their knowledge, skills, and behaviors as teachers and educators, leaders and managers, and researchers and scholars, in both individual and group settings."[2]. Faculty development is what clinical teachers and educators choose to pursue in order to improve their capabilities. While I may facilitate learning and practice through faculty development, it is the participants who pursue and engage with faculty development activities.

Lesson #2 - The improvement in teaching that is possible is influenced by values, beliefs, and norms

Teaching is complex. There are many instructional activities that constitute "effective teaching". Teachers need to select and apply instructional methods or activities in specific educational contexts for learning to occur. Experience and practice are also important. Prior experiences and interests allow some teachers to appear to be more intuitive in their teaching. As D'Eon and colleagues[3] argue, effective teaching is more than simply the application of technique or a craft. Teaching is a social practice that is guided by the values, beliefs, and norms of the workplace community and institutional culture. As the facilitator of the teaching scholars program, I need to be attentive to the beliefs and values about "effective teaching" that any cohort of participants has at the beginning of the fellowship. I am able to influence and guide the development of group norms and expectations about teaching and learning through my own teaching and role modeling. Not only to I demonstrate the instructional skills that are an essential part of the *curriculum*, I also strive to embody an attitude towards learners. Collaborative learning activities are also important in providing participants with peer support as they move from a more teacher-centered to a more learner-centered approach to teaching.

Lesson #3 - Clinical teachers are seeking a community of like-minded colleagues

The participants in the faculty fellowship are genuinely motivated to enhance their teaching skills. Some perceive the organizational culture as one that does not value teaching as highly as they do. They join the fellowship because they are looking for like-minded colleagues who share their passion for teaching. As a faculty developer I use processes of negotiating, constructing, and attuning[4] to shape the teaching commons of the fellowship. Negotiating is the process of acknowledging and working within the goals, structures, and routines of the workplace community. I design and refine program activities so that the participants learn to work more effectively within changing educational environments. Some participants need to learn new teaching methods for a medical education curriculum renewal. Others need to learn how to respond to evolving accreditation standards. I help participants make sense of the educational environment and to align their goals with those of the educational workplace. In constructing sessions within the program, I create opportunities to demonstrate and practice teaching skills that are required in the workplace community – and that reflect the values and beliefs of learner-centered teaching that are central to the faculty development community. I use the process of attuning during each session to recognize and respond to participants' learning needs. Over time working with many different participants, I have developed an understanding of the questions and challenges faced by clinical teachers that allows me to adjust the focus and pace of activities in the moment. Reflective discussion, building relationships among participants, and introducing the language and frameworks of education contribute to a supportive community within which participants develop their identities as clinical teachers and educators[5].

In closing, in my experiences over fifteen years of practice I have learned important lessons about the participants' motivations to participate in the teaching scholars program, the culture that we create together within the teaching commons, and the processes that I use to create a community of clinical teachers.

References

1. O'Sullivan PS, Irby DM. Reframing research on faculty development. Acad Med. 2011;86(4):421-428. doi: 10.1097/ACM.0b013e31820dc058

2. Steinert Y. Faculty development: core concepts and principles. In Steinert Y, editor. Faculty Development in the Health Professions: A Focus on Research and Practice. Dordrecht: Springer; 2014; p.4.

3. D'Eon M, Overgaard V, Rutledge S. Teaching as social practice: implications for faculty development. Adv Health Sci Educ Theory Pract. 2000;5(2):151-162. doi: 10.1023/A:1009898031033

4. Baker L, Leslie K, Panisko D, Walsh A, Wong A, Stubbs B, Mylopoulos M. Exploring faculty developers' experiences to inform our understanding of competence in faculty development. Acad Med. 2018;93(2):265-273. doi: 10.1097/ACM.0000000000001821

5. Lieff S, Baker L, Mori B, Egan-Lee E, Chin K, Reeves S. Who am I? Key influences on the formation of academic identity within a faculty development program. Med Teach. 2012;34(3):e208-215. doi: 10.3109/0142159X.2012.642827

2016, 38: 64–74

Medical education practice-based research networks: Facilitating collaborative research

ALAN SCHWARTZ[1,3], ROBIN YOUNG[3] & PATRICIA J. HICKS[2,3]; FOR APPD LEARN[3]

[1]University of Illinois at Chicago, USA, [2]Children's Hospital of Philadelphia, USA, [3]Association of Pediatric Program Directors, USA

Abstract

Background: Research networks formalize and institutionalize multi-site collaborations by establishing an infrastructure that enables network members to participate in research, propose new studies, and exploit study data to move the field forward. Although practice-based clinical research networks are now widespread, medical education research networks are rapidly emerging.

Aims: In this article, we offer a definition of the medical education practice-based research network, a brief description of networks in existence in July 2014 and their features, and a more detailed case study of the emergence and early growth of one such network, the Association of Pediatric Program Directors Longitudinal Educational Assessment Research Network (APPD LEARN).

Methods: We searched for extant networks through peer-reviewed literature and the world-wide web.

Results: We identified 15 research networks in medical education founded since 2002 with membership ranging from 8 to 120 programs. Most focus on graduate medical education in primary care or emergency medicine specialties.

Conclusions: We offer four recommendations for the further development and spread of medical education research networks: increasing faculty development, obtaining central resources, studying networks themselves, and developing networks of networks.

Introduction

Multi-site research offers several compelling advantages for medical education research. First, multi-site studies help ameliorate the inherent limitations in sample size at individual medical schools and training programs, allowing for opportunities to pursue both smaller effect sizes and more nuanced hypotheses about interaction, mediation, and moderation of educational effects. Second, multi-site studies enable comparisons of effects among sites, potentially illuminating both overall generalizability of effects as well as contextual sources of variability in educational effects. In combination with a data repository for storing research data (Schwartz et al. 2010; Cleland et al. 2013), multi-site research encourages efforts by educational communities to share and leverage research resources (O'Sullivan et al. 2010; Huggett et al. 2011).

Research networks formalize and institutionalize multi-site collaborations by establishing infrastructure to enable network members to participate in multiple studies, propose new studies, and exploit study data to maximize scholarly output. Research networks also facilitate the dissemination of evidence-based practices to network members. Scientific research networks and clinical research networks have a long history, with primary care practice-based research networks (PBRNs) emerging in the 1960s (Green & Hickner 2006). On the

Practice points

- Medical education practice-based research networks (MEPBRNs) offer exciting opportunities to conduct multi-site studies in medical education and provide meaningful scholarship for members.
- Faculty development for investigators at sites participating in MEPBRNs is necessary for network success.
- MEPBRNs require some central resources, and must select a funding model that is agreeable to network members and stakeholders.
- As MEPBRNs are relatively new, formal relationships among networks for sharing best practices and multi-network projects have yet to be established, and are likely to be an important future development.

other hand, calls for research networks in medical education are comparatively recent (Carney et al. 2004; Beeson & Deiorio 2010). Network activities in support of collaborative research may include review, refinement, and approval of study proposals; coordination of study funding, human subjects approval, and site recruitment; faculty development and professional networking for participating network member faculty; data collection infrastructure and assistance;

© 2015 The Author(s). Published by Taylor & Francis. This is an Open Access article distributed under the terms of the Creative Commons Attribution License (http://creativecommons.org/Licenses/by/4.0/), which permits unrestricted use, distribution, and reproduction in any medium, provided the original work is properly cited.

Correspondence: Alan Schwartz, Department of Medical Education (mc 591), University of Illinois at Chicago, 808 S. Wood St., 986 CME, Chicago, IL 60612, USA. Tel: + 1 312 996 2070; Fax: + 1 312 413 2048; E-mail: alansz@uic.edu

data warehousing; development and dissemination of scholarly products; and recognition of participating sites.

In this article, we offer a definition of the medical education PBRN, a brief description of networks in existence in July 2014 and their features, and a more detailed case study of the development, evolution, and activities of one such network, the Association of Pediatric Program Directors Longitudinal Educational Assessment Research Network (APPD LEARN). Our goal is to provide a common terminology and a catalog of medical education PBRNs to allow future investigators to study the features and life courses of these networks. Along the way, and in conclusion, we outline several challenges and opportunities for the further development and spread of medical education research networks.

Defining networks

We define a medical educational practice-based research network as an organization or consortium consisting of multiple educational sites (e.g. schools or training programs) formed for the primary purpose of facilitating multiple research studies each using all or a subset of the network sites. The several components of this definition place specific conditions on what we categorize as an educational research network for the purposes of this article.

First, the practice-based network must consist of educational sites, as opposed to individual researchers. Although research teams consisting of groups of individual scholars are of critical importance to medical education, and may persist for years, our focus is on research networks with institutional members who implicitly or explicitly are committing program resources to network participation. Of course, institutions conduct research through affiliated individuals, so we expect that each member institution in a medical education PBRN will be represented by one or more individuals.

The network members must be primarily medical educational organizations, directly involved in educational practice – the instruction or assessment of learners. This component of the definition is broad enough to allow for certifying boards or other regulatory institutions involved in assessment to be network members although they may not be directly responsible for instruction, although as a rule most members will be continuing medical education providers, training programs, or medical schools. We exclude by design networks whose only educational focus is either patient education or the education of network members themselves in the absence of educational research conducted by the network. A notable feature of the medical education research network is that most network members will have a primary education mission, rather than a research mission – this presents particular challenges we discuss later.

Second, our definition requires that the network intends to consider research its primary purpose and to engage in multiple research studies over time. In this, we mirror the Agency for Healthcare Research and Quality (AHRQ)'s description of PBRNs as including "a sense of ongoing commitment to network activities and an organizational structure that transcends a single research project". In particular, we do not consider one-time consortia or study groups formed for the purposes of a single multisite research project to fit our definition of a research network. Similarly, we exclude from this manuscript networks whose primary purpose is developing or disseminating educational materials and only engage in data collection to the extent necessary to assess the needs for, or satisfaction with, such materials. AHRQ maintains a registry of practice-based research networks that fit its criteria (including educational research networks), but as there is no definitive registry of medical education research networks in particular, it can be difficult to determine whether a collaborative not listed in AHRQ's registry is a research network. One potential indicator is the use of a group author on publications (Flanagin et al. 2002), which generally necessitates a description of the group and the contributions of member sites and their personnel, including sites involved in the research but not authorship of the publication.

Networks may conduct studies that do not involve all of their members at once; indeed, for larger PBRNs, this is typical. Nevertheless, even when only a subset of members are collaborating on a network project, the project is likely to be identified with the network if it partakes of centralized network resources (such as management or statistical support). The same group of sites may collaborate on non-network projects as well.

Existing networks

The development of research networks themselves may not be documented in the peer-reviewed literature. Although some practice-based clinical research networks publish manuscripts describing their formation (Wasserman et al. 1998; Deshefy-Longhi et al. 2002; Dickerson et al. 2007), there may be fewer journals in medical education research that publish such descriptions. In light of this gap, we sought to document existing networks at this historical moment.

Accordingly, we searched both peer-review literature sources (PubMed, OVID, and Wiley Online) and the broader web (via Google and Yahoo search engines) to attempt to identify medical education research networks in operation in July 2014. Our search was restricted to English- and Korean-language publications and web sites. Keywords used for search included "medical education" and "research" combined with each of the keywords "network", "collaborative", "consortium", and "database", as well as PubMed searches using each of those keywords as "corporate names" (group authors). We also hand-searched the AHRQ's Practice-Based Research Network portal to identify networks focused on medical education. We did not attempt to identify networks that may have existed in the past and are no longer in operation, and excluded networks when contact with their (former) directors indicated that the network was no longer operational.

In addition to APPD LEARN, which we describe in greater detail as a case study later in this article, we located 15 research networks in medical education. Figure 1 displays the founding year, size, and focus of these networks. We provide a brief summary of key network information in Table 1 to

65

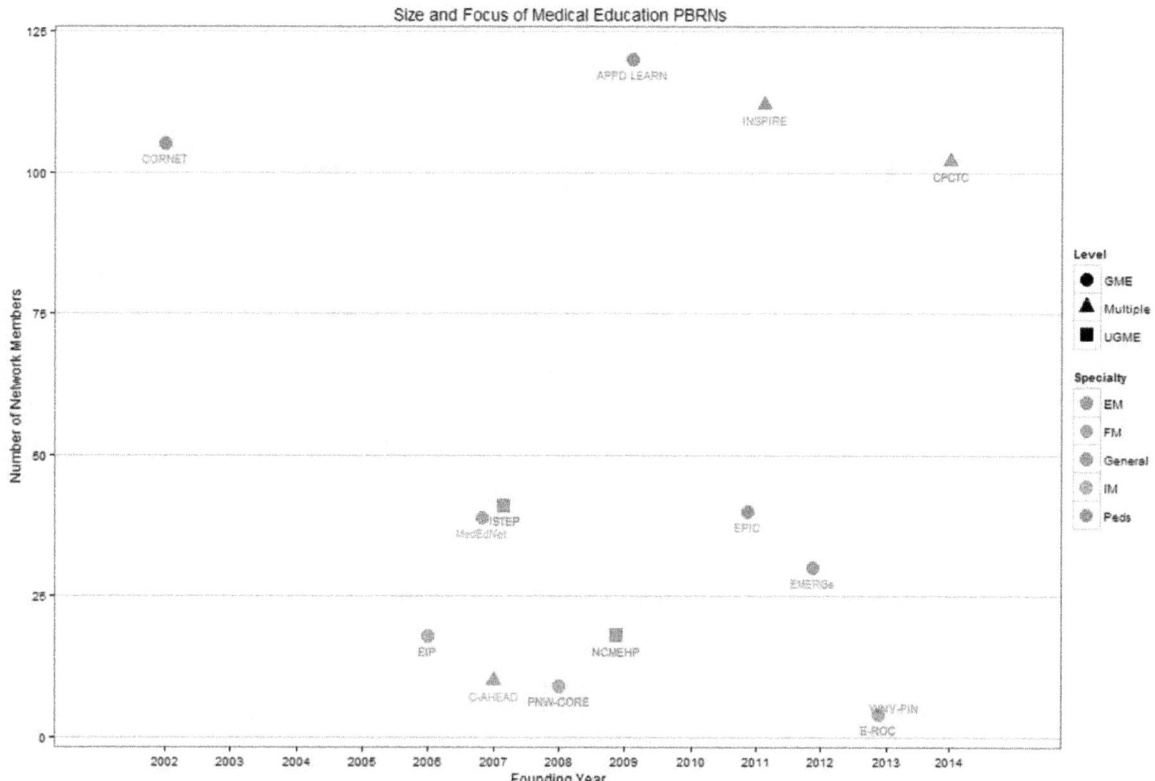

Figure 1. Founding years and current membership size (as of July 2014) for 15 medical education practice-based research networks.

identify common features as well as to document and record their existence. When possible, we contacted the network director or coordinator to inform them about this paper and to verify this information, and we provide an overview below of those networks for which we could obtain additional information from their directors.

Innovative Strategies for Transforming the Education of Physicians

The American Medical Association (AMA) began organizing Innovative Strategies for Transforming the Education of Physicians (ISTEP) in 2005 through a competitive process in which medical schools or consortia applied to receive planning grants for the network, with the network itself officially established in 2007. ISTEP's mission is "To be the premier transformational medical education research collaborative focused on identifying the connections between educational efforts across all learner levels (students, residents/fellows and practicing physicians) and improved patient care outcomes" (American Medical Association 2010). ISTEP currently comprises 41 medical schools in the US and Canada. Ongoing research includes a longitudinal investigation (in its third year as of this writing) into the relationship between educational climate and the development of professional attributes among students (the "Learning Environment Study" with 29 participating sites). ISTEP also received funding from the National Institute on Drug Abuse to develop educational resources and curriculum on substance abuse and to survey residents and students on their attitudes and beliefs surrounding intervening when a patient presents with a substance abuse problem. AMA provides administrative coordination for ISTEP studies, and provides support to ISTEP sites to act as data coordination centers for particular studies.

Center for the Advancement of Healthcare Education and Delivery

Center for the Advancement of Healthcare Education and Delivery (C-AHEAD) is a family medicine network of six practices, one family practice residency, and three medical schools, that engages in both health care delivery and medical education research. Examples of recent projects include a study of osteopathic distinctiveness and its role in education, and evaluation of an online educational module in care transitions for medical students, funded by the American Association of Colleges of Osteopathic Medicine.

Medical Education Research Network

Medical Education Research Network (MedEdNet) is a national research network with a primary focus on family medicine. The network was founded in 2007 by 14 Family Medicine residency programs engaged in the P^4 Initiative

Table 1. Summary of existing medical education practice-based research networks.

Network name (acronym)	Sponsoring organizations	Founded	Focus	Members	Number of members	Contact URL
COntinuity Research NETwork (CORNET)	Academic Pediatric Association	2002	Pediatrics health care delivery, disparities, and resident education	Pediatrics continuity clinics (US)	105	http://www.ambpeds.org/research/research_cornet.cfm
Educational Innovations Project (EIP)	ACGME (Internal Medicine Residency Review Committee)	2006	Internal Medicine education, particularly GME	Internal Medicine residency programs (US), approved by RRC	18	http://www.im.org/AcademicAffairs/EducationalInnovations/Pages/default.aspx
Innovative Strategies for Transforming the Education of Physicians (ISTEP)	American Medical Association	2007	Medical education, all levels	Medical schools (North America)	41	http://www.ama-assn.org/ama/pub/education-careers/istepinnovative-strategies-transforming-education-physicians.page
Medical Education Research Network (MedEdNet)	Oregon Health & Science University, Association of Family Medicine Residency Directors, American Board of Family Medicine	2007	Primary care education, particularly GME	Primary care residency programs (US)	39	https://fmresearch.ohsu.edu/medednet.org
Pacific Northwest Consortium for Outcomes in Residency Education (PNW-CORE)	American Board of Internal Medicine	2008	Internal Medicine GME	Internal Medicine residency programs (US)	9	None yet
Longitudinal Educational Assessment Research Network (APPD LEARN)	Association of Pediatric Program Directors	2009	Pediatrics education, particularly GME	Pediatrics residency programs (US)	123	http://learn.appd.org
Education in Pediatric Intensive Care (EPIC)		2011	Pediatric intensive care education	Pediatric critical care fellowship programs	40	http://epicstudy.com for current study; None yet for network.
International Network for Simulation-Based Pediatric Innovation, Research, and Education (INSPIRE)	RBaby Foundation & Laerdal Foundation	2011 (merger of EXPRESS, and POISE)	Simulation-based education in Pediatrics	Medical centers and schools (International)	112	http://inspiresim.com
Emergency Medicine Educational Research Group (EMERGe)	None	2012	Emergency Medicine	Emergency Medicine training programs	30	None yet
Educational Research Outcomes Collaborative (E-ROC)		2013	Internal Medicine, GME	Internal Medicine residency programs (US)	23	None yet
Canadian Network for Simulation in Healthcare (CNSH)	None	2012	Simulation (interprofessional)	Canadian investigators and institutions	Unknown	http://www.cnsh.ca
Center for the Advancement of Healthcare Education and Delivery PBRN (C-AHEAD)	None	2007	Family Medicine	Family Medicine practices and medical school programs	10	None currently
Western New York Pediatric Innovation Network (WNY-PIN)		2013	Pediatrics	Pediatric clinics (New York)	8	None identified
National Consortium for Multicultural Education for Health Professionals	NHLBI	2009	Health disparities	Medical schools (US)	18	http://culturalmeded.stanford.edu/about/initiatives.html
Collaborative of the Primary Care Training Collaborative (Patient-Centered Primary Care Collaborative)	Patient-Centered Primary Care Collaborative	2014	Educational outcomes of patient-centered medical homes	Network of 5 networks of practices	102 total (4, 10, 19, 25, and 44 in the member networks)	http://www.pcpcc.org/

(Preparing the Personal Physician for Practice) sponsored by the American Board of Family Medicine, the Association of Family Medicine Residency Directors, and TransforMED (Carney & Green 2011; Agency for Healthcare Research and Quality 2013; MedEdNet 2013). It currently includes 39 programs. MedEdNet focuses on physician education through longitudinal assessments of learners to evaluate which aspects of the residency experience correlate with primary care practice and innovation, with the ultimate goal of improving the health of populations served by primary care practices. The network is currently funded to conduct three national studies: an extension of the P^4 study to collect two additional years of graduate data; the Accreditation Council for Graduate Medical Education (ACGME) Family Medicine Length of Training Pilot to compare 3- and 4-year FM residencies; and the Primary Care Faculty Development Initiative, a pilot program of the American Boards of Family Medicine, Internal Medicine, and Pediatrics funded by HRSA and the Macy Foundation that is studying how to train residents in primary care disciplines to practice safely and effectively in a rapidly evolving health care system.

Membership is open to all family medicine, general internal medicine residency and general pediatrics residency programs, with a membership fee based on participation level (participation in a single study versus full membership in the network). MedEdNet offers services to help programs with study design, program evaluation and instrumentation, and fulfilling accreditation requirements for scholarly activity. Members have access to a relational database with information on more than 800 residents linked to 6+ years of data from resident, program, continuity clinic, and graduate surveys (administered 18 months after residency completed). The network also provides IRB support and consultative services for research and faculty development. MedEdNet is governed by a Board of Directors and operated by a Scientific Director and an Administrative Director.

Educational Innovations Project

The Educational Innovations Project (EIP) was launched in 2006 by the Internal Medicine Residency Review Committee of the ACGME. EIP programs "are expected to develop, study, and disseminate methods for competency-based education and evaluation" (Accreditation Council for Graduate Medical Education 2011) Programs with excellence in past accreditation cycles were invited to join the EIP. Collaborative activities among the 18 Internal Medicine residency programs currently engaged in the EIP include studies to evaluate continuity experiences for residents and to operationalize the use of milestones for resident assessment.

Pacific Northwest Consortium for Outcomes in Residency Education

The Pacific Northwest Consortium for Outcomes in Residency Education (PNW-CORE) began in 2008 with support from the American Board of Internal Medicine. Nine Internal Medicine programs are currently members. The network is currently engaged in a study of assessment of resident leadership in codes. PNW-CORE recently published a cultural consensus analysis among patients, nurses, residents, physicians, and administrators at eight of its member programs that provided evidence for construct validity of ACGME's six-competency framework (Smith et al. 2013).

Education Research Outcomes Collaborative

The Education Research Outcomes Collaborative (E-ROC) is a consortium of 13 Internal Medicine programs with analytic support from investigators at ACGME. E-ROC has been studying the impact of milestones on the training of residents and methods to increase engagement of residents with milestones (Meade et al., 2013a,b).

APA Continuity Research Network

Continuity Research Network (CORNET) is a national (US) practice-based research network composed of pediatric resident continuity practices and organized by the Academic Pediatric Association (APA). CORNET currently includes 104 pediatric training program continuity practices as members. CORNET focuses on research in primary care, health care delivery and medical education that improves the training of future pediatricians and the health care of children, with special attention to underserved children (Academic Pediatric Association 2013). Current CORNET studies include a three-phase CDC-funded quality improvement study of adolescent immunization (now in phase 3, with 12 CORNET sites participating), the second phase of a study examining resident education in mental health integration models, and a pilot study of an interactive DVD on methods to decrease aggressive behavior in young children in preparation for a larger randomized trial. Past studies have included a variety of topics and research designs involving 4–27 sites, as well as collaborations with the clinical PBRN Pediatric Research in Outpatient Settings (PROS).

Membership is free and open to any APA member. CORNET is governed by a Steering Committee, and operated by a Network Director and a Lead Research Associate/Research Network Coordinator. CORNET is organized into 11 regions with research chairs for each region. The Steering Committee and Regional Research Chairs together form an Executive Committee which reviews submitted research proposals, provides feedback, and designates approved proposals.

Emergency Medicine Educational Research Group

The Emergency Medicine Educational Research Group (EMERGe) is a newly formed network independent of other academic organizations. The network's initial development was reported by Newgard et al. (2012). Members to date include 30 Emergency Medicine training programs. The network's efforts are driven by the principal investigators of proposed studies, with the network providing review of studies, infrastructure to recruit sites, and guidelines for authorship and division of labor. The network is beginning two studies, one on burnout among academic emergency physicians and the other on evaluation of a feedback tool for Emergency Medicine milestones (Hansen, personal communication).

Education in Pediatric Intensive Care

Education in Pediatric Intensive Care (EPIC) is a research collaborative focused on education-based research in pediatric intensive care involving 30 institutions, independent of other academic organizations. Network members are individual investigators, of whom there are currently approximately 40 (Turner, personal communication). It recently published its first study, an investigation of teaching modalities used by pediatric critical care medicine (PCCM) fellowship programs to teach communication and professionalism (Turner & Goodman 2011). Three other investigations are ongoing which include a follow-up investigation of how PCCM fellows perceive their teaching in communication and professionalism, the development of a valid and reliable tool to assess central venous catheter placement, and development of a mechanism to assess leadership competence. The network is developing an oversight committee and is in the process of formalizing its structure.

International Network for Simulation-based Pediatric Innovation, Research, and Education

The International Network for Simulation-based Pediatric Innovation, Research, and Education (INSPIRE) network was formed in 2011 through the merger of the examining pediatric resuscitation education through simulation and scripting (EXPRESS) and patient outcomes in simulation education (POISE) networks, and is supported by the Laerdal Foundation for Acute Medicine and the RBaby Foundation. INSPIRE's membership is international (North America, Europe, Middle East, and Australia) and includes 112 institutions. INSPIRE seeks to improve the delivery of medical care to acutely ill children through research in pediatric resuscitation, technical skills, behavioral skills, and simulation-based education. INSPIRE investigators have 15 studies planned, ongoing, or completed in areas including debriefing methods, teamwork, and simulation instruction in procedural and psychomotor skills, as well as simulation studies of clinical innovations. For example, the improving pediatric acute care through simulation (IMPACTS) study has developed and validated cases to study care of simulated infants by different emergency department teams; site enrollment has begun, with an anticipation that 32 hospitals will be involved (INSPIRE 2013).

INSPIRE's Executive Committee reviews and approves proposals, and develops policies and procedures for the network. An external Network Advisory Board provides counsel on study conduct and publications. INSPIRE has a consultative submission process (to obtain consultation to inform a submission) as well as a new project submission process. INSPIRE proposals with external support are expected to allocate 0.1 FTE for administrative support of the network (INSPIRE 2012).

Other networks

Our search identified several additional networks for which we did not receive additional information from network directors. Accordingly, we are not sure whether these networks fully meet our definition of the medical education PBRN, but we list them to improve the comprehensiveness of this review. These networks include the Canadian Network for Simulation in Healthcare (CNSH; Chiniara et al. 2013), the Western New York Pediatric Innovation Network (WNY-PIN), the National Consortium for Multicultural Education for Health Professionals (Lie et al. 2009; Carter-Pokras et al. 2010; Crenshaw et al. 2011), the Society for Academic Primary Care Special Interest Group in Educational Research, and the Asia neTwork to reguLAte Sepsis care (ATLAS; Li et al. 2011).

APPD LEARN: A case study of the emergence of a medical education research network

In this section, we describe in greater detail the formation and early development of a single medical education research network (in which the authors are involved). In this case study, we highlight challenges that we believe will be typical for new medical education research networks.

Formation

The Association of Pediatric Program Directors Longitudinal Educational Assessment Research Network (APPD LEARN) grew from APPD's experiences with sharing of assessment tools and instructional materials (APPD Share Warehouse; Roberts et al. 2012). Sharing educational materials naturally led to questions about the value, validity, and transferability of the materials; an educational (residency program-based) research network was proposed as the approach for coordinating residency programs who sought to study these questions. Brainstorming for the creation of APPD LEARN began in 2006, with a strategic plan formulated by APPD leaders in 2008 and incorporated into APPD's 2010 strategic planning initiative (Burke et al. 2010).

As a parallel process, the American Board of Pediatrics (ABP) engaged the community in a four-year self-study of residency education, the Residency Review and Redesign Project (R^3P; Jones et al. 2009) concluding that no prescription for training could withstand the test of time. Health needs of patients and the delivery systems in which we care for them are evolving and changing, and medical education needs to keep pace. The Initiative for Innovation in Pediatric Education (IIPE), a program supported by the ABP Foundation to foster and disseminate educational innovations in Pediatrics, was developed in response to this challenge. Members of APPD were invited to become members of the IIPE infrastructure, and matching funds from APPD's annual operating budget and the ABP Foundation were directed to support APPD LEARN from 2009 to 2012. An initial Advisory Committee (see the discussion of governance below) and the first APPD LEARN Director were selected in 2009. APPD LEARN registered as a PRBN with AHRQ in 2012.

Mission

In developing the mission for APPD LEARN, leadership was cognizant of the need to define the network's distinctive aims, particularly in light of the existence of APA CORNET, and APPD's own Research and Scholarship Task Force, which coordinates survey research on program directors themselves. Through advisory committee meetings, and informed by discussions between APPD LEARN leaders and other stakeholders, APPD LEARN defined its mission around the needs of Pediatrics program directors and a focus on learner (as opposed to patient or program director) outcomes.

The mission of APPD LEARN is "to conduct meaningful educational research that advances the training of future Pediatricians by developing and promoting participation and collaboration in research by program directors for the purpose of improving the health and well-being of children". Based in APPD, a member organization, APPD LEARN seeks to serve the educational research needs of pediatric training programs and their program directors by undertaking studies proposed by members as well as engaging in national initiatives and collaborations with other education organizations.

APPD LEARN's initial strategic plan defined six core interconnected network activities:

- Managing a collaborative research network of Pediatric Programs working together to conduct multi-site studies of educational methods and instruments.
- Maintaining an online repository of educational research study materials, raw data, and findings for dissemination to APPD members and collaborators.
- Promoting learning opportunities to enhance educational research participation and scholarship by Program Directors.
- Providing expert consultation for research conducted within APPD LEARN.
- Communicating regularly with the APPD membership and the larger medical education community about activities, opportunities, and outcomes.
- Exploring, conducting, and coordinating research with other organizations and initiatives across a continuum of medical and non-medical education (e.g., the education of other health professionals).

The first two activities embody the research operations, particularly data collection, management, dissemination, and sharing. The second two activities address the needs of program directors for specific faculty development and support to translate insights and questions arising out of the lived reality of directing a residency program into research questions, hypotheses, study designs, and analysis plans. The final two activities emphasize the aspiration of reaching out beyond APPD to enable members to advance the study of medical education broadly.

Organization and participation

Membership in APPD LEARN is open to any APPD member program. Programs are asked to name a liaison to APPD LEARN when they join (frequently the program director or an associate program director). There is no membership fee, but members are expected to complete an annual needs assessment survey and to participate in at least one study every two years when there are active studies available. In practice, most, but not all, member programs comply with these expectations.

Operating personnel

The APPD LEARN Director is responsible for scientific and management oversight of all APPD LEARN activities. The APPD LEARN Director serves for a term of two years, renewable by the APPD Board indefinitely, at a time commitment of at least 0.4 FTE. This position is currently filled by a PhD social scientist working remotely through a contract with his home institution.

The APPD LEARN Project Manager facilitates communications among the participating institutions and funding agencies, develops and tracks project timelines, and ensures that regulatory requirements are satisfied; she also has a large role in assisting PIs with study management, including IRB submissions, data collection, and other study processes. She serves as liaison with research administration at all participating institutions. A full-time Master's or PhD-level project manager based at the APPD administrative headquarters fills this position.

Governance and operating committees

Three standing committees (Advisory, Educational Development, and Proposal Review) currently guide the major functions of the network. The APPD LEARN Director and Project Manager serve ex officio on each committee.

The APPD LEARN Advisory Committee provides guidance to the APPD LEARN Director, sets policies for APPD LEARN activities and resources, develops calls for proposals in specific research areas, and conducts annual formative and summative evaluations of the APPD LEARN Director. The Committee consists of five voting members (one of whom serves as the Chair, and another of whom is the Past Chair), and may include additional non-voting members representing external stakeholders or partners. APPD LEARN Advisory Committee terms are two years long, staggered, and renewable. APPD's Executive Director also serves ex officio on the Advisory Committee. This committee meets monthly by phone.

The APPD LEARN Educational Development Committee advises the APPD LEARN Director in determining the faculty development needs of APPD LEARN members in the area of educational research, designing and interpreting the annual APPD LEARN needs assessment survey, and identifying training opportunities. The APPD LEARN Proposal Review Committee assists the APPD LEARN Director in the review of proposals to conduct research using the network and its member programs. During proposal review, the committee identifies areas of strength and weakness in each proposal, and makes recommendations to the Director and the proposal investigators about whether the proposal is suitable for the network and what kinds of additional support (e.g., statistical consultation) APPD LEARN can provide to enhance its likelihood of success.

Study committees

Each approved study using the APPD LEARN network has an ad hoc project oversight committee, composed of the project principal investigator, APPD LEARN Director, APPD LEARN Project Manager, and other members selected by the principal investigator and APPD LEARN Director. These committees hold regular conference calls during the period of the study to refine study protocols, monitor the progress of the study, and set guidelines for authorship of study manuscripts and presentations.

Infrastructure

APPD LEARN maintains an online data repository using the Dataverse Network system (King 2007), which provides support for permanent data and document archiving, data subsetting, simple online statistical analysis, and assignment of unique citable identifiers to data sets. Each APPD LEARN study archives the study protocol and materials, IRB documentation, study data, and manuscripts arising from the study. APPD LEARN members and other medical education researchers are eligible to request access to archived data for secondary analyses. Proposals for data access require both scientific and budgetary approval, as well as agreement to a standard set of terms and conditions intended to ensure uniform citation of the investigators and sites involved in the primary study. Oversight for the data repository is provided by the IRB at University of Illinois at Chicago.

An important goal of APPD LEARN is to permit learner data to be linked longitudinally and across studies. APPD LEARN member programs can generate an APPD LEARN data collection ID for each learner based on a one-way encryption system. The data collection ID is known only to the program director, is fixed over time and across studies, and cannot be feasibly decrypted to obtain any learner information. Member programs participating in a study obtain approval from their IRBs to provide their data sets to APPD LEARN with only these IDs, preventing APPD LEARN from obtaining identifiable data.

APPD LEARN then re-encrypts the IDs with a second one-way encryption to create a data storage ID before archiving the data, making the archived data de-identified even to the program that contributed the data. Figure 2 illustrates the process. APPD LEARN does not collect patient identifiers.

In early network studies, programs generated data collection IDs "just-in-time" as learners were enrolled into the study or as each learner completed the study and the program was preparing to provide the data to APPD LEARN. Although this process decreased the likelihood of misidentifying data in studies conducted with learners over several rotations (e.g., if a different learner participated than originally expected), it became more cumbersome for site investigators to generate and maintain the identifiers on an *ad hoc* basis. Because the identifiers are the same whenever they are generated, APPD LEARN is now encouraging programs to generate these identifiers for all their learners en masse in advance of any data collection, to avoid these delays.

APPD LEARN provides regular updates to the APPD membership at its annual meetings and maintains a web site for public updates. Administrative support for APPD LEARN activities is provided by Degnon Associates, Inc., APPD's association management company. Other infrastructure components include an online survey platform (LimeService) and an online project management system (5pm(TM)).

Support for infrastructure is a standard challenge for research networks, and may be particularly irksome for medical education research networks in light of the relative scarcity of large-scale funding for medical education, particularly in the United States. Accordingly, most medical education research networks are supported by one or more sponsoring medical education organizations; this support typically extends to core network functions including the conduct of a limited number of modest studies, usually without compensation to participating sites. Following this model, APPD LEARN does

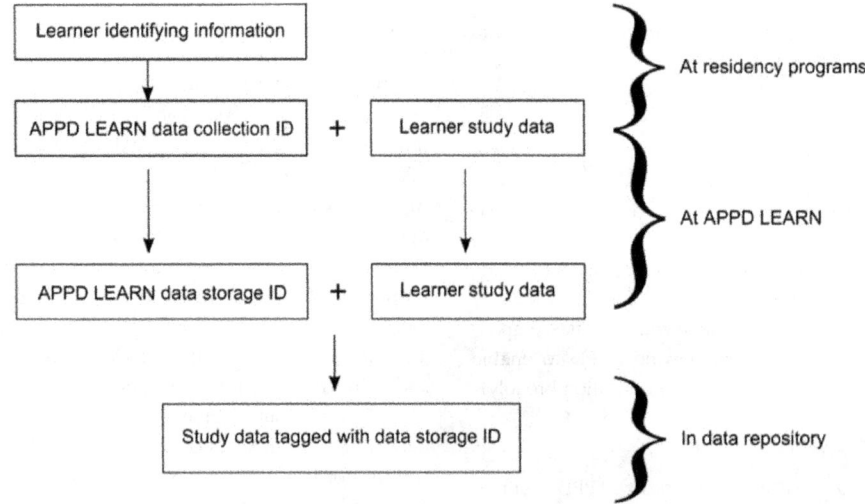

Figure 2. The APPD LEARN de-identification process. Residency programs collect data on (identified) learners. Programs generate permanent non-reversible APPD LEARN data collection IDs for their learners and transmit study data, tagged by data collection ID, to APPD LEARN. APPD LEARN re-encrypts the data collection ID to a data storage ID, and archives study data, tagged by data storage ID, in the data repository.

not typically provide direct funding to participating sites. The network instead encourages members proposing more extensive projects to seek external funding, and provides assistance in such proposals.

Past, current, and future activities

As an early proof-of-concept for the network's infrastructure, APPD conducted a study entitled "The New Duty Hour Regulations–Were Changes Necessary? A Survey of Pediatric Program Directors". This study sought to identify what, if any, changes in Pediatric Residency Program structure were necessary to achieve compliance with the new duty hour regulations by July 2011. Fifty-five APPD LEARN member sites responded to the survey, and (qualitative) data analysis and reporting continues. Although APPD LEARN focuses on residents, rather than program directors, as the unit of analysis, this study provided insights about network operations and serves as a model for the annual needs assessment survey of members. Once the data analysis is completed, the data set will also present a challenge to APPD LEARN's data sharing function, as the network will need to develop methods to archive and share qualitative data with appropriate de-identification.

In the same period, APPD LEARN in collaboration with the National Board of Medical Examiners (NBME) began collecting data in the Pediatrics Milestones Assessment Pilot, a study in which 18 sites have collected structured clinical observation, multisource feedback, and milestone classification data (summative performance level described by a given milestone for a competency) on interns and subinterns involving nine of the Pediatrics competencies and their corresponding Milestones (Hicks et al. 2010). Data were collected between June 2012 and June 2013. In 2013, APPD, NBME, and ABP announced the formation of the Pediatrics Milestones Assessment Collaborative, which will engage in further study of the reliability and validity of instruments for assessing competencies informed by the Pediatrics Milestones with the goal of offering a national assessment platform. Following the example of the Pediatrics Milestones Assessment Pilot, APPD LEARN serves as the primary vehicle for program director involvement and data collection. Validity evidence for a national assessment platform can only be developed with the active and coordinated participation of many residency programs, and APPD LEARN is ideally poised to conduct this potentially high-impact research.

In 2012, APPD LEARN issued its first call for member-initiated proposals with three deadlines per year. Since that time, eight proposals from members have been received by the proposal review committee; four have been approved for the network, and one is pending review. One, a year-long study of resident self-assessment using the Pediatrics Milestones, has recruited 44 sites and collected data for one of its two time points. Another, a study of resident perceptions of social media and professionalism across 13 sites has completed its data collection and is preparing manuscripts. The third and fourth, focused on medical errors and the balance of service and education in training programs, are still preparing to proceed. Additional submissions and a collaboration with Pediatrics subspecialty program networks are expected in 2014.

Future directions for research networks

The emergence of collaborative educational research networks in medical education is an exciting development for the field. To date, many of these networks have been focused on graduate medical education in Pediatrics, Family Medicine, and Emergency Medicine, but if these networks prove successful in increasing meaningful educational scholarship and uptake of evidence-based educational practices, additional networks are likely to be formed spanning other specialties and the full continuum of medical education. Our experience with the formation and growth of APPD LEARN has identified several core challenges to this process, and we conclude with four recommendations for the future development of medical education research networks:

(1) Most medical school faculty, even those experienced as teachers or clinical researchers, are not trained in educational (or other social scientific) research, and will require faculty development efforts to participate in an educational research network. Faculty may need education in human subjects regulations and ethics in educational research, educational research design, qualitative and quantitative analysis of behavioral data, and processes in team science such as authorship and data sharing. As it is possible to participate meaningfully at several different levels of commitment (e.g., as a study site investigator, as a principal investigator or co-investigator, or as a network committee member), faculty development should be tailored to the involvement of the audience, and take place at a time and in a setting appropriate to the audience. Proposal development and review processes provide teachable moments for both proposing investigators and review committee members. Each study run by a network is a chance to provide training to faculty at participating sites. Providing CME to network members is also an opportunity for the network to recognize and reward participation.

(2) In addition to the skills and energy of participating sites, collaborative research networks need sufficient central resources to be productive and sustainable. These include program management staff time, access to expertise in educational research, technological infrastructure to support project management, data collection, and data analysis. In particular, the network director or steering committee should expect to invest substantial time in building and maintaining network infrastructure and operations, such as communications, technology, and policy. In addition, funding to support investigator meetings, study expenses, faculty development, and other network needs is ideal. There are several viable models for network funding, including direct sponsorship by an educational organization, network membership fees, and direct or indirect cost charges to external funders of individual network studies; our key recommendation is

that the network finds a model that serves its members' needs and that potential sponsors embrace the value of collaborative research in medical education.

(3) This is a propitious time to begin to study medical education research networks themselves. Little is known about the organizational life cycle of such networks, including processes such as founding and failure and mechanisms such as legitimation and competition that characterize other organizational populations (Carroll & Hannan 1992), or about the perspectives of network members and leaders on the value of medical education research networks. IRB handling of network studies, which we have found to have substantial variability both in study classification and time to decision, is another area for investigation and potentially process improvement. Although, the networks reviewed here are relatively young, measures of effectiveness and cost-effectiveness of network research should be developed that go beyond tallying publications or funding support to look at the transfer and impact of the research on institutions, educators, learners, and patients.

(4) Finally, as collaborative medical education research networks become more prevalent, we recommend looking ahead to the development of an international network of networks (NON) that can share best practices and coordinate multinational, multi-specialty, and cross-continuum studies run on multiple networks. Perhaps most importantly, the NON can promulgate specifications, standards, and practices for intellectual property and data sharing, such as those now emerging from Medbiquitous (Smothers et al. 2008) and Data Commons, LLC (2013; a partnership of the Federation of State Medical Boards, National Board of Medical Examiners, Association of American Medical Colleges, Educational Commission for Foreign Medical Graduates, American Board of Family Medicine, and American Board of Pediatrics). The NON might itself be organized as a member organization, with each member network contributing a membership fee to support periodic NON conference calls and meetings. An early example of such a network of networks is the Collaborative of the Primary Care Training Collaboratives, a network of five networks (ranging from 4 to 44 members per network) each interested in educational effectiveness of teaching methods for implementing patient-centered medical homes. The "Collaborative of the Collaboratives" is working to disseminate common methods used across its constituent networks (Warning W, personal communication).

Glossary

Medical educational practice-based research network (MEPBRN): An organization or consortium consisting of multiple educational sites (e.g., schools or training programs) formed for the primary purpose of facilitating multiple research studies each using all or a subset of the network sites.

Glossary of abbreviations (other than network/study names)
ABP, American Board of Pediatrics; ACGME, Accreditation Council for Graduate Medical Education; AHRQ, Agency for Healthcare Research and Quality; AMA, American Medical Association; APA, Academic Pediatric Association; APPD, Association of Pediatric Program Directors; HRSA, Health Resources and Services Administration; IRB, Institutional Review Board; NBME, National Board of Medical Education; PBRN, Practice-Based Research Network

Notes on contributors

Dr. ALAN SCHWARTZ, PhD, is a Professor and an Associate Head, Department of Medical Education, and Research Professor, Department of Pediatrics, University of Illinois at Chicago. He is also Director of the Association of Pediatric Program Directors Longitudinal Educational Assessment Research Network (APPD LEARN).

Ms. ROBIN YOUNG, MS, is a Project Manager, Association of Pediatric Program Directors Longitudinal Educational Assessment Research Network (APPD LEARN).

Dr. PATRICIA J. HICKS, MD, MHPE, is a Professor of Pediatrics, Perelman School of Medicine, University of Pennsylvania, and Attending Physician, Children's Hospital of Philadelphia. She is also Past President, Association of Pediatric Program Directors (APPD) and Past Chair, Advisory Committee, Association of Pediatric Program Directors Longitudinal Educational Assessment Research Network (APPD LEARN).

APPD LEARN is a research network composed of over 120 member programs, listed at http://learn.appd.org. Members and past members of the APPD LEARN Advisory Committee who met the ICMJE Criteria for Authorship of this article are: Alan Schwartz, PhD; Robin Young, MS; Patricia J. Hicks, MD, MHPE; Ann Burke, MD; Carol Carraccio, MD; Hilary Haftel, MD, MHPE; Robert McGregor, MD; and Laura Degnon, CAE.

Acknowledgments

We thank the directors and coordinators of research networks who responded to requests to confirm our information about their networks. We thank Dr. Yoon Soo Park for Korean-language assistance.

Declaration of interest: This study was funded in part by a contract from the Association of Pediatric Program Directors to the Department of Medical Education at the University of Illinois at Chicago that supports Schwartz's role as APPD LEARN Director. Patricia Hicks, MD, MHPE has been supported by the American Board of Pediatrics Foundation for her work as Director of the national work on the development of the Pediatrics Milestones. Except insofar as authors are members or officers of APPD, the sponsor had no role in the design and conduct of the study, collection, management, analysis, and interpretation of the data, or preparation, review, or approval of the report. All authors had full access to all the data in the study and take responsibility for the integrity of the data and the accuracy of the data analysis. Alan Schwartz is the guarantor for this article.

The work and opinions reported herein do not represent the official viewpoint of the Association of Pediatric Program

Directors, American Board of Pediatrics, or any other organization named herein.

References

Academic Pediatric Association. 2013. CORNET. [Accessed 28 May 2013] Available from http://www.ambpeds.org/research/research_CORNET.cfm.

Accreditation Council for Graduate Medical Education. 2011. ACGME program requirements for graduate medical education in internal medicine – Educational innovations project (EIP). [Accessed 6 June 2013] Available from http://www.acgme.org/acgmeweb/Portals/0/PFAssets/ProgramRequirements/140_EIP_PR205.pdf.

Agency for Healthcare Research and Quality. 2013. Medical education research network. AHRQ PBRN Registry. [Accessed 28 May 2013] Available from http://pbrn.ahrq.gov/pbrn-registry/medical-education-research-network.

American Medical Association. 2010. Key dates/activities in ISTEP history. [Accessed 28 May 2013] Available from http://www.ama-assn.org/ama/pub/education-careers/istepinnovative-strategies-transforming-education-physicians/history.page.

Beeson MS, Deiorio NM. 2010. It's time: An argument for a national emergency medicine education research center. Acad Emerg Med 17(s2):S11–S12.

Burke AE, Guralnick S, Hicks P. 2010. The Association of Pediatric Program Directors' strategic plan: An opportunity for transformational change. Acad Pediatr 10(4):220–221.

Carney PA, Green LA. 2011. An emerging epidemic of innovation in family medicine residencies. Fam Med 43(7):461–463.

Carney PA, Nierenberg DW, Pipas CF, Brooks W, Stukel TA, Keller AM. 2004. Educational epidemiology: Applying population-based design and analytic approaches to study medical education. JAMA 292(9):1044–1050.

Carroll GR, Hannan MT. 1992. Dynamics of organizational populations: Density, competition and legitimation. New York, NY: Oxford University Press.

Carter-Pokras O, Bereknyei S, Lie D, Braddock III CH. 2010. Surmounting the unique challenges in health disparities education: A multi-institution qualitative study. J Gen Intern Med 25(2):108–114.

Chiniara G, Cole G, Brisbin K, Huffman D, Cragg E, Lamacchia M, Norman D, Canadian Network For Simulation In Healthcare, Guidelines Working Group. 2013. Simulation in healthcare: A taxonomy and a conceptual framework for instructional design and media selection. Med Teach 35(8):e1380–e1395.

Cleland J, Scott N, Harrild K, Moffat M. 2013. Using databases in medical education research: AMEE Guide No. 77. Med Teach 35(5):e1103–e1122.

Crenshaw MK, Shewchuk RM, Qu H, Staton LJ, Bigby JA, Houston TK, Allison J, Estrada CA. 2011. What should we include in a cultural competence curriculum? An emerging formative evaluation process to foster curriculum development. Acad Med 86(3):333.

Data Commons LLC. 2013. Data Commons. [Accessed 28 May 2013] Available from http://mydatacommons.org.

Deshefy-Longhi T, Swartz MK, Grey M. 2002. Establishing a practice-based research network of advanced practice registered nurses in southern New England. Nurs Outlook 50(3):127–132.

Dickerson LM, Kraus C, Kuo GM, Weber CA, Bazaldua OV, Tovar JM, Hume AL, Ives TJ, Gums JG, Carter BL. 2007. Formation of a primary care pharmacist practice-based research network. Am J Health Syst Pharm 64(19):2044–2049.

Flanagin A, Fontanarosa PB, DeAngelis CD. 2002. Authorship for research groups. JAMA 288(24):3166–3168.

Green LA, Hickner J. 2006. A short history of primary care practice-based research networks: From concept to essential research laboratories. J Am Board Fam Med 19(1):1–10.

Hicks PJ, Schumacher DJ, Benson BJ, Burke AE, Englander R, Guralnick S, Ludwig S, Carraccio C. 2010. The Pediatrics Milestones: Conceptual framework, guiding principles, and approach to development. J Grad Med Educ 2(3):410–418.

Huggett KN, Gusic ME, Greenberg R, Ketterer JM. 2011. Twelve tips for conducting collaborative research in medical education. Med Teach 33(9):713–718.

INSPIRE. 2012. The INSPIRE network submission process. [Accessed 28 May 2013] Available from http://www.slideshare.net/INSPIRE_Network/the-inspire-network-submission-process.

INSPIRE. 2013. INSPIRE Meeting @ IPSSW 2013. New York, NY: New York Simulation Center for the Health Sciences.

Jones MD, McGuinness GA, Carraccio CA. 2009. The residency review and redesign in Pediatrics (R3P) project: Roots and branches. Pediatrics 123(suppl):S8–S11.

King G. 2007. An introduction to the Dataverse Network as an infrastructure for data sharing. Sociol Methods Res 32(2):173–199.

Li C-H, Kuan W-S, Mahadevan M, Daniel-Underwood L, Chiu T-F, Nguyen HB, ATLAS Investigators (Asia neTwork to reguLAte Sepsis care). 2011. A multinational randomised study comparing didactic lectures with case scenario in a severe sepsis medical simulation course. Emerg Med J 29(7):559–564.

Lie D, Bereknyei S, Braddock III CH, Encinas J, Ahearn S, Boker JR. 2009. Assessing medical students' skills in working with interpreters during patient encounters: A validation study of the Interpreter Scale. Acad Med 84(5):643–650.

Meade LB, Caverzagie KJ, Swing SR, Jones RR, O'Malley CW, Yamazaki K, Zaas AK. 2013a. Playing with curricular milestones in the educational sandbox: Q-sort results from an internal medicine educational collaborative. Acad Med 88(8):1142–1148.

Meade LB, Zaas A, O'Malley C, Jones R. 2013b. Workshop 203. Engaging Residents in the Milestones: Results of the Education Research Outcomes Collaborative (E-ROC). Paper presented at the Association of Program Directors in Internal Medicine, Lake Buena Vista, FL. Available from http://www.im.org/Meetings/CurrentMeetings/2013APDIMSpringConference/Presentations/Documents/Spring%20Meeting/Wksp%20203_Jones.pdf.

MedEdNet. 2013. About MedEdNet. [Accessed 28 May 2013] Available from https://fmresearch.ohsu.edu/medednet/static/about.

Newgard CD, Beeson MS, Kessler CS, Kuppermann N, Linden JA, Gallahue F, Wolf S, Hatten B, Akhtar S, Dooley-Hash SL, Yarris L. 2012. Establishing an emergency medicine education research network. Acad Emerg Med 19(12):1468–1475.

O'Sullivan PS, Stoddard HA, Kalishman S. 2010. Collaborative research in medical education: A discussion of theory and practice. Med Educ 44(12):1175–1184.

Roberts KB, Degnon LE, McGregor RS. 2012. The Association of Pediatric Program Directors: The first 25 years. Acad Pediatr 12(3):166–170.

Schwartz A, Pappas C, Sandlow LJ. 2010. Data repositories for medical education research. Acad Med 85(5):837–843.

Smith CS, Morris M, Francovich C, Tivis R, Bush R, Sanders SS, Graham J, Niven A, Kai M, Knight C, et al. 2013. A multisite, multistakeholder validation of the Accreditation Council for Graduate Medical Education competencies. Acad Med 88(7):997–1001.

Smothers V, Greene P, Ellaway R, Detmer DE. 2008. Sharing innovation: The case for technology standards in health professions education. Med Teach 30(2):150–154.

Turner D, Goodman D. 2011. 64: Development of a multicenter collaborative for education based research – Birth of the Education in Pediatric Intensive Care (Epic) Investigators. Crit Care Med 39(12):18.

Wasserman RC, Slora EJ, Bocian AB, Fleming GV, Baker AE, Pedlow SE, Kessel W. 1998. Pediatric research in office settings (PROS): A national practice-based research network to improve children's health care. Pediatrics 102(6):1350–1357.

Perspective

AMIA Board White Paper: AMIA 2017 core competencies for applied health informatics education at the master's degree level

Annette L Valenta,[1,2] Eta S Berner,[3] Suzanne A Boren,[4] Gloria J Deckard,[5] Christina Eldredge,[6] Douglas B Fridsma,[7] Cynthia Gadd,[8] Yang Gong,[9] Todd Johnson,[10] Josette Jones,[11] E LaVerne Manos,[12] Kirk T Phillips,[13] Nancy K Roderer,[14,15] Douglas Rosendale,[16] Anne M Turner,[17,18] Guenter Tusch,[19] Jeffrey J Williamson,[20] and Stephen B Johnson[21]

[1]Department of Biomedical and Health Information Sciences, University of Illinois at Chicago, Chicago, Illinois, USA, [2]Department of Medical Education, University of Illinois at Chicago, Chicago, Illinois, USA, [3]Department of Health Services Administration, University of Alabama at Birmingham, Birmingham, Alabama, USA, [4]Department of Health Management and Informatics, University of Missouri, Columbia, Missouri, USA, [5]Department of Information Systems and Business Analytics, Florida International University, Miami, Florida, USA, [6]School of Information, University of South Florida, Tampa, Florida, USA, [7]Executive Office, AMIA, Bethesda, Maryland, USA, [8]Department of Biomedical Informatics, Vanderbilt University, Nashville, Tennessee, USA, [9]School of Biomedical Informatics, University of Texas Health Science Center, Houston, Texas, USA, [10]School of Biomedical Informatics, University of Texas Health Science Center, Houston, Texas, USA, [11]Department of BioHealth Informatics, Indiana University-Purdue University, Indianapolis, Indiana, USA, [12]University of Kansas Center for Health Informatics, University of Kansas Medical Center, Kansas City, Kansas, USA, [13]Department of Health Management and Policy, University of Iowa, Iowa City, Iowa, USA, [14]Division of Health Sciences Informatics, Johns Hopkins University, School of Medicine, Baltimore, Maryland, USA, [15]iSchool, University of Maryland, College Park, Maryland, USA, [16]Deloitte Consulting for Federal Healthcare, Washington, District of Columbia, USA, [17]Department of Health Services, University of Washington, Seattle, Washington, USA, [18]Department of Biomedical Informatics and Medical Education, University of Washington, Seattle, Washington, USA, [19]Department of Computer Science and Information Systems, Grand Valley State University, Allendale, Michigan, USA, [20]Education, AMIA, Bethesda, Maryland, USA, and [21]Division of Health Informatics, Healthcare Policy and Research, Weill Cornell Medicine, New York, New York, USA

This paper was formally approved by the AMIA Board on May 7, 2018.

Corresponding Author: Jeffrey J. Williamson, AMIA, 4720 Montgomery Lane, Suite 500, Bethesda, MD 20814, USA (jeff@amia.org)

Received 27 July 2018; Revised 24 August 2018; Editorial Decision 4 September 2018; Accepted 2 October 2018

ABSTRACT

This White Paper presents the foundational domains with examples of key aspects of competencies (knowledge, skills, and attitudes) that are intended for curriculum development and accreditation quality assessment for graduate (master's level) education in applied health informatics. Through a deliberative process, the AMIA Accreditation Committee refined the work of a task force of the Health Informatics Accreditation Council, establishing 10 foundational domains with accompanying example statements of knowledge, skills, and attitudes that are components of competencies by which graduates from applied health informatics programs can be assessed for competence at the time of graduation. The AMIA Accreditation Committee developed the domains for application across all the subdisciplines represented by AMIA, ranging from translational bioinformatics to clinical and public health informatics, spanning the spectrum from molecular to population levels of health and biomedicine. This document will be periodically updated, as part of the responsibility of the AMIA Accreditation Committee, through continued study, education, and surveys of market trends.

Key words: professional competence, professional practice, education, graduate, accreditation, curriculum

INTRODUCTION AND BACKGROUND

In 2012, a committee of the AMIA Academic Forum published as an AMIA Board White Paper the definition of biomedical informatics and specification of core competencies for graduate education in the discipline.[1] The White Paper drew on a series of task force meetings with stakeholders and sought to provide broad competency statements that programs could use in curriculum and course development.

Recognizing the importance of supporting the emerging profession of health informatics, in January 2015, AMIA joined the Commission on Accreditation for Health Informatics and Information Management Education (CAHIIM) as an Organizational Member to work on one aspect of a maturing profession: accreditation.[2] CAHIIM is an independent accrediting organization whose mission is to serve the public interest by establishing and enforcing quality accreditation standards for health informatics (HI) and health information management (HIM) educational programs.

AMIA and CAHIIM began working together on an update of accreditation standards for professionals in applied health informatics at the master's degree level. The collaboration sought to move from an accreditation model of standards driven by curriculum content to a model driven by attainment of competence. AMIA and CAHIIM agreed that the foundation for the new model should be based on the 2012 White Paper. To accomplish this goal, two separate committees were created. AMIA worked with CAHIIM to establish the Health Informatics Accreditation Council (HIAC) and AMIA established the AMIA Accreditation Committee (AAC).

Health Informatics Accreditation Council

The HIAC was initially charged with updating the existing CAHIIM Curriculum Requirements document and the CAHIIM *2010 Standards and Interpretations for Accreditation of Master's Degree Programs in Health Informatics* (http://www.cahiim.org/documents/2012_HI_Masters_Stndrds.pdf). The Curriculum Requirements were to be reframed as new graduate outcome "Health Informatics Competencies" and were to be formally referenced within the curriculum section of the CAHIIM accreditation standards so as to reflect the emergent knowledge, skills, and attitudes associated with the foundational domains for health informatics. It is the role of HIAC within CAHIIM to:

1. Review and revise accreditation standards in conjunction with the CAHIIM board of directors;
2. Establish decisions for accreditation action, based on review of the documentation provided by programs and site visits;
3. Report accreditation decisions to the CAHIIM board;
4. Review outcome reports and dashboard data from CAHIIM staff; and
5. Oversee peer reviewers who serve the council.

AMIA Accreditation Committee

The AMIA AAC (a subcommittee of the AMIA Education Committee) is to serve as the primary interface between AMIA and CAHIIM to achieve the goals of participation by AMIA in CAHIIM and the HIAC. The AAC was charged with establishing a set of foundational domains that reflected the intent of the 2012 White Paper and an outline of competencies to guide graduate programs seeking accreditation. It is the role of AAC within AMIA to:

1. Provide validation examples and guidelines to assist programs in interpreting domains and competencies;
2. Collaborate in monitoring and refining domains and competencies to keep them current;
3. Provide guidelines to assist programs in interpreting domains for competency-driven curricula;
4. Collaborate for the purpose of coordination and communication across health informatics education-focused groups;
5. Help identify educational activities that can assist academic programs through shared ideas for curriculum evaluation and student assessment as it relates to the foundational domains; and
6. Maintain/update the foundational domains and core competencies.

ESTABLISHING THE FOUNDATIONAL DOMAINS FOR HEALTH INFORMATICS EDUCATION

In reviewing the CAHIIM *2010 Standards and Interpretations for Accreditation of Master's Degree Programs in Health Informatics* to begin its update, HIAC found the curriculum requirements aligned with the 2012 White Paper, yet the requirements had become somewhat dated, were difficult to interpret, lacked specifics on the depth of instruction, and focused on content of the curriculum rather than the expected competence to be demonstrated by a graduate with a master's degree in Health Informatics. While the White Paper described a core set of competencies that were shared by many informatics subdisciplines, the broadly stated competencies were not sufficiently succinct for use in a formal accreditation process.

The updated accreditation standards related to curriculum sought to provide a framework to define HI competencies broadly enough to be applicable to a wide variety of established programs. Additionally, the scope of the discipline, and, therefore, the curriculum standards, needed to span the spectrum from translational bioinformatics to public health, including clinical informatics, consumer health informatics, and clinical research informatics. As a general guideline, AMIA and CAHIIM agreed that the new framework should define roughly 10 areas of competence.

In 2015, a task force that was a subgroup of HIAC (Johnson, Boren, and Tusch) created an initial vision for HI competencies. The HIAC task force analyzed the 5 broad areas defined in the AMIA White Paper: 1) professional skills; 2) scope and breadth of discipline; 3) theory and methodology; 4) technologic approach; and 5) human and social context. The task force began by reorganizing the content in areas 2 to 5, drawing on related publications.[3–6] The outcome of this work was a Venn diagram with 3 intersecting circles corresponding to the broad "parent" disciplines that inform health informatics: health science, information science, and social science.

Table 1. Timelines for establishing AMIA foundational domains

Time Period	Committee/Organization	Deliverable/Activity
2015	HIAC Task Force	1. Venn diagram describing 7 foundational domains 2. Venn diagram describing 7 professional skills
April 2015	HIAC - CAHIIM	Model of Venn diagrams presented at AMIA Academic Forum
October 2015	HIAC – CAHIIM	Model of Venn diagrams presented during an AMIA webinar
November 2015	HIAC – CAHIIM	Model of Venn diagrams and accreditation process overview presented at AMIA Annual Symposium
March 18, 2016	HIAC—AAC—AMIA Leadership	Committee charters discussed; transition of work effort from HIAC to AAC
April 2016	AAC	AAC model, reducing HIAC model to 10 foundational domains
June 2016	AAC	First draft of AMIA domains presented at AMIA InSpire Conference
September 14 – October 14, 2016	AAC and members of AMIA leadership	AMIA foundational domains and examples of key aspects of competencies disseminated for public comment to Academic Forum and AMIA community
November 2016	AAC and members of AMIA leadership	AMIA foundational domains and examples of key aspects of competencies incorporate both stakeholder and public comments
December 2016	AMIA Board of Directors	Final version of AMIA foundational domains and examples of key aspects of competencies submitted and approved by email vote
January 12, 2017	AMIA Board of Directors	*AMIA 2017 Core Competencies for Health Informatics Education at the Master's Degree Level* formally accepted by vote of the Board
January 2017	HIAC	Newly approved *AMIA 2017 Core Competencies...* embedded in CAHIIM revised 2017 *Standards for Accreditation of Master's Degree Programs in Health Informatics*
March 2017	CAHIIM	*2017 Standards for Accreditation...* disseminated for public comment
June 2017	CAHIIM	*2017 Standards for Accreditation...* approved by CAHIIM Board

The regions of intersection among the circles produced 7 distinct combinations: health science, information science, social science, health information science, social health science, social information science, and social health information science.

In analyzing the remaining area from the AMIA White Paper (professional skills), the HIAC task force was influenced by the Health Leadership Competency Model™ of the National Center for Healthcare Leadership, which is also represented by a Venn diagram of 3 intersecting circles.[7,8] The team adapted this model to produce a second Venn diagram with 7 regions, which were labeled analyze, execute, communicate, manage, conduct, collaborate, and lead, drawing on related literature.[9,10] The skill for lead was defined broadly to include many forms of leadership that students could exhibit through methods, projects, innovation, and studies, and was placed at the center to align with the AMIA motto: *informatics professionals leading the way*.

The final model produced by the HIAC task force defined 14 focal areas for HI: 7 describing knowledge areas, and 7 describing areas of skills. The model was presented at multiple venues in 2015 (Table 1).

Subsequent to the work of the HIAC task force, the AAC launched its work effort with an inaugural meeting among members of HIAC, AAC, and AMIA leadership on March 18, 2016. The AAC understood that the foundational domains and accompanying example statements of knowledge, skills, and attitudes had to be written in a manner that provided a common core for competency building that could apply across the subdisciplines represented by all AMIA constituents (translational bioinformatics, clinical informatics, public health informatics, consumer health informatics, and clinical research informatics) as well as within the focus of individual programs.

In the process of establishing the foundational domains, the AAC examined the output of the HIAC task force and reviewed the 2012 White Paper, the literature published on the skills and practices related to the field of health informatics, as well as the literature on the general concepts of competency and the mastery of learning. The committee incorporated scholarship written for the three domains of learning, ie, cognitive, affective, and psychomotor by Bloom, Krathwohl, Dave, and others, in its deliberations.[11–13] Embracing the Dreyfus Model of Skill Acquisition (later adapted by Patricia Benner in her seminal nursing theory on stages of clinical competence), the committee adopted a "competent/proficient level of skills acquisition at the time of graduation" to frame its discussions.[14–16]

As a standard point of reference for its work, AAC adopted the following definitions for the terms competence and competency (Table 2).

In updating curriculum standards and requirements, particularly the framework, content, and processes represented in the HIAC task force Venn diagrams, the AAC employed a deliberative process of review and revision to refine each of the HIAC domains as well as to explore additional domains that may have been needed, given the evolution of the profession since the 2012 White Paper.[18] The process for establishing the foundational domains for accreditation required completing 3 tasks: 1) identifying and naming the domains needed in the present health informatics field, 2) describing each domain clearly and succinctly, and 3) describing examples of key aspects of competencies (knowledge, skills, and attitudes) associated with each domain—capabilities to be demonstrated by a student at the time of graduation from an applied master of science in health informatics program. Following the March inaugural meeting, the members of AAC deliberated and through an iterative process, at the next meeting in April, reduced the 14 areas originally proposed by HIAC to 10 foundational domains, in concept. The committee then drafted and/or edited the domain name, wrote a description for each domain, and proposed example statements of knowledge, skills, and attitudes—the components of a competency—expected of new graduates. Seeking input during the process of deliberation,

Table 2. Definitions (KSA acronym for Knowledge, Skills, and Attitudes)

Competency – "An observable ability of a health professional, integrating multiple components such as knowledge, skills, values, and attitudes. Since competencies are observable, they can be measured and assessed to ensure their acquisition. Competencies can be assembled like building blocks to facilitate progressive development."[17]

Competence – "The array of abilities across multiple domains or aspects of performance in a certain context. Statements about competence require descriptive qualifiers to define the relevant abilities, context, and stage of training. Competence is multi-dimensional and dynamic. It changes with time, experience, and setting."[17]

---

committee members presented the first draft of the domains to attendees of the InSpire conference in Columbus, Ohio, in June 2016, as part of the session by CAHIIM on accreditation standards for programs.

Public comment and board approval

By September 2016, the AAC had refined the work of the HIAC taskforce and established a set of foundational domains and descriptions with accompanying examples of knowledge, skills, and attitudes necessary to succeed as health informatics professionals or health informaticians. AAC and members of AMIA Leadership prepared the document for dissemination for public comment. Table 1 summarizes the timelines for developing and vetting the AMIA foundational domains document and its insertion into the CAHIIM 2017 accreditation standards. Under the 2017 standards, new programs seeking accreditation must comply with the officially termed *AMIA 2017 Core Competencies for Health Informatics Education at the Master's Degree Level* that are part of the *2017 Standards for Accreditation of Master's Degree Programs in Health Informatics*.[19] All programs either currently accredited by CAHIIM or in the initial accreditation process must be in compliance by January 1, 2020.

AMIA 2017 CORE COMPETENCIES FOR APPLIED HEALTH INFORMATICS EDUCATION AT THE MASTER'S DEGREE LEVEL

The newly refined foundational domains with example statements of knowledge, skills, and attitudes (key components of competencies) are intended for curriculum development and accreditation quality assessment for graduate (master's level) education in applied health informatics. The application areas of health informatics, ranging from translational bioinformatics to clinical and public health informatics, span the spectrum from molecular to population levels of health and biomedicine. An in-depth discussion of each of the application areas can be found under The Science of Informatics at the AMIA website https://www.amia.org/about-amia/science-informatics

For the purposes of the foundational domains, the AAC used the following definitions:

- Clinical informatics is the application of informatics and information technology to deliver healthcare services, including medical, nursing, pharmacy, and dental informatics.
- Public health informatics is the application of informatics in areas of public health, including population health, surveillance, prevention, preparedness, and health promotion.
- Consumer health informatics is the field devoted to informatics from multiple consumer or patient views.
- Translational bioinformatics includes the development of storage, analytic, and interpretive methods to optimize the transformation of increasingly voluminous biomedical data and genomic data, into proactive, predictive, preventive, and participatory health.
- Clinical research informatics (CRI) includes the use of informatics in the discovery and management of new knowledge relating to health and disease. CRI and translational bioinformatics are the primary informatics domains supporting translational research.

The discipline of health informatics exists at the confluence of 3 major domains: Health, Information Science and Technology, and Social and Behavioral Science (represented by F1, F2, and F3 in Figure 1). Graduate students in this discipline are expected to have working knowledge of these 3 domains, as these domains define and affect the practice of health informatics. Where 2 foundational domains intermingle, each affects the other, and the graduate student is expected to demonstrate the knowledge, skills, and attitudes that exist in these co-mingled domains: Health Information Science and Technology, Human Factors and Socio-technical Systems, and Social and Behavioral Aspects of Health (F4, F5, and F6). Where all 3 domains intermingle, the graduate student is expected to demonstrate the knowledge, skills, and attitudes that exist in this most complex domain: Social, Behavioral, and Information Science and Technology Applied to Health (F7). As with all other health professions, the work of health informaticians affects the health, safety, and effectiveness of those working and being cared for within the system of health care delivery. Graduate students are also expected to demonstrate the knowledge, skills, and attitudes reflecting the domains of Professionalism, Interprofessional Collaborative Practice, and Leadership (Figure 1).

Table 3 summarizes the 10 foundational domains. Please see the Appendix for full descriptions of the domains along with their accompanying example statements of knowledge, skills, and attitudes, which can be used to develop program-specific competencies to reflect the program's focus within an AMIA Application Area.

DISCUSSION

These foundational domains and example statements of knowledge, skills, and attitudes provide a step forward in defining the core competencies for applied health informatics education and practice, reflecting the expansion of the field as it has evolved since 2012. The embedding of these domains into the accreditation standards provides a basis for curriculum development and quality assurance across a wide variety of health informatics programs by applying the competency framework to a program's specific application area of expertise.

Why change from content to competencies?

Knox and colleagues proposed in 2014 that we can no longer continue to emphasize only rote performance based on content. Rather, we should cultivate performance that demonstrates an understanding and application of principles and processes that will prepare graduates for continuous learning of new skills and techniques as their futures evolve.[20] The endpoint of all curricula—clinical informatics, public health informatics, consumer health informatics, translational bioinformatics, clinical research informatics—must

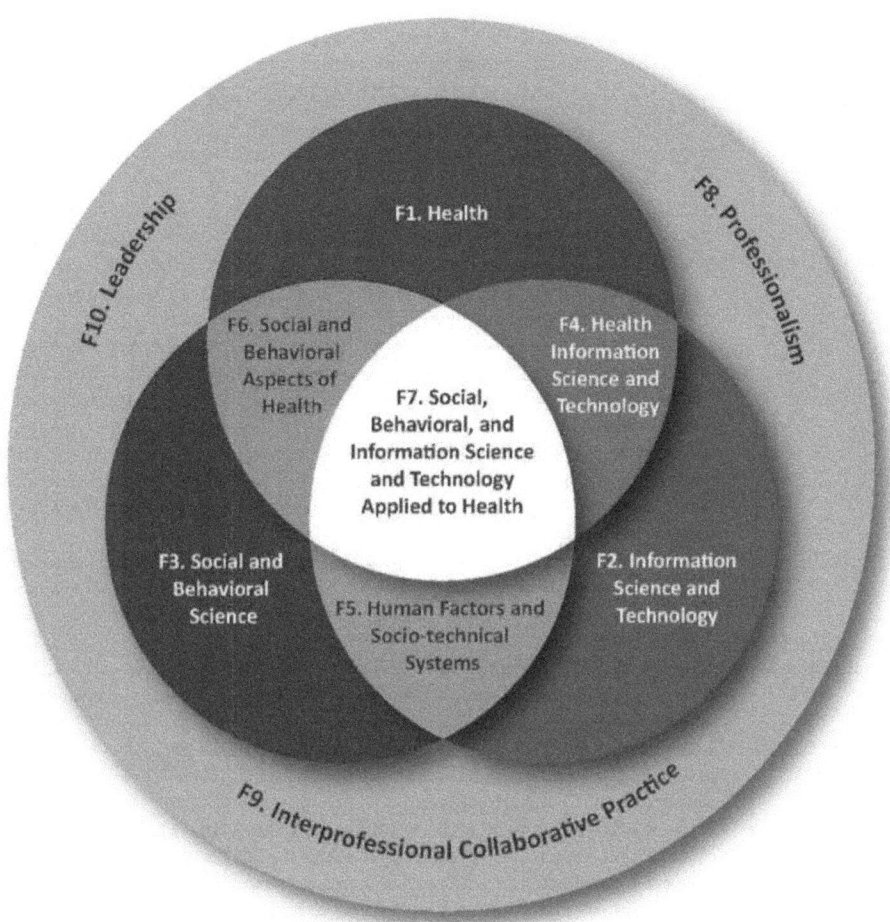

Figure 1. Foundational domains of applied health informatics. Graphic: Christina Lorenzo, MS in Biomedical Visualization, 2017, Department of Biomedical and Health Information Sciences, University of Illinois at Chicago.

integrate all 10 domains illustrated in Figure 1; however, the relative weight of any particular competency will differ depending on the program focus or purpose, and may be adjusted to reflect the job market demands.

Transforming curriculum

The AAC envisions the best way to integrate programmatic competencies reflecting the foundational domains is through *competency-driven curricula*. Health informatics education, as proposed, is more open to interdisciplinary learning and focuses more on problem solving and critical thinking than on traditional "sit and get" learning. Moving to a *competency-driven* educational approach will require an intensive educational process and multiple assessments involving all educational and professional stakeholders (Figure 2). The approach asks programs to rethink outcomes and course expectations, moving away from rote memory to the incorporation of essential knowledge, skills, and attitudes and assessed performance of defined competencies.

Where do program directors start?

The introduction of the foundational domains within a program starts with mapping the current curriculum. Program directors should start at the endpoint of their program and identify those competencies students are expected to demonstrate at graduation that align with the foundational domains. Essentially, program directors should define the program outcomes as competencies that offer a meaningful reflection of what a graduate "knows" and what he/she can "do with that knowledge." Competencies are observable and can be measured and assessed. The content as taught in the current curriculum can be reused and reorganized to address the competencies defined in the program outcomes, resulting in a more comprehensive curriculum that integrates the domains and culminates in the acquisition of the higher level, more complex competencies.

The content of each course in a curriculum should be a stepping stone to the next one, adhering to the principles of instructional scaffolding.[21] Instructional scaffolding encompasses iterative and interconnected assessment of the intended learning objectives of each course and the instructional support and didactic approaches needed to attain the intended levels of competence. Reflecting its theoretical frameworks of Activity Theory and Knowledge Integration, instructional scaffolding facilitates the development of cohesive mental models—in this case, the scientific foundations of the health informatics.[22] Ultimately, the placement and sequence of courses leading to the program outcome competencies are determined by each individual program.

How do programs assess (measure) performance?

For decades, whether formative or summative, regardless of the format or type of assessment, all health professions educational

Table 3. Foundational domain titles and short descriptions

Domain	Name	Brief Description
F1	Health	The background knowledge of the history, goals, methods, and current challenges of the major health sciences, including human biology, genomics, clinical and translational science, healthcare delivery, personal health, and public health.
F2	Information Science and Technology	The background knowledge of the concepts, terminology, methods, and tools of information science and technology for managing and analyzing data, information, and knowledge.
F3	Social and Behavioral Science	The background knowledge of the effects of social, behavioral, legal, psychological, management, cognitive, and economic theories, methods, and models applicable to health informatics from multiple levels including individual, social group, and society.
F4	Health Information Science and Technology	The knowledge, skills, and attitudes to use concepts and tools for managing and analyzing biomedical and health data, information, and knowledge. Key foci include systems design and development, standards, integration, interoperability, and protection of biomedical and health information.
F5	Human Factors and Socio-technical Systems	The knowledge, skills, and attitudes to apply social behavioral theories and human factors engineering to better understand the interaction between users and information technologies within the organizational, social, and physical contexts of their lives, and apply this understanding in information system design.
F6	Social and Behavioral Aspects of Health	The knowledge, skills, and attitudes to use social determinants of health and patient-generated data to analyze problems arising from health or disease, to recognize the implications of these problems on daily activities, and to recognize and/or develop practical solutions to managing these problems.
F7	Social, Behavioral, and Information Science and Technology Applied to Health	The knowledge, skills, and attitudes to apply the diverse foundational concepts and facets in order to develop integrative approaches to the design, implementation, and evaluation of health informatics solutions.
F8	Professionalism	The conduct that reflects the aims or qualities that characterize a professional person, encompassing especially a defined body of knowledge and skills and their lifelong maintenance as well as adherence to an ethical code.
F9	Interprofessional Collaborative Practice	Behavior that reflects the foundations of values/ethics, roles/responsibilities, interprofessional communication practices, and interprofessional teamwork for team-based practice.
F10	Leadership	Behavior that demonstrates the following characteristics: credibility, honesty, competence, ability to inspire, and ability to formulate and communicate a vision.

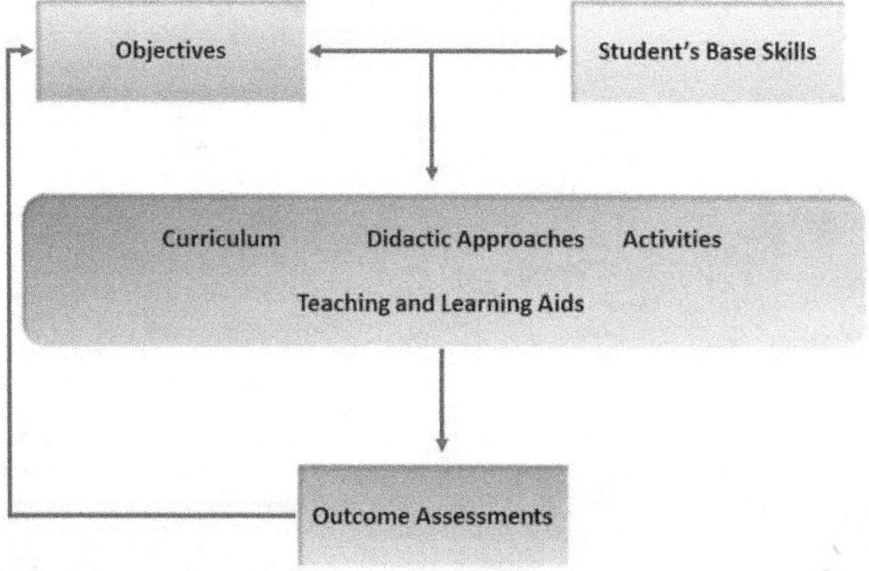

Figure 2. Path from content- to competency-driven curriculum.

programs have assessed students' attainment of knowledge. Graduate programs in health informatics, however, have far less experience in assessing attainment of technical skills and desired attitudes. Fortunately, the discipline can draw on the experiences of other health professions that have sought to build conceptual frameworks for such assessment. Conceptual frameworks for assessment of competence, such as the work of Miller and Cruess et al. in medical education, and the work of Lenburg for nursing competence, among others, can inform the assessment efforts of the discipline as it moves to a new paradigm of graduate education.[23–29]

CONCLUSION

Ultimately, the value of the competencies that programs develop will be demonstrated as graduates of health informatics programs gain employment in this field. They may become teachers or practitioners in any number of industries, based upon their and their employers' ability to articulate and apply these skills. AMIA has surveyed and analyzed industries' view of health informatics, and fosters strong relationships with public and private employers. As a past Chair of the AMIA Board of Directors stated, "I hope the move will lend some clarity to employers who seek skills, competencies, and talent that informatics graduates possess, in the nation's effort to proliferate clinical information systems using informatics tools and techniques."

Building standards across programs and the change from content-driven to competency-driven curricula is an evolutionary process. The definition of core competence is part of any accreditation standard; accreditation is one step in the journey toward professionalism of a discipline. Professional societies and their contribution to professional education (as opposed to formal graduate education) is an essential component of a profession.[30] This document will be periodically updated, as part of the responsibility of the AMIA Accreditation Committee, through continued study, education, and surveys of market trends. The active participation of AMIA within CAHIIM provides a pathway for the member programs of AMIA to speak in a more unified voice, while respecting the unique differences and diversity that make informatics such a dynamic field.

Finally, the 10 foundational domains emerged from the comprehensive review of the field in the 2012 article authored by Kulikowski and colleagues.[1] These domains define the field. Competencies are created and anchored to the level of skills acquisition appropriate for the population under consideration. Competencies can be adapted for different stages of education, including that of the baccalaureate or, potentially, doctoral program, by modifying the level of knowledge, skills, and attitudes to be expected at the time of graduation of the baccalaureate (or doctoral) student; other competencies may be required for those stages. Over time, through the iterative process of building competency-driven curricula, through national conversations at the AMIA Academic Forum and its annual Informatics Educators Forum, and through the work of the AMIA Education Committee and its subcommittee, the AMIA Accreditation Committee, insight on the foundational domains and the knowledge, skills, and attitudes required of informaticians will grow. This has been the path to the professionalization of every other health profession and will be the path taken for those in the discipline of health informatics.

REFERENCES

1. Kulikowski CA, Shortliffe EH, Currie LM, et al. AMIA Board White Paper: definition of biomedical informatics and specification of core competencies for graduate education in the discipline. *J Am Med Inform Assoc* 2012; 19 (6): 931–8.
2. Ford G, Gibbs N. *A Mature Profession of Software Engineering*. Pittsburgh, PA: Software Engineering Institute, Carnegie Mellon University; 1996. Technical Report CMU/SEI-96-TR-004. https://resources.sei.cmu.edu/asset_files/TechnicalReport/1996_005_001_16460.pdf.
3. Hersh W. A stimulus to define informatics and health information technology. *BMC Med Inform Decis Mak* 2009; 9: 24–30.
4. Friedman CP. What informatics is and isn't. *J Am Med Inform Assoc* 2013; 20 (2): 224–6.
5. Gardner RM, Overhage JM, Steen EB, et al. Core content for the subspecialty of clinical informatics. *J Am Med Inform Assoc* 2009; 16 (2): 153–7.
6. Mantas J, Ammenwerth E, Demiris G, et al. Recommendations of the International Medical Informatics Association (IMIA) on education in biomedical and health informatics. *Methods Inf Med* 2010; 49 (2): 105–20.
7. National Center for Healthcare Leadership. NCHL Health Leadership Competency Model™. Chicago: NHCL; 2017. http://www.nchl.org/static.asp?path=2852, 3238. Accessed August 24, 2018.
8. Calhoun JG, Dollett L, Sinioris ME, et al. Development of an interprofessional competency model for healthcare leadership. *J Healthc Manag* 2008; 53 (6): 375–91.
9. Valerius J, Mohan V, Doctor D, et al. Collaboration leads to enhanced curriculum. *Appl Clin Inform* 2015; 06 (01): 200–9.
10. Gibson CJ, Dixon BE, Abrams K. Convergent evolution of health information management and health informatics: a perspective on the future of information professionals in health care. *Appl Clin Inform* 2015; 06 (01): 163–84.
11. Wilson LO. Anderson and Krathwohl–Bloom's Taxonomy revised. [Place Unknown: The Second Principle]; 2018. http://thesecondprinciple.com/teaching-essentials/beyond-bloom-cognitive-taxonomy-revised/. Accessed August 24, 2018.
12. Wilson LO. Three Domains of Learning—Cognitive, Affective, Psychomotor. [Place Unknown: The Second Principle]; 2018. http://thesecondprinciple.com/instructional-design/threedomainsoflearning/. Accessed August 24, 2018.
13. Clark D. Bloom's Taxonomy: The Psychomotor Domain. [Place Unknown: Donald Clark]; c1999-2015. http://www.nwlink.com/~donclark/hrd/Bloom/psychomotor_domain.html. Accessed August 24, 2018.
14. Dreyfus HL, Dreyfus SE. *Mind over Machine: The Power of Human Intuition and Expertise in the Era of the Computer*. New York, NY: The Free Press; 1986.
15. Benner P. From novice to expert. *Am J Nurs* 1982; 82 (3): 402–7.
16. Benner P. The Dreyfus Model of Skill Acquisition applied to nursing In: Benner P, ed. *From Novice to Expert*. Menlo Park, CA: Addison-Wesley; 2001: 13–38.
17. Frank JR, Snell LS, Cate OT, et al. Competency-based medical education: theory to practice. *Med Teach* 2010; 32 (8): 638–45.
18. Harris I. Deliberative inquiry: the arts of planning. In: Short EC, ed. *Forms of Curriculum Inquiry*. Albany, NY: SUNY Press; 1991: 285–308.
19. CAHIIM. 2017 *Health Informatics Accreditation Standards—Masters Degree*. Chicago: Commission on Accreditation for Health Informatics and Information Management Education; 2018. http://www.cahiim.org/hi/accreditationstandards.html. Accessed August 24, 2018.
20. Knox AD, Gilardino MS, Kasten SJ, et al. Competency-based medical education for plastic surgery: where do we begin? *Plast Reconstr Surg* 2014; 133 (5): 702e–10e.
21. Belland BR. Instructional scaffolding: foundations and evolving definition. In: *Instructional Scaffolding in STEM Education: Strategies and Efficacy Evidence*. Cham. Switzerland: Springer International Publishing; 2017: 17–54.
22. Raes A, Schellens T. The effects of teacher-led class interventions during technology-enhanced science inquiry on students' knowledge integration and basic need satisfaction. *Comput Educ* 2016; 92-93: 125–41.

23. Accreditation Council for Pharmacy Education. Guidance for the Accreditation Standards and Key Elements for the Professional Program in Pharmacy Leading to the Doctor of Pharmacy Degree (Guidance for Standards 2016). Chicago: Accreditation Council for Pharmacy Education; 2015. https://www.acpe-accredit.org/pdf/GuidanceforStandards2016FINAL.pdf. Accessed August 24, 2018.
24. American Health Information Management Association. *Academic Curricula Competencies.* Chicago: AHIMA; 2017. http://www.ahima.org/education/academic-affairs/academic-curricula. Accessed August 24, 2018.
25. American Occupational Therapy Association. Occupational therapy practice framework: domain and process (3rd edition). *Am J Occup Ther* 2014; 68: S1–S48.
26. Council on Social Work Education Commission on Accreditation and Commission on Educational Policy. *Educational Policy and Accreditation Standards for Baccalaureate and Master's Social Work Programs.* Alexandria, VA: Council on Social Work Education; 2015. https://www.cswe.org/getattachment/Accreditation/Standards-and-Policies/2015-EPAS/2015EPASandGlossary.pdf.aspx. Accessed August 24, 2018.
27. Lenburg CB. The framework, concepts and methods of the competency outcomes and performance assessment (COPA) model. *Online J Issues Nurs* 1999; 4 (2): 1–2.
28. Miller GE. The assessment of clinical skills/competence/performance. *Acad Med* 1990; 65 (9 suppl): S63–S7.
29. Cruess RL, Cruess SR, Steinert Y. Amending Miller's Pyramid to include professional identity formation. *Acad Med* 2016; 91 (2): 180–5.
30. McConnell S. Novum Organum. In: *Professional Software Development: Shorter Schedules, Higher Quality Products, More Successful Projects, Enhanced Careers.* Boston, MA: Addison-Wesley Longman Publishing; 2004: 49–58.

APPENDIX

AMIA 2017 core competencies for applied health informatics education at the master's degree level

INTRODUCTION

Competencies describe what a student will be able to do at a point in time. For the purpose of this document, the point in time is set at graduation from an applied master of science in health informatics program. A given competency is built upon an integrated set of knowledge, skills, and attitudes needed to perform an activity. For each of the 10 foundational domains presented here, every program must develop competency statements that reflect the individual AMIA Application Area that is the focus of the program. For each domain described below, examples are provided of knowledge, skills, and attitudes that could be reflected in competencies for those domains.

As an example, in looking at Foundational Domain F9, Interprofessional Collaborative Practice, a competency reflecting that domain from a program focusing on preparing students for an applied clinical informatics role might be "Collaborate with clinicians and administrative and technical personnel to implement a communication plan for a new EHR system." A competency for a program in translational bioinformatics from the same domain might be "Participate with clinical researchers on a team science project." Both of these competencies reflect the integration of a knowledge component that includes the knowledge about different professions, stakeholders, and team dynamics; a skill component related to relationship-building and interprofessional communication; and an attitude component related to mutual respect and shared values. The example statements of knowledge, skills, and attitudes listed within each of the domains below can be used to develop the program-specific competencies that reflect an individual program's focus within an AMIA Application Area. Programs may also define competencies within a given foundational domain that are an integration of other knowledge, skills, and attitudes that are not listed here.

As a final note, the discipline of health informatics exists at the confluence of 3 major domains: Health, Information Science and Technology, and Social and Behavioral Science (represented by F1, F2, and F3), which define and affect the practice of health informatics. During its deliberations, members of the AAC concluded that graduate students in this discipline should have working knowledge of these 3 domains as they enter their graduate work. As a result, only a statement of knowledge was developed for each of these 3 major domains.

F1. HEALTH

Health refers to the biomedical and health sciences underlying AMIA's 5 major informatics areas: translational bioinformatics, clinical research informatics, clinical informatics, consumer health informatics, and public health informatics. The biomedical and health sciences aim to understand and improve human health. To identify and develop solutions to biomedical informatics problems, students must understand the history, goals, methods (including data and information used and produced), and current challenges of the major health sciences, including human biology, genomics, clinical and translational science, healthcare delivery, personal health, and public health.

Knowledge

At the time of graduation from an applied master of science in health informatics program, the graduate student should be able to....

Describe the history, goals, methods (including data and information used and produced), and current challenges of the major health science fields. These include biology, genomics, clinical and translational science, healthcare delivery, personal health, and public health.

F2. INFORMATION SCIENCE AND TECHNOLOGY

Information Science and Technology refers to the key concepts, methods, and tools for creating, acquiring, storing, representing, accessing, merging, organizing, processing, transferring, analyzing, reporting, and visualizing data, information, and knowledge. It also includes the methods and tools for protection of the data, information, and knowledge from unauthorized access. Included are understanding how information is used and the ability to assess the information needs of users. Familiarity is required with basic computer science terminology and concepts, including terms and concepts related to information systems and computer programming, information retrieval, ontologies, business intelligence, analytics, and user interface design.

Knowledge

At the time of graduation from an applied master of science in health informatics program, the graduate student should be able to....

Identify the applicable information science and technology concepts, methods, and tools, which may be dependent upon the application area of the training program, to solve health informatics problems. These include the concepts, methods, and tools related to managing data, information, and knowledge, the basic information and computer science terms and concepts, the principles of information security, as well as the methods of assessing users' information needs.

F3. SOCIAL AND BEHAVIORAL SCIENCE

Social and Behavioral Science refers to basic social, behavioral, psychological, and management theories, methods, and models as well as the legal and regulatory frameworks that seek to describe human actions and interactions as well as human behavior in society. It includes concepts from fields such as sociology, economics, anthropology, political science, law, psychology, and management and cognitive sciences. It is concerned with the application of social, behavioral, psychological, and management theories, methods, and models to the design, implementation, and evaluation of health information behaviors at the levels of individual, social group, organizations, and society, which are influenced by laws and regulations. The purpose is to contribute to decreasing health-damaging behaviors and improving health-promoting behaviors and psychosocial well-being through health informatics perspectives.

Knowledge

At the time of graduation from an applied master of science in health informatics program, the graduate student should be able to....

Identify the effects of social, behavioral, legal, psychological, management, cognitive, and economic theories, methods, and models applicable to health informatics from multiple levels, including individual, social group, and society.

F4. HEALTH INFORMATION SCIENCE AND TECHNOLOGY

Health Information Science and Technology refers to the array of health information science and technology methods, tools, and standards for collecting, organizing, representing, sharing, integrating, using, governing, and learning from biomedical and health data, information, and knowledge across the entire spectrum of informatics domains. Systems design and development addresses standards, integration, interoperability, and protection of information. These competencies also address computational thinking, which includes problem solving, systems design, and understanding human behavior, as associated with computer science.

Knowledge

At the time of graduation from an applied master of science in health informatics program, the graduate student should be able to....

Identify possible biomedical and health information science and technology methods and tools for solving a specific biomedical and health information problem. Core health information technology tools may be dependent upon the application area of the training program.

Skills

At the time of graduation from an applied master of science in health informatics program, the graduate student should be able to....

Design a solution to a biomedical or health information problem by applying computational and systems thinking, information science, and technology.

Attitudes/abilities

At the time of graduation from an applied master of science in health informatics program, the graduate student should be able to....

Demonstrate consideration of the advantages and limitations of using information science and technology to solve biomedical and health information problems as well as the needs of the different stakeholders and context.

F5. HUMAN FACTORS AND SOCIO-TECHNICAL SYSTEMS

Human Factors and Socio-technical Systems refers to the interactions between human behaviors (physical, social, cognitive, and psychological) and information technologies. People and organizations are the ultimate users of health information and technologies. This domain draws on the social, behavioral, cognitive, economic, human factors engineering, and management and systems sciences in considering the needs, workflows, and practices of individuals and organizations in the context of information systems and technology.

Knowledge

At the time of graduation from an applied master of science in health informatics program, the graduate student should be able to....

Draw on socio-technical knowledge regarding the social behavioral sciences and human factors engineering to apply to the design and implementation of information systems and technology.

Skills

At the time of graduation from an applied master of science in health informatics program, the graduate student should be able to....

Apply social behavioral theories and human factors engineering to the design and evaluation of information systems and technology.

Attitudes/abilities

At the time of graduation from an applied master of science in health informatics program, the graduate student should be able to....

Demonstrate consideration and respect for the role of users in the design and application of information systems and technology.

F6. SOCIAL AND BEHAVIORAL ASPECTS OF HEALTH

Social and Behavioral Aspects of Health refers to action(s) taken by an individual, groups of individuals, or an organization to manage the health of an individual or population. It entails social determinants and patient-generated data, analyses of problems arising from health or disease, the implications of these problems on daily activities, and the practical solutions to managing these problems. Patient behavior (that may be affected by genotypes and phenotypes), health literacy, informed decision making, patient engagement, and patient activation are examples of issues in this domain. Other common topics in this domain, depending on the program focus, may include health-behavioral paradigms, such as health and healthcare self-management, substance abuse, utilization of healthcare services, characteristics of nutrition, exercise/physical activity habits, organizational network analyses, precision medicine and individualized care, etc.

Knowledge
At the time of graduation from an applied master of science in health informatics program, the graduate student should be able to....

Identify theories or models that explain and modify patient or population behaviors related to health and health outcome.

Skills
At the time of graduation from an applied master of science in health informatics program, the graduate student should be able to....

Apply models, which may be dependent upon the application area of the training program, to address social and behavioral problems related to health of individuals, populations, and organizations.

Attitudes/abilities
At the time of graduation from an applied master of science in health informatics program, the graduate student should be able to....

Acknowledge the importance of social and behavioral aspects of health and their contribution to the health of individuals and populations.

F7. SOCIAL, BEHAVIORAL, AND INFORMATION SCIENCE AND TECHNOLOGY APPLIED TO HEALTH

Social, Behavioral, and Information Science and Technology Applied to Health refers to the integration of social, business, human factors, behavioral, and information sciences and technology on the design, implementation, and evaluation of health informatics solutions. The application of health technologies and clinical and/or business processes can impact individual and community health outcomes at numerous levels from molecular and biological systems, to healthcare and organizational protocols, to social systems and public health.

Knowledge
At the time of graduation from an applied master of science in health informatics program, the graduate student should be able to....

Identify the theories, models, and tools from social, business, human factors, behavioral, and information sciences and technologies for designing, implementing, and evaluating health informatics solutions. Theories, models, and tools may be dependent upon the application area of the training program.

Skills
At the time of graduation from an applied master of science in health informatics program, the graduate student should be able to....

Integrate and apply the theories, models, and tools from social, business, human factors, behavioral, and information sciences and technologies to design, implement, and evaluate health informatics solutions. Theories, models, and tools may be dependent upon the application area of the training program.

Attitudes/abilities
At the time of graduation from an applied master of science in health informatics program, the graduate student should be able to....

Demonstrate an awareness of the interrelatedness of social, business, human factors, behavioral, and information sciences and technology in the design, implementation, and evaluation of health informatics solutions.

F8. PROFESSIONALISM

Professionalism refers to the level of excellence or competence that is expected of a health informatics professional and includes such concepts as the maintenance and utilization of knowledge and technical skills, which may be dependent upon the application area of the training program; commitment to professional ethical principles including those in AMIA's Code of Ethics; and maintenance of the highest standards of excellence in the field including professional development. In health informatics, there is a particular emphasis on preserving the confidentiality, privacy, and security of patient and other health data and information, and balancing it with appropriate stakeholder access.

Knowledge
At the time of graduation from an applied master of science in health informatics program, the graduate student should be able to....

Define and discuss ethical principles and the informaticians' responsibilities to the profession, their employers, and ultimately to the stakeholders of the informatics solutions they create and maintain.

Skills
At the time of graduation from an applied master of science in health informatics program, the graduate student should be able to....

Demonstrate professional practices that incorporate ethical principles and values of the discipline.

Attitudes/abilities
At the time of graduation from an applied master of science in health informatics program, the graduate student should be able to....

Demonstrate awareness of the value of information literacy and lifelong learning, maintenance of skills, and professional excellence.

F9. INTERPROFESSIONAL COLLABORATIVE PRACTICE

Interprofessional Collaborative Practice (ICP) refers to the shared, coordinated work among peers from different professions in order to achieve a common goal or mission. The work may range from local projects to those on a national and international scale, and should be performed in an ethical manner that involves honesty, integrity, trust, and respect. Part of this domain is teamwork and team science, which involves drawing on individual team members' strengths and expertise and assigning designated roles and methods to achieve the goals and mission. ICP requires effective communication skills. In summary, the domain requires mastery of values/ethics, roles/responsibilities, interprofessional communication, and team/teamwork.

Knowledge

At the time of graduation from an applied master of science in health informatics program, the graduate student should be able to....

Define and discuss the scope of practice and roles of different health professionals and stakeholders including patients, as well as the principles of team science and team dynamics to solve complex health and health information problems.

Skills

At the time of graduation from an applied master of science in health informatics program, the graduate student should be able to....

Apply relationship-building skills and the principles of interprofessional communication in a responsive and responsible manner that supports a team approach to solve complex health and health information problems.

Attitude/abilities

At the time of graduation from an applied master of science in health informatics program, the graduate student should be able to....

Recognize the importance of mutual respect and shared values, as well as one's own role, the role of other professions and stakeholders including patients, and the role of teamwork and team science to solve complex health and health information problems.

F10. LEADERSHIP

Leadership refers to the interactive process for which the output is vision, guidance, and direction. Essentials of leadership include vision, communication skills, stewardship, acting as a change agent, and the developing and renewing of followers and future leaders. Leaders must envision goals, set priorities, manage change, make decisions, communicate, serve as a symbol of one who is willing to take risks and has credible expertise, and guide others by motivating other leaders as well as those who will follow. The concept of followership refers to a role held by certain individuals in an organization, team, or group. Specifically, it is the capacity of an individual to actively follow a leader. For leaders to be successful at leadership, they must possess the following characteristics: credibility, honesty, competence, ability to inspire, and the ability to formulate and communicate a vision.

Knowledge

At the time of graduation from an applied master of science in health informatics program, the graduate student should be able to....

Articulate the methods, concepts, tools, and characteristics of leading and leadership.

Skills

At the time of graduation from an applied master of science in health informatics program, the graduate student should be able to....

Employ leadership and followership methods, concepts, and tools to motivate others toward accomplishing a health informatics vision.

Attitude/abilities

At the time of graduation from an applied master of science in health informatics program, the graduate student should be able to....

Demonstrate leadership behaviors for achieving a vision for health informatics solutions.

BIBLIOGRAPHIC MATERIALS DRAWN UPON FOR DEVELOPMENT OF FOUNDATIONAL DOMAINS AND CORE COMPETENCIES

AMIA. The Science of Informatics. Bethesda, MD: AMIA; 2018. https://www.amia.org/about-amia/science-informatics. Accessed August 24, 2018.

Amin TT. Competency-Based Education in Public Health [PowerPoint slides]. 2014 Mar 20:[30 slides]. http://www.slideshare.net/Tawfikzahran/competency-based-education-in-public-health-32522626. Accessed August 24, 2018.

Association for Computing Machinery (ACM). New York: ACM; 1992. ACM Code of Ethics and Professional Conduct; [about 12 screens]. https://www.acm.org/about-acm/acm-code-of-ethics-and-professional-conduct. Accessed August 24, 2018.

Association for Information Science and Technology (ASIS&T). Silver Spring, MD: ASIS&T; 1992. ASIS&T Professional Guidelines; [about 3 screens]. http://www.asis.org/AboutASIS/professional-guidelines.html. Accessed August 24, 2018.

Berg M. Patient care information systems and health care work: a sociotechnical approach. *Int J Med Inform* 1999; 55 (2): 87–101.

Caldwell C, Voelker C, Dixon RD, LeJeune A. Transformative leadership: an ethical stewardship model for healthcare. *Organ Ethic* 2008; 4 (2): 126–34.

Choi J. A motivational theory of charismatic leadership: envisioning, empathy, and empowerment. *J Leadersh Organizational Stud* 2006; 13 (1): 24–43.

Duffy VG, ed. *Advances in Human Factors and Ergonomics in Healthcare.* Boca Raton, FL: CRC Press; 2011.

Frank JR, Snell LS, Cate OT, et al. Competency-based medical education: theory to practice. *Med Teach* 2010; 32 (8): 638–45.

Glanz K, Rimer BK, Viswanath K, eds. *Health Behavior: Theory, Research, and Practice.* 5th ed. San Francisco: John Wiley & Sons, Inc; 2015.

Goetsch DL, Davis SB. *Quality Management for Organizational Excellence: Introduction to Total Quality.* 7th ed. Essex, England: Pearson Education Limited; 2014.

Goodman KW, Adams S, Berner ES, et al. AMIA's code of professional and ethical conduct. *J Am Med Inform Assoc* 2013; 20 (1): 141–3.

Google for Education. CT [Computational Thinking] Overview; [about 3 screens]. https://www.google.com/edu/resources/programs/exploring-computational-thinking/#!ct-overview. Accessed August 24, 2018.

Hill J, Nielsen M, Fox MH. Understanding the social factors that contribute to diabetes: a means to informing health care and social policies for the chronically ill. *Perm J* 2013; 17 (2): 67–72.

Holt-Lunstad J, Uchino BN. Social support and health. In: Glanz K, Rimer BK, Viswanath K, eds. *Health Behavior: Theory, Research, and Practice*. 5th ed. San Francisco: John Wiley & Sons, Inc.; 2015: 183–204.

Human Factors and Ergonomics Society (HFES). Santa Monica, CA: HFES; No Date. Educational Resources: Definitions of Human Factors and Ergonomics; [about 12 screens]. http://cms.hfes.org/Resources/Educational-and-Professional-Resources/Educational-Resources/Definitions-of-Human-Factors-and-Ergonomics.aspx. Accessed August 24, 2018.

International Medical Informatics Association (IMIA). Geneva, Switzerland: IMIA; c2002. The IMIA Code of Ethics for Health Information Professionals; [10 pages]. http://www.imia-medinfo.org/new2/pubdocs/Ethics_Eng.pdf. Accessed August 24, 2018.

Interprofessional Education Collaborative Expert Panel. *Core Competencies for Interprofessional Collaborative Practice: Report of an Expert Panel*. Washington, DC: Interprofessional Education Collaborative; 2011: 47. https://www.ipecollaborative.org/resources.html.

Interprofessional Education Collaborative. *Core Competencies for Interprofessional Collaborative Practice*: 2016 Update. Washington, DC: Interprofessional Education Collaborative; 2016: 19. https://www.ipecollaborative.org/resources.html.

Kulikowski CA, Shortliffe EH, Currie LM, et al. AMIA Board White Paper: definition of biomedical informatics and specification of core competencies for graduate education in the discipline. *J Am Med Inform Assoc* 2012; 19 (6): 931–8.

Mcdougal JA, Brooks CM, Albanese M. Achieving consensus on leadership competencies and outcome measures: the Pediatric Pulmonary Centers' experience. *Eval Health Prof* 2005; 28 (4): 428–46.

National Cancer Institute Team Science Toolkit. Bethesda, MD: National Cancer Institute at the National Institutes of Health. https://www.teamsciencetoolkit.cancer.gov/Public/Home.aspx. Accessed August 24, 2018.

Red River College. Winnipeg and Manitoba, Canada: Red River College; c2004-2006. KSA Verbs Related to Bloom's Taxonomy; [2 pages]. http://www.rrc.ca/LearningOutcomeSupport/modules.asp?module=1&type=2&page=3. Accessed April 26, 2016.

Society of Hospital Medicine. Professionalism and medical ethics. *J Hosp Med* 2006; 1(S1): 90–1.

Riggio RE, Chaleff I, Blumen-Lipman J. *The Art of Followership: How Great Followers Create Great Leaders and Organizations*. San Francisco: Jossey-Bass; 2008.

Trastek VF, Hamilton NW, Niles EE. Leadership models in health care—a case for servant leadership. *Mayo Clin Proc* 2014; 89 (3): 374–81.

University of Minnesota Duluth, Office of the Vice Chancellor for Academic Affairs. Duluth: UMN; 2015. Bloom's Taxonomy: Three Learning Domains; [3 pages]. http://www.d.umn.edu/vcaa/assessment/bloomoverviw.docx. Accessed August 3, 2015.

Vicente KJ. *Cognitive Work Analysis: Toward Safe, Productive, and Healthy Computer-Based Work*. Mahwah, NJ: Lawrence Erlbaum Associates; 1999.

Wing JM. Computational thinking. *Commun ACM* 2006; 49 (3): 33–5.

Yale School of Public Health. New Haven, CT: Yale University; 2015. Social and Behavioral Sciences: MPH Competencies; [about 2 screens]. http://publichealth.yale.edu/sbs/curriculum/mph/competencies.aspx. Accessed August 24, 2018.

Part II: Advances in Assessment

Overview

Rachel Yudkowsky
Professor, Department of Medical Education

Assessment is "a systematic process to measure or evaluate the characteristics or performance of individuals ... for purposes of drawing inferences".[1] High quality, evidence-based assessment undergirds our ability to select students and residents for training in the health professions; to determine whether learners are ready to progress to later stages of training, or require remediation; and ultimately, to decide who will be licensed for independent practice.

The quality or validity of an assessment reflects the claim that it is reasonable to make a particular decision, in a particular context, based on the results of a given assessment. Validity investigations are studies that gather evidence and present an argument to support that claim. The four papers in this section present validity evidence for a broad range of assessments in medical education. They describe traditional and innovative assessments; explore written tests, performance tests, and workplace-based assessments; and span from medical school through post-graduate training to licensure examinations.

The papers are exceptional in that each addresses a critical and often-neglected aspect of validity: an evaluation of the consequences or impact of an assessment. Consequences validity evidence extends far beyond pass/fail outcomes. It can include investigations of the impact of assessment-based information, of assessment-based decisions, and of the experience of the assessment, as well as an exploration of consequences at the level of the learner, the patient, and the institution.[2]

In "The key-features approach to assess clinical decisions: validity evidence to date" Bordage and Page conduct a systematic review of validity evidence for the key-features (KF) approach that they pioneered in 1984. The KF approach focuses on the outcomes of clinical reasoning: key clinical decisions known to be challenging to the targeted examinees. Validity evidence gathered across 164 papers confirms that the KF approach can provide both a reliable estimate of skills and an information-rich source of formative feedback, including identifying decision errors that can lead to patient harm. (Impact at the level of the patient: potential to reduce patient harm.)

Assessment at an earlier stage of clinical reasoning is addressed by Yudkowsky and DME coauthors Riddle and Bordage in "A hypothesis-driven physical examination learning and assessment procedure for medical students: initial validity evidence". The hypothesis-driven physical exam (HDPE) assessment approach aims to avoid rote performance of the PE and to promote clinical reasoning by asking students to anticipate, elicit, and interpret PE findings in the context of a standardized patient-based diagnostic challenge. Students who participated in an HDPE encounter performed better than students who did not when facing a similar challenge later in training. (Consequences at the level of the learner: promoting clinical reasoning.)

Park, with DME coauthors Riddle and Tekian, report on "Validity evidence of resident competency ratings and the identification of problem residents". End-of-rotation evaluations can be an important source of information regarding resident progress but suffer from many challenges, including rater biases and delayed submission. This study of internal medicine resident evaluations suggests that, notwithstanding their imperfections, end-of-rotation ratings can provide reliable information and aid in the early detection of struggling residents. (Consequences for learner and for program: early detection and remediation.)

Finally, resident assessment is also the focus of "Developing an institution-based assessment of resident communication and interpersonal skills" by Sandlow, with DME coauthors Downing and Yudkowsky. We describe validity evidence for a centrally-developed standardized patient-based assessment of communication, patient care, and professionalism. The assessment was implemented with minimal modifications across six specialties, conserving resources and providing actionable information regarding individual resident deficiencies and curricular gaps. (Consequences for institution: reduced cost and faculty time.)

George Miller, founder of DME, famously declared that "assessment drives the curriculum", reminding us that assessments have consequences beyond learner-specific inferences. The papers in this section demonstrate well this broader impact of assessment, ranging from assessment affecting learning to consequences for nations and global regions.[3]

Following in the tradition of George Miller, DME continues at the cutting edge of assessment research, exploring innovations in mastery learning and competency-based medical education, simulation-based assessment, student and resident selection, and the consequences of assessments for our learners, our institutions, and society itself.

References

1. American Educational Research Association, American Psychological Association, National Council on Measurement in Education. *Standards for educational and psychological testing.* Washington, DC: American Educational Research Association; 2014.
2. Cook DA, Lineberry M. Consequences validity evidence: evaluating the impact of educational assessments. *Acad Med.* 2016;91(6):785-795.
3. Lineberry M. From: Assessment affecting Learning. In: Yudkowsky R, Park YS, Downing SM, editors. *Assessment in Health Professions Education* (2nd edition), New York: Routledge; 2019.

Adv in Health Sci Educ (2018) 23:1005–1036
https://doi.org/10.1007/s10459-018-9830-5

REVIEW

The key-features approach to assess clinical decisions: validity evidence to date

G. Bordage[1] · G. Page[2]

Received: 4 November 2017 / Accepted: 7 May 2018 / Published online: 17 May 2018
© Springer Science+Business Media B.V., part of Springer Nature 2018

Abstract The key-features (KFs) approach to assessment was initially proposed during the First Cambridge Conference on Medical Education in 1984 as a more efficient and effective means of assessing clinical decision-making skills. Over three decades later, we conducted a comprehensive, systematic review of the validity evidence gathered since then. The evidence was compiled according to the *Standards for Educational and Psychological Testing*'s five sources of validity evidence, namely, Content, Response process, Internal structure, Relations to other variables, and Consequences, to which we added two other types related to Cost-feasibility and Acceptability. Of the 457 publications that referred to the KFs approach between 1984 and October 2017, 164 are cited here; the remaining 293 were either redundant or the authors simply mentioned the KFs concept in relation to their work. While one set of articles reported meeting the validity standards, another set examined KFs test development choices and score interpretation. The accumulated validity evidence for the KFs approach since its inception supports the decision-making construct measured and its use to assess clinical decision-making skills at all levels of training and practice and with various types of exam formats. Recognizing that gathering validity evidence is an ongoing process, areas with limited evidence, such as item factor analyses or consequences of testing, are identified as well as new topics needing further clarification, such as the use of the KFs approach for formative assessment and its place within a program of assessment.

Keywords Medical examinations · Key features · Validity

✉ G. Bordage
bordage@uic.edu

[1] Department of Medical Education, College of Medicine, University of Illinois at Chicago, Chicago, USA

[2] Department of Medicine, Faculty of Medicine, University of British Columbia, Vancouver, Canada

Introduction

Gathering validity evidence is an ongoing process. Since the inception of the key features (KFs) approach for the assessment of clinical decision-making skills in 1984, there have been many studies published on its use. However, these studies focus mostly on limited, and sometimes outdated, aspects of validity; few contain reviews with cumulative and overall evidence. Using Messick's unitary framework of construct validity, the purpose of this study was to conduct a comprehensive and systematic review of all the sources of validity evidence gathered to date regarding the use of the KFs approach to assess clinical decision-making skills.

Historically, the KFs approach originated during the First Cambridge Conference on Medical Education held in 1984 in Cambridge England (Norman et al. 1984). By then, Elstein, Shulman and Sprafka (1978) had shown that problem solving in medicine was not a general skill but rather was highly case specific, as indicated by low inter-case correlations, typically in the .1–.3 range, meaning that the resolution of a clinical problem is "highly contingent on the successful manipulation of a few key elements in it." (in Norman et al. 1984) Consequently, testing time would be best used by focusing only on those unique challenges in each case, the case's KFs (Bordage and Page 1987). This meant a shift in the object of assessment from general problem-solving skills, as was then the case with the use of oral exams (Miller 1966) and written Patient Management Problems (McGuire et al. 1976), to focusing only on the most challenging decisions and actions in each case, resulting in tests that contain many short, focused cases. The increased number of cases per testing time would result in better content representation of the domain assessed. Furthermore, the oral and written exams at the time tended to overly reward thoroughness, that is, the more "good" things the examinees did, the higher their scores, despite the fact that Elstein et al. (1978) had also shown that thoroughness was a poor predictor of performance. Thus, scoring that rewarded only key decisions would also contribute to more reliable and valid test scores.

Box 1a. Example of a Key-Features case and questions: 2 Parts, 2 Questions, 3 Key Features

Adapted from the American College of Surgeons' Entering Resident Readiness Assessment program, with permission from the Division of Education, American College of Surgeons.

Part 1

Case Scenario. You are called by the surgical-ward nurse to see a 67-year-old woman because she became disoriented and combative. She had a total abdominal hysterectomy 3 days ago.

When you arrive at the bedside, her pulse is 115/min, BP of 90/50 mmHg, temperature of 39.2 °C, and an oxygen saturation of 98% on room air. She is using a morphine pump for pain control.

Question-1. What diagnosis(es) are you considering at this time? You may list up to 3.

———————————————
———————————————
———————————————

Attention. Once you go to the next part, you cannot come back and change your answers to the current part.

Part 2 (on a separate page)

Question-2. How will you manage this patient at this time? You may select up to 7.

    1. Administer empiric antibiotics
    2. Administer haloperidol and reassess in 2 h
    3. Administer thiamine and folate
    4. Blood cultures

5. Call senior resident or attending

6. CBC

7. Chest X-ray

8. CT scan of the abdomen and pelvis

9. CT scan of the brain

10. Examine the abdomen

11. Examine the chest

12. MRI of the brain

13. Open midline wound at bedside

14. Order incentive spirometry and chest physiotherapy

15. Place patient in soft wrist restraints

16. Request psychiatry consultation

17. Stop morphine and reassess in 2 h

18. Ultrasound of the pelvis

19. Urinalysis

End of case

Box 1b: Scoring keys (3 KFs, each worth 1 point)

Question 1

Scoring key for KF-1: Consider sepsis in the differential diagnosis

1	Listed any one of the following: Sepsis, infection, septic shock, systemic inflammatory response syndrome, or SIRS
0	Listed more than 3 diagnoses

Question 2

Scoring key for KF-2: Examine the abdomen and order blood cultures, chest X-ray, and urinalysis

.25	4. Blood cultures
.25	7. Chest X-Ray
.25	10. Examine the abdomen
.25	19. Urinalysis
0	Selected more than 7 options

Scoring key for KF-3: Administer empiric antibiotic and call senior resident or attending; avoid giving sedation or stopping pain medication

.5	1. Administer empiric antibiotic
.5	5. Call senior resident or attending
0	Selected more than 7 options or selected one of the following:
	2. Administer haloperidol and reassess in 2 h
	17. Stop morphine and reassess in 2 h

Case score $= \sum (\text{KF1 score} + \text{KF2 score} + \text{KF3 score})/3$

A KFs case typically begins with a brief clinical scenario followed by 2 or 3 questions aimed at assessing only the unique challenges in each case. An example a KFs case, intended for beginning surgery interns, is presented in Box 1a, along with its scoring keys in Box 1b; note that only the KFs are scored and rewarded.

Methods

We used Messick's unitary framework of construct validity as our conceptual basis, as embodied in the *Standards for Educational and Psychological Testing* (American Educational Research Association 2014). The *Standards* define validity as, "the degree to which evidence and theory support the interpretation of test scores entailed by [the] proposed uses of tests." Accordingly, validity evidence will be presented using the *Standards*' five types of evidence, namely, Content, Response process, Internal structure, Relations to other variables, and Consequences, to which we added two other types regarding Cost-feasibility and Acceptability, based on van der Vleuten's model for the utility of assessment methods (1996) and Norcini et al.'s criteria for good assessment (2011). In our interpretation of the *Standards*, we also used complementary resources from Downing (2004, 2009), Downing and Haladyna (2009), and Downing and Yudkowsky (2009)) for topics related to responses process, scoring, item analysis, and consequences and from Zieky and Perie (2006) for cut scores.

We conducted sequential literature searches, starting with ResearchGate followed by PubMed, Google Scholar, SCOPUS, and Web of Science, of various publication formats (such as scientific articles, chapters, reports, and theses and dissertations) published between 1984 and October 2017 and using the search terms "key feature[s]" in medical education, health professions education, veterinary education, and educational measurement. These searches yielded 620 articles (including some duplicates) to which we added 63 references from Hrynchak, Takahashi and Nayer's 2014 review, for a total of 683 publications. Each publication was read by the first author (GB) for its relevance to the KFs approach and its contribution to validity evidence. Both authors then reviewed together the evidence in detail to discuss and settle any discrepancies, of which there were very few.

Results

The literature search yielded 457 publications that referred to the KFs approach, of which 164 are cited here; the remaining 293 (available on request) were either redundant with the ones already cited or the authors simply mentioned the KFs concept in relation to their work; 21 additional references were used as background or complementary resources. Overall, two types of evidence were gathered, one describing how the validity standards were met and one reporting research findings on test development choices and score interpretation.

The KFs' approach has been used for three different purposes, namely, (1) to assess students, residents, and practicing health professionals and veterinarians, (2) as stimulus material or outcome measures in research studies, and (3) as a method for defining learning objectives or instructional plans. A detailed list of these different uses is presented in the "Appendix". The subjects in the studies listed in Appendices Tables 3 and 4 were undergraduates (54%), postgraduates (20%), and clinicians in practice (24%); the evidence in this review is mostly related to the assessment purpose.

Over the years, different definitions of "key features" have emerged and a word of caution is in order. Not all clinically discriminating (Gauthier and Lajoie 2014; Renaud et al. 2016) or essential and critical clinical findings (Heist et al. 2016: Sturmberg and Martin 2016) are automatically KFs, only those that are particularly challenging in a given clinical situation or most likely to be missed and lead to errors in practice (Norman et al. 1984; Bordage and Page 1987; Page et al. 1995). For example, while ordering a CBC may be generically defined as an essential step in the diagnosis of a particular condition, if it is

likely that all the candidates taking the test would order a CBC in practice, such as during an emergency room visit for an urgent problem, then ordering a CBC is not a KF in that situation because it is not likely to effectively discriminate competent from non-competent clinicians within that group of examinees. Yet in another situation, such as during an office visit for an undifferentiated complaint, ordering a CBC for the same diagnosis may often be overlooked by that group of examinees, then it would be considered a KF. Thus, a "critical or essential" decision is only considered a KF if it represents a challenge in the clinical situation chosen. Furthermore, KFs will likely vary depending on the examinees being tested; for example, eliciting some characteristics of hyperthyroidism may be considered KFs when assessing medical students but not so for internal medicine fellows or practicing endocrinologists. Thus, KFs for assessment purposes are both situation dependent and examinee dependent. Finally, the term "key features" is sometimes used in the literature to designate a totally different construct than the one that emanated from the Cambridge Conference; for example, "key features" was used to refer to any short-answer question format without specific reference to the KFs approach or to highlight the distinguishing elements of a concept, as in "this method's key features," but again having nothing to do with the KFs approach.

Results of validity evidence for KFs-based assessment are presented under seven subsections: Content, Response process, Internal structure, Relations to other variables, Consequences, Cost-Feasibility, and Acceptability.

Evidence based on content

The construct that the KFs approach purports to measure is the challenging decisions that clinicians make when interpreting patient findings in a given clinical situation. It is not a measure of the clinician's reasoning per se, but only the ensuing outcomes, the clinical decisions or actions taken. Evidence based on content is presented according to three subheadings: Domain-test blueprint; Representativeness and adequacy of content tested to domain; and Quality of the test materials.

Domain-test blueprint

The type of test blueprint used to select cases from the domain of interest will directly impact the specific KFs that are defined. For example, KFs will vary depending on patient age groups (e.g., asthma in an infant versus an elderly person) or context of care (e.g., an undifferentiated complaint during an office visit versus a life-threatening event in the emergency room). Various types of blueprint have been used in conjunction with the KFs approach. For example, the blueprint can be based on:

- Clinical disciplines (Pediatrics, Medicine, Surgery, Obstetrics-Gynecology, Psychiatry; Bloch and Burgi 2002; Fischer et al. 2005; Nikendei et al. 2009; Lang 2015),
- Clinical situations (e.g., undifferentiated complaint, single, typical or atypical presentation, multi-system disorders, life-threatening event, preventive care, and health promotion; Bordage and Page 1987),
- Frequency or priority of problems in practice (Hatala and Norman 2002; Farmer and Hinchy 2005; Allen 2005; Trudel et al. 2008; Pinnock and Jones 2008; Lawrence et al. 2011),

- Patient age groups from health services data (Page et al. 1995), or
- Physician activities and dimensions of care (Touchie and Streefkerk 2014).

Studies of the impact of test blueprints on KF definition will be discussed later in the sections on Generalizability (sources of test score variance) and Factor analysis.

Representativeness and adequacy of content tested to domain

For a test to have content validity, it must contain both an adequate and representative sample of cases from the domain of interest.

A number of studies have been conducted to verify the extent to which the content of KF-based tests represents the domain of interest. In a study of clerkship directors across Canada (Page and Bordage 1995; Bordage et al. 1995a), almost all directors retrospectively confirmed the KFs (92%) defined by the test committee members and prospectively generated similar KFs (94%) to those from the test committee members. They also felt that their medical students were exposed to the problems presented on the KFs exam. Similarly, the majority of students (76%) rated the competencies tested by the KFs as "very critical" or "critical" to the resolution of the cases presented (Page et al. 1995). Dutch students also thought that the KF-based test they took as "highly relevant and adequately reflecting the practice in the rotation." (Schuwirth et al. 1996a) Other types of KFs test takers also confirmed these results, for example, family physicians (Ali and Bordage 1995), colo-rectal surgeons (Trudel et al. 2008), and medical students during their internal medicine clerkship rotations (Bronander et al. 2015).

Assessing candidates' decision-making skills for high stakes, patient safety and quality-of-care cases is a domain of particular interest for credentialing agencies responsible for protecting the public. Using 59 practice indicators that contribute to causing or preventing suboptimal care and adverse events, Bordage et al. (2013) found that three fifths of these indicators were tested on the 2008–2009 Medical Council of Canada Qualifying Examination (MCCQE). Of the three fifths tested, 30% were part of the KF-based Clinical Decision Making (CDM) section of the MCCQE.

In his analysis of the content of the KF-based decision-making part of the MCCQE, Page (2008) found that "the lack of factual recall questions in the CDM examination, coupled with the more appropriate distribution of CDM questions across clinical tasks [i.e., data gathering, data interpretation, and patient management], supports it as a more 'content valid' assessment relative to the MCQ examination of a candidate's ability to enter supervised practice."

The issue of the adequacy of the number of KF cases on a test is an empirical matter that will be addressed later in relation to internal structure and the reliability of KFs scores. Also, related aspects of content validity will be discussed in the sections on Divergent and Convergent validity.

Quality of the test material

Test developers have made available to item writers and staff various KFs training and development guidelines (e.g., Page et al. 1995; Schuwirth et al. 1999a; Haladyna 2004; Farmer and Page 2005; Kopp et al. 2006 (in German); Kwa et al. 2007; Medical Council of Canada 2012 (in French and English), Medical Council of Canada 2017a, b; Wearne 2008; Bronander et al. 2015) to minimize construct under-representativeness (e.g., how to select

an adequate number of cases) and construct irrelevant variance (e.g., how to define KFs and formulate test questions).

Evidence based on response process

Evidence based on response process, "such that all sources of error associated with the test administration are controlled or eliminated to the maximum extent possible" (Downing and Haladyna 2009), is presented under 10 subheadings.

Candidate familiarity with format

To further minimize construct irrelevant variance in the scores, test administrators offer candidates opportunities to practice taking a KFs test before actually sitting a live exam (e.g., Kwa et al. 2007; Wearne 2008; Medical Council of Canada 2017a, c, d, e, f, h).

Question and response formats

A variety of question and response formats have been used with KFs cases, from traditional multiple-choice questions (MCQs) and short-answer, written constructed-responses, to short and long menus, and oral questions. KFs tests have also been administered as open and closed-book tests. The effect of these various response formats on response frequency, item difficulty, and test score reliability have been studied by many researchers.

The use of single-question cases and latent-image short-menus (i.e., responses to options are revealed by using a special highlighter pen) has yielded the least reliable test scores, and, when using the long-menu format (as in a catalogue of alphabetically coded options) examinees selected more responses (in search of cues), took longer to respond, had lower scores, and gave the format low ratings. (Page and Bordage 1995; Page 2008) Similarly, Fischer et al. (2005) found that students complained about not finding the answers they were looking for. Thus, a variation on the long-menu format was developed, the "constructed long-menu questions" format, whereby "students enter their answer in a dialog box and the computer compares it with a list of more than 2500 possible answers" (Schuwirth et al. 1966c). In a comparative study, Rotthoff et al. (2006a) found that the "average number of correct answers for constructed long-menu questions and open-ended questions showed no significant difference ($p=.93$) [and] response time for constructed long-menu questions did not significantly differ from that of open-ended questions ($p=.65$)." They however cautioned that "constructed long-menu questions should only be used when the answers can be clearly phrased, using a few, precise synonyms."

The short-menu, selected-response format, with as few as 3 or 4 options to as many as 15–30 options, elicited more responses than the write-in response format and increased the average score by about 20% (Page and Bordage 1995) Page et al. (2000a) found that, in general, "the relative performance of candidates on write-in and short-menu questions was a function of the candidates' level of competence, and write-in questions, relative to short-menu questions, provide[d] a more reliable assessment and [were] more effective at identifying weaker candidates" at or around the pass/fail cut score (see also Page et al. 1990a, b, 2000b; Page 2008; Desjardins et al. 2014).

Schuwirth (1998a) studied the use of various question formats and noted that, "it is most sensible to use the number of alternatives in a question (either infinite in an open-ended question or finite in a multiple-choice question) that most closely resembles the number of realistic options in real practice." He concluded that, "simply adding the scores of all the items without adjustment or weighting for the different numbers could be perceived as too simplistic an approach. The results, however, indicate that this is not the case. The homogeneity of the scores within each question format is about equal. Therefore, no empirical objections to this approach exist."

One advantage of the KF-based Structured Oral Interviews used by Jacques et al. (1995) was that the examiners, once the examinee had verbally answered a question, would provide the correct answer to that question before moving on to the next question, thus avoiding cumulative errors within a case. They found that agreement between interviewers was high (91.2%) and stable throughout a given session. A similar sequential approach was used by Schaper et al. (2013).

Finally, Trudel et al. (2008), using an open-book administration of a KF-based test as a learning tool during recertification, found that colo-rectal surgeons did score better on the open-book KFs test than a closed-book version. This type of test administration will depend on the intended goal of the test, such as assessment for learning (versus of learning) in the context of an open-book test.

In summary, the KFs approach is not a test or item format per se but an approach to assess challenging clinical decisions or actions likely to lead to errors in practice. The choice of question and response formats for KFs cases is dictated largely by the type of decisions to be assessed and the circumstances in actual practice to achieve an as authentic assessment of clinical decision making as possible (Schuwirth 1998a).

Scoring rationale

A unique attribute of the KFs approach is that each KF may have one or more correct answers depending on the complexity of the challenge involved (e.g., multiple diagnoses, lab tests, or treatments) as is often the case in actual practice. This poses two scoring challenges: use of differential weighing of options within a KF, that is, giving different options different weights depending on the perceived relative clinical importance of each option [e.g., for the scoring key for third KF in Box 1b: giving .66 point for option 1 (Administer empiric antibiotic) and .33 point for option 5 (Call senior resident or attending)], and use of dichotomous or partial-credit scoring algorithms, that is, getting a score of 1 for having all the correct options for a given KF and 0 for missing one or more correct options versus getting partial credit for as many correct responses provided.

Norcini et al. (1983) and Norcini and Guille (2002) showed that, in general, differential weighting does not improve test score reliability. Both Norman et al. (1983) and Norcini et al. (1983) found that "scores derived from different weighting methods are frequently inter-correlated at the .9 level or higher" (in Norman et al. 1984). Given that discussions about the relative importance of various response options within a KF usually consume a lot of test committee time, in the end, that time does not translate into better test scores. As for dichotomous and partial-credit scoring, and based on test score reliability estimates, partial-credit scores yielded marginally higher estimates than dichotomous scores because more information about the examinees' ability goes into the scoring (Page and Bordage 1995). Consequently, Page et al. (1995) have used equal weights for KFs within each case, that are averaged to generate a KFs case score; and then case scores within an exam are averaged to generate a total exam score that represents the average proportion (percentage) of KFs mastered for each case on the exam.

Negative marking is also not recommended (Fowell and Jolly 2000), except when a negative action or decision is proscribed as part of a KF, such as ordering a potentially harmful and unnecessary investigation, or prescribing an inappropriate or contra-indicated medication or procedure. This raises the issue of examinee errors in a KFs exam.

Childs et al. (2003) categorized examinee errors into three types: failing to select any correct responses, going over the maximum limit of responses, or selecting a response that is inappropriate or harmful to the patient. They noted that by distinguishing among these types of errors, the accuracy of pass–fail decisions might be improved. In a subsequent 2007 study, they found that, the reliability and validity evidence "support the use of a compensatory scoring approach […] (1) with killer and max errors counted as zero; (2) with killer and max errors combined with no correct responses into a single category; [and] (3) with killer and max errors treated as separate categories." However, they found it "troubling that examinees who make several killer and/or max errors can pass the test through strong performance on other items. [and suggested that] given the small number of examinees who fit this profile, it may be possible to review these cases individually [and] examinees could be notified of their errors and remediation recommended." By taking advantage of the detailed information contained in the KFs scoring keys, this type of formative assessment will be discussed later as a topic of future research and development.

In their study of practice indicators mentioned earlier, Bordage et al. (2013) also found a discrepancy between the percentage of questions (i.e., 39%) or cases (i.e., 44%) per exam testing a practice indicator and the percentage of the total test score attributed to practice indicators [i.e., 30% (vs. 39%) and 5% (vs. 44%) respectively for questions and cases]. Such discrepancies between test content and scoring further attenuates the contribution of these patient-safety and quality-of-care cases that are of particular interest for agencies responsible for protecting the public.

While being a more authentic assessment of clinical decision making than selected-response formats, one of the challenges of open-ended responses is marking and scoring the many synonymous answers. This led the MCC for example to develop a software application, the Scoring Aggregator (Medical Council of Canada 2016, 2017g). Gierl et al. (2014) found that this type of automated scoring yielded scores that are "at a level as high, if not higher, as the level of agreement among human raters themselves [and] offer[s] medical educators many benefits for scoring constructed-response tasks, such as improving the consistency of scoring, reducing the time required for scoring and reporting, minimizing the costs of scoring, and providing students with immediate feedback on constructed-response tasks." Latifi et al. (2016), using a three-stage, computer scoring of English or French responses to open-ended questions, found computer scoring better (5.4% improvement) than human scoring.

Finally, and based on the item independence assumption in psychometrics (Downing 2004), the unit of measurement for KFs exams is the case, not individual KFs. The independence assumption is important because, as will be seen later, some reliability estimates have been calculated using KFs as the unit of measurement, not the cases, thus inappropriately inflating these estimates.

Language used in clinical scenarios

In an effort to maximize authenticity and construct relevant variance on a KFs exam, one may consider the use of lay language instead of medical terminology in the case scenarios as would be the case in real life; for example, instead of "he had tonic–clonic muscle activity," the case vignette would state, "he twitched and jerked for a minute or two" (in Bronander et al. 2015). In their studies of the effects of language on test score discrimination and reliability, Eva and collaborators (2003, 2010) found that while Canadian medical graduates were not influenced by the language used in the clinical scenarios, international medical graduates performed better in cases using medical terminology compared to lay terms, especially among the low performers. Overall, the uniform use of lay terminology yielded the highest test score reliability, requiring "16 fewer cases and a third less testing time (29 cases) relative to the lay versus medical terminology condition (45 cases) to achieve a reliability of .80." They recommended that, "the use of lay terms to describe clinical cases should continue to be encouraged."

Rater training and accuracy for write-in responses

In early studies, trained lay, non-physician raters, with oversight, performed similarly to physician raters, both achieving 90.0% agreement (Page and Bordage 1995). Developments in automated essay scoring have achieved superior inter-rater results, compared to previous human scoring (Schuwirth et al. 2005; Stark et al. 2011; Gierl et al. 2014; Latifi et al. 2016) and offer new time-saving and feedback resources to test developers.

The issue of evaluating inter-rater reliability is also present with KF-based Structured Oral Interviews (as seen above in the section on Item format) and OSCEs, but in this type of assessment the interviewers or observers have to pick up keyed responses on the fly as the interview or case unfolds, with little or no time to think about what was just said or done by the examinee. Fuller et al. (2017), using a global rating and a KF-based checklist for OSCEs, studied extremes of assessor judgments [i.e., low inter-rater agreement] and cautioned that, "care must be taken when assuming that apparent aberrant examiner behavior is automatically that," thus highlighting the fact that these so-called "extreme" raters may actually be picking up keyed behaviors that the other rater(s) did not see. Another alternative when there are multiple raters present is to simply average rater scores as Schuwirth et al. (2005) did.

Quality control of final scores or grades

In a spirit of full disclosure and transparency, testing agencies publish publicly available technical reports on the quality of their exams. For example, each year the MCC publishes a technical report that "summarizes the fundamental psychometric characteristics, test development, and test administration activities of the MCCQE Part I [that includes a CDM, KF-based component] and candidate performance on the exam," (Medical Council of Canada 2016), including validity evidence in support of score interpretation.

Validation of test materials (pilot studies) and preliminary scores

Pilot testing, often with as few as 20 subjects (Page and Bordage 1995), provides a means of verifying whether the test cases and questions are unambiguous and that the scoring keys focus exclusively on the KFs, and nothing else and thus can help minimize construct irrelevant variance. Bronander et al. (2015) gathered both quantitative and qualitative information from the test takers regarding their time spent to complete the pilot test, level of difficulty of the items, acceptability, case and question formats, authenticity, feedback, technical issues, cognitive level tested, and clarity of instructions. Only when the test cases, questions, and scoring keys meet performance requirements are they then used as live items for scoring (Medical Council of Canada 2016; Doucet et al. 1998; Bernabeo et al. 2013).

Accuracy in combining scores from different formats

The issue of combining scores from different formats occurs both within cases and across exam formats. As indicated in the previous section on Question and response formats, Schuwirth (1998a) showed that combining scores from different formats does not impact generalizability.

Results from a KF-based test can also be used on their own or combined with other formats or sections for an overall test score. In the latter case, for example, the MCCQE1 score used to be calculated "as the weighed sum of the multiple choice (weight=.75) and clinical decision-making skills components (weights=.25), where weights reflect the amount of testing time devoted to each component" (Wenghofer et al. 2009). More recently the MCC is using a Rasch model to score the MCQ and CDM components of the MCCQE, and thus "establish[ed] a scale that is expressed in such a way that candidate attributes (such as ability) and item attributes (such as item difficulty) are on the same unit of measurement." (Medical Council of Canada 2016)

Accuracy of pass-fail decision rule

Various standard-setting methods have been used to set a pass-fail cut score. Page and Bordage (1995) used a modified Angoff approach that included examinee performance data to set a pass/fail cut score. They found that, "The average alpha reliability coefficient for minimum pass indices for cases was .82. By using this average coefficient with the average [standard deviation] (SD) of committee members' minimum pass indices for cases, a standard error of measurement (SEM) for the cut score was calculated to be 1.85, indicating a relatively narrow confidence interval within which the "true" cutting score existed."

Standards (cut score) can change over time because of changes in the exam or the candidates. The MCC, for example, now uses a Bookmark method to set standards and "conducts a standard-setting exercise every three to 5 years to ensure the standard and the pass score remains appropriate" (Medical Council of Canada 2016)—for the Bookmark method, all the items in the test are ordered from least difficult to most difficult (using item response theory (IRT) data) and each standard setter then reads the items and indicates, "bookmarks at the point between the hardest question borderline [minimally competent] test takers would be likely to answer correctly and the easiest question the borderline test takers would not be likely to answer correctly" (Zieky and Perie 2006).

Quality of score reporting to candidates, institutions

The accuracy of the results reported to candidates and institutions depends on careful test blueprinting and in large part on test score reliability and pass/fail decisions. For example, for the 2015–2016 cohort of examinees taking the MCCQE, that includes MCQs and KF-based CDM cases, the standard error of measurement is "the lowest [containing as little error as possible] near the pass score, which indicates the highest precision of ability estimates, thus supporting more accurate and consistent pass/fail decisions. [...] both the decision consistency estimate and the decision accuracy estimate for each of the two administrations of 2016 indicate reliable and valid pass/fail decisions based on MCCQE Part I scores." (Medical Council of Canada 2016).

Evidence based on internal structure

Evidence based on internal structure, that is, "the degree to which the relationship among items and test components conform to the construct on which the proposed test score interpretations are based" (American Educational Research Association 2014), is presented under five subheadings.

Item analysis

Item analysis of individual KF scores can be used to flag items that are too easy or too difficult (Amini et al. 2011a) or non-discriminating, either because of some deficiency or pitfalls in the case scenario, question formulation, or scoring key, or because of actual performance levels among the candidates taking the test. The best measure of case performance is the index of discrimination, that is, the ability of a case, or a KF, to best capture various levels of performance among the candidates taking the test. While there is no steadfast rule about an acceptable level of discrimination, Downing (2009) recommends indices of at least +.30 or higher or mid-to-high 0.20s for locally developed tests. Negative discrimination indexes are mostly indicative of some misleading information in the case scenario or the questions. Item-total correlation coefficients are most often used to measure discrimination; the higher the level, the better. For example, Fischer et al. (2005) found that "Three KFs problems did not contribute to the differentiation between high and low achieving students. When analyzing the KFs within these problems it became clear that they were either too easy or contained cueing answers. However, the content validation process showed a high relevance for these specific questions. The analysis of the item-total correlation and the difficulty level in respect to content relevance will lead to a change of some questions for the next version of our KF-test." Thus, case selection for KFs test is best done based on prior information about discrimination levels, either through pilot testing or through retrospective analyses of past administrations.

Analysis of item difficulty data can also reveal possible discrepancies between the perception of test takers and their actual level of performance. When test takers were asked whether the KF questions tested a competency that was "too trivial, too ambitious, or at the correct level of difficulty for a graduating student?" almost all (96%) answered "at the correct level"; however, "the average score on the examination was only 50%." (Page and Bordage 1995) Jacques et al. (1995) found similar discrepancies for physicians taking the KF-based Structured Oral Interviews and highlighted the "need for objective assessment tools […] instead of relying on physicians' own perceptions of their educational needs." This issue of feedback will be revisited in the Conclusion.

Score reliability

The initial estimates for the number of KFs cases needed to reach a test score reliability of .8 were based on findings of case specificity from Elstein, Shulman, and Sprafka (1978) and from studies of problem-solving performance, with inter-case correlations on the order of .1–.3 (Norman and Feightner 1981; Norman et al. 1984). Using the Spearman-Brown Prophecy formula to estimate test length from test score reliability, 40 cases were needed to reach a .80 level, requiring 4.1 hours of testing time (Page and Bordage 1995). Thirty years later (except for higher levels in Allen's 2005 study), Hrynchak et al. (2014) confirmed these initial estimates with reports of internal consistency reliability coefficients from six studies between ".49 and .95, with the majority at the upper end when 25–40 cases were used." Building on Hrynchak et al.'s findings, we reviewed 17 publications that reported reliability coefficients, some with projected testing time and corresponding reliability coefficients, remembering that the unit of measurement should be the case and not the questions or KFs; see Table 1.

Evidence over time has shown that a reasonably large number of KFs cases (e.g., > 35–40) are needed to obtain acceptable levels of test score reliability to make decisions about individual examinees. Many factors contribute to test score reliability, some related to the discriminating ability of the KFs themselves (i.e., focusing on the true challenges and difficulties in practice) and some related to the heterogeneity of the candidates taking the test. As observed by Hrynchak et al. (2014), some general advice to maximize test score reliability can be gleaned from the findings to date, such as: selecting cases and questions based on prior information about their discrimination level; having a majority of multi-question cases compared to single-question cases (more on this in the section on generalizability); using open-ended questions for diagnosis and management questions with short answers (e.g., 2–3 words) because they are more discriminating, especially among weaker candidates; using a partial-credit, equal-weighting system for scoring options within a KF; using lay language over medical terms in the clinical scenarios; and using the case as the unit of measurement, not the questions or KFs, to satisfy the item independence assumption.

Furthermore, the more homogenous the group of candidates, the harder it will be to differentiate among them and more cases will be needed. Conversely, the more heterogeneous the candidates are, the easier it will be to differentiate among them and fewer cases will be needed, as in the Trudel et al. (2008) study with general and subspecialty colo-rectal surgeons, with as few as 9 KFs cases. Schuwirth and van der Vleuten (2011a) noted that, "The biggest advantage of the KFs approach is that a large number (roughly 30) short cases can be asked per hour of testing time. Thus, the sampling is broad."

Generalizability

Another approach to maximizing test score reliability is to conduct G and D generalizability studies to better understand the various sources of variance contributing to the scores and thus better design the exams. During the early pilot testing of KFs cases, the types of clinical situation presented in the cases (e.g., a life-threatening event versus an undifferentiated complaint) accounted for a significant percentage of score variance in some booklets, whereas the clinical disciplines (e.g., medicine, surgery, pediatrics) and the age group of the patients did not. The main source of score variance (30%) came from cases nested within these three factors [disciplines, age groups, situations], and "thus the importance of constructing exams with large samples of cases (e.g., 40), as each case makes a large independent contribution to score variance." (Page and Bordage 1995) Brailovsky et al. (1998) also found that, of the same three factors, only the clinical situations "appeared as an important factor."

Table 1 Number of Key-Features cases with reported and projected reliability coefficients

KFs cases	Number of KFs	Cronbach-α	Candidates	n	Projected hours and reliability	Authors
11	31	–	Graduating medical students	156		Page and Bordage (1995)
38	107			395	4.1 h	
59	172		Canadian and foreign graduates	2800	(40 prob.), .80	Page and Bordage (2004)
36		.64 (median)	MCCQE candidates	~20,000 (1992–2002)		
15	1–4/case	.49	Clerks, int. med.	101	3 h, .60	Hatala and Norman (2002)
					4 h, .67	
					5 h, .71	
					1 h .32	van der Vleuten and Schuwirth (2005) (based on Hatala and Norman 2002)
					2 h .49	
					4 h .66	
					8 h .79	
25		.64 (in 1999)	General practitioners	–	–	Farmer and Hinchy (2005)
		.83 (in 2004)				
15	60	.65	5th-yr med. students	37	25 probl., .75	Fischer et al. (2005)
9	30	.95	General and colo-rectal surgeons	256	–	Trudel et al. (2008)
10	10	.72 (KF as unit)	Med. students	153	–	Kopp et al. (2008)
10	10	.77 (KF as unit)	Med. students	124	–	Kopp et al. (2009a)
10	10	.78 (KF as unit)	Med. students	61	–	Kopp et al. (2009b)
16	75	.71 (pre)	Final-yr med. stud. (internal med.)	74	–	Nikendei et al. (2009)
		.75 (post)				
11	55	.83	Med. students	148	–	Raupach et al. (2009)
12	Not spec.	.36	Clerks	129	–	Monnier et al. (2011)
12	24	.75	Med. students	23	–	Schreiner et al. (2011)
15		$\varphi = .36 - .52$	Clerks, int. med.	759	+ 5 cases, .59 - low discriminating cases, .58, .59	Lang (2015)

Table 1 (continued)

KFs cases	Number of KFs	Cronbach-α	Candidates	n	Projected hours and reliability	Authors
20		.83	Medical students from 45 schools	135	–	Amini et al. (2011a)
10	29	.72 (KF as unit)	Medical students in clinical years	153	–	Stark et al. (2011)
10	30	.77 (KF as unit)	Medical students in clinical years	124		

In a subsequent and more detailed analysis, Norman et al. (2006) challenged the traditional notion of case specificity (i.e., that error variance due to cases should be high and variance due to questions within cases be low) and found indeed, using data from the KF-based CDM component of the MCCQE (6342 examinees), that, "relatively little variance was due to differences between cases; conversely, about 80% of the error variance was due to variability in performance among items [KFs] within cases." Similar results were found for OSCE scores (Daniels et al. 2014) and extended-matching scores (Dory et al. 2010).

The D-study from Norman et al. (2006) showed that, "the optimal strategy in terms of enhancing reliability would [be to] use cases with 2–3 items per case." This finding has important practical implications for KFs test developers, namely to prepare tests that contain a majority of multi-question (KFs) cases rather than single-question cases (not enough information) to maximize test score reliability; and limit the number of KFs tested to 2 or 3 per case because beyond 3 KFs, no new information is contributing to the reliability of the scores and thus testing time is wasted.

Item factor analysis

A factor analysis of the three main components of the MCCQE showed that the KF-based CDM exam and the problem-solving portion of the OSCE occupied an intermediate position between knowledge (MCQs) and performance (OSCEs), which "is in keeping with the accepted notion that clinical expertise involves both knowledge and other skills gained through experience" (Dauphinee et al. 1998).

More recently, De Champlain (2015) conducted a study "to compare the fit of a number of exploratory and confirmatory factor analysis models to the 2010 combined spring and fall MCCQE1 CDM item response matrix." His results suggest that, "knowledge of broad disciplinary domains best account for performance on [KF-based] CDM cases. In test development, particular effort should be placed on developing CDM cases according to broad discipline and patient age domains [with significantly less attention paid to the setting and clinical situation]; CDM testlets should be assembled largely using the criteria of discipline and age." However, and by definition, KFs will vary depending on the clinical situation; for example, the challenging decisions related to managing diabetes are totally different depending on whether the situation is a life-threatening event in an emergency room versus an undifferentiated complaint during an office visit. And thus, sampling (blueprinting) across clinical situations has its relevance.

A more detailed discussion of what KFs cases are measuring compared to other types of items is presented later in the section on Divergent Evidence.

Differential item functioning (DIF)

Differential item functioning (DIF) is a method used to determine whether test items behave differently for different groups of test takers, such as candidates with different cultural or linguistic backgrounds. Early studies of possible French–English differences on the KF-based CDM portion of the MCCQE showed that while there were 16% more words in French and the candidates took 8.47 min longer to complete the exam, a DIF study of English-to-French translation confirmed the high quality of the translation (Page and Bordage 1995; Bordage et al. 1955b) De Champlain et al. (2003) criticized the Bordage et al. study because of insufficient sample sizes for this type of study and the assumption that the

construct underlying the examination in both its English and French forms was the same. The planned follow-up studies by De Champlain have yet to be conducted, a topic awaiting future inquiry, as discussed in the Conclusion section.

Evidence based on relations to other variables

KFs exams purports to measure decision-making skills that uses higher-order cognitive processes beyond simple factual recall. Evidence based on relations to other variables, either measuring similar or different constructs, is presented under three subheadings: convergent and divergent evidence, and test-criterion relationships.

Convergent evidence

A number of studies using KFs cases have shown that KF scores were highest for the group expected to have greater decision-making or problem-solving skills. For example, subspecialists colo-rectal surgeons performed better than general surgeons (Trudel et al. 2008); students in a Team-Based Learning (TBL) group, "optimized for teaching clinical reasoning," performed significantly better than those in a non-TBL group ($p=.026$) (Jost et al. 2017); and "the higher a person's rested [post-call] KFP score, the greater the negative change between their rested and post-call scores" (Flinn and Armstrong 2011). These results, and those from similar studies (Doucet et al. 1998; Schuwirth et al. 1999b; Spike and Hays 1999; Korestein et al. 2003; Nikendei et al. 2009; Schreiner et al. 2011; Bernabeo et al. 2013; Lehmann et al. 2015; Leung et al. 2016), provide convergent evidence that KFs cases assess the construct of clinical decision making.

Divergent evidence

Validity studies investigating correlations of KF-based tests with other measures show moderate correlations, typically in the .35 to .50 range (Hatala and Norman 2002; Fischer et al. 2005; Lang 2015; Zamani et al. 2017). These results raise the question of whether KFs cases measure something different than other formats, especially in the sense of higher-order thinking beyond simple factual recall.

More compelling than correlations are studies that use think-aloud strategies when comparing formats (Schuwirth et al. 1998b; Schuwirth et al. 2001; Skakun 1994; van der Vleuten et al. 2008). For example, Schuwirtz et al. (2001) analyzed verbatim protocols and found that, "Short case-based questions [like KFs questions] lead to thinking processes which represent problem-solving ability better than those elicited by factual knowledge questions."

Hurtz et al. (2012) conducted a series of mixed-method studies comparing KFs cases and MCQ questions in gerontology and oncology dietetics. They measured subject-matter experts' ratings of the cognitive complexity elicited by the questions (i.e., 1. Factual, 2. Application, 3. Interpretation, and 4. Synthesis) and test takers' response time and correct-incorrect and total exam scores. While KFs cases were rated more complex (2.73 vs. 1.93), "it is not only reading time and item difficulty that produces longer response times to KFPs but also more complex problem-solving and decision-making processes. This again supports the validity of KFPs as measures of higher-level cognitive processes." They concluded that, "As measures of clinical decision making, KFPs play a key role in helping to ensure that licensed and certified allied health practitioners have the skills they need

to make important decisions on the job and improve their practice and quality of patient care."

Test-criterion relationships

How well do KFs scores predict performance in practice? Tamblyn and collaborators conducted three studies that looked at the predictive relationship between MCCQ scores and complaints to medical regulatory authorities (Tamblyn et al. 2007, 2009) and persistence with antihypertensive therapy (2010). They showed that complaints were mainly associated with the KF-based CDM sub-scores and the OSCE-based communication sub-scores. They noted that, KF-based "clinical decision-making assessment was specifically designed to select problems and test aspects of the decision-making process where physicians were more likely to make errors that would have an effect on patient outcome." (Tamblyn et al. 2007) and prompted them to suggest selecting cases and test questions for the problem-solving part of the OSCE-based clinical exam on the same basis as KF written problems.

In a follow-up study of acute and chronic care, and prevention, they found that the KF-based CDM sub-score "was most strongly associated with the likelihood of receiving a complaint about a communication or quality of care problem [and] the risk of having an ER visit for asthma after a visit to the study physicians was reduced by 36% (relative risk: .64; *p* value .008) for every two-standard deviation increase in the [KF-based] clinical decision-making sub-score of the MCCQE1. All other examination scores had no significant relationship to outcomes for patients with out-of-control asthma." (Tamblyn et al. 2009).

In their study of predicting persistence with antihypertensive medication, Tamblyn et al. (2010) found that KF-based "clinical decision-making ability was the strongest predictor, for which the risk of non-persistence was reduced by 23% per 2-SD increase in examination score and by 65% when comparing physicians who were 3 SDs above versus below the mean score." Wenghofer et al. (2009), who also worked with Tamblyn, showed that "doctors in the bottom quartile of MCCQE1 scores [that included KF-based CDM scores] had a greater than threefold increase in the risk of an unacceptable quality-of-care assessment outcome (odds ratio [OR] 3.41, 95% confidence interval [CI] 1.14–10.22)." Overall, the Tamblyn studies provide compelling evidence that KF-based test scores predict future practice.

Although scores from KF-based computerized testing (CCT) were not predictive of incognito standardized-patient (SP) visits (the criterion) to rheumatologists, Schuwirth et al. (2005) noted that, "although SP-scores were more authentic, they were less valid than [KF-based] CCT scores, mainly because they focused more on thoroughness than on efficiency in data gathering," echoing Tamblyn's suggestion to better focus on aspects of care where physicians were more likely to make errors, the very essence of a KFs' approach.

In a prospective sense, predicting performance on a national qualifying exam from admission data to medical school, the Multiple Mini Interviews (MMI) significantly predicted two components of MCCQE scores, that is, the CLEO-PHELO scores (Cultural, Communication, Legal, Ethical, and Organizational—Population Health, Ethical, Legal and Organizational) and the [KF-based] clinical decision-making (CDM) scores. These two scores were not predicted by other non-cognitive admissions measures or by the undergraduate grade point average (Reiter et al. 2007).

Evidence based on consequences of testing

The scores, decisions, and intended, and unintended, outcomes of assessment can have a positive or negative impact on examinees, teachers, patients, and society (Downing and Haladyna 2009).

Two studies reported KFs testing consequences. Fifth-year German medical students felt that, from an educational perspective, KFPs steered their learning towards clinical reasoning during their clerkships (Huwendiek et al. 2017). American medical students during their internal medicine clerkships preferred using the KFE format for formative rather than summative purposes because they were "reluctant to add an exam format specifically targeting decision-making ability that would count as part of the grade." (Lang 2015) The paucity of consequential validity evidence will be revisited in the Conclusion.

Evidence based on cost and feasibility

Generally speaking, the development and maintenance of KFs exams are costly in time and resources; "The main downside of the KFs approach is that test preparation is very labor intensive. It takes a lot of time to produce a good case and the key decisions are often difficult to define." (Schuwirth and van der Vleuten 2003) For example, Schuwirth (1998a) estimated that it takes about 2 to 3 hours to develop and review a KF case by experienced item writers. However burdensome and time consuming the production of high-quality exams, he also noted that, as the case writers gain experience, "the production time decreases to some extent." This was also the case for Trudel et al. (2008) in developing a KF-based self-assessment exam for colon and rectal surgeons; however, "the gains from the examination can begin to offset the investments, gains such as a reliable and valid test of higher-order competencies, the promotion of better patient care by focusing exclusively on case-specific critical decisions, and recent evidence of predictive validity." Similarly, Bronander et al. (2015) in administering a high-stakes [KF-based] examination via the internet found that "the web-based format allowed us to administer the test to multiple sites easily and automate the marking of the exam."

As stated above, efficiency addresses both test development procedures (e.g., selecting case developers and rater training) and test validity characteristics. This is especially true compared to long simulations: "…almost all of the major certification institutes have abandoned the long simulations. Currently, short case-based assessment is being used with more success, typical examples of which are the KFs cases." (Schuwirth and van der Vleuten 2010) While the development and implementation of a KF-based exam is work intensive, its widespread use to assess clinical decision-making skills (see "Appendix"), both at local institutions and by regulatory agencies, provides evidence of its feasibility. Another example of maximizing efficiency (i.e., improving consistency of scoring) while reducing cost (i.e., time required for scoring and reporting) is the use of automated scoring of KFs write-in questions (Gierl et al. 2014; Latifi et al. 2016).

Evidence based on acceptability

Norcini et al. (2011) define acceptability as "Stakeholders find[ing] the assessment process and results to be credible." Candidates taking a KF-based test from various countries (Australia, Canada, Germany, and United States) concur that KF-based tests are credible,

Table 2 Suggested lines of inquiry regarding the Key-Features approach according to types of validity evidence

Content
  What type of 'reasoning tasks' are assessed in KFs cases? (Goldszmidt et al. 2013)

Response process
  What is the theoretical basis for the extended-matching format and how does it compare to the KFs approach? (Winslade 2001)

Internal structure
  How does giving answers to questions sequentially during a KF case effect the generalizability of the scores versus the usual accumulation of errors? (Jacques et al. 1995; Schaper et al. 2013)
  From a DIF analysis perspective, what factor structures underlie different language forms of a KF exam? How are the two linguistic groups cross-culturally equivalent? (De Champlain et al. 2003)

Relations to other variables
  What basic science justifications accompany clinical decisions (Rademakers et al. 2005)?
  How prevalent is the occurrence of candidates making potentially harmful decisions? Are candidates making harmful decisions at higher risk of providing suboptimal care or the object of complaints or disciplinary actions? (Childs et al. 2007)
  To what extent is a statistically significant increase in KFs test scores related to a significant increase in clinical performance? (Nikendei et al. 2009)
  Are physicians with better clinical decision-making and data-collection skills more likely to incorporate patient preferences into their treatment decision-making process? (Tamblyn et al. 2010)
  Is assessing the reasoning process, compared to focusing on multiple outcomes (as with KFs cases), more or less predictive of overall performance? (Schuwirth and van der Vleuten 2011b)
  Which scoring procedures would best represent suboptimal care and adverse events in KFs cases? (Bordage et al. 2013)

Consequences
  What might be the advantage of having KF-based progress testing? (Winslade, 2001)
  What are the consequences for examinees and classification accuracy on changing the pass-fail cut score? (Medical Council of Canada 2016)

Cost and feasibility
  How much does it cost to develop a new KFs exam de novo? To maintain a KFs exam? (van der Vleuten 1996; Reznick et al. 1993)

including the process and format, the authenticity and relevance of the cases, and the decision-making competencies tested (Page and Bordage 1995; Jacques et al. 1995; Farmer and Hinchy 2005; Fischer et al. 2005; Krautter et al. 2012; Schaper et al. 2013; Bronander et al. 2015; Huwendiek et al. 2017).

Conclusion and future directions

The accumulation of validity evidence gathered since the inception of the KFs approach in 1984 has provided support for the decision-making construct measured and its use to assess clinical decision-making skills at all levels of training and practice and with various types of exam formats. However, gathering validity evidence is an ongoing process. The validity evidence gathered to date, as extensive as it is, still points to areas in need of additional evidence, as seen, for example, with the limited evidence in certain sections such as factor analyses or consequences of testing. New and ongoing lines of research needing further clarification were proposed by many researchers; a sample of which is summarized in Table 2.

More broadly, the ongoing gathering of validity evidence and the pursuit of clarification studies are not limited to individual assessment methods, such as KFs exams, but also "the utility of the assessment program as a whole" (van der Vleuten and Schuwirth 2005; Schuwirth, and van der Vleuten 2012). Thus, we suggest two novel areas of future research and development, one related to formative assessment, the other to assessment as a program.

Educators such as van der Vleuten et al. (2010) and Eva et al. (2016) have steered our attention towards assessment for learning, compared to the ubiquitous assessment of learning. The KFs approach offers the distinct opportunity of providing examinees with detailed information about their clinical decisions, as contained for example in the KFs scoring keys. This information could be used to better identify areas of strength and weakness, not only related to specific clinical situations or disciplines, but also to the type of potentially harmful decisions examinees made during a KFs test, an element that is especially important in promoting patient safety. The detailed information from a KFs test can be used by the examinees to compare their self-assessment with an information-rich external source (Eva and Regehr 2013) and then, in collaboration with their supervisors, prepare a more specific and targeted learning plan. Also, one might add a justification component to the KFs exam, à la Williams et al. (2014), to directly assess the quality of the reasoning behind the decisions, for example, by revisiting the decisions after completing the cases.

Second, how do KFs exams, with their specific focus on clinical decisions, fit within a program of assessment, not only in term of its unique object of assessment compared with other measures of clinical competence (as highlighted by Schuwirth et al. (2005) in the Test-criterion relationship section) but also, in combining the summative and formative functions of assessment. To quote van der Vleuten et al. (2010), "without formative value, the summative function would be ineffective, leading to trivialization of the assessment. As soon as the learner sees no learning value in an assessment, it becomes trivial."

Both of these initiatives push the KFs approach forward and call for new research and validation studies.

Acknowledgements We are grateful to Hrynchak, Takahashi and Nayer for sharing their 2014 references and to Maureen Clark, librarian at the University of Illinois at Chicago for her exceptional skills with database searches and Kimberly Hu for her unflagging assistance in retrieving the papers and preparing the references. We are also grateful for the judicious and helpful comments from the external reviewers.

Funding This study was supported in part by a travel grant from the Medical Council of Canada for which we are grateful. The views expressed here are not necessarily those of the MCC.

Compliance with ethical standards

Conflict of interests The authors wish to indicate that they were among those who created the Key-Features concept and have led various research and development projects related to the Key-Features approach reported here. To the best of their ability, the authors remained as impartial as possible. The authors alone are responsible for the content and writing of the article.

Appendix: Uses of the Key-Features' approach

See Tables 3, 4, and 5.

Table 3 Uses of the Key-Features approach for assessment according to clinical disciplines

Clinical disciplines		Authors
Athletic training		Geisler et al. (2014)
Dentistry		Gerhard-Szep et al. (2016)
Dietetics		Litchfield et al. (2000, 2002), Hurtz et al. (2012)
Allopathic medicine	Admissions	Reiter et al. (2007)
	Anatomy	Shiozawa et al. (2017)
	Clinical teachers	Gauthier and Lajoie (2014)
	Colo-rectal surgery	Trudel et al. (2008)
	Continuing education	Jacques et al. (1995, 2006), Page et al. (1995b), Miller et al. (1997), Doucet et al. (1998), Schenowitz (2000), Goulet et al. (2010), Burrows et al. (2012)
	Emergency medicine	Allen (2005), Carriere et al. (2009)
	Family medicine	Ali and Bordage (1995), Bordage et al. (1996), Spike and Hays (1999), Page et al. (2000b), Farmer and Hinchy (2005), Kwa et al. (2007), Goulet et al. (2010), Lawrence et al. (2011), Laughlin et al. (2012), Wetmore et al. (2012), Leung et al. (2016)
	Intensive care	Lee et al. (2009)
	Medical ethics, law, communication	Schubert et al. (2008)
	Post-graduate residents	Flinn and Armstrong (2011), Heist et al. (2016), Korenstein et al. (2003)
	Multi-level: Students, residents, physicians	Schuwirth et al. (1996b)
	Otolaryngology	Carr et al. (2002)
	Rheumatology	Schuwirth et al. (2005)
	Pediatrics	Lehmann et al. (2015)
	Professionalism	Bernabeo et al. (2013)
	Undergraduate students	Schuwirth et al. (1996b, 1999b), Page et al. (2000a), Mandin and Dauphinee (2000), Hatala and Norman (2002), Sturmberg et al. (2003), Smith et al. (2003), Fischer et al. (2005), Norman et al. (2006), Heid et al. (2006), Rotthoff et al. (2006b), Pinnock and Jones (2008), Kopp et al. (2008, 2009a), Nikendei et al. (2009), Raupach et al. (2009); Norman et al. (2010), Amini (Amini, Moghadami, et al. 2011a, b), Stark et al. (2011), Krautter et al. (2012), Schmidmaier et al. (2013), Reinert et al. (2014), Bosner et al. (2015), Consorti et al. (2015), Lang (2015), Renaud et al. (2016)
Midwifery		Zamani et al. (2017)

Table 3 (continued)

Clinical disciplines	Authors
Nursing	Buisson and Lévesque-Cardinal (2000)
Nutrition	Maiburg et al. (2003)
Osteopathic medicine	Vaughan and Morrison (2015), National Board of Osteopathic Medical Examiners (2017)
Pharmacy, pharmacology	Duncan-Hewitt et al. (2007), Matthes et al. (2008), Benedict et al. (2017)
Physical therapy	Ladyshewsky (2000), Clark (2010), Manns and Darrah (2012)
Physician assistant	Winslade (2000)
Veterinary medicine	Schaper et al. (2013)

Table 4 Uses of the Key-Features approach as stimulus material or outcome measures in research studies

Cueing effects: OEQs versus, MCQs (Schuwirth et al. 1996a)
PBL versus lectures (Doucet et al. 1998)
PBL versus non-PBL schools (Schuwirth et al. 1996b)
On-line instruction in dietetics (Litchfield et al. 2002)
Reciprocal peer coaching (Ladyshewsky 2002)
Buprenorphine and LAAM training (Lintzeris et al. 2002)
Domestic violence education program (Korenstein et al. 2003)
Web-based tutorial on critical thinking reasoning (Kumta et al. 2003)
Computer-based versus standard vocational training (Maiburg et al. 2003)
Case-based worked examples (Kopp et al. 2008, 2009a, b; Stark et al. 2011)
Web-based versus face-to-face instruction (Raupach et al. 2009)
Supplementary curriculum on clinical reasoning skills (Nikendei et al. 2009)
Quality of asthma management and patient morbidity (Kawasumi 2009)
Pre-post call decision making (Flinn and Armstrong 2011)
New curriculum on pain diagnosis and management (Schreiner et al. 2011)
Learning effects of assessment (Cilliers et al. 2012)
Reasoning, personality, and emotional intelligence (Ashoorion et al. 2012)
Virtual patients designs and clinical reasoning (Bateman et al. 2013)
Vignettes to stimulate reflection on professionalism (Bernabeo et al. 2013)
Understanding of competent clinical reasoning (Gauthier and Lajoie 2014)
Self-explanation prompts and adaptable feedback (Heitzmann et al. 2015)
Inverted classroom to teach differential diagnosis (Bosner et al. 2015)
Virtual patients and case summary skills (Heist et al. 2016)
Short-term workshop on reasoning skills (Yousefichaijan et al. 2016)
Spaced versus massed delivery of procedural knowledge (Breckwoldt et al. 2016)
Question sequence in OSCEs (LaRochelle et al. 2016)
Virtual patients in the acquisition of clinical reasoning skills (Schubach et al. 2017)
Supplemental Team-based learning on clinical reasoning (Jost et al. 2017)

Table 5 Uses of the Key-Features approach for defining learning objectives or instruction plan

Clinical reasoning in a community-based medical course (Sturmberg et al. 2003)
Clinical reasoning skills in emergency medicine (Allen 2005)
Professional behavior (Schubert et al. 2008)
Pediatrics undergraduate curriculum (Pinnock and Jones 2008)
Speech-language pathology and audiology curriculum (Naude et al. 2011)
Family medicine (Lawrence et al. 2011; Wetmore et al. 2012; Laughlin et al. 2012; Keegan et al. 2017)
Clinical reasoning in adult cardiology (de la Calzada 2015)
Summary Statements in Virtual Patient Cases (Smith et al. 2016)

References

Ali, K., & Bordage, G. (1995). Validity of key features for a family medicine pilot exam at the college of physicians and surgeons Pakistan. *Journal of the College of Physicians and Surgeons of Pakistan, 5,* 256–260.

Allen, T. (2005). A comparison of the performance of an oral certification examination of clinical reasoning skills in emergency medicine with the performance of similar North American examinations. Master's thesis, Université Laval.

American Educational Research Association, American Psychological Association, & National Council on Measurement in Education. (2014). *Standards for educational and psychological testing* (pp. 11–21). Washington: American Education Research Association.

Amini, M., Kojuri, J., Karimian Lofti, F., Moghadami, M., Dehghani, M. R., Azarpyra, N., et al. (2011a). Talents for Future: Report of the Second National Medical Science Olympiad in Islamic Republic of Iran. *Iranian Red Crescent Medical Journal, 13,* 377–381.

Amini, M., Moghadami, M., Kojuri, J., Abbasi, H., et al. (2011b). An innovative method to assess clinical reasoning skills: Clinical reasoning tests in the second national medical science Olympiad in Iran. *BMC Research Notes, 4,* 418–425.

Ashoorion, V., Liaghatdar, M. J., & Adibi, P. (2012). What variables can influence clinical reasoning? *Journal of Research in Medical Sciences, 17,* 1170–1175.

Bateman, J., Allen, M. E., Samani, D., Kidd, J., & Davis, D. (2013). Virtual patients design: exploring what works and why. *A grounded theory study. Medical Education, 47,* 595–606.

Benedict, N., Smithburger, P., Donihi, A. C., Empey, P., Kobulinsky, L., Seybert, A., et al. (2017). Blended simulation progress testing for assessment of practice readiness. *American Journal of Pharmaceutical Education, 81,* 1–13.

Bernabeo, E. C., Holmboe, E., Ross, K., Chesluk, B., & Ginsburg, S. (2013). The utility of vignettes to stimulate reflection on professionalism: Theory and practice. *Advances in Health Sciences Education, 18,* 463–484.

Bloch, R. D., & Burgi, H. (2002). The Swiss catalogue of learning objectives. *Medical Teacher, 24,* 144–150.

Bordage, G., Brailovsky, C., Carretier, H., & Page, G. (1995a). Content validation of key features on a national examination of clinical decision-making skills. *Academic Medicine, 70,* 276–281.

Bordage, G., Brailovsky, C. A., Cohen, T., & Page, G. (1996). Maintaining and enhancing key decision-making skills from graduation into practice: an exploratory study. In A. J. J. A. Scherpbier, C. P. M. van der Vleuten, & J. J. Rethans (Eds.), *Advances in Medical Education* (pp. 128–130). Dordrecht: Kluwer Academic.

Bordage, G., Carretier, H., Bertrand, R., & Page, G. (1995b). Comparing times and performance of french- and english-speaking candidates taking a national examination of clinical decision-making skills. *Academic Medicine, 70,* 359–365.

Bordage, G., Meguerditchian, A., & Tamblyn, R. (2013). Practice indicators of suboptimal care and avoidable adverse events: A content analysis of a national qualifying examination. *Academic Medicine, 88,* 1493–1498.

Bordage, G., & Page, G. (1987). An alternative to PMPs: The "key feature concept". In I. R. Hart & R. Harden (Eds.), *Further developments in assessing clinical competence* (pp. 59–75). Ottawa: Can-Heal Publications.

Bosner, S., Pickert, J., & Stibane, T. (2015). Teaching differential diagnosis in primary care using an inverted classroom approach: student satisfaction and gain in skills and knowledge. *BMC Medical Education, 15,* 1–7.

Brailovsky, C., Bordage, G., & Page, G. (1998). Components of variance on a Key-Feature (Q4) Paper of the medical council of canada's exam. In *Proceedings of the 8th Ottawa Conference on Medical Education* (pp. 169–175). Philadelphia.

Breckwoldt, J., Ludwig, J. R., Plener, J., Schröder, T., Gruber, H., & Peters, H. (2016). Differences in procedural knowledge after a "spaced" and a "massed" version of an intensive course in emergency medicine, investigating a very short spacing interval. *BMC Medical Education, 16,* 249.

Bronander, K. A., Lang, V., Nixon, J., Harrell, H. E., Kovach, R., Hingle, S., et al. (2015). How we developed and piloted an electronic key features examination for the internal medicine clerkship Based on a US National Curriculum. *Medical Teacher, 37,* 807–812.

Buisson, S., & Lévesque-Cardinal, S. (2000). Nouvel examen professionnel de l'O.I.I.Q.—volet pratique : une ttawace préparatoire au ttawa de l'Outaouais. *Pédagogie collégiale, 14,* 41–42.

Burrows, P., Khan, A., Trafford, P., & Whiteman, J. (2012). The induction and refresher scheme simulated surgery. *Education in Primary Care, 23,* 335–341.

Carr, M. M., Hewitt, J., Scardamalia, M., & Reznick, R. K. (2002). Internet-based otolaryngology case discussions for medical students. *Journal of Otolaryngology, 31,* 197–201.

Carriere, B., Gagnon, R., Charlin, B., Downing, S., & Bordage, G. (2009). Assessing clinical reasoning in pediatric emergency medicine: Validity evidence for a script concordance test. *Annals of Emergency Medicine, 53,* 647–652.

Childs, R. A., Dunn, J. L., van Barneveld, C., & Jaciw, A. P. (2007). Does It Matter if You "Kill" the Patient or Order Too Many Tests? Scoring Alternatives for a Test of Clinical Reasoning Skill. *International Journal of Testing, 7,* 127–139.

Childs, R. A., Dunn, J. L., van Barneveld, C., Jaciw, A. P., & McIlroy, J. H. (2003). Differential weighting of errors on a test of clinical reasoning skills. *Academic Medicine, 78,* S62–S64.

Cilliers, F. J., Schuwirth, L. W. T., & van der Vleuten, C. P. M. (2012). Modelling the pre-assessment learning effects of assessment: Evidence in the validity chain. *Medical Education, 46,* 1087–1098.

Clark, M. (2010). *Continuing competence: Overcoming our blind spots. Instep newsletter.* Victoria: College of Occupational Therapists of British Columbia.

Consorti, F., Della Rocca, C., Familiari, G., Gallo, P., Riggio, O., Sperandeo, F., et al. (2015). Verso una Laurea professionalizzante. Certificazione delle Competenze professionali. *Medicina e Chirurgia., 65,* 2931–2941.

Daniels, V. J., Bordage, G., Gierl, M. J., & Yudkowsky, R. (2014). Effect of clinically discriminating, evidence-based checklist items on the reliability of scores from an Internal Medicine residency OSCE. *Advances in Health Sciences Education, 19,* 497–506.

Dauphinee W.D., Boulais A.P., Smee S.M., Rothman A.I., Reznick R., & Blackmore D. (1998). Examination Results of the Licentiate of the Medical Council of Canada: Trends, Issues, and Future Considerations. In: *Proceedings of the 8th Ottawa Conference on Medical Education* (pp. 92–98). Philadelphia.

De Champlain, A. F. (2015). Best-fit model of exploratory and confirmatory factor analysis of the 2010 Medical Council of Canada Qualifying Examination Part I clinical decision-making cases. *Journal of Educational Evaluation for Health Professions., 12,* 11. https://doi.org/10.3352/jeehp.2015.12.11.

De Champlain, A. F., Melnick, D., Scoles, P., et al. (2003). Assessing medical students' clinical sciences knowledge in France: A collaboration between the NBME and a consortium of french medical schools. *Academic Medicine, 78,* 509–517.

de la Calzada, C. S. (2015). A framework for clinical reasoning in adult cardiology. *Advances in Medical Education Practice, 6,* 489–495.

Desjardins, I., Touchie, C., Pugh, D., Wood, T. J., & Humphrey-Murto, S. (2014). The impact of cueing on written examinations of clinical decision making: a case study. *Medical Education, 48,* 255–261.

Dory, V., Gagnon, R., & Charlin, B. (2010). Is case-specificity content-specificity? An analysis of data from extended-matching questions. *Advances in Health Sciences Education, 15,* 55–63.

Doucet, M. D., Purdy, R. A., Kaufman, D. M., & Langille, D. B. (1998). Comparison of problem-based learning and lecture format in continuing medical education on headache diagnosis and management. *Medical Education, 32,* 590–596.

Downing, S. M. (2004). Reliability: On the reproducibility of assessment data. *Medical Education, 38,* 1006–1012.

Downing, S. M. (2009). What is good item discrimination? In S. M. Downing & R. Yudkowsky (Eds.), *Assessment in Health Professions Education* (p. 108). New York: Routledge.

Downing, S. M., & Haladyna, T. M. (2009). Validity and its threats. In S. M. Downing & R. Yudkowsky (Eds.), *Assessment in Health Professions Education* (p. 33). New York: Routledge.

Downing, S. M., & Yudkowsky, R. (Eds.). (2009). *Assessment in health professions education.* New York: Routledge.

Duncan-Hewitt, W., Jungnickel, P., & Evans, R. L. (2007). Development of an office of teaching, learning, and assessment in a pharmacy school. *American Journal of Pharmaceutical Education, 71*(35), 1–8.

Elstein, A. S., Shulman, L. S., & Sprafka, S. A. (1978). *Medical problem solving.* Cambridge: Harvard University Press.

Eva, K., Bordage, G., Campbell, C., Galbraith, R., Ginsburg, S., Holmboe, E., et al. (2016). Towards a program of assessment for health professionals: From training into practice. *Advances in Health Sciences Education, 21,* 897–913.

Eva, K. W., & Regehr, G. (2013). Effective feedback for maintenance of competence: From data delivery to trusting dialogues. *Canadian Medical Association Journal, 185,* 463–464.

Eva, K., & Wood, T. (2003). Can the strength of candidates be discriminated based on ability to circumvent the biasing effect of prose? Implications for evaluation and education. *Academic Medicine, 78,* S78–S81.

Eva, K. W., Wood, T., Riddle, J., Touchie, C., & Bordage, G. (2010). How clinical features are presented matters to weaker diagnosticians. *Medical Education, 44,* 775–785.

Farmer, E. A., & Hinchy, J. (2005). Assessing general practice decision-making skills—The Key features approach. *Australian Family Physician, 34,* 1059–1061.

Farmer, E. A., & Page, G. A. (2005). Practical guide to assessing clinical decision-making skills using the key features approach. *Medical Education, 39,* 1188–1194.

Fischer, M. R., Kopp, V., Holzer, M., Ruderich, F., & Junger, J. (2005). A modified electronic key feature examination for undergraduate medical students: validation threats and opportunities. *Medical Teacher, 27,* 450–455.

Flinn, F., & Armstrong, C. (2011). Junior doctors' extended work hours and the effects on performance: The Irish Case. *International Journal of Quality Health Care, 2011*(23), 210–217.

Fowell, S. L., & Jolly, B. (2000). Combining marks, scores and grades. Reviewing common practices reveals some bad habits. *Medical Education, 34,* 785–786.

Fuller, R., Homer, M., Pell, G., & Hallam, J. (2017). Managing extremes of assessor judgment within the OSCE. *Medical Teacher, 39,* 58–66.

Gauthier, G., & Lajoie, S. P. (2014). Do expert clinical teachers have a shared understanding of what constitute a competent reasoning performance in case-based teaching? *Instructional Science, 42,* 579–594.

Geisler, P., Hummel, C., & Piebes, S. (2014). Evaluating evidence-informed clinical reasoning proficiency in oral practical examinations. *Athletic Training Education Journal, 9,* 43–48.

Gerhard-Szep, S., Guentsch, A., Pospiech, P., et al. (2016). Assessment formats in dental medicine: An overview. *GMS Journal for Medical Education, 33,* 1–43.

Gierl, M. J., Latifi, S., Lai, H., Boulais, A.-P., & DeChamplain, A. (2014). Automated essay scoring and the future of educational assessment in medical education. *Medical Education, 48,* 950–962.

Goldszmidt, M., Minda, J. P., & Bordage, G. (2013). Developing a unified list of physicians' reasoning tasks during Clinical Encounters: Time to be more explicit. *Academic Medicine, 88,* 390–394.

Goulet, F., Jacques, A., Gagnon, R., Charlin, B., & Shabah, A. (2010). Poorly performing physicians: does the script concordance test detect bad clinical reasoning? *Journal of Continuing Education in the Health Professions, 30,* 161–166.

Haladyna, T. M. (2004). Chapter 7. Item generation: Key features—Steps in developing key features problems. In T. M. Haladyna (Ed.), *Developing and validating multiple-choice test items* (pp. 165–170). Mahwah: Lawrence-Erlbaum Associates.

Hatala, R., & Norman, G. R. (2002). Adapting the key features examination for a clinical clerkship. *Medical Education, 36,* 160–165.

Heid, J., Bauch, M., Brass, K., Hess, F., Junger, J., Haag, M., et al. (2006). Development and usage of a secure assessment software system for the medical education. *GMS Medizinische Informatik, Biometrie und Epidemiologie, 10,* 1–6.

Heist, B. S., Kishida, N., Deshpande, G., Hamaguchi, S., & Kobayashi, H. (2016). Virtual patients to explore and develop clinical case summary statement skills amongst Japanese resident physicians: A mixed methods study. *BMC Medical Education, 16,* 39–46.

Heitzmann, N., Fischer, F., Kühne-Eversmann, L., & Fischer, M. R. (2015). Enhancing diagnostic competence with self-explanation prompts and adaptable feedback. *Medical Education, 49,* 993–1003.

Hrynchak, P., Takahashi, S. G., & Nayer, N. (2014). Key-feature questions for assessment of clinical reasoning: A literature review. *Medical Education, 48,* 870–883.

Hurtz, G. M., Chinn, R. N., Barnhill, G. C., & Hertz, N. R. (2012). Measuring clinical decision making: Do key features problems measure higher level cognitive processes? *Evaluation in the Health Professions, 35,* 396–415.

Huwendiek, S., Reichert, F., Duncker, C., de Leng, B. A., van der Vleuten, C. P. M., Muijtjens, A. M. M., et al. (2017). Electronic Assessment of Clinical Reasoning in Clerkships: A Mixed-Methods Comparison of Long-menu Key-Feature Problems with Context-Rich Single Best Answer Questions. *Medical Teacher, 39,* 476–485.

Jacques, A. (2006). Maintaining competence: A professional challenge. *Bulletin of the Kuwait Institute for Medical Specializations, 5,* 74–79.

Jacques, A., Sindon, A., Bourque, A., Bordage, G., & Ferland, J. J. (1995). Structured oral interview One way to identify family physicians' educational needs. *Canadian Family Physician, 41,* 1346–1352.

Jost, M., Brüstle, P., Giesler, M., Rijntjes, M., & Brich, J. (2017). Effects of additional team–based learning on students' clinical reasoning skills: a pilot study. *BMC Research Notes, 10,* 282. https://doi.org/10.1186/s13104-017-2614-9.

Kawasumi, Y. (2009) The association between physician competence at licensure and the quality of asthma management and patient morbidity. Master's thesis. McGill University. Montreal.

Keegan, D. A., Scott, I., Sylvester, M., Tan, A., Horrey, K., & Weston, W. (2017). Shared Canadian Curriculum in Family Medicine (SHARC-FM). Creating a national consensus on relevant and practical training for medical students. *Canadian Family Physician, 63,* e223–e231.

Kopp, V., Moltner, A., & Fisher, M. R. (2006). Key feature problems for the assessment of procedural knowledge: a practical guide. *GMS Zeitschrift für Medizinische Ausbildung, 23,* 1–6.

Kopp, V., Stark, R., & Fischer, M. R. (2008). Fostering diagnostic knowledge through computer supported, case-based worked examples: effects of erroneous examples and feedback. *Medical Education, 42,* 823–829.

Kopp, V., Stark, R., Heitzmann, N., & Fischer, M. R. (2009a). Self-regulated learning with case-based worked examples: effects of errors. *Evaluation and Research in Education, 22,* 107–119.

Kopp, V., Stark, R., Kuhne-Eversmann, L., & Fischer, M. R. (2009b). Do worked examples foster medical students' diagnostic knowledge of hyperthyroidism? *Medical Education, 43,* 1210–1217.

Korenstein, D., Thomas, D. C., Foldes, C., Ross, J., Halm, E., & McGinn, T. (2003). An evidence-based domestic violence education program for internal medicine residents. *Teaching and Learning in Medicine, 15,* 262–266.

Krautter, M., Junger, J., Koehl-Hackert, N., Nagelmann, L., & Nikendei, C. (2012). Evaluation of a structured, longitudinal training program for the preparation for the second state exam (M2)—A quantitative analysis. *Zeitschrift für Evidenz, Fortbildung und Qualität im Gesundheitswesen., 106,* 110–115.

Kumta, S. M., Tsang, P. L., Hung, L. K., & Cheng, J. C. Y. (2003). Fostering critical thinking skills through a web-based tutorial programme for final year medical students—A randomized controlled study. *Journal of Educational Multimedia and Hypermedia, 12,* 267–273.

Kwa, S. K., Amin, S. M., & Ng, A. C. (2007). Avoiding common errors in key feature problems. *Malaysian Family Physician, 2,* 18–21.

Ladyshewsky, R. K. (2002). A quasi-experimental study of the differences in performance and clinical reasoning using individual learning versus reciprocal peer coaching. *Physiotherapy Theory and Practice, 18,* 17–31.

Ladyshewsky, R., Baker, R., Jones, M., & Nelson, L. (2000). Evaluating clinical performance in physical therapy with simulated patients. *Journal of Physical Therapy Education, 14,* 31–37.

Lang, V. (2015). Validity Evidence for a Key Features Examination in the Internal Medicine Clerkship. Master's thesis. University of Illinois at Chicago.

LaRochelle, J., Durning, S. J., Boulet, J. R., van der Vleuten, C. P. M., van Merrienboer, J., & Donkers, J. (2016). Beyond standard checklist assessment: Question sequence may impact student performance. *Perspectives in Medical Education, 5,* 95–102.

Latifi, S., Gierl, M. J., Boulais, A. P., & DeChamplain, A. (2016). Using automated scoring to evaluate written responses in English and French on a high-stakes clinical competency examination. *Evaluation in the Health Professions, 39,* 100–113.

Laughlin, T., Wetmore, S., Allen, T., Brailovsky, C., Crichton, T., Bethune, C., et al. (2012). Defining competency-based evaluation objectives in family medicine: Communication skills. *Canadian Family Physician, 58,* e217–e224.

Lawrence, K., Allen, T., Brailovsky, C., Crichton, T., Bethune, C., Donoff, M., et al. (2011). Carpentier MP, Visser S. Defining competency-based evaluation objectives in family medicine Key-feature approach. *Canadian Family Physician, 57,* e373–e380.

Lee, R. P., Venkatesh, B., & Morley, P. (2009). Evidence-based evolution of the high stakes postgraduate intensive care examination in Australia and New Zealand. *Anaesthesia and Intensive Care, 37,* 525–531.

Lehmann, R., Thiessen, C., Frick, B., Bosse, H. M., Nikendei, C., Hoffmann, G. F., et al. (2015). Improving pediatric basic life support performance through blended learning with web-based virtual patients: Randomized controlled trial. *Journal of Medical Internet Research, 17,* e162.

Leung, F. H., Herold, J., & Iglar, K. (2016). Family medicine mandatory assessment of progress: Results of a pilot administration of a family medicine competency-based in-training examination. *Canadian Family Physician, 62,* e263–e267.

Lintzeris, N., Ritter, A., Dunlop, A., & Muhleisen, P. (2002). Training primary health care professionals to provide buprenorphine and LAAM treatment. *Substance Abuse, 23,* 245–254.

Litchfield, R. E., Oakland, M. J., & Anderson, J. A. (2000). Improving dietetics education with interactive communication technology. *Journal of the American Dietetic Association, 100,* 1191–1194.

Litchfield, R. E., Oakland, M. J., & Anderson, J. (2002). Promoting and evaluating competence in on-line dietetics education. *Journal of the American Dietetic Association, 102,* 1455–1458.

Maiburg, B. H., Rethans, J. J., Schuwirth, L. W., Mathus-Vliegen, L. M., & van Ree, J. W. (2003). Controlled trial of effect of computer-based nutrition course on knowledge and practice of general practitioner trainees. *American Journal of Clinical Nutrician, 77,* 1019S–1024S.

Mandin, H., & Dauphinee, W. D. (2000). Conceptual guidelines for developing and maintaining curriculum and examination objectives: the experience of the Medical Council of Canada. *Academic Medicine, 75,* 1031–1037.

Manns, P. J., & Darrah, J. (2012). A structured process to develop scenarios for use in evaluation of an evidence-based approach in clinical decision making. *Advances in Medical Education Practice, 3,* 113–119.

Matthes, J., Look, A., Kahne, A. K., Tekian, A., & Herzig, S. (2008). The semi-structured triple jump—a new assessment tool reflects qualifications of tutors in a PBL course on basic pharmacology. *Archives of Pharmacology, 377,* 55–63.

McGuire, C. H., Solomon, L. M., & Forman, P. M. (1976). *Clinical simulations: Selected problems in patient management* (2nd ed.). New York, NY: Appleton-CenturyCrofts.

Medical Council of Canada. (2012) Guidelines for the Development of Key Feature Problems and Test Cases. Ottawa: Medical Council of Canada. August, 2012. http://mcc.ca/wp-content/uploads/CDM-Guidelines.pdf; http://mcc.ca/wp-content/uploads/Lignes-directrices-PDC.pdf Accessed January 19, 2017.

Medical Council of Canada. (2016) 2016 MCCQE Part I Annual Technical Report. http://mcc.ca/wp-content/uploads/MCCQE-Part-I-Annual-Technical-Report-2016-EN.pdf Accessed June 26, 2017.

Medical Council of Canada. (2017a). Online Demo MCCEE Sample Test. Ottawa: Medical Council of Canada.

Medical Council of Canada. (2017b). Test Committee Resources. Ottawa: Medical Council of Canada. http://mcc.ca/about/test-committee-resources/Accessed January 23, 2017.

Medical Council of Canada. (2017c). Clinical decision making – Exam tips. Ottawa: Medical Council of Canada. https://www.youtube.com/watch?v=ln6X_sVenWc Accessed April 1, 2017.

Medical Council of Canada. (2017d). Self-Administered Examination (SAE). Ottawa: Medical Council of Canada. http://mcc.ca/examinations/self-administered-exam/Accessed April 1, 2017.

Medical Council of Canada. (2017e). MCC Part-I Examination Demo. Ottawa: Medical Council of Canada. http://mcc.ca/examinations/mccqe-part-i/exam-preparation-resources/Accessed June 19, 2017.

Medical Council of Canada. (2017f). When and how you will receive your MCCQE Part I results. http://mcc.ca/examinations/mccqe-part-i/result/Accessed June 19, 2017.

Medical Council of Canada. (2017 g). Scoring Aggregator. http://mcc.ca/scoring-aggregator/Accessed June 20, 2017.

Medical Council of Canada. (2017 h). Scoring. http://mcc.ca/examinations/mccqe-part-i/scoring/Accessed June 27, 2017.

Miller, G. E. (1966). New Thoughts on Old Examinations. *Federation Bull., 53,* 390–396.

Miller, F., Jacques, A., Brailovsky, C., Sindon, A., & Bordage, G. (1997). When to recommend compulsory versus optional CME programs? A study to establish criteria. *Academic Medicine, 72,* 760–764.

Monnier, P., Bedard, M. J., Gagnon, R., & Charlin, B. (2011). The relationship between script concordance test scores in an obstetrics-gynecology rotation and global performance assessments in the curriculum. *International Journal of Medical Education, 2,* 3–6.

National Board of Osteopathic Medical Examiners (NBOME). COMLEX-USA, Level 3. *Assessment of Competencies for Osteopathic Medical Licensure.* https://www.nbome.org/exams-assessments/comlex-usa/comlex-usa-level-3/Accessed September 08, 2017.

Naude, A., Wium, A. M., & duPlessis, S. (2011). Re-engineering the curriculum at a rural institution: Reflection on the process of development. *South African Journal of Health Education, 25,* 760–783.

Nikendei, C., Mennin, S., Weyrich, P., Kraus, B., Zipfel, S., Schrauth, M., et al. (2009). Effects of a supplementary final year curriculum on students' clinical reasoning skills as assessed by key-feature examination. *Medical Teacher, 31,* e438–e442.

Norcini, J. J., Anderson, B., Bollela, V., Burch, V., Costa, M. J., Duvivier, R., et al. (2011). Criteria for good assessment: consensus statement and recommendations from the ttawa 2010 conference. *Medical Teacher, 33,* 206–214.

Norcini, J. J., & Guille, R. (2002). Chapter 25: Combining tests and setting standards. In G. R. Norman, C. P. M. van der Vleuten, & D. I. Newble (Eds.), *International handbook of research in medical education* (pp. 811–834). Berlin: Springer.

Norcini, J.J., Swanson, D.S., Grosso, L.J., & Webster, G.D. (1983) A comparison of several methods for scoring Patient Management Problems. In *Proceedings of the 22nd research in medical education conference.* Association of American Medical Colleges.

Norman, G., Alan, N., Blake, J. M., & Mueller, B. (2010). Assessment steers learning down the right road: Impact of progress testing on licensing examination performance. *Medical Teacher, 32,* 496–499.

Norman, G., Bordage, G., Curry, L., Dauphinee, D., Jolly, B., Newble, D., et al. (1984). Review of recent innovations in assessment. In R. Wakeford (Ed.), *Directions in Clinical Assessment. Report of the Cambridge Conference on the Assessment of Clinical Competence* (pp. 9–27). Cambridge: Office of the Regius Professor of Physic. Cambridge University School of Clinical Medicine.

Norman, G., Bordage, G., Page, G., & Keane, D. (2006). How specific is case specificity? *Medical Education, 40,* 618–623.

Norman, G. R., & Feightner, J. W. (1981). A comparison of behavior on simulated patients and patient management problems. *Medical Education, 15,* 26–32.

Norman, G.R., Tugwell, P., Jacoby, L.L., & Muzzin, L.J. (1983). The Generalizability of Measures of Clinical Problem Solving. In *Proceedings of the 22nd Conference on Research in Medical Education* (pp. 110–114). Washington: Association of American Medical Colleges.

Page, G. (2008). *An Exploratory Review of Content, Format and Performance Differences on the MCQ and CDM Components of the 2008 QE Part 1 Examination* (p. 17). Ottawa: Report to the Medical Council of Canada.

Page, G., & Bordage, G. (1995). The Medical Council of Canada's Key Feature Project: A more valid written examination of clinical decision-making skills. *Academic Medicine, 70,* 104–110.

Page, G., & Bordage, G. (2004). Better test score reliability with multi-question key feature cases: refining our view of case specificity. In *Presented at the Asian Pacific Medical Education Conference*. Singapore.

Page, G., Bordage, G., & Alen, T. (1995). Developing key-feature problems and examinations to assess clinical decision-making skills. *Academic Medicine, 70,* 194–201.

Page, G., Bordage, G., Harasym, P., Bowmer, I., & Swanson, D. (1990b). A revision of the Medical Council of Canada's qualifying examlnatlon: Pilot test results. In R. Zwierstra, W. Bender, W. Hiemstra, & R. Scherpbier (Eds.), *Teaching and assessing clinical competence* (pp. 403–407). Groningen: Boekwerk Publ.

Page, G., Boulais, A.P., Blackmore, D., & Dauphinee, D. (2000a). Justifying the use of short answer questions in the KF Problems of the MCCC's qualifying exam. In *Presented at the 9th Ottawa Conference*. Cape Town.

Page, G., Broudo, D., Blackmore, D., Schulzer, M., Bordage, G., (1990a). Cueing as a factor in written examinations of clinical decision-making skills. In *Proceedings of the international conference on current developments in assessing clinical competence* (pp. 184–191), Ottawa.

Page, G., Farmer, L., Spike, N., & McDonald, E. (2000b). The use of short-answer questions in the key features problems on the Royal Australian College of General Practitioners Fellowship Examination. In *Presented at the 9th Ottawa Conference*. Cape Town.

Pinnock, R., & Jones, A. (2008). An undergraduate paediatric curriculum based on clinical presentations and 'key features'. *Journal of Paediatrics and Child Health, 44,* 661–664.

Rademakers, J., Ten Cate, T. H. J., & Bar, P. R. (2005). Progress testing with short answer questions. *Medical Teacher, 27,* 578–582.

Raupach, T., Muenscher, C., Anders, S., Steinbach, R., Pukrop, T., Hege, I., et al. (2009). Web-based collaborative training of clinical reasoning: A randomized trial. *Medical Teacher, 31,* e431–e437.

Reinert, A., Berlin, A., Swan-Sein, A., Nowygrod, R., & Fingeret, A. (2014). Validity and reliability of a novel written examination to assess knowledge and clinical decision-making skills of medical students on the surgery clerkship. *American Journal of Surgery, 207,* 236–242.

Reiter, H., Eva, K. W., Rosenfeld, J., & Norman, G. R. (2007). Multiple mini-interviews predict clerkship and licensing examination performance. *Medical Education, 41,* 378–384.

Renaud, J. S., Ratté, F., Theriault, J. F., Roy, A. M., & Cote, L. (2016). Questions de planification clinique: un nouvel outil pour évaluer la capacité des étudiants en médecine à identifier les éléments-clés discriminants d'un diagnostic différentiel. *Pédagogie Médicale, 17,* 65–75.

Reznick, R. K., Smee, S., Baumber, J. S., et al. (1993). Guidelines for estimating the real cost of an objective structured clinical examination. *Academic Medicine, 68,* 513–517.

Rotthoff, T., Baehring, T., Dicken, H. D., Fahron, U., Fischer, M. R., Adler, M., et al. (2006a). Case-based computerized examinations for medical students—objective, implementation and experiences. *GMS Medizinische Informatik, Biometrie und Epidemiologie, 2,* 11.

Rotthoff, T., Baehring, T., Dicken, H. D., Fahron, U., Richter, B., Fischer, M. R., et al. (2006b). Comparison between long-menu and open-ended questions in computerized medical assessments. a randomized controlled trial. *BMC Medical Education, 6,* 50.

Schaper, E., Tipold, A., & Ehlers, J. P. (2013). Use of key feature questions in summative assessment of veterinary medicine students. *Irish Veterinary Journal, 66,* 3.

Schenowitz, G. (2000). Le projet STEP ou l'évaluation des besoins de formation revisitée. *Acta Endoscopica, 30,* 265–268.

Schmidmaier, R., Eiber, S., Ebersbach, R., Schiller, M., Hege, I., Holzer, M., et al. (2013). Learning the facts in medical school is not enough: which factors predict successful application of procedural knowledge in a laboratory setting? *BMC Medical Education, 13,* 28–37.

Schreiner, U., Haefner, A., Gologan, R., & Obertacke, U. (2011). Effective teaching modifies medical student attitudes toward pain symptoms. *European Journal of Trauma Emergency Surgery., 37,* 655–659.

Schubach, F., Goos, M., Fabry, G., Vach, W., & Boeker, M. (2017). Virtual patients in the acquisition of clinical reasoning skills: does presentation mode matter? A quasi-randomized controlled trial. *BMC Medical Education, 17*(1), 165.

Schubert, S., Ortwein, H., Dumitsch, A., Schwantes, U., Wilhelm, O., & Kiessling, C. (2008). A situational judgement test of professional behaviour: development and validation. *Medical Teacher, 30,* 528–533.

Schuwirth, L.W.T. (1998a). An approach to the assessment of medical problem solving: Computerised case-based testing. Doctoral dissertation. University of Maastricht.

Schuwirth, L. W. T., Blackmore, D. E., Mom, E., van den Wildenberg, F., Stoffers, H. E. J. H., & van der Vleuten, C. P. M. (1999a). How to write short cases for assessing problem-solving skills. *Medical Teacher, 21,* 144–150.

Schuwirth, L. W. T., Gorter, S., van der Heijde, D., Rethans, J. J., Brauer, J., Houben, H., et al. (2005). The role of a computerised case-based testing procedure in practice performance assessment. *Advances in Health Sciences Education, 10,* 145–155.

Schuwirth, L. W. T., & van der Vleuten, C. P. M. (2003). The use of clinical simulations in assessment. *Medical Education, 37*(Suppl. 1), 65–71.

Schuwirth, L. W. T., & van der Vleuten, C. P. M. (2010). Cost-affective assessment. In K. Walsh (Ed.), *Cost Effectiveness in Medical Education* (pp. 94–100). Oxford: Radcliffe.

Schuwirth, L. W. T., & van der Vleuten, C. P. M. (2011a). General overview of the theories used in assessment: AMEE Guide No. 57. *Medical Teacher, 33,* 783–797.

Schuwirth, L. W. T., & van der Vleuten, C. P. M. (2011b). Conceptualising surgical education assessment. In H. Fry & R. Kneebone (Eds.), *Surgical education: Theorising an emerging domain* (pp. 75–90). Berlin: Springer.

Schuwirth, L. W. T., & van der Vleuten, C. P. M. (2012). Programmatic assessment and Kane's validity perspective. *Medical Education, 46,* 38–48.

Schuwirth, L. W. T., van der Vleuten, C. P. M., De Kock, C. A., Peperkamp, A. G. W., & Donkers, H. H. L. M. (1996a). Computerized case-based testing: a modern method to assess clinical decision making. *Medical Teacher, 18,* 294–299.

Schuwirth, L. W. T., van der Vleuten, C. P. M., & Donkers, H. H. L. M. (1996b). A closer look at cueing effects in multiple-choice questions. *Medical Education, 30,* 44–49.

Schuwirth, L. W. T., van der Vleuten, C. P. M., Stoffers, H. E. J. H., & Peperkamp, A. G. W. (1996c). Computerized long-menu questions as an alternative to open-ended questions in computerized assessment. *Medical Education, 30,* 50–55.

Schuwirth, L.W.T., Verheggen, M.M., Boshuizen, H.P.A., van der Waarten, Th.H.A.M., & van der Vleuten, C.P.M. (1998b). Validation of key-feature assessment using think-aloud protocols. In *Proceedings of the 8th Ottawa Conference on Medical Education* (p. 655), Philadelphia.

Schuwirth, L. W. T., Verheggen, M. M., van der Vleuten, C. P. M., Boshuizen, H. P. A., & Dinant, G. J. (2001). Do short cases elicit different thinking processes than factual knowledge questions do? *Medical Education, 35,* 348–356.

Schuwirth, L. W. T., Verhoeven, B. H., Scherpbier, A. J. J. A., Mom, E. M. A., Cohen-Schotanus, J., Van Rossum, H. J. M., et al. (1999b). An inter- and intra-university comparison with short case-based testing. *Advances in Health Sciences Education, 4,* 233–244.

Shiozawa, T., Butz, B., Herlan, S., Kramer, A., & Hirt, B. (2017). Interactive anatomical and surgical live stream lectures improve students' academic performance in applied clinical anatomy. *Anatomical Sciences Education, 10,* 46–52.

Skakun, E. N., Maguire, T. O., & Cook, D. A. (1994). Strategy Choices in Multiple-choice Items. *Academic Medicine, 69,* S7–S9.

Smith, S. R., Dollase, R. H., & Boss, J. A. (2003). Assessing students' performances in a competency-based curriculum. *Academic Medicine, 78,* 97–107.

Smith, S., Kogan, J. R., Berman, N. B., Dell, M. S., Brock, D. M., & Robins, L. S. (2016). The Development and Preliminary Validation of a Rubric to Assess Medical Students' Written Summary Statements in Virtual Patient Cases. *Academic Medicine, 91,* 94–100.

Spike, N. A., & Hays, R. B. (1999). Analysis by training status of performance in the certification examination for Australian family doctors. *Medical Education, 33,* 612–615.

Stark, R., Kopp, V., & Fischer, M. R. (2011). Case-based learning with worked examples in complex domains: Two experimental studies in undergraduate medical education. *Learning and Instruction, 21,* 22–33.

Sturmberg, J. P., Crowe, P., & Hughes, C. (2003). Computer-assisted instruction: guiding learning through a key features approach in a community-based medical course. *Medical Teacher, 25,* 332–335.

Sturmberg, J. P., & Martin, C. M. (2016). Diagnosis—The limiting focus of taxonomy. *Journal of Evaluation in Clinical Practice, 22,* 103–111.

Tamblyn, R., Abrahamowicz, M., Bartlett, G., Winslade, N., Jacques, A., Klass, D., Wenghofer, E., Smee, S., Dauphinee, D., Blackmore, D., Bartman, I., Buckeridge, D., & Hanley, J. (2009). The Quebec-ontario follow-up study of the association between scores achieved on the MCCQE Part II examination and performance in clinical practice. Report to the Medical Council of Canada.

Tamblyn, R., Abrahamowicz, M., Dauphinee, D., Wenghofer, E., Jacques, A., Klass, D., et al. (2007). Physician scores on a national clinical skills examination as predictors of complaints to medical regulatory authorities. *JAMA, 298,* 993–1001.

Tamblyn, R., Abrahamowicz, M., Dauphinee, D., Wenghofer, E., Jacques, A., Klass, D., et al. (2010). Influence of physicians' management and communication ability on patients' persistence with antihypertensive medication. *Archives of Internal Medicine, 170,* 1064–1072.

Touchie C., & Streefkerk C. for the Blueprint Project Team. (2014). Blueprint Project – Qualifying Examinations Blueprint and Content Specifications. Ottawa, Ontario: Medical Council of Canada. September 2014. http://mcc.ca/wp-content/uploads/Blueprint-Report.pdf Accessed April 12, 2017.

Trudel, J. L., Bordage, G., & Downing, S. M. (2008). Reliability and validity of key feature cases for the self-assessment of colon and rectal surgeons. *Annals of Surgery, 248,* 252–258.

van der Vleuten, C. P. M. (1996). The assessment of professional competence: developments, research and practical implications. *Advances in Health Sciences Education, 1,* 41–67.

van der Vleuten, C. P. M., Norman, G. R., & Schuwirth, L. W. T. (2008). Assessing clinical reasoning. In J. Higgs, M. Jones, S. Loftus, & N. Christensen (Eds.), *Clinical reasoning in the health professions* (pp. 413–421). Philadelphia: Elsevier.

van der Vleuten, C. P. M., & Schuwirth, L. W. T. (2005). Assessing professional competence: from methods to programmes. *Medical Education, 39,* 309–317.

van der Vleuten, C. P. M., Schuwirth, L. W. T., Scheele, F., Driessen, E. W., & Hodges, B. (2010). The assessment of professional competence: building blocks for theory development. *Best Practice & Research in Clinical Obstetrics and Gynaecology, 24,* 703–719.

Vaughan, B., & Morrison, T. (2015). Assessment in the final year clinical practicum of an Australian osteopathy program. *International Journal of Osteopathic Medicine, 18,* 278–286.

Wearne, S. (2008). The RACGP Fellowship examination: 10 tips for answering key feature problems. *Australian Family Physician, 37,* 559–561.

Wenghofer, E., Klass, D., Abrahamowicz, M., Dauphinee, D., Jacques, A., Smee, S., et al. (2009). Doctor scores on national qualifying examinations predict quality of care in future practice. *Medical Education, 43,* 1166–1173.

Wetmore, S., Laughlin, T., Lawrence, K., Donoff, M., Allen, T., Brailovsky, C., et al. (2012). Defining competency-based evaluation objectives in family medicine—Procedure skills. *Canadian Family Physician, 58,* 775–780.

Williams, R., Klamen, D., Markwell, S. J., Cianciolo, A. T., Colliver, J. A., & Verhulst, S. J. (2014). Variations in senior medical student diagnostic justification ability. *Academic Medicine, 89,* 790–798.

Winslade, N. (2000). Assessment of Medical Assistant's Knowledge of Authorized Pharmaceuticals. Master's thesis, University of Maastricht.

Winslade, N. (2001). A System to Assess the Achievement of Doctor of Pharmacy Students. *American Journal of Pharmaceutical Education, 65,* 363–392.

Yousefichaijan, P., Jafari, F., Kahbazi, M., Rafiei, M., & Pakniyat, A. G. (2016). The effect of short-term workshop on improving clinical reasoning skill of medical students. *Medical Journal of the Islamic Repubublic of Iran, 30,* 396.

Zamani, S., Amini, M., Masoumi, S. Z., Delavari, S., Namaki, M. J., & Kojuri, J. (2017). The comparison of the key feature of clinical reasoning and multiple-choice examinations in clinical decision makings ability. *Biomedical Research, 28,* 1115–1119.

Zieky, M. J., & Perie, M. (2006). *A primer on setting cut scores on tests of educational achievement* (p. 20). Princeton, NJ: Educational Testing Service Inc.

Validity evidence of resident competency ratings and the identification of problem residents

Yoon Soo Park, Janet Riddle & Ara Tekian

OBJECTIVES This study examined validity evidence of end-of-rotation evaluations used to measure progress toward mastery of core competencies in residents. In addition, this study investigated whether end-of-rotation evaluations can be used to detect problem residents during their training.

METHODS Historical data for a 4-year period (2009–2012), containing 4986 observations of 291 internal medicine residents, were examined. Residents were observed and assessed by fellows, faculty members and programme directors on nine domains, including the six Accreditation Council for Graduate Medical Education core competencies, as part of their end-of-rotation evaluations. Descriptive statistics were used to collect evidence of the response process. Correlations between competencies and a generalisability study were used to examine the internal structure of the end-of-rotation evaluations. Hierarchical regression was used to estimate the increase in scores across years of training. Scores on end-of-rotation evaluations were compared with trainees identified as problem residents by programme directors.

RESULTS Compared with fellows, faculty and programme directors had significantly greater variability in assigning scores across different competencies. Correlations between competencies ranged from 0.69 to 0.92. The reliability of end-of-rotation evaluations was adequate (fellows, phi coefficient [φ] = 0.68; faculty [including programme directors], φ = 0.71). Mean scores increased by 0.21 points (95% confidence interval 0.18–0.24) per postgraduate year. Mean scores were significantly correlated with classification as a problem resident ($r = 0.33$, $p < 0.001$); problem residents also had significantly lower ratings across all competencies during PGY-1 compared with all other residents.

CONCLUSIONS End-of-rotation evaluations are a useful method of measuring the growth in resident performance associated with core competencies when sufficient numbers of end-of-rotation evaluation scores are used. Furthermore, end-of-rotation evaluation scores provide preliminary evidence with which to detect and predict problem residents in subsequent postgraduate training years.

Medical Education 2014; 48: 614–622
doi: 10.1111/medu.12408

Discuss ideas arising from the article at "www.mededuc.com discuss"

Department of Medical Education, College of Medicine, University of Illinois at Chicago, Chicago, Illinois, USA

Correspondence: Yoon Soo Park, PhD, Department of Medical Education (MC 591), College of Medicine, University of Illinois at Chicago, 808 South Wood Street, 963 CMET, Chicago, Illinois 60612-7309, USA. Tel: 00 1 312 355 5406; E-mail: yspark2@uic.edu

INTRODUCTION

Residency programmes in the USA are undergoing major transitions with respect to the training and assessing of residents. With the implementation of the Next Accreditation System (NAS) and the Milestone Project by the Accreditation Council for Graduate Medical Education (ACGME), ongoing data collection and trend analysis of resident performance are mandated on a biannual basis.[1] Given these changes in residency education, a validated assessment system for measuring residents' growth and progress toward the mastery of core competencies at different levels of training is required. A key feature of a valid assessment system is the ability to identify and monitor underperforming residents at early stages of training so that they can be given proper remediation.

Nearly all residency programmes have problem residents.[2] Generally, problem residents are trainees who demonstrate significant difficulties and require intervention by a person of authority.[3,4] Problem residents have also been viewed as learners who fail to acquire the necessary competencies or progress at a slower rate than other residents toward the acquisition of competencies.[5] The literature provides a wide array of remediation plans for problem residents.[6,7] These studies emphasise the early identification of and intervention with problem residents because the needs of these learners can lead to difficulties in their completion of residency and can require substantial resources for remediation.

According to a national survey conducted in 1999, 82% of programme directors reported to have discovered problem residents through observations; problem residents were reported to have difficulties in medical knowledge and in clinical judgement.[8] More recently, a 10-year review of resident records in Canada (July 1999 to June 2009) found medical expertise and professionalism to be two competencies in which problem residents were reported to have difficulties.[9] Although previous research describes the characteristics of problem residents and provides methods for identifying them, there is a lack of empirically driven studies providing the necessary data and results to support these findings.[10] For example, it is unclear whether end-of-rotation evaluations measuring core competencies can reproduce consistent scores representing growth in a learner's performance over time. End-of-rotation evaluations are global judgements completed by supervising faculty members or fellows and are based on a form on which core competencies during residency training are rated; they are similar to the In-Training Evaluation Reports (ITERs) used in Canada. End-of-rotation evaluations are not based on a specific observation or direct encounter, but, rather, on a prolonged observation of a resident throughout a rotation (typically one month in duration) and can include second-hand reports and case presentations, in addition to direct observations.[11,12] Although guidelines on the number of evaluations are emerging in the multi-source feedback literature,[13] it is unclear how many evaluations are required when measuring core competencies or whether evaluations provided by fellows or faculty, respectively, are more accurate and reliable. There is also a lack of empirical evidence on whether end-of-rotation evaluations can be used to identify problem residents during the early stages of residency training. End-of-rotation evaluations are based on several factors, including direct observations and multi-source feedback (discussions between the rater and the resident's peers, nurses and students in order to obtain their input); direct observations and multi-source feedback are assessment methods considered by ACGME in the Milestone Project. Therefore, there is an increasing and urgent need for studies that provide psychometric evidence to support the theoretically based frameworks cited in the literature.

End-of-rotation evaluations are a type of workplace-based assessment, which has been shown to be effective in changing the behaviour of learners through feedback.[14,15] However, concerns regarding end-of-rotation evaluations have also been raised because evaluation forms are not completed directly following an actual educational experience and thus may not provide meaningful feedback to the learner.[16] End-of-rotation evaluations have also been subject to the 'failure to fail' phenomenon, whereby raters become reluctant to provide accurate feedback on a resident's performance as a result of multiple social factors, such as pressure from peers and administration to comply, the consequences of reporting underperformance, and conflicting demands and time constraints among instructors who have both clinical and educational duties.[17] Kogan and colleagues have also noted variability in observers' rating processes and in the translation of the observation to numeric scores, which presents a challenge in end-of-rotation evaluations that may be conducted by a wide pool of observers who lack rater training.[18] Despite these concerns that call into question the validity of end-of-rotation evaluations, recent studies on ITERs have shown that evaluation scores in postgraduate years 1 (PGY-1) and 2 predict performance in PGY-3, providing evidence to support their validity.[19]

A valid assessment system may provide useful information for the early detection of problem residents who can benefit from remediation and feedback. Ratings of internal medicine residents have been electronically stored in the New Innovations™ (NI) platform since 2009 based on nine domains, which include six ACGME core competencies (interpersonal and communication skills, medical knowledge, patient care, practice-based learning and improvement, professionalism, systems-based practices) and three domains relevant to the local internal medicine programme (medical interviewing, physical examination, procedural skills). Residents are rated at the end of each monthly rotation and programme directors use their scores, among other sources of information, to assess residents on their biannual performance as mandated by ACGME. As accreditation agencies in the USA and Canada move toward data-driven systems to measure trends in resident performance, the need to evaluate the validity of assessment systems, such as end-of-rotation evaluations, becomes critical.

The purpose of this study is to investigate the validity of end-of-rotation evaluations that are based on ACGME core competencies. Validity evidence will be investigated using Messick's unified validity framework, focusing on response process, internal structure, relationship to other variables, and consequences.[20] Scores from end-of-rotation evaluations will be examined for their association with learners identified as problem residents. Findings from this study will guide residency programmes as they undergo the changes required in the NAS.

METHODS

Historical data for end-of-rotation evaluations were extracted from an electronic database (NI) at a single institution, which contains ratings of 291 internal medicine residents in residency during 2009–2012, resulting in a total of 4986 assessments. Ratings of residents (PGY-1–3) were obtained from 146 fellows, 144 faculty members and 21 programme directors (associate programme directors or programme directors, including subspecialty fellowship programme directors) on nine domains. Faculty and fellows providing summative evaluations for residents serve as supervisors on clinical rotations. Residents were observed by other groups, including peers, but their ratings were not included in the analysis because the focus of this study was on assessments by fellows, faculty and programme directors. Raters used a 9-point scale on which scores of 1–3 represent 'unsatisfactory' performance, scores of 4–6 represent 'satisfactory' performance, and scores of 7–9 represent 'superior' performance in an ordinal scale; qualitative comments were also collected as part of end-of-rotation evaluations, but were not analysed in this study. The unit of analysis was the residents; multiple ratings of competencies by different raters were averaged by year and by resident to create an annual rating index for each competency; a composite mean, which averaged ratings across the nine domains, was also calculated.

Descriptive statistics were examined to study characteristics of the data and to collect evidence of the response process. Descriptive statistics are presented for fellows, faculty and programme directors. Pairwise correlations between competencies were calculated to examine their association. A generalisability study (G study) was conducted to examine the reliability and internal structure of the end-of-rotation evaluation using the r (rater) : p (person) × i (competencies) design, in which raters are nested in residents and crossed with ratings of competencies. The selection of this G study design was based on the 'unbalanced' nature of the data, which included unequal numbers of observations by different raters, following recommendations from Brennan.[21] A similar design was used by Kreiter et al. to resolve issues in the unbalanced ratings of observations.[22] Details of variance component estimation for unbalanced random effects are beyond the scope of this study. The G study was conducted using rating data from fellows and faculty members. Variance components from the G study were used to examine sources of error variance and the reliability of end-of-rotation evaluations. A decision study (D study) was conducted to project the number of required observations to reach a sufficient level of reliability (phi coefficient [φ] > 0.70).

To measure the longitudinal progression of competency ratings over time, hierarchical regression was used by specifying cross-classified random effects for residents and raters.[23] This analysis was conducted to identify whether ratings of a particular competency increased at a faster rate than those of other competencies. To examine whether scores from end-of-rotation evaluations can be used in the early detection of problem residents, as part of consequential validity evidence, mean ratings at PGY-1 were correlated with learners identified as problem residents. Problem residents were identified by programme directors based on their holistic judgement of resident performance documented in a portfolio assessment system, which includes mean competency ratings based on end-of-rotation evaluations, assessment scores and qualitative comments, among other sources of information. Mean competency ratings were compared between problem and all other residents using t-tests. Data compilation and analyses were conducted using STATA Version 12 (StataCorp LP, College Station, TX, USA). This study was approved by the institutional review board of the study institution.

RESULTS

Assessments based on end-of-rotation evaluations were recorded, on average, 14.9 (standard deviation [SD] 8.1) times per year for each resident (by fellows, $n = 5$; by faculty members, $n = 8$; by programme directors, $n = 2$). The mean ± SD length of time spent supervising residents was 23.2 ± 7.7 days. Raters logged their ratings of competency scores a mean ± SD of 41.3 ± 51.7 days after the completion of the observation period. Institutional policy requires raters to complete scoring within 6 months of the completion of observation.

Response process

Average ratings across competencies by rater and postgraduate year are shown in Table 1. The composite mean ± SD rating was 7.74 ± 0.40. Compared with fellows, faculty and programme directors showed significantly greater variability in scores assigned across different competencies assessed during the first 2 years of residency training (F-test for homogeneity of variance, $p < 0.001$). During PGY-1, the variability of scores assigned across the nine domains by fellows had an SD of 0.27; for faculty members and programme directors, the SD was 0.39. The SDs of scores assigned by fellows, faculty and programme directors during PGY-2 were 0.23, 0.33 and 0.41, respectively. These differences in variability indicate that fellows provided similar ratings across the nine domains (e.g. assigning values of '7' across all nine domains), whereas faculty members and programme directors provided different ratings. Across the 3 years, the mean ± SD composite rating increased from 7.54 ± 0.95 in PGY-1, to 7.83 ± 0.86 in PGY-2, and 7.97 ± 0.83 in PGY-3. Table 1 also shows the increase in mean composite scores by rater.

Internal structure

Pairwise correlations between core competencies ranged from 0.69 to 0.92; however, after adjusting for multiple comparisons, there were no significant

Table 1 Average ratings across competencies by rater and postgraduate year (PGY): descriptive statistics

PGY	Raters	Evaluations, n	Composite score, mean ± SD	Min	Max
1 (2092 observations)	Fellows	997	7.57 ± 0.27	1.00	9.00
	Faculty	817	7.49 ± 0.39	2.20	9.00
	PDs	141	7.55 ± 0.39	5.10	9.00
2 (1447 observations)	Fellows	656	7.83 ± 0.23	4.63	9.00
	Faculty	616	7.83 ± 0.33	3.50	9.00
	PDs	93	7.76 ± 0.41	5.00	9.00
3 (1447 observations)	Fellows	700	7.90 ± 0.20	3.88	9.00
	Faculty	582	8.04 ± 0.24	4.78	9.00
	PDs	95	8.01 ± 0.22	4.56	9.00

Missing values were excluded from the calculations. Composite refers to the mean rating across the nine domains. Raters scored on a 9-point scale, on which scores of 1–3 represent 'unsatisfactory', scores of 4–6 represent 'satisfactory' and scores of 7–9 represent 'superior' performance. The median number of evaluations completed by a rater per year was four by fellows, five by faculty, and six by programme directors.
SD = standard deviation; PDs = programme directors.

Table 2 Variance components by fellows and faculty members: generalisability study

	Fellows		Faculty members	
Facet	Variance component	Variance component, %	Variance component	Variance component, %
p	0.117	12.3	0.097	11.5
r : p	0.687	72.1	0.538	63.6
i	0.008	0.9	0.017	2.0
p × i	0.002	0.2	0.007	0.9
r × i : p	0.139	14.6	0.187	22.1

The G study was conducted using an r (raters) : p (residents) × i (competencies) design in order to consider unbalanced data structure. Faculty results include data from both faculty members and programme directors.

differences in correlations to indicate greater association between any two competencies.

Variance decomposition for ratings conducted by fellows and faculty members are presented in Table 2. Ratings by programme directors were combined with those of faculty for this analysis in view of the small number of programme directors. Percentage variance components were similar between the two rater types, for which 12.3% and 11.5%, respectively, of total variance represented resident variance. However, the greatest source of error variance derived from raters nested in residents ($r : p$), which accounted for 72.1% of variance for fellows and 63.6% of variance for faculty members. This indicates differential levels of severity depending on the fellow or faculty member observing and assessing the resident; greater variability in severity was noted among fellows than among faculty. The reliability of end-of-rotation evaluations had a phi coefficient of about 0.70 (fellows ratings, $\varphi = 0.68$; faculty ratings, $\varphi = 0.71$). To reach sufficient levels of reliability ($\varphi > 0.70$), projections from the D study indicate at least 14 end-of-rotation evaluations.

Relationship to other variables

Scores from end-of-rotation evaluations were examined in relation to postgraduate year of training. Figure 1 presents average ratings by competency and by postgraduate year. The x-axis denotes the 3 years of postgraduate residency training. Within each year, 10 plots are presented (nine domains and an overall summary rating). As Figure 1 illustrates, medical knowledge and professionalism, respectively, were awarded relatively lower and higher mean ratings than other competencies dur-

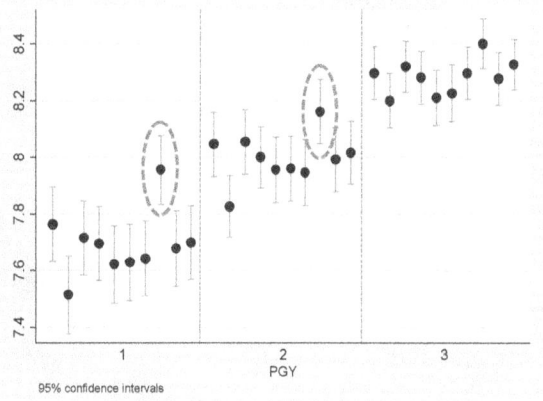

Figure 1 Mean ratings by competency and postgraduate year. The 10 bars per year group represent ratings on (from left to right): interpersonal and communication skills; medical knowledge; patient care; medical interviewing; physical examination; procedural skills; practice-based learning and improvement; professionalism; systems-based practice; and overall summary. Bars represent 95% confidence intervals; ●, mean ratings. Y-axis indicates mean rating. X-axis indicates postgraduate year. Average ratings for professionalism are circled for PGY-1 and PGY-2

ing the first 2 years of postgraduate training. The plot shows a gradual increase in the mean ratings of competencies over the 3 years. Results of a hierarchical regression show that on average ratings increased by 0.21 points per postgraduate year (95% confidence interval [CI] 0.18–0.24). Among the nine domains, medical knowledge had the lowest baseline mean rating, but the fastest rate of increase of 0.28 points per postgraduate year (95% CI 0.25–0.31); this rate of increase was significantly greater than those of the other competencies. Professionalism had the slowest rate of increase of 0.12 points per postgraduate year (95% CI 0.09–0.15), which was significantly lower than those of the other competencies.

Consequence

Of the 210 PGY-1 residents referred to in the data, nine (4.3%) were identified as problem residents by programme directors. Although the prevalence of problem residents was small, correlation (point-biserial) between mean composite ratings and a dichotomous indicator of problem residents and all other residents was 0.33 ($p < 0.001$) (correlations ranged between 0.28 and 0.34 by competency; all $p < 0.001$). However, there were no significant differences in the magnitude of correlation for a specific competency; moreover, there were no significant differences in correlations by fellow or faculty raters. A comparison of mean ratings by ACGME core competencies between problem and all other residents is presented in Table 3. Results indicate significant differences in mean ratings, even after adjusting for the type I error rate using Bonferroni correction, for all competencies with differences ranging between 0.70 and 0.85 ($p < 0.001$). Although there were no significant differences in the magnitude of mean ratings between competencies, these results show a meaningful difference in ratings between problem and all other residents. The average ratings of problem residents were generally 1.5 SD below those of all other residents; a cross-classified random-effects model accounting for resident and rater effects indicated that a resident with a mean composite rating below 1.5 SD had significantly higher odds of being classified as a problem resident (odds ratio: 4.48; $p = 0.039$).

DISCUSSION

The general trends found in this study are consistent with results from the workplace-based assessment literature.[24] Findings from this study also support recent results of ITERs that produced reasonable reliability indices and demonstrated predictive validity.[19] This study provides several meaningful implications for end-of-rotation evaluations used to measure core competencies in residents at various levels of training and for identifying problem residents. Results show that compared with fellows, faculty and programme directors showed significantly greater variability in their ratings of different competencies. Given the 'failure to fail' concept raised in clinical skills assessments, the greater variability in scores assigned by faculty and programme directors may contribute to the detection of underperforming residents.[17] Although this does not suggest that faculty and programme directors necessarily assign more accurate scores, this finding provides empirical evidence that they may have greater ability to detect and discriminate differences between competencies when observing and assessing residents. To date, there has not been any response process validity evidence suggesting differences in the quality of ratings provided by fellows or by faculty observers. Furthermore, when sufficient numbers of end-of-

Table 3 Comparison of ratings of problem and other residents: descriptive statistics and t-test results

ACGME core competency	Difference*	Problem residents Rating, mean ± SD	All other residents Rating, mean ± SD
Interpersonal skills and communication	0.79	6.86 ± 0.76	7.65 ± 0.49
Medical knowledge	0.75	6.56 ± 0.47	7.31 ± 0.52
Patient care	0.85	6.76 ± 0.53	7.61 ± 0.47
Practice-based learning and improvement	0.75	6.79 ± 0.48	7.54 ± 0.48
Professionalism	0.70	7.19 ± 0.55	7.89 ± 0.47
System-based practices	0.80	6.79 ± 0.46	7.59 ± 0.48

* $p < 0.001$; all comparisons of mean ratings between problem and all other residents are based on *t-tests*. Results remain significant, even with Bonferroni adjustment for multiple comparisons. Comparisons are based on nine problem residents and 201 other residents during postgraduate year 1.
ACGME = Accreditation Council for Graduate Medical Education; SD = standard deviation.

rotation evaluations are used (14 or more evaluations per year), the reliability of end-of-rotation evaluations achieve phi coefficients of an acceptable level, supporting internal structure validity evidence within Messick's[20] unified validity framework. However, the greatest source of error was rater differences in severity, which were larger among fellows than among faculty raters. The variability between raters may also reflect differences in frame of reference among groups of raters who process ratings differently when translating the observation into numeric values.[18] These findings provide information on the value of using faculty, rather than fellows, to assess residents' core competencies. These findings also indicate the need to further train faculty and fellows to become better evaluators of resident performance.

The plot of average ratings by competency and by postgraduate year in Figure 1 presents an empirical validation of theoretical trends illustrated in the NAS. Nasca[25] emphasised that standards in professionalism need to be higher regardless of the training level of the resident, including in PGY-1 residents; this is empirically replicated in this study, in which ratings of professionalism were relatively higher than ratings of other competencies during PGY-1 and PGY-2. By PGY-3, mean ratings of all competencies converged to relatively similar scores. The increase in competency ratings over the 3 years of postgraduate training provides additional evidence of the validity of end-of-rotation evaluations.

As part of consequential validity evidence, mean ratings of competencies were significantly associated with whether or not a learner was classified as a problem resident. Although the number of problem residents in this study represented only 4.3% of the total number of residents during PGY-1, the relatively moderate, but significant correlation of 0.33 shows promise that end-of-rotation evaluations can be used to predict problem residents. Comparisons of mean ratings by competencies also showed significant differences. Although this study does not provide absolute evidence that end-of-rotation evaluation scores can be used to identify problem residents, ratings based on this system send a signal to programme directors who base their judgement of global resident performance on various sources of information; moreover, end-of-rotation evaluations can be used to inform programme directors of specific residents who may warrant further investigation. Despite the score inflation by raters, within the score ranges assigned, there was variability that supported the detection of underperforming residents. For example, based on the results of this study, programme directors may define end-of-rotation evaluation ratings of 1.5 SD below the mean ratings of all 'non-problem' residents as criteria for concern. Replications of this study should be conducted with a larger sample of problem residents to increase the precision of the results.

Institutional support and programme coordination are important for effective measurement of resident performance. A database that tracks these ratings and stores data for analysis is a basic necessity for an effective assessment system based on end-of-rotation evaluations. Even with electronic reminders and follow-up by the programme coordinator, the average number of evaluations recorded per resident per year amounted to only 14.9, and raters completed their ratings 41.3 days after the end of the observation period. Although it is unclear whether significant delays in logging ratings in NI have an impact on the accuracy of the recording of observations, this study indicates the need to investigate how this might affect the validity of scores; the methods and resources required to minimise delays should also be examined.

End-of-rotation evaluations included in this study can be viewed as components of multi-source feedback. As studies in multi-source feedback indicate the need to identify learners who are receptive to feedback and who are facing difficulties, the validity of end-of-rotation evaluations by fellows, faculty and other observers demands greater attention.[26,27] Although guidelines for using the evaluation form and ongoing rater training sessions were provided as part of faculty development, some raters may need additional training. Rater training sessions consisted of periodic meetings among core internal medicine faculty (programme directors, associate programme directors and chief residents), who discussed and recalibrated on the rating form, using criterion-based frame-of-reference training. However, a rigorous rater training session for all raters was not provided. As such, fellows may benefit from rater training in order to increase their discrimination among different levels of resident performance because efforts to improve evaluations could lead to a higher quality of resident assessment and feedback.[28] This study provides empirical evidence for the support and further development of effective assessment systems based on end-of-rotation evaluations, which includes direct observations and multi-source feedback, for postgraduate medical education.

There are some limitations to this study. This study was conducted in only one residency programme at a single institution. However, given the exploratory nature of this study and the timing of this work in relation to the NAS, these results provide meaningful implications for the field. Additional studies replicating the procedures in this study using larger and more heterogeneous samples across multiple institutions should be conducted to increase the generalisability of the results presented. Analyses pertaining to problem residents are based on programme directors' overall review of resident performance, which includes end-of-rotation evaluation scores. However, the programme director also bases the classification of the problem resident on other assessment scores, including test scores, conference attendance, and direct observation performance.

When sufficient numbers of evaluation scores are used, end-of-rotation evaluations are a useful method for measuring the growth of resident performance associated with core competencies. Furthermore, end-of-rotation evaluation scores provide preliminary evidence with which to detect and predict problem residents in subsequent postgraduate training years. Additional studies are underway to examine the link between qualitative comments and the quantitative scores reported, including whether feedback differs among different groups consisting of peers, fellows, faculty members and programme directors.

Contributors: YSP contributed to the study design, acquisition of data, analysis and interpretation of results, and wrote the primary draft of the manuscript. JR contributed to the study design and the interpretation of results. AT contributed to the study conceptualisation, the plan for data analysis, and the interpretation of results. All authors contributed to the revision of the paper and approved the final manuscript for publication.
Acknowledgements: none.
Funding: none.
Conflicts of interest: none.
Ethical approval: this study was approved by the Institutional Review Board of the University of Illinois at Chicago.

REFERENCES

1 Nasca TJ, Philibert I, Brigham T, Flynn TC. The next GME accreditation system. *N Engl J Med* 2012;**366**:1051–6.
2 Yao DC, Wright SM. The challenge of problem residents. *J Gen Intern Med* 2001;**16**:486–92.
3 American Board of Internal Medicine. Materials from Association of Program Directors in Internal Medicine (APDIM) Chief Residents' Workshop on Problem Residents, 19 April 1999, New Orleans, LA.
4 Steinert Y, Levitt C. Working with the 'problem' resident: guidelines for definition and intervention. *Fam Med* 1993;**25**:627–32.
5 Lucey CR, Boote RM. Working with problem residents: a systematic approach. In: Holmboe ES, Hawkins RE, eds. *Practical Guide to the Evaluation of Clinical Competence.* Philadelphia, PA: Mosby 2008;201–15.
6 Roberts NK, Williams RG, Klingensmith M *et al.* The case of the entitled resident: a composite case study of a resident performance problem syndrome with interdisciplinary commentary. *Med Teach* 2012;**34**:1024–32.
7 Samenow CP, Worley LL, Neufeld R, Fishel T, Swiggart WH. Transformative learning in a professional development course aimed at addressing disruptive physician behaviour: a composite case study. *Acad Med* 2013;**88**:117–23.
8 Yao DC, Wright SM. National survey of internal medicine residency programme directors regarding problem residents. *JAMA* 2000;**284**:1099–104.
9 Zbieranowski I, Takahashi SG, Verma S, Spadafora SM. Remediation of residents in difficulty: a retrospective 10-year review of the experience of a postgraduate board of examiners. *Acad Med* 2013;**88**:111–6.
10 Hauer KE, Ciccone A, Henzel TR, Katsufrakis P, Miller SH, Norcross WA, Papadakis MA, Irby DM. Remediation of the deficiencies of physicians across the continuum from medical school to practice: a thematic review of the literature. *Acad Med* 2009;**84**:1822–32.
11 Kogan JR, Holmboe ES, Hauer KE. Tools for direct observation and assessment of clinical skills of medical trainees. *JAMA* 2009;**302**:1316–26.
12 Epstein RM. Assessment in medical education. *N Engl J Med* 2007;**356**:387–96.
13 Overeem K, Wollersheim HC, Arah OA, Cruijsberg JK, Grol RP, Lombarts KM. Evaluation of physicians' professional performance: an iterative development and validation study of multi-source feedback instruments. *BMC Health Serv Res* 2012;**12**:1–11.
14 Norcini J, Burch V. Workplace-based assessment as an educational tool: AMEE guide no. 31. *Med Teach* 2007;**29**:855–71.
15 Schwind CJ, Williams RG, Boehler ML, Dunnington GL. Do individual attendings' post-rotation performance ratings detect residents' clinical performance deficiencies? *Acad Med* 2004;**79**:453–7.
16 Iobst WF, Sherbino J, ten Cate O, Richardson DL, Dath D, Swing SR, Harris P, Mungroo R, Holmboe ES, Frank JR. Competency-based medical education in postgraduate medical education. *Med Teach* 2010;**32**:651–6.

17 Cleland JA, Knight LV, Rees CE, Tracey S, Bond CM. Is it me or is it them? Factors that influence the passing of underperforming students. *Med Educ* 2008;**42**:800–9.
18 Kogan JR, Conforti L, Bernabeo E, Iobst W, Holmboe E. Opening the black box of clinical skills assessment via observation: a conceptual model. *Med Educ* 2011;**45**:1048–60.
19 Ginsburg S, Eva K, Regehr G. Do in-training evaluation reports deserve their bad reputations? A study of the reliability and predictive ability of ITER scores and narrative comments. *Acad Med* 2013;**88**:1539–44.
20 Messick S. Standards of validity and the validity of standards in performance assessment. *Educ Meas* 1995;**14**:5–8.
21 Brennan RL. *Generalizability Theory.* New York, NY: Springer-Verlag 2001.
22 Kreiter CD, Ferguson K, Lee WC, Brennan RL, Densen P. A generalisability study of a new standardised rating form used to evaluate students' clinical clerkship performances. *Acad Med* 1998;**73**:1294–8.
23 Hox J. *Multilevel Analysis: Techniques and Applications.* New York, NY: Routledge 2010.
24 Davies H, Archer J, Southgate L, Norcini J. Initial evaluation of the first year of the Foundation Assessment Programme. *Med Educ* 2009;**43**:74–81.
25 Nasca T. Graduate Medical Education in the United States: Vision and General Directions for the Next 10 Years. Association of American Medical Colleges, 7 November 2010, Washington, DC.
26 Smither JW, London M, Reilly RR. Does performance improve following multi-source feedback? A theoretical model, meta-analysis and review of empirical findings. *Pers Psychol* 2005;**58**:33–66.
27 Archer J, Swanwick T, Smith D, O'Keefe C, Cater N. Developing a multi-source feedback tool for postgraduate medical educational supervisors. *Med Teach* 2013;**35**:145–54.
28 Holmboe ES, Fiebach NH, Galaty LA, Huot S. Effectiveness of a focused educational intervention on resident evaluations from faculty: a randomised controlled trial. *J Gen Intern Med* 2001;**16**:427–34.

Received 19 June 2013; editorial comments to author 13 September 2013, 8 November 2013; accepted for publication 14 November 2013

Residents' Education

Developing an Institution-Based Assessment of Resident Communication and Interpersonal Skills

Rachel Yudkowsky, MD, MHPE, Steven M. Downing, PhD, and Leslie J. Sandlow, MD

Abstract

Purpose
The authors describe the development and validation of an institution-wide, cross-specialty assessment of residents' communication and interpersonal skills, including related components of patient care and professionalism.

Method
Residency program faculty, the department of medical education, and the Clinical Performance Center at the University of Illinois at Chicago College of Medicine collaborated to develop six standardized patient-based clinical simulations. The standardized patients rated the residents' performance. The assessment was piloted in 2003 for internal medicine and family medicine and was subsequently adapted for other specialties, including surgery, pediatrics, obstetrics–gynecology, and neurology. We present validity evidence based on the content, internal structure, relationship to other variables, feasibility, acceptability, and impact of the 2003 assessment.

Results
Seventy-nine internal medicine and family medicine residents participated in the initial administration of the assessment. A factor analysis of the 18 communication scale items resulted in two factors interpretable as "communication" and "interpersonal skills." Median internal consistency of the scale (coefficient alpha) was 0.91. Generalizability of the assessment ranged from 0.57 to 0.82 across specialties. Case-specific items provided information about group-level deficiencies. Cost of the assessment was about $250 per resident. Once the initial cases had been developed and piloted, they could be adapted for other specialties with minimal additional effort, at a cost saving of about $1,000 per program.

Conclusion
Centrally developed, institution-wide competency assessment uses resources efficiently to relieve individual programs of the need to "reinvent the wheel" and provides program directors and residents with useful information for individual and programmatic review.

Acad Med. 2006; 81:1115–1122.

The Accreditation Council for Graduate Medical Education (ACGME)[1] mandates that residency programs begin to develop valid and reliable assessments of six core competencies: medical knowledge, patient care, interpersonal and communication skills, professionalism, systems-based practice, and practice-based learning and improvement. The ACGME Website provides a toolbox of assessment methods and examples of their application, but specialty-specific application of the methods is left to the creative ingenuity of individual programs.

In this article we describe the development and validation of an institution-wide, cross-specialty assessment of communication and interpersonal skills. Program directors often lack the time, educational expertise, and funds to develop new assessment programs.[2] The challenge is particularly acute because the ACGME recommends nontraditional assessment methods, such as standardized patients (SPs), for several of the competencies. To assist programs in meeting the ACGME requirements, the University of Illinois at Chicago College of Medicine (UIC-COM) embarked on an initiative to develop institution-based competency assessments for residency programs. In this collaborative effort, the department of medical education provided the educational expertise, program faculty provided specialty-specific content expertise, the UIC-COM's Clinical Performance Center (CPC) provided simulation resources and a testing facility, and sponsoring hospitals provided funding.

As suggested by the ACGME, we measure communication and interpersonal skills (CIS) through clinical simulations in which trainees interacted with multiple SPs under realistic conditions. This type of assessment is referred to as an objective structured clinical examination (OSCE)[3]; hence, we called our assessment the CIS-OSCE. The use of SPs to assess residents' communication skills has been described previously[4–6]; our innovation is in leveraging the expertise of an institutional center to develop assessments for multiple residency programs, adapting cases across programs to conserve department and residency program resources.

The CIS-OSCE was first developed for internal medicine (IM) and family medicine (FM) residents, then modified for surgery, pediatrics, neurology, and obstetrics–gynecology. In this article we report on the first administration of the CIS-OSCE to residents in the IM and FM programs at UIC in 2003. We also report comparative data from the surgery,

Dr. Yudkowsky is assistant professor and director of the UIC Clinical Performance Center, Department of Medical Education, University of Illinois at Chicago College of Medicine, Chicago, Illinois.

Dr. Downing is associate professor, Department of Medical Education, University of Illinois at Chicago College of Medicine, Chicago, Illinois.

Dr. Sandlow is senior associate dean for Medical Education and professor and head, Department of Medical Education, University of Illinois at Chicago College of Medicine, Chicago, Illinois.

Correspondence should be addressed to Dr. Yudkowsky, Department of Medical Education MC 591, University of Illinois at Chicago College of Medicine, 808 S. Wood Street, Chicago IL 60612; telephone: (312) 996-3598; e-mail: (rachely@uic.edu).

pediatrics, neurology, and obstetrics–gynecology assessments, and we discuss the lessons learned to date.

Method

Developing the CIS-OSCE

There is an extensive evidence base for the effective assessment of communication and interpersonal skills using SPs—lay persons who are trained to simulate a patient in a consistent, reliable manner.[7,8] Studies focus on a variety of communication behaviors; we selected patient-centered communication for our conceptual framework, because this approach is effective in promoting the doctor–patient alliance, improving compliance, and increasing patient satisfaction.[9] Because communication skills are case specific,[10] residents were assessed on their ability to maintain a patient-centered approach across several different communication tasks. We selected existing cases from our own SP case library and from public-domain casebooks.[11,12] We chose tasks for their salience to clinical practice, and tasks were designed to allow residents to demonstrate their skills across a range of patient ages, genders, and problems. Residency program faculty reviewed and modified the cases to ensure appropriateness for their second- and third-year residents.

A variety of different instruments are used to assess communication and interpersonal skills. The American Board of Internal Medicine (ABIM) Patient Satisfaction Questionnaire[13] (PSQ) measures patient satisfaction with patient-centered physician behaviors. We used an expanded 17-item version of the PSQ and added one global item asking SPs whether they would choose this resident as their personal physician. The result was an 18-item instrument to assess patient-centered communication, with all items scored on a 5-point Likert scale ranging from "strongly disagree" to "strongly agree" (Appendix).

We also generated a few essential content-specific items for each scenario. For example, we added "resident elicited the history of abuse" to the domestic violence case assessment, and "resident reviewed risks of the procedure" to the informed consent case assessment. These dichotomously scored items were not included in residents' CIS scores, because

---

List 1
Accreditation Council for Graduate Medical Education competencies addressed by the CIS-OSCE at the University of Illinois at Chicago College of Medicine, 2003 to present

Interpersonal and Communication Skills
- Ability to create and sustain a therapeutic and ethically sound relationship with patients
- Ability to use effective listening skills and to elicit and provide information using effective nonverbal, explanatory, questioning, and writing skills

Patient Care
- Ability to communicate effectively and demonstrate caring and respectful behaviors when interacting with patients and their families
- Ability to gather essential and accurate information about patients
- Ability to counsel and educate patients and their families

Professionalism
- Ability to demonstrate respect, compassion, and integrity
- Ability to demonstrate a commitment to ethical principles pertaining to provision or withholding of clinical care, confidentiality of patient information, informed consent, and business practices
- Ability to demonstrate sensitivity and responsiveness to patients' culture, age, gender, and disabilities

---

they did not involve generalizable patient-centered behaviors. At the completion of the exam, residents completed a survey indicating how much previous experience they had had with each task (never, 1–3, 4–6, 7–10, or more than 10 times). Group-level scores were reported to the program director for curriculum evaluation purposes.

To generate cases for additional specialty programs, faculty from each specialty modified the IM/FM presenting scenario and task content to ensure that these were relevant to their own residents' clinical experience. CIS items and task-specific items on the SP instruments stayed the same across specialties.

Financing the exam

The cost of developing and administering the CIS-OSCE was about $250 per resident. This cost covered CPC staff time to recruit and train SPs and to set up and administer the exam, SP time for training and for the assessment itself, and the cost of generating the report. Faculty time to develop the cases was donated in kind. Funding was provided by the affiliated teaching hospitals via the GME office. There was no direct charge to the residency programs.

Once the initial cases had been developed, the assessment was adapted for new programs at a cost saving of about $1,000 per program. The decreased cost was a result of significant reductions in faculty time needed to modify cases (rather than developing cases from scratch), in staff time to set up the exam, and in SP-training time.

Conducting the exam

Each of the six SP stations consisted of a 10-minute encounter with the SP followed by a five-minute postencounter interval, during which the SP completed the CIS rating scale and case-specific item checklist. After the postencounter interval, the resident returned to the SP for five minutes of verbal feedback. This feedback focused only on the communication and interpersonal elements of the encounter, identifying effective and ineffective resident behaviors and the SPs' subjective reactions to them; no feedback was given regarding case-specific items or the clinical content of the case. At the conclusion of the six encounters, residents completed the survey, including items regarding demographic information and previous task experience.

The assessment was conducted in the UIC-COM CPC, an established SP facility. Six professional actors were trained to portray the patients, complete the rating scale, and provide feedback to the residents according to standard CPC protocols. All SPs were experienced

Table 1

Factor Loadings of CIS Scale Items in the CIS-OSCE for the Internal Medicine and Family Medicine Residency Programs at the University of Illinois at Chicago College of Medicine, 2003.

CIS scale item	Factor Communication	Interpersonal skills
Discussed options	0.841	
Made sure patient understood options	0.826	
Answered questions	0.799	
Explained what to expect next	0.784	
Explained problem	0.783	
Was frank	0.762	
Encouraged questions	0.711	
Had patience for patient's questions	0.588	0.500
Asked patient's opinion	0.544	
Was friendly		0.837
Offered a warm greeting		0.806
Showed interest in patient as person	0.518	0.755
Patient would choose as personal physician	0.561	0.738
Did not talk down to patient		0.705
Was not judgmental		0.661
Let patient tell story		0.653
Accepted feedback		0.638
Did not use jargon		0.503

veterans of several CPC-assessment programs. All encounters were videotaped, and each resident's six encounters were recorded on a single tape. At the 2003 administration of the CIS-OSCE, SP data entry was done on sheets that could later be scanned, and the resident chart note was done on paper. Since 2004, however, SP data entry has been done by computer, using WebSP,[14] a data-management system for performance assessments.

The first two sessions of the exam (each with six residents) served to pilot the assessment and the cases. We conducted separate focus groups with all residents and SPs after each session, and we used their feedback to improve the cases and conduct of the exam.

Resident and program director reports were generated by the UIC-COM testing center in 2003 and by WebSP software since 2004. Residents received reports that included their case-level scores for the CIS scale and global item and their overall CIS score across cases. Program directors received reports that included the individual resident reports, the group-level CIS scale, global and case-specific checklist scores for each case and across cases, and a group-level item analysis showing the response distribution for each case-specific item and survey item. We also provided the program director with the residents' written chart notes for optional scoring. Program directors could also opt to obtain the residents' videotapes for a number of uses, including review by the resident with or without a faculty preceptor for additional feedback, especially for residents who needed some remediation. They could also be used as part of the resident's portfolio documenting their competency.

We conducted informal interviews with each of the program directors after the completion of the CIS-OSCE to obtain their feedback and to determine how they used the results of the assessment.

Reliability/validity analysis

The 2003 administration of the CIS-OSCE to IM and FM residents served as the data source for all psychometric analyses unless otherwise specified. We did all analyses using SPSS version 11.5 (SPSS Inc., Chicago, IL).

Following recommendations by Downing[15] based on the Standards for Educational and Psychological Testing,[16] we looked for validity evidence in the content, internal structure, and response process of the exam, as well as from the relationship of CIS-OSCE scores to other variables.

We obtained validity evidence for the content of the CIS-OSCE by matching the communication tasks we assessed to the ACGME competency descriptions.[1] We explored the internal structure of the CIS scale by factor analysis. Factors were extracted using principal component analysis with Varimax rotation and Kaiser normalization based on mean item rating across cases. Internal consistency reliability of the CIS scale was estimated with coefficient alpha. We estimated reliability of the composite exam score using generalizability analysis. We did not formally assess the response process in this study; however, high interrater reliability of SPs after CPC protocol has been previously established.[17] We explored the relationship of CIS scores to other variables by examining effects of gender and level of training on CIS scores.

After the first two groups of residents completed the pilot exam, we explored the feasibility and acceptability of the assessment in focus groups with the SPs and residents. We obtained additional triangulation on acceptability and impact of the assessment from interviews with the program directors.

The University of Illinois IRB approved the study.

Results

Seventy-nine IM and FM residents participated in the initial administration of the CIS-OSCE in 2003. Of these, 41 (52%) were second-year residents, and 38 (48%) were third-year residents. Of the 70 records with identified gender, 44 residents (56%) were male.

List 1 shows the ACGME competencies assessed by the CIS-OSCE. Although we had set out to assess only communication and interpersonal skills, components of patient care and professionalism were also embedded in the challenges presented to the residents.

Table 1 shows the results of the rotated factor analysis of the 18 CIS scale items, specifying two factors, with factor loadings below 0.5 suppressed. Factor one, accounting for 34% of the variance,

Table 2
CIS-OSCE Scores for Internal Medicine and Family Medicine Residents at the University of Illinois at Chicago College of Medicine, 2003.*

Case	Global score mean† (SD)	Scale score mean‡ (SD)	Correlation scale versus global score	Coefficient alpha
Informed consent (HIV testing)	2.8 (1.1)	3.7 (0.53)	0.91**	0.92
Patient education (smoking cessation)	3.0 (1.0)	3.6 (0.62)	0.82**	0.92
Domestic violence (elder abuse)	3.3 (.91)	3.6 (0.52)	0.89**	0.92
Hx and PE (appendicitis)	3.4 (1.1)	3.8 (0.59)	0.84**	0.87
Giving bad news (mammogram)	3.8 (1.2)	4.5 (0.48)	0.84**	0.91
Treatment refusal (transfusion)	3.9 (1.1)	4.7 (0.37)	0.88**	0.88
Exam mean§	3.4 (0.4)	4.0 (0.5)	0.90 (0.04)	0.91 (0.02)
Generalizability (G)	0.72	0.66		

* n = 79; second- and third-year internal medicine and family medicine residents.
† Global item: given a choice, I would choose this resident as my personal physician. 1 = strongly disagree, 5 = strongly agree.
‡ Scale score 1 = strongly disagree, 5 = strongly agree. See Appendix for items.
§ Mean (SD) for case and global scores, median (SD) for coefficient alpha and correlations.
** Correlations significant at $P < .01$.

is interpretable as a "communication" factor, and factor two (30% of the variance) seems to represent an "interpersonal skills" factor. In fact, all four factors with eigenvalues above 1.0 were easily interpretable, including warmth (accounting for 28% of the variance), shared decision making (21%), encouraging questions (16%), and reciprocal communication (not using jargon, letting patient tell their story; 10%), for a total of 76% of variance explained.

Table 2 presents global and scale scores for the 79 IM and FM residents, as well as case-level and exam-level reliability indices. The standard error of measurement (SEM) was 0.1 for the treatment-refusal case and 0.2 for all other cases. Internal consistency reliability was high for all cases, with median coefficient alpha of 0.91 (SD 0.02). Generalizability was 0.66 based on case scores and 0.72 based on global scores. Global scores were highly correlated with case scores, with correlations ranging from 0.82 to 0.91 (median correlation 0.90, SD 0.04).

Resident gender and level of training

Female residents had higher scores than male residents. Mean global scores were 3.2 (SD 0.68) for men and 3.5 (0.65) for women (two-tailed $t = -2.21$, $df = 68$, $P = 0.03$, effect size d = 0.43). Mean CIS-scale scores were 3.9 (3.1) for men and 4.1 (0.30) for women, (two-tailed $t = -2.67$, $df = 68$, $P = 0.01$, effect size d = 0.63). However, 9 of 79 residents did not provide gender data on the survey. After a worst-case sensitivity analysis, the difference between male and female residents was no longer significant. The mean scores of second- and third-year residents were identical.

Case-specific items

Sixty-six of 68 IM residents (97%) discussed risk factors in the informed consent (HIV) case, but only 55 (81%) thoroughly explained the pros and cons of testing. In the elder-abuse case, only 50 of 63 residents (79%) elicited the history of elder abuse; when asked by the patient, 9 residents (14%) said they would confront the patient's son about the problem despite her request not to do so. One resident agreed to the patient's request not to make note of the abuse on her clinic chart.

Acceptability and feasibility

In focus groups after the first two pilot administrations of the CIS-OSCE, all residents (n = 6 for each of the two groups) felt that the SP portrayals were realistic, but some felt that there had not been enough time to play some of the scenarios through to conclusion. Residents particularly valued encounters in which they had little prior experience, such as elder abuse. All residents appreciated the verbal feedback from the SPs and felt that the assessment experience was helpful overall. In a similar debriefing of the six SPs, all the SPs felt that the encounters were realistic. Although several of the scenarios could not be played out to a conclusion, SPs felt adequately able to assess the residents' interpersonal and communication skills based on the 10-minute encounter. In the survey after the CIS-OSCE, 36 of 45 IM residents (78%) agreed or strongly agreed that the cases had allowed them to demonstrate their interpersonal and communication skills.

Experience across programs

Table 3 shows the generalizability of the CIS-OSCE for the five residency programs assessed to date: IM/FM, general surgery, pediatrics, obstetrics–gynecology, and neurology. Generalizability ranged from 0.57 to 0.82, with a median of 0.72 (SD 0.12). Results of the surgery CIS-OSCE have been previously published.[18] Detailed results of the CIS-OSCE assessments of other specialties are pending.

Educational impact

Interviews with the program director "consumers" of the CIS-OSCE indicated that the reports generated by the CIS-OSCE were acceptable and useful for both resident assessment and program evaluation. Reports were used in diverse ways (List 2). Most program directors used the individual CIS-OSCE report as a focus of discussion in their semiannual resident feedback/evaluation meetings. In some programs, residents and preceptors reviewed videotapes of the encounters to facilitate individual remediation, whereas group debriefing of residents afforded remedial instruction of frequently missed content-specific and CIS items. Program directors reported that group-level reports helped them identify curricular gaps, such as lack of experience with elder abuse, sometimes resulting in educational interventions, the outcomes of which could be assessed in the following year's exam. All programs stated that they had used the CIS-OSCE as only one component of their formative assessment process.

Table 3

Communication Task Variants Across Specialties for Residents Participating in the CIS-OSCE at the University of Illinois at Chicago College of Medicine, 2003 to Present

	Internal Med/Family Med (n=79)	Pediatrics (n=27)	General Surgery (n=22)	Neurology (n=6)	OBG (n=11)
Bad news	Mammogram	Down syndrome	Breast biopsy	Brain tumor	Mammogram
Informed consent	HIV testing	Lumbar puncture	HIV testing	HIV testing	HIV testing
Treatment refusal	Blood transfusion (GI bleed)	Transfusion (GI bleed)	Transfusion (GI bleed)	Transfusion (aplastic anemia)	Transfusion (postpartum bleeding)
Patient education	Smoking cessation	Toilet training	Smoking cessation	Smoking cessation (poststroke)	Smoking cessation (prenatal)
Domestic violence	Elder abuse	Child abuse	Elder abuse	Elder abuse	Elder abuse
H&P	Appendicitis	Appendicitis	Appendicitis	Loss of vision	Ectopic pregnancy
Generalizability	0.72	0.57	0.82	0.81	0.59

Discussion

This article describes the development and validation of an SP-based assessment of resident communication and interpersonal skills. The use of SPs to assess CIS at the resident level is not novel; our innovation is in leveraging the expertise of an institutional clinical performance center to develop assessments for multiple residency programs while conserving department and residency program resources. Accordingly, we have presented information about the CIS-OSCE at one particular program, as well as some comparative data across programs. On the basis of these data, we conclude that the institutional approach is both effective and efficient.

Validity issues

As for any assessment, validity questions are paramount. As recommended,[16] we have described validity evidence based on the CIS-OSCE's content, internal structure, response process, relationship to other variables, and consequences of the exam. Thus, the content of the CIS-OSCE included a variety of common and clinically important communication challenges and a spread of patient ages, gender, and cultural backgrounds. Cases included in this assessment reflected components of three of the six ACGME competencies. The factor analysis of our ABIM-derived scale confirmed that the expanded item set represented both communication and interpersonal skills of examinees. We ensured the response process, including data entry, test security, and rater reliability, by following standard CPC protocols for patient training and quality assurance. These sources of evidence relate to all versions of the CIS-OSCE across residency programs.

The internal structure of the exam is reflected by moderate to high internal consistency at the case level (coefficient alpha). The variation in coefficient alpha across cases reflects the variable salience of different items within different case scenarios. Generalizability (a measure of the reproducibility of exam scores under similar conditions) was sufficient for a local formative exam. Interestingly, the generalizability of the exam varied across residency programs. This variation may be attributable to changes in the cases across programs, resulting in nonequivalent forms. Alternatively, a wider range of performance among the residents in a specific program would result in a higher generalizability, even though the exam is roughly comparable across programs. Thus, the low generalizability of the pediatrics exam compared with the IM exam may be attributable to the relatively extensive modifications made in the original IM cases to adapt them for pediatric residents. After these changes, perhaps the pediatrics cases were no longer comparable with the IM cases. Alternatively, the low generalizability may simply have reflected a more consistent (less variable) level of performance among the pediatric residents. The high generalizability of the surgery and neurology resident exam, despite the low number of residents, is probably attributable to the wide range of performance observed among those residents. The implication is that the generalizability (reliability) of the assessment in a given residency program will not necessarily be predicted by the results of the generalizability analysis for a different program. Whenever possible, reliability or generalizability should be established for each context or group of examinees individually, as we have done here.

As for any performance assessment, the ideal way to increase the generalizability of the exam would be to increase the number of cases assessed. For this low-stakes formative assessment, we chose to dedicate time to feedback at the cost of limiting the number of encounters that could be accomplished in the time available. That decision could be reversed for a summative exam used for pass/fail decisions.

The relationship of the residents' performance to other variables was assessed by comparing scores across gender and level of training. Previous studies have consistently shown that women tend to achieve higher scores on SP-based assessments of communication and interpersonal skills,[19] and that little or no change occurs across levels of training.[20] Our findings of higher scores for female residents and no differences between second- and third-year residents are consistent with these studies, providing some reassurance that the CIS-OSCE is sensitive to real differences and is not spuriously sensitive to differences that do not exist. The relationship between prior experience and task comfort and performance on the CIS-OSCE has been reported elsewhere.[21] Additional studies are in progress to relate CIS-OSCE scores to other measures of resident communication, such as global ratings of communication in the context of a mini-CEX.

Finally, we estimated the predictive validity of the exam score by correlating the case-level score with the score on the global item. For a resident physician soon to be in practice, the question of whether

List 2
How residency programs at the University of Illinois at Chicago College of Medicine used the CIS-OSCE scores, 2003 to present

Individual Level
- Discussion focus during semiannual resident evaluation
- Individual review of videotapes with preceptor
- Baseline assessment of new residents
- Component of overall resident formative evaluation program

Group Level
- Needs assessment for entering resident group
- Group discussion and remediation of frequently missed items

Program Level
- Document compliance with resident review committee requirements
- Identify curricular strengths and weaknesses
- Pre/post assessments of educational interventions

---

a patient would choose him or her as a physician is consequential indeed. The high correlation of the scale score with the global score, on both the case level and exam level, confirms findings that patient-centered communication is central to patient satisfaction with a physician. However, because the scale and global ratings were provided together, the global rating may have been contaminated by the scale ratings. Better predictive validity studies would correlate CIS-OSCE scores with the same global item asked of clinic patients the following year. Formal consequential validity studies await standard setting for the exam.

Van der Vleuten[22] suggests that the acceptability, feasibility, and educational impact of an assessment are as important to evaluate as its reliability and validity. The weight of each of these characteristics depends on the specific context of the exam: "if any of these equals zero, the utility of the assessment is zero." The CIS-OSCE was acceptable to residents, standardized patients, and program directors—three important stakeholder groups. Anecdotal evidence indicated that the assessment was also well regarded by the residency review committee as a component of a program's resident competency assessment program.

The CIS-OSCE has considerable potential for educational impact[23] as an integral part of a residency program curriculum. Our residency programs are using the reports as a new focus for individual-, group-, and program-level discussion, diagnosis, and remediation. Residents' comments about the particular usefulness of scenarios with which they were *not* familiar (such as elder abuse) highlight the potential uses of the CIS-OSCE as an instructional intervention. We are planning additional follow-up studies to investigate the long-term impact on resident learning and curriculum.

The feasibility aspect of the CIS-OSCE is its particular strength. Many medical schools sponsoring multiple residency programs have an inhouse SP facility. For these institutions, the CIS-OSCE demonstrates the feasibility and efficiency of developing and implementing an SP-based core competency assessment program on an institutional level. The original cases we used were almost all existing medical student SP cases. Adapting these cases to the residency level required minimal effort, as did adapting the cases across specialty programs. Because of the similarity of cases across specialties, once the SPs were trained to the original IM version of the case, little additional training was required when switching to surgery, obstetrics–gynecology, or neurology versions. There was even considerable crossover in many of the pediatric cases, which had been more substantively modified. The rating scales, report formats, and logistical arrangements were identical across versions, providing even more savings of time and effort.

Next steps and lessons learned

Program directors tell us that case-specific items are particularly useful for program evaluation purposes. Accordingly, over the years we have added case-specific items based on "best practices" for specific scenarios. For example, the informed-consent scenario checklist now includes items on discussing risks, benefits, alternatives, and other information that must be disclosed in any informed-consent situation. We have also added a "structure of communication" scale to assess communication behaviors that are not specifically patient centered, such as "moved from open-ended to closed questions" and "uses segment summaries to check accuracy of understanding." Like the CIS scale, both the case-specific and structural communication items are constant across specialties.

Because UIC provides an institutional online cross-program core-competency curriculum in areas such as communication skills, confidentiality, and informed consent, the CIS-OSCE also provides a way to evaluate the effectiveness of components of this curriculum. Indeed, one of the things we have learned in the course of developing and administering this assessment is that one cannot disentangle CIS from other core competencies. Resident CIS must be assessed in the context of an encounter with another person in a health care–related situation. Inevitably, this situation will also contain aspects of professionalism, knowledge, and patient care. Rather than attempting to assess each competency in isolation, efforts should focus on developing a system that provides opportunities to assess competencies in various combinations and in multiple settings. The CIS-OSCE can be a valuable component of such a system.

We are currently developing a second set of six cases for the CIS-OSCE, including new challenges, such as obtaining advance directives, notification of patient death, and discussing a medical mistake. These "Form B" cases will be administered on alternate years, providing the opportunity to evaluate remediation at the individual resident level as well as group-level curricular interventions.

Limitations

The CIS-OSCE has been piloted in only one institution, with a limited number of residency programs and residents. Interrater reliability was not established. Several residents did not provide gender data on the survey, and a worst-case sensitivity analysis did not result in a significant difference between genders. Therefore, the gender-difference finding will need to be replicated in future studies with full gender data. The acceptable level of generalizability found when assessing our residents may not be replicated in programs with more homogenous levels of performance. Some specialties may require more substantive modification of the scenarios, with unpredictable effects on the psychometric properties of the assessment. The psychometric properties reported for the IM/FM exam are not necessarily transferable across residency programs. Reliability indices were acceptable for a local, formative exam, but would not be acceptable for a high-stakes summative exam. We have not set pass/fail standards for the exam, and we do not recommend that it be used summatively at this stage. However, as we accumulate more data about resident performance both within and across programs, standard-setting exercises with both faculty and SPs will provide guidelines to residency programs wishing to use the CIS-OSCE as a component of their resident-promotion decision process.

The institutional cost savings achieved by assessing CIS across specialties might not be realized in assessing skills more dependent on specialty-specific content knowledge (e.g., diagnostic reasoning or disease management). On the other hand, cross-specialty competencies such as professionalism, practice-based learning, and systems-based practice are good candidates for a centrally coordinated assessment program such as ours.

Conclusion

The ACGME lists SPs and OSCEs as the preferred methods for demonstrating resident competence in interpersonal and communication skills. Cases developed to elicit and assess communication and interpersonal skills in one program can be modified across specialties with minimal additional effort, conserving faculty time and development costs. Institutional-level competency assessments use resources efficiently to relieve individual programs of the need to "reinvent the wheel," and provide program directors and residents with useful information for individual and programmatic review.

References

1 Accreditation Council for Graduate Medical Education. Outcome project. Chicago, IL: Accreditation Council for Graduate Medical Education; 2005. Available at: ⟨http://www.acgme.org/Outcome⟩. Accessed August 24, 2006.

2 Heard JK, Allen RM, Clardy J. Assessing the needs of residency program directors to meet the ACGME general competencies. Acad Med. 2002;77:750.

3 Harden RM, Stevenson M, Downie WW, Wilson GN. Asessment of clinical competence using objective structured examination. BMJ. 1975;1:447–451.

4 Donnelly MB, Sloan D, Plymale M, Schwarz R. Assessment of residents interpersonal skills by faculty proctors and standardized patients: a psychometric analysis. Acad Med. 2000; 75(10 Suppl):S93–S95.

5 Wilson BE. Performance-based assessment of internal medicine interns: evaluation of baseline clinical and communications skills. Acad Med. 2002;77:1158.

6 Roth CS, Watson KV, Harris IB. A communication assessment and skill-building exercise (CASE) for first-year residents. Acad Med. 2002;77:746–747.

7 Barrows HS. An overview of the uses of standardized patients for teaching and evaluating clinical skills. Acad Med. 1993;68: 443–451.

8 Aspegren K. BEME guide no. 2: teaching and learning communication skills in medicine—a review with quality grading of articles. Med Teach. 1999;21:563–570.

9 Stewart M, Brown JB, Weston WW, McWhinney IR, McWilliam CL, Freeman TR. Patient-Centered Medicine: Transforming the Clinical Method. Thousand Oaks, California: Sage; 1995.

10 Hodges B, Turnbull J, Cohen R, Bienenstock A, Norman G. Evaluating communication skills in the objective structured clinical examination format: reliability and generalizability. Med Educ. 1996;30:38–43.

11 Yedidia MJ, Gillespie CC, Kachur E, et al. Effect of communications training on medical student performance. JAMA. 2003; 290:1157–1165.

12 Schimpfhauser FT, Sultz H, Zinnerstrom KH, Anderson DR. Communication cases involving standardized patients for medical student and resident training. Buffalo, NY: The State University of New York at Buffalo School of Medicine and Biomedical Sciences; 2000.

13 American Board of Internal Medicine. Final report on the patient satisfaction questionnaire project. ABIM internal document; 1989.

14 WebSP LIONIS, Inc. 2002–2005. Available at: ⟨http://lionis.net⟩. Accessed August 24, 2006.

15 Downing SM. Validity: on the meaningful interpretation of assessment data. Med Educ. 2003;37:830–837.

16 American Educational Research Association, American Psychological Association, National Council on Measurement in Education. Standards for educational and psychological testing. Washington DC: American Eductional Research Association; 1999.

17 Yudkowsky R, Downing S, Klamen D, Valaski M, Eulenberg B, Popa M. Assessing the head-to-toe physical examinations skills of medical students. Med Teach. 2004;26:415–419.

18 Yudkowsky R, Alseidi A, Cintron J. Beyond fulfilling the core competencies: an objective structured clinical examination to assess communication and interpersonal skills in a surgical residency. Curr Surg. 2004;61:499–503.

19 Roter DL, Hall JA, Aoki Y. Physician gender effects in medical communication: a meta-analytic review. JAMA. 2002;288:756–764.

20 Mangione S, Kand GC, Caruso JW, Gennella JS, Nasca TJ, Hojat M. Assessment of empathy in different years of internal medicine training. Med Teach. 2002;24:370–373.

21 Yudkowsky R, Downing SM, Ommert D. Prior experiences associated with residents' scores on a communication and interpersonal skill OSCE. Patient Educ Couns. Patient Educ Couns. 2006;62:368–373.

22 van der Vleuten CPM. The assessment of professional competence: developments, research and practical implications. Adv Health Sci Educ. 1996;:41–67.

23 van der Vleuten CPM, Schuwirth LWT. Asessing professional competence: from methods to programmes. Med Educ. 2005;39: 309–317.

Appendix
Patient-Centered Communication and Interpersonal Skills (CIS) Scale, University of Illinois at Chicago College of Medicine CIS-OSCE

Patient-Centered Communication

- I felt you were telling me everything; being truthful, up front, and frank; not keeping things from me.
- I felt that you discussed options with me.
- I felt you made sure that I understood those options.
- I felt you asked my opinion, allowing me to make my own decision.
- I felt you encouraged me to ask questions.
- I felt you answered my questions, never avoiding them.
- I felt you clearly explained what I needed to know about my problem; how and why it occurred.
- I felt you clearly explained what I should expect next.

Interpersonal Skills: Personal Warmth and Sensitive Respect

- I felt you greeted me warmly upon entering the room.
- I felt you were friendly throughout the encounter. You were never crabby or rude to me.
- I felt that you treated me like we were on the same level. You never "talked down" to me or treated me like a child.
- I felt you let me tell my story and were careful not to interrupt me while I was speaking.
- I felt you showed interest in me as a "person." You never acted bored or ignored what I had to say.
- I felt you were patient when I asked questions
- I felt you were careful to use plain language and not medical jargon when speaking to me.
- I felt you approached sensitive/difficult subject matters with sensitivity and without being judgmental.
- I felt the resident displayed a positive attitude during the verbal feedback session.

Global Item

- Given a choice, I would choose this resident as my personal physician.

Source: Yudkowsky R, Alseidi A, Cintron J: Beyond fulfilling the core competencies: an objective structured clinical examination to assess communication and interpersonal skills in a surgical residency. Curr Surg. 2004;61:499–503.

A hypothesis-driven physical examination learning and assessment procedure for medical students: initial validity evidence

Rachel Yudkowsky,[1] Junji Otaki,[2] Tali Lowenstein,[1] Janet Riddle,[1] Hiroshi Nishigori[3] & Georges Bordage[1]

CONTEXT Diagnostic accuracy is maximised by having clinical signs and diagnostic hypotheses in mind during the physical examination (PE). This diagnostic reasoning approach contrasts with the rote, hypothesis-free screening PE learned by many medical students.
A hypothesis-driven PE (HDPE) learning and assessment procedure was developed to provide targeted practice and assessment in anticipating, eliciting and interpreting critical aspects of the PE in the context of diagnostic challenges.

OBJECTIVES This study was designed to obtain initial content validity evidence, performance and reliability estimates, and impact data for the HDPE procedure.

METHODS Nineteen clinical scenarios were developed, covering 160 PE manoeuvres. A total of 66 Year 3 medical students prepared for and encountered three clinical scenarios during required formative assessments. For each case, students listed anticipated positive PE findings for two plausible diagnoses before examining the patient; examined a standardised patient (SP) simulating one of the diagnoses; received immediate feedback from the SP, and documented their findings and working diagnosis. The same students later encountered some of the scenarios during their Year 4 clinical skills examination.

RESULTS On average, Year 3 students anticipated 65% of the positive findings, correctly performed 88% of the PE manoeuvres and documented 61% of the findings. Year 4 students anticipated and elicited fewer findings overall, but achieved proportionally more discriminating findings, thereby more efficiently achieving a diagnostic accuracy equivalent to that of students in Year 3. Year 4 students performed better on cases on which they had received feedback as Year 3 students. Twelve cases would provide a reliability of 0.80, based on discriminating checklist items only.

CONCLUSIONS The HDPE provided medical students with a thoughtful, deliberate approach to learning and assessing PE skills in a valid and reliable manner.

Medical Education 2009: 43: 729–740
doi:10.1111/j.1365-2923.2009.03379.x

[1]Department of Medical Education, College of Medicine, University of Illinois at Chicago, Chicago, Illinois, USA
[2]Department of General Medicine and Primary Care, Tokyo Medical University Hospital, Tokyo, Japan
[3]International Research Centre for Medical Education, University of Tokyo, Tokyo, Japan

Correspondence: Rachel Yudkowsky MD, MHPE, Department of Medical Education 963 CME, M/C 591, University of Illinois at Chicago College of Medicine, 808 South Wood Street, Chicago, Illinois 60612, USA. Tel: 00 1 312 996 3598; Fax: 00 1 312 413 2048; E-mail: rachely@uic.edu

INTRODUCTION

The physical examination (PE) is an essential component of almost all clinical encounters, providing data that are critical to the diagnosis and management of the patient. At the University of Illinois at Chicago College of Medicine, as in many other medical schools, students learn to perform PE manoeuvres in system-based workshops during the pre-clinical years and later assemble these manoeuvres into a head-to-toe (HTT) screening PE performed on a healthy patient with no presenting complaint.[1] A checklist containing 140 PE manoeuvres (e.g. 'Test cranial nerve VII motor function [upper division] by asking patient to close his eyes as student tries to force the eyelids open') is then used to assess the student's mastery of the HTT PE prior to the beginning of clinical rotations. Although an HTT assessment ensures that students are prepared to examine patients during their clerkships, it is not, as suggested by van der Vleuten and Schuwirth,[2,3] well integrated into the larger programme of clinical studies. The PE manoeuvres are not linked to patient complaints and students do not learn to appreciate how an abnormal finding would appear or what it might mean. This de-contextualisation may help explain why students have difficulty in selecting relevant PE manoeuvres and interpreting patient findings to reach a diagnosis later in their clerkships.[4-7] Instead of facilitating diagnostic reasoning, an HTT assessment of PE skills encourages students to perform a rote PE without thinking, thereby negatively impacting learning and compromising the consequential validity of the assessment.[3,8] It also tends to minimise the diagnostic function of the PE.[9] The overall goal of this project was to develop a PE assessment procedure that would support learning by embedding PE manoeuvres within diagnostic reasoning tasks and providing a situated learning approach[10] while retaining the focus on the PE.

Diagnostic reasoning is a complex skill which is comprised of several constituent skills, such as eliciting the history, generating diagnostic hypotheses, anticipating PE findings to confirm or refute hypotheses, performing PE manoeuvres to elicit findings, and interpreting patient findings to reach a working diagnosis or generate new hypotheses. Van Merriënboer and colleagues[11,12] have proposed an instructional framework for learning complex skills comprised of an integrated and co-ordinated set of recurrent and non-recurrent constituent skills. Recurrent skills, such as PE manoeuvres, are invariant across problems: for example, cardiac auscultation is performed in the same manner across cases. Non-recurrent skills, such as generating hypotheses and interpreting patient findings, vary across problem situations and are dependent on cognitive strategies to guide reasoning and problem solving. Part-task practice of recurring skills, such as PE manoeuvres, can help novices automate PE procedures but does not promote the integration of the recurring skills into the complex task as a whole. Instead of teaching novices constituent skills in isolation, as with the HTT approach, instructors can regulate the complexity of whole-task practice by controlling the number of skills to be practised and the interactions allowed between skills by embedding, for instance, the performance of PE manoeuvres within a patient encounter (the 'whole task') in a context that involves a controlled history and limited diagnostic challenge.

A variety of analytical and non-analytical strategies are involved in the development of diagnostic reasoning.[13-15] In deciding which constituent tasks to include in a learning and assessment procedure for PE manoeuvres, we considered research on the recognition of clinical signs, on learning prototypical disorders, and on the effect of highlighting discriminating features for clinical diagnosis. Other strategies and more complex cases can be added in more advanced physical diagnosis courses and in other elements of the curriculum.

Norman and collaborators[16-18] have shown that PE signs are more readily identified when the doctor has the correct diagnosis or differential diagnosis in mind, a process they called 'co-selection' of diagnoses and signs. When the doctor is 'just looking', simply being thorough, or going through the motions mechanically, as in the HTT examination, the number of signs recognised decreases significantly. Thus learning PE manoeuvres could be optimised by incorporating the constituent tasks of *anticipating* and *recognising* PE findings within a relevant diagnostic task. By contrast, the complexity of the learner's task can be controlled by focusing on a limited number of prototypical diagnoses, consistent with Bordage's findings[19] that categories of disorders are better learned when the initial exposure is limited to a few prototypical members of the category rather than a broad range of disorders.

Wigton and others[20-23] have shown that correct diagnosis most often rests on a limited number of key findings that discriminate between competing diagnoses (e.g. localised pain present in diagnosis A but absent in diagnosis B). Mangione and Pietzman[5] and St-Clair et al.[7] also advocate a selective approach to physical diagnosis, concentrating on key discriminating manoeuvres and findings. Assessment checklists that focus on discriminating items would encourage students to develop more efficient PE strategies and facilitate reliable assessment by eliminating PE items that do not reflect increasing diagnostic expertise. As Ericsson et al. demonstrated through their theory of expertise,[24] or deliberate mixed practice with feedback, Wigton et al. showed that giving cognitive feedback to medical students is most likely to bring about changes in practice.[25]

The purpose of this study was to develop and gather initial validity evidence for a hypothesis-driven PE (HDPE) assessment of Year 3 medical students, including content validation, performance and reliability estimates of scores, and impact on learning; specific hypotheses will be presented after the procedure has been described in more detail.

METHODS

Materials

The HTT manoeuvres at the University of Illinois at Chicago were grouped around 19 presenting complaints chosen to include all anatomical regions of the body. Twenty manoeuvres were added to address specific complaints, resulting in a total of 160 PE items. Each PE manoeuvre is represented at least once; some appear two or three times across different complaints, if clinically appropriate. For each complaint, three of the authors (JO, GB, HN) prepared a set of three to four prototypical diagnoses that could be associated with the complaint, a list of relevant PE manoeuvres highlighting the findings that best discriminate between the diagnoses, and a sample clinical scenario consistent with two of the possible diagnoses (Appendix S1). Prototypical diagnoses were selected to cover a range of pathophysiological aetiologies for each complaint, which represented a range that might serve as a solid foundation for a medical student. The scenarios are brief and deliberately ambiguous in order to render several hypotheses plausible and ensure that the final diagnosis is based on physical findings rather than history.

Content validation

An international panel of eight doctors from the USA, Canada, Japan, Belgium and Switzerland, selected on the basis of their experience with teaching the physical examination, was established. These doctors were asked to independently evaluate the 19 sets of complaints, differential diagnoses and manoeuvres for plausibility, relevance and completeness. They were also asked to provide additional references related to the discriminating value of the signs in order to select as many manoeuvres and findings for which there were reproducibility, sensitivity and specificity data.[26] The judges received a stipend for their participation. Members of the research team (RY, TL, JR, GB) later reviewed each comment and agreed upon appropriate revisions.

Procedure

Guided by the conceptual frameworks presented earlier, an HDPE learning and assessment procedure was developed around the diagnostic challenges provided by the 19 presenting complaints. During the learning phase, the students are given a study guide with which to compare and contrast the PE findings for the prototypical diagnoses for each complaint (i.e. a two-dimensional grid with diagnoses at the top and manoeuvres on the left-hand side). To foster meaningful learning, the students are asked to identify on their own the manoeuvres that will best discriminate among pairs of diagnoses (e.g. a normal test for cranial nerve VII [raising eyebrow] in a central facial palsy compared with an abnormal finding for a Bell's palsy). (The study guide is available from the authors upon request.)

During the assessment phase, the student encounters a number of standardised patients (SPs) (the whole task), each of whom presents with one of the complaints. The assessment focuses on five constituent tasks of diagnostic reasoning, which are listed below. Before each encounter, the student receives a brief history (scenario) and two of the prototypical diagnoses, both plausible in the context of the scenario. Before seeing the SP, the student is asked (i) to *anticipate* in writing the positive findings for each diagnosis. The student then enters the examination room and (ii) *elicits* findings by selecting and executing the relevant PE manoeuvres for the complaint and differentiating between the two diagnoses; when this is done, the student (iii) *interprets* the clinical findings by expressing his or her working diagnosis to the SP. Specialised SPs portray the PE findings appropriate to one of the two diagnoses in each scenario and assess and teach the PE manoeuvres associated with the case. The student is expected to relate to the SP in a professional manner, but no additional history is available from the SP during the PE. Physical examination manoeuvres that are incorrectly performed by the student do not elicit findings from the SP. Simulator models are sometimes used to complement the SPs by providing realistic clinical findings that cannot be simulated by the SP, such as abnormal lung sounds or retinal abnormalities. After the initial interpretation of the findings by the student, the SP provides immediate corrective feedback on the execution of the PE manoeuvres and prompts the student to redo any incorrectly performed manoeuvres and perform any omitted manoeuvres. This ensures that each student has the opportunity to elicit all embedded findings. The student is then asked by the SP to redo the incorrect or omitted manoeuvres and (iv) to *revise* his or her working diagnosis based on any additional findings; this revised diagnosis is called the 'prompted diagnosis', as opposed to the 'unprompted diagnosis' described in (iii) above. Finally, upon exiting the room, the student is asked (v) to *document* the clinical findings associated with his or her working diagnosis. The uniqueness of the HDPE assessment procedure is its facility to embed the learning and assessment of PE skills within a clinical reasoning task of carefully limited complexity. As such, it can serve as a model for constructing similarly graded assessments of other complex skills; for example, more advanced students can be asked to differentiate between more than two competing diagnoses or to generate the diagnoses from a more elaborate history without help.

Scoring

The five constituent tasks for each case are scored according to two algorithms. The first scoring method is based only on the performance of manoeuvres and signs that discriminated between the two diagnoses provided for that case. The second is based on all the manoeuvres and signs included in the study guide for that complaint, including items that were relevant to other prototypical diagnoses for that complaint but not salient to the specific scenario and differential provided for testing.

Pilot testing

The HDPE procedure was piloted with two groups of Year 3 medical students, using one group to refine the materials and procedures and another to obtain performance and reliability estimates.

The Year 3 medical students had completed 2 years of pre-clinical studies during which they demonstrated mastery of the HTT examination. Year 3 consists of a series of core clerkships in which students conduct a large number of workups on hospitalised and ambulatory patients and document the history, physical examination, differential diagnosis and plan, with feedback from residents and faculty. Each group of Year 3 students beginning a 1-month ambulatory clerkship in internal medicine (IM) were given a preparatory study guide covering six of 18 presenting complaints (complaint 19, heart murmur, was excluded from the study because at the time we had no model to simulate cardiovascular findings). Students were asked to compare and contrast the discriminating findings for each PE manoeuvre across the diagnostic options for each of the six complaints. No coaching or feedback were provided with the study guide. Each group of students received a different subset of complaints, systematically selected to represent different organ systems, such that all 18 complaints were piloted several times over the course of the year.

Towards the end of the 1-month rotation, students were assessed on their ability to use the PE to diagnose patients with complaints contained in their study guide. Students encountered the SPs individually during a mandatory formative assessment of the ambulatory rotation (Table 1).

At the end of the assessment session, students completed a questionnaire regarding their use of the study guide and their preparation for the examination. About a week later, students convened in small groups with a faculty member to review (debrief) the technical and clinical reasoning challenges associated with each case.

Students who completed the IM ambulatory clerkship from July to December 2005 comprised the pilot group. Each student encountered two SPs, providing feedback for additional refinement of the cases. Students who completed the clerkship between January and June 2006 encountered three SPs and provided data for the reliability studies (Figure 1).

Impact on learning

We evaluated the impact of the HDPE procedure on learning and retention by assessing the performance of the same students in a mandatory summative clinical skills examination during the summer of their Year 4, up to 1 year after the initial HDPE experience. Six of the 18 cases piloted during the Year 3 studies were selected for the Year 4 examination, including: shoulder pain; wrist pain; back pain; ankle pain; hearing loss, and blurred vision. The cases were chosen because they could be completed during the

Table 1 Hypothesis-driven physical examination procedures for Year 3 and 4 medical students

Year 3, weeks 1–2: preparation	Prepare with self-study guide: identify expected findings for a short list of PE manoeuvres across three to four prototypical diagnoses
Year 3, week 3: formative assessment	
(A) Immediately before entering room for encounter with SP	(1) Read clinical vignette and two competing diagnoses. List anticipated findings for each of the diagnoses
(B) During encounter with SP	(2) Select and correctly perform appropriate PE manoeuvres to elicit PE findings from SP
	(3) Interpret the findings and commit to a working diagnosis
	(4) SP corrects any incorrectly performed manoeuvres and prompts for and teaches any omitted manoeuvres. Student performs corrected and omitted manoeuvres, eliciting remaining findings. Commit to a revised final (prompted) diagnosis
(C) After encounter with SP	(5) Document findings that support diagnosis
Year 3, week 4: debriefing	Group workshop to review clinical reasoning strategies
Year 4: clinical skills examination	
(A) Immediately before entering room for encounter with SP	(1) Read clinical vignette and two competing diagnoses. List anticipated findings for each of the diagnoses
(B) During encounter with SP	(2) Select and correctly perform appropriate PE manoeuvres to elicit PE findings from SP
	(3) Interpret the findings and commit to a working diagnosis
(C) After encounter with SP	(4) Document findings that support diagnosis

PE = physical examination; SP = standardised patient

time allotted for the examination and because of SP training considerations. Each student encountered three of the cases during their Year 4 examination. Consequently, the Year 4 students might have one of three levels of prior experience with a case, represented by no prior experience with the case as a Year 3 student; preparation of the presenting complaint as one of the six presented in the study guide, but without testing or any immediate SP feedback, or testing on the case as a Year 3 student and receipt of immediate SP feedback. Year 4 students were not prompted to correct inappropriately executed or omitted manoeuvres or asked to revise their working diagnoses (step iv above).

Hypotheses

The HDPE procedure allowed us to test hypotheses that extend our understanding of performance assessments for medical education. Because a thoughtful HDPE should focus on eliciting findings that best discriminate between competing diagnoses rather than simply accumulating findings in the absence of a diagnostic task, we hypothesised that performance on the subset of discriminating PE manoeuvres would be a more reliable measure than performance on the entire set of manoeuvres listed for a given complaint. If true, this would have important implications for the construction of effective PE checklists for SP-based performance tests. We also hypothesised that long-term retention (learning) would be enhanced by the experience of performing the HDPE and receiving immediate feedback, consistent with the testing effect described in cognitive psychology for written tests.[27,28]

Analyses

We calculated the mean percent score for each constituent task in each case and across all 18 cases for Year 3 students in the reliability study and Year 4 students in the impact study. Student's t-tests were used to assess differences between scores of students in Years 3 and 4 and ANOVA for differences across

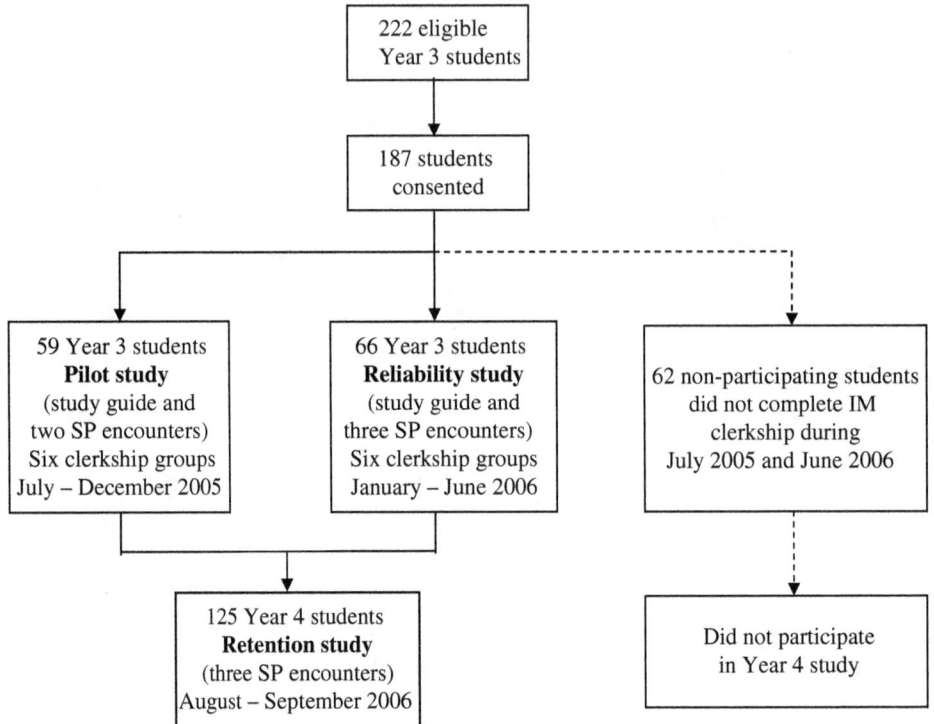

Figure 1 Flow diagram showing students participating in the pilot, reliability and retention studies for the hypothesis-driven physical examination assessment procedure. SP = standardised patient; IM = internal medicine

levels of experience with the cases as a Year 4 student. We conducted a generalisability study using Year 3 student scores on four clinical tasks (anticipation, elicitation, working diagnosis and documentation) as the items for each case, using an 'items crossed with cases nested in persons' design (i × c : p), with items and cases as fixed and random facets, respectively. Using G-String II (3.1.1),[29] we computed the phi (φ) coefficient and estimated the number of cases that would be needed to reach a generalisability of 0.80, sufficient for a moderate-stakes, criterion-based local examination.

RESULTS

Content validation

The panel of judges made numerous suggestions to improve the set of prototypical diagnoses and corresponding PE manoeuvres. Their suggestions led to a total of 226 modifications to the initial set of complaints, scenarios and manoeuvres. The great majority of changes represented slight refinements and fine-tuning to the initial set of complaints and manoeuvres (e.g. changing the patient's age to better fit the differential diagnosis). However, some of the recommendations were substantial and led to significant modifications. The most frequent changes affected the manoeuvres and signs (65.4%) and the diagnoses (20.7%) (e.g. refining, deleting or adding discriminating manoeuvres or modifying some of the prototypical diagnoses). Special attention was paid to selecting manoeuvres and findings for which reproducibility, sensitivity and specificity data were available. The most important change, however, occurred in the general approach used to group the manoeuvres around chief complaints. Initially, the manoeuvres and complaints represented distinct anatomical regions, such as the neck or the chest, and the PE was limited to that anatomical region. Both the judges and the students who pilot-tested the cases suggested that the manoeuvres be organised around diagnoses within complaints. For example, if the student is examining the lungs for congestive heart failure, manoeuvres relevant to the neck jugular venous pulse (JVP) and the lower limbs (pedal oedema) should also be included to create a diagnostically logical PE. Changes were made to accommodate the shift from an anatomic to a diagnostic organisation. The final set of

Table 2 Mean proportions (standard deviations in parentheses) of signs anticipated, physical examination manoeuvres elicited, findings documented and correct diagnoses achieved by Year 3 students

Complaints	n	Signs anticipated	Physical examination elicitation	Findings documented	Diagnosis before prompting
Upper abdominal pain	11	0.73 (0.20)	0.92 (0.16)	1.00 (0.00)	1.00 (0.00)
Lower abdominal pain	9	0.93 (0.09)	0.94 (0.05)	1.00 (0.00)	1.00 (0.00)
Back pain	11	0.42 (0.13)	0.85 (0.17)	0.66 (0.11)	0.91 (0.30)
Blurred vision	9	0.67 (0.22)	0.93 (0.09)	0.75 (0.25)	1.00 (0.00)
Claudication	12	0.52 (0.24)	0.87 (0.21)	0.56 (0.36)	0.58 (0.51)
Funny feeling face	9	0.65 (0.25)	0.95 (0.10)	0.83 (0.35)	0.78 (0.44)
Hearing loss	12	0.75 (0.22)	0.78 (0.13)	0.68 (0.26)	0.75 (0.45)
Itchy scalp	8	0.49 (0.26)	1.00 (0.00)	0.63 (0.52)	0.63 (0.52)
Lump in breast	11	0.64 (0.16)	0.95 (0.08)	0.61 (0.36)	0.82 (0.40)
Painful ankle	8	0.52 (0.21)	1.00 (0.00)	0.28 (0.36)	0.75 (0.46)
Painful hip	11	0.53 (0.20)	0.93 (0.11)	0.16 (0.06)	1.00 (0.00)
Painful shoulder	11	0.36 (0.22)	0.76 (0.20)	0.36 (0.28)	0.36 (0.50)
Painful wrist	15	0.71 (0.19)	0.91 (0.08)	0.67 (0.18)	1.00 (0.00)
Shortness of breath	15	0.78 (0.16)	0.93 (0.11)	0.87 (0.30)	0.87 (0.35)
Sore knee	12	0.91 (0.13)	0.60 (0.25)	0.72 (0.24)	0.75 (0.45)
Stuffy nose and sore throat	15	0.68 (0.19)	0.93 (0.07)	0.11 (0.21)	0.40 (0.51)
Swollen neck and fatigue	11	0.66 (0.30)	0.79 (0.23)	1.00 (0.00)	0.27 (0.47)
Unsteadiness	8	0.63 (0.20)	0.93 (0.09)	0.54 (0.32)	0.88 (0.35)
All cases (total)	66	0.65 (0.24)	0.88 (0.16)	0.61 (0.36)	0.76 (0.43)

complaints and prototypical diagnoses is presented in Table S1.

Performance estimates

Of the Year 3 students in the reliability study ($n = 66$), 86% reported having used the study guide to prepare for the assessment. On average, students anticipated 65% of the signs, performed 88% of the PE manoeuvres and documented 61% of the findings. Diagnostic accuracy was 76% after the unprompted portion of the PE (step iii) and 82% after the prompted portion of the PE (step iv; see Table 2). Discriminating manoeuvres comprised 57% of manoeuvres overall; students elicited 83% of the discriminating manoeuvres compared with 88% of all manoeuvres (paired t-test = -4.752, $P < 0.001$). Anticipation and documentation of the subset of discriminating items did not significantly differ from those for all items.

Although only 12 out of 195 students (6%) successfully completed all three tasks of anticipation, elicitation and interpretation of the findings, about half ($n = 91$, 47%) reached the correct diagnosis despite incomplete anticipation of signs and execution of manoeuvres, as did almost a fifth of the students ($n = 35$; 18%) with incomplete anticipation and good execution of manoeuvres. Another fifth (17%) were unsuccessful in all three tasks (Table 3).

Reliability studies

Reliability calculations were based on 61 of 66 Year 3 students from whom complete reliability datasets were available. The generalisability (φ) reliability coefficient across three cases was 0.50 when scoring was based on the discriminating findings and PE manoeuvres, compared with 0.35 when scoring was based on all possible findings and PE manoeuvres. A D study showed that a reliability of 0.80 could be reached with 12 cases using only discriminating item scores, compared with 22 cases using scores from all items.

Impact on learning

The 125 Year 3 students from the pilot and reliability studies subsequently encountered three of six cases

Table 3 Number and percentage of Year 3 student encounters according to various performance profiles (anticipation, execution and interpretation)

	Profile type	n	%
A	All correct: anticipation, manoeuvres, interpretation	12	6
B	Good anticipation and manoeuvres, wrong interpretation	4	2
C	Good anticipation, incomplete manoeuvres, correct interpretation	9	5
D	Good anticipation, incomplete manoeuvres, wrong interpretation	1	1
E	Incomplete anticipation, incomplete manoeuvres, correct interpretation	91	47
F	Incomplete anticipation, good manoeuvres, correct interpretation	35	18
G	Incomplete anticipation, good manoeuvres, wrong interpretation	10	5
H	All incorrect: incomplete anticipation, incomplete manoeuvres, wrong interpretation	33	17
	Total	195	100

during their Year 4 clinical skills examination, about 7 months after their initial Year 3 experience (range 2–13 months). In almost all encounters (98%), patients were portrayed by different SPs than in the Year 3 studies. Although Year 4 students anticipated, elicited and documented fewer signs than Year 3 students, more than half of the manoeuvres performed by Year 4 students were discriminating manoeuvres (59%), whereas less than half (49%) of the manoeuvres performed by Year 3 students were discriminating (t-test = − 3.28, P = 0.001). There was no significant difference in diagnostic accuracy on the six cases between students in Year 3 (accuracy of unprompted diagnosis was 0.80, standard deviation [SD] = 0.29) and Year 4 (accuracy 0.71, SD = 0.37) (t = − 2.78, P = 0.18).

Year 3 students with incorrect diagnoses had difficulty interpreting discriminating signs: almost all the Year 3 students (96%) elicited discriminating findings by performing at least one discriminating manoeuvre correctly and two-thirds (69%) elicited at least half of the discriminating signs correctly, but did not interpret the findings correctly to reach the correct diagnosis. Year 4 students with incorrect diagnoses had trouble eliciting findings: they performed about half (49%) of their discriminating manoeuvres incorrectly, thus failing to elicit all the discriminating signs (Table 4).

There was a significant linear increase in performance across the three levels of experience for the number of signs anticipated, discriminating signs anticipated, PE manoeuvres performed correctly, discriminating PE items performed correctly, and correct diagnosis (linear contrast F = 5.6, 3.9, 8.1, 5.8, 6.3, respectively; all P < 0.05). For example, the correct diagnosis was reached by 68% of the students with no prior experience, 73% of students who prepared with the study guide, and 85% of students who were tested on the case in Year 3 (linear contrast F = 6.3; P = 0.01).

DISCUSSION

The results from these content validation and reliability and impact studies indicate that the HDPE procedure can be used to learn and assess PE skills in a valid and reliable manner while encouraging a thoughtful approach towards the use of PE in the service of diagnostic reasoning.

The content validation procedure proved to be extremely valuable, not only in improving the editorial quality of the material, but also in obtaining a greater alignment between the nature of the material used and the conceptual basis of the HDPE procedure. For example, the external judges suggested shifting from a purely anatomical grouping of the PE manoeuvres to a multi-system grouping that is more clinically relevant to the complaint and the prototypical diagnoses. The judges were also helpful in suggesting more relevant discriminating manoeuvres and in providing references. As more studies are conducted on the discriminating power of PE findings, these can be incorporated into the reference list for each complaint. The take-home message states that once the designer has developed a 'best' set of materials, he should show it to external judges for feedback. They will look at the material with fresh eyes and make valuable suggestions, even in cases the designer believes to be complete.

Table 4 Mean proportions (standard deviations in parentheses) of students with correct and incorrect working diagnoses according to skills measured for Year 3 (n = 66) and Year 4 (n = 125) students

	Students with correct diagnosis	Students with incorrect diagnosis
Year 3 students	n = 147 encounters	n = 48 encounters
All signs anticipated	0.68 (23)*	0.56 (26)*
Discriminating signs anticipated	0.69 (25)	0.67 (27)
PE manoeuvres performed	0.91 (14)*	0.80 (21)*
Discriminating PE manoeuvres performed	0.87 (18)*	0.71 (28)*
Discriminating PE manoeuvres performed correctly	0.97 (09)*	0.89 (18)*
Year 4 students	n = 268 encounters	n = 102 encounters
All signs anticipated	0.39 (19)	0.37 (22)
Discriminating signs anticipated	0.56 (23)	0.55 (25)
PE manoeuvres performed	0.64 (20)*	0.58 (18)*
Discriminating PE manoeuvres performed	0.68 (28)†	0.75 (30)†
Discriminating PE manoeuvres correctly	0.69 (32)*	0.51 (38)*

* t-test, $P = 0.01$
† t-test, $P < 0.05$
Unmarked results are not statistically significant
PE = physical examination

The performance profiles shown in Table 3 provided students and faculty with detailed information about areas of strength and weakness for both individuals and groups. Although documentation was not part of the original study design, it could be included in future profiles. As shown, Year 3 students reached the correct working diagnosis in three-quarters of the encounters (n = 147), despite incomplete anticipation and elicitation of signs. Apprehending only one or two of the discriminating signs was sufficient to decide between the competing hypotheses. An increased reliance on discriminating manoeuvres may also explain why Year 4 students achieved diagnostic accuracy equivalent to that of Year 3 students despite demonstrating significantly poorer anticipation and elicitation skills overall.

The results from the performance study showed that the procedure was sensitive enough to pick up differences in performance within and across levels of experience. For Year 3 students, incorrect diagnosis was often the result of incorrect interpretation or attribution of meaning: they correctly elicited discriminating signs, but did not appreciate their implication. For Year 4 students, incorrect diagnosis reflected a failure to elicit discriminating signs as a result of incorrect performance of the PE manoeuvres, suggesting a decay of previously acquired PE skills, as previously shown by Mangione and Pietzman[5] and St-Clair et al.[7] These findings have important implications for curriculum planning. Early in their training, students need experiences which link specific PE manoeuvres and findings with diagnoses: they require deliberate practice[24] which integrates the constituent skills of diagnostic reasoning. This represents a type of practice that cannot be acquired through the performance of a traditional HTT screening examination, but precisely the type of practice that can be obtained by repeated experience with an HDPE approach. Later in their training, students can continue to benefit from an HDPE approach to monitor and maintain the correct performance of discriminating PE manoeuvres[30] and to highlight the consequences of incorrect execution of the PE manoeuvres in the context of sorting diagnostic alternatives.

The HDPE assessment procedure allowed us to advance our understanding of several aspects of performance assessment. As hypothesised, the performance on the subset of discriminating PE manoeuvres was more reliable than performance based on all the items on the checklist: 12 cases were needed to reach a 0.80 level of reliability, compared with 22 cases. The non-discriminating signs added noise rather than useful information. This is consistent with the findings of Hodges et al.[31] that traditional checklist scores do not reflect expertise. The salience of PE manoeuvres is highly case-specific; non-discriminating items for a given scenario may become significant in other scenarios. This is emphasised in the HDPE approach by having the students compare and contrast sets of diagnostic hypotheses in order to identify discriminating findings, an approach suggested long ago by Wigton and colleagues.[20] The present results indicate that checklist scores could benefit by deleting signs and manoeuvres that reflect rote thoroughness rather than a discriminating diagnostic function.

The second hypothesis about the long-term test effect of an HDPE assessment with immediate feedback was also corroborated by the results. A previous encounter with a case in which the SP provided feedback had the strongest impact on later performance. This effect probably reflects the intense engagement of a live teaching–learning encounter that fosters double encoding, which is both experiential and cognitive, in memory.[30,31] Strong performance on previously encountered cases is consistent with findings from Roediger, Marsh and Karpicke concerning written tests, which showed that prior testing resulted in a stronger performance on a subsequent test than prior studying.[27,28] They also found that prior response to a multiple-choice question (MCQ) increased the probability of the same response occurring if that MCQ was encountered again, whether the initial response was correct or incorrect.[32] They concluded that immediate feedback was important to prevent any incorrect response from solidifying. Prior testing with immediate feedback from SPs during the HDPE provided a unique teaching–learning moment to help consolidate correct selection and performance of PE manoeuvres. The HDPE assessment's impact on learning implies that the 'test effect' previously demonstrated with MCQs extends to the realm of performance tests; this is further supported by recent findings from Kromann et al.[33] showing that students tested on a cardiac arrest simulation scenario performed better on later testing than did students who discussed the scenario as part of a learning exercise.

The present results suggest key areas for future research. When is a hypothesis-driven approach best implemented in the curriculum? Butter et al.[34] showed that adding ultrasound training to initial PE training did not improve PE performance; competence and confidence were improved only if the students had already acquired basic PE skills. This raises the question of whether the HDPE is best implemented early in the curriculum when students first learn the PE, or later, during clinical rotations when they have more clinical knowledge and experience. Secondly, what assessment strategies best reinforce (deteriorating) PE skills over time? Given that Williams et al.[30] recommend that subsets of PE skills should be periodically tested during the clinical years, would the HDPE procedure enrich such reviews by incorporating the reasoning component of the PE? These are two important questions about learning and mastering the art and science of the PE that can be addressed now that the materials and procedures for an HDPE approach are available.

Unlike the traditional HTT assessment, the HDPE provides students with targeted practice and feedback in an analytic process of anticipating, eliciting, interpreting and revising discriminatory aspects of the PE in the context of controlled diagnostic challenges. Whether deployed as an instructional method or an assessment approach, the HDPE has the potential to promote the development of effective clinical reasoning by encouraging the learning and integration of constituent skills.

Contributors: JO, GB and HN developed the initial set of complaints and case scenarios. All authors were involved in the case development and revisions or data acquisition and analysis. RY wrote the first draft of the paper and all authors were involved in revising the manuscript.
Acknowledgements: we are most grateful for the thoughtful reviews from the content validity judges, namely: Drs. S. Aaron (U. Alberta), N. Ban (Nagoya U.), M. Goldszmidt (U. Western Ontario), M. Nendaz (U. de Geneve), A. Nofziger (U. Rochester), D. Vanpee (U. Catholique de Louvain), and R. Wigton (U. Nebraska). We would like to acknowledge Bob Kiser and the standardised patients of the Dr. Allan L. and Mary L. Graham Clinical Performance Center for their assistance and professionalism.
Funding: this study was funded in part by a grant from the Edward J Stemmler Medical Education Research Fund of the National Board of Medical Examiners (NBME), Philadelphia, to RY and GB and a grant-in-aid for scientific research from the Japanese Ministry of Education, Culture, Sports, Science and Technology, Tokyo. This article does not necessarily reflect NBME policy and NBME support represents no official endorsement.
Conflicts of interest: GB chairs the international editorial board of *Medical Education*. The authors are not aware of other conflicts of interest.

Ethical approval: this study received ethics approval from the University of Illinois at Chicago's Internal Review Board.

REFERENCES

1 Yudkowsky R, Downing S, Klamen D, Valaski M, Eulenberg B, Popa M. Assessing the head-to-toe physical examination skills of medical students. *Med Teach* 2004;**26**:415–9.
2 van der Vleuten CPM. The assessment of professional competence: developments, research and practical implications. *Adv Health Sci Educ* 1996;**1** (1):41–67.
3 van der Vleuten CPM, Schuwirth L. Assessing professional competence: from methods to programmes. *Med Educ* 2005;**39**:309–17.
4 Mangione S, Nieman LZ, Gracely E, Kaye D. The teaching and practice of cardiac auscultation during internal medicine and cardiology training: a nationwide survey. *Ann Intern Med* 1993;**119**:47–54.
5 Mangione S, Pietzman SJ. Physical diagnosis in the 1990s: art or artefact? *J Gen Intern Med* 1996;**11**:490–3.
6 Mangione S, Nieman LZ. Cardiac auscultatory skills of internal medicine and family practice trainees: a comparison of diagnostic proficiency. *JAMA* 1997;**278**:717–22.
7 St-Clair EW, Oddone EZ, Waugh RA, Corey GR, Feussner JR. Assessing house staff diagnostic skills using a cardiology patient simulator. *Ann Intern Med* 1992;**117**:751–6.
8 Downing SM. The metric of medical education. Validity: on the meaningful interpretation of assessment data. *Med Educ* 2003;**37** (9):830–7.
9 Hampton JR, Harrison MJG, Mitchell JRA, Prichard JS, Seymour C. Relative contributions of history taking, physical examination, and laboratory investigation to diagnosis and management of medical outpatients. *Br Med J* 1975;**2**:486–9.
10 Brown J, Collins A, Duguid P. Situated cognition and the culture of learning. *Educ Res* 1989;**18**:32–42.
11 van Merriënboer JJG, Jelsma O, Paas F. Training for reflective expertise: a four-component instructional design model for training complex cognitive skills. *Educ Tech Res Dev* 1992;**40**:23–43.
12 van Merriënboer J, Clark RE, De Croock M. Blueprints for complex learning: the 4C/ID-model. *Educ Tech Res Dev* 2002;**50**:39–64.
13 Boshuizen HPA, Schmidt HG. The development of clinical reasoning expertise. In: Higgs J, Jones M, eds. *Clinical Reasoning in the Health Professions*, 2nd edn. Oxford: Butterworth Heinemann 2000;15–22.
14 Eva KW. What every teacher needs to know about clinical reasoning. *Med Educ* 2004;**39**:98–106.
15 Fletcher J, Fox R. Pattern recognition versus Bayesian approach for diagnosis in primary care. *BMJ* 2006;**332**:646–7.
16 Norman GR, Brooks LR, Regehr G, Marriott M, Shali V. Impact of feature identification on medical student diagnostic performance. *Acad Med* 1996;**71** (**Suppl**):108–9.
17 Norman GR, Leblanc V, Brooks LR. On the difficulty of noticing obvious features in patient appearance. *Psychol Sci* 2000;**11**:112–7.
18 Hatala RM, Norman GR, Brooks LR. Impact of a clinical scenario on accuracy of electrocardiogram interpretation. *J Gen Intern Med* 1999;**14**:126–9.
19 Bordage G. The curriculum: overloaded and too general? *Med Educ* 1987;**21**:183–8.
20 Wigton RS, Connor JL, Centor RM. Transportability of a decision rule for the diagnosis of streptococcal pharyngitis. *Arch Intern Med* 1986;**146**:81–3.
21 Wigton RS. Use of linear models to analyse physicians' decisions. *Med Decis Making* 1988;**8**:241–52.
22 Poses RM, Cebul RD, Wigton RS, Centor RM, Collins M, Fleischli G. Controlled trial using computerised feedback to improve physicians' diagnostic judgements. *Acad Med* 1992;**67**:345–7.
23 Tape TG, Kripal J, Wigton RS. Comparing methods of learning clinical prediction from case simulations. *Med Decis Making* 1992;**12**:213–21.
24 Ericsson KA, Krampe RT, Tesch-Römer C. The role of deliberate practice in the acquisition of expert performance. *Psychol Rev* 1993;**100**:363–406.
25 Wigton RS, Patil KD, Hoellerich VL. The effect of feedback in learning clinical diagnosis. *J Med Educ* 1986;**61**:816–22.
26 McGee SR. *Evidence-based Physical Diagnosis*. Philadelphia, PA: Saunders 2007.
27 Roediger HL, Marsh EJ. The positive and negative consequences of multiple-choice testing. *J Exp Psychol Learn Mem Cogn* 2005;**31** (5):1155–9.
28 Roediger HL, Karpicke JD. Test-enhanced learning: taking memory tests improves longterm retention. *Psychol Sci* 2006;**17**:249–55.
29 Block R, Norman G. G-String II program for urGENOVA. http://www.fhs.mcmaster.ca/perd/download/g_string/index.htm. [Accessed 30 March 2008.]
30 Williams RG, Klamen DL, Mayer D, Valaski M, Roberts NK. A sampling strategy for promoting and assessing medical student retention of physical examination skills. *Acad Med* 2007;**82** (**Suppl**):22–5.
31 Hodges B, Regehr G, McNaughton N, Tiberius R, Hanson M. OSCE checklists do not capture increasing levels of expertise. *Acad Med* 1999;**74**:1129–34.
32 Marsh EJ, Roediger HL, Bjork RA, Bjork EL. The memorial consequences of multiple-choice testing. *Psychon Bull Rev* 2007;**14**:194–9.
33 Kromann C, Jensen M, Ringsted C. The effect of testing on skills learning. *Med Educ* 2009;**43**:21–7.
34 Butter J, Grant TH, Egan M, Kaye M, Wayne DB, Carrion-Carire V, McGaghie WC. Does ultrasound

training boost Year 1 medical student competence and confidence when learning abdominal examination? *Med Educ* 2007;41:843–8.

SUPPORTING INFORMATION

Additional Supporting Information may be found in the online version of this article:

Appendix S1. A chief complaint and related prototypical diagnoses, and an example of a clinical scenario and manoeuvres and references.

Table S1. Prototypical diagnoses for each of the 19 chief complaints, representing an average of 3.5 diagnoses per complaint, for a total of 60 distinct diagnoses (number of physical examination manoeuvres per complaint in parentheses).

Please note: Wiley-Blackwell are not responsible for the content or functionality of any supporting materials supplied by the authors. Any queries (other than for missing material) should be directed to the corresponding author for the article.

Received 25 June 2008; editorial comments to authors 3 October 2008; accepted for publication 24 February 2009

Part III: Selection, Access, and Retention

Overview

Jorge Girotti
Past Director, Hispanic Center of Excellence, Department of Medical Education

This section highlights the scholarship of faculty in the area of selection processes, access, and retention in health professions education. We present four articles that describe the issues and challenges that educational institutions must address as they attempt to meet societal expectations, spanning programs nationally and internationally. The topics range from the transferability of knowledge and skills acquired in medical schools across the globe; educational initiatives that aim to sustain community to improve access and care for underserved communities; novel mechanisms to select candidates for medical school admission that go beyond traditional academic metrics; to the persistent challenge of patient communication in languages other than English and its impact on access and quality.

Tekian and Boulet tackle the very pressing topic of the increasingly global movement of physicians because of unstable political situations abroad and the search for better professional or financial opportunities. Their article, "A longitudinal study of the characteristics and performances of medical students and graduates from the Arab countries", provides a comprehensive view of educational outcomes for graduates of fifteen Arab countries. Specifically, the authors examine the career trajectory of learners as they seek certification from the Educational Commission for Foreign Medical Graduates, which is required to pursue graduate training in the United States. Tekian and Boulet's analysis shows wide variability in performance on U.S. licensing examinations (i.e., USMLE Steps 1 and 2 CK), from a high rate of 91% on first attempt for students from Jordan, to as low as 47% for those from Kuwait. The authors posit that, while performance on U.S. licensing examinations is not a perfect proxy for the quality of medical education in Arab countries, it does offer some insights into areas that may need more attention, particularly for those nations with graduates who pursue advanced training opportunities outside their borders.

In "The Urban Medicine Program: developing physician-leaders to serve underserved urban communities," Girotti, Loy, Michel and Henderson discuss the development and early outcomes of an educational program that aims to prepare physicians to improve outcomes in underserved urban communities through advocacy, research, policy change, and culturally-competent care. The premise of the UMed program is that medical students who demonstrate a commitment to community service can be nurtured throughout studies to enhance leadership skills and improve their potential effectiveness. While the article describes the issues that impact urban areas in the United States, these challenges cross national boundaries.

Yingling, Park, Curry, Monson, and Girotti provide evidence of the effectiveness of non-academic measures to evaluate applicants for admission to medical school. In their article, "Beyond cognitive measures: empirical evidence supporting holistic medical school admissions practices and professional identity formation", the authors aim to establish a potential link between measures used at admissions and those later used to evaluate the formation of professional identity among medical students as they proceed through the curriculum and training. Early results demonstrate the connection of situational judgment instruments and identity formation measures; this can positively impact the initial review of applicants that best fit the mission and educational environment of the school.

Ortega's "Spanish language concordance in U.S. medical care: a multifaceted challenge and call to action", examines the dire shortage of physicians who can communicate directly with Spanish-speaking patients, especially in light of demographic shifts. The author argues that current practices fall woefully short of legal and quality standards. Ortega provides recommendations on how medical schools in the United States may begin to tackle the shortfall through more standardized instruction in the Spanish language, including the validation of resources used in the curriculum; certification of competency for those who intend to use Spanish in the clinical setting; and the use of incentives for physicians that demonstrate linguistic competence.

The four articles in this section represent a valuable cross-sectional sampling of the contributions of DME faculty in a critical area of discourse: professional educational programs in medicine and other health professions share a societal responsibility to admit, educate and graduate health care professionals who are competent in their clinical field, and can also make a positive and personalized contribution to the quality, access, and appropriateness of care for all patients.

Research Report

The Urban Medicine Program: Developing Physician–Leaders to Serve Underserved Urban Communities

Jorge A. Girotti, PhD, MA, Gary L. Loy, MD, MPH, Joanna L. Michel, PhD, and Vida A. Henderson, PharmD, MPH, MFA

Abstract

Purpose
Medical school graduates are poorly prepared to address health care inequities found in urban, underserved communities. The University of Illinois College of Medicine developed the Urban Medicine Program (UMed) to prepare students for the roles of advocate, researcher, policy maker, and culturally competent practitioner through a four-year curriculum integrating principles of public health with direct interventions in local, underserved communities. This study assessed the program's effectiveness and evaluated early outcomes.

Method
The authors analyzed data for UMed students (graduating classes 2009–2013) from pre- and postseminar assessments and longitudinal community project progress reports. They also compared UMed and non-UMed outcomes from the same classes, using graduation data and data from two surveys: Medical Students' Attitudes Toward the Underserved (MSATU) and the Intercultural/Professional Assessment.

Results
UMed students were more likely than non-UMed students to endorse MSATU constructs ("Universal medical care is a right" [$P = .01$], "Access to basic medical care is a right" [$P = .03$], "Access is influenced by social determinants" [$P = .03$]); to be selected for the Gold Humanism Honor Society ($P < .0001$); to complete joint degrees ($P < .0001$); and to enter primary care residencies ($P = .002$).

Conclusions
Early outcomes reveal that a longitudinal, experiential curriculum can provide students with competencies that may prepare them for leadership roles in advocacy, research, and policy making. Contact with diverse communities inculcates—in medical students with predispositions toward helping underserved populations—the self-efficacy and skills to positively influence underserved, urban communities.

Calls for the integration of public/population health content into medical education have come from influential organizations and agencies.[1–3] The consensus is that lasting improvements in the health of populations necessitate the application of both clinical care and established public health principles.[1] Medical schools are in a key position to bridge the paradigms of public health and clinical care.[3] Curricular approaches that integrate community-based components represent one potential way to link the two traditions.

The Institute of Medicine[1] defined several principles for successful integration of primary care medicine and public health, principles that are applicable to clinical care in general. They include the following:

Please see the end of this article for information about the authors.

Correspondence should be addressed to Jorge A. Girotti, Department of Medical Education, University of Illinois College of Medicine at Chicago, 808 S. Wood St. (MC 591), Chicago, IL 60612-7309; telephone: (312) 996-4493; e-mail: jorgeg@uic.edu.

Acad Med. 2015;90:1658–1666.
First published online October 16, 2015
doi: 10.1097/ACM.0000000000000970

a common goal of improving population health; engagement of community members in defining and addressing their own needs; aligned leadership that bridges disciplines, programs, and jurisdictions; sustainability; and collaborative use of data and analysis.[1] Medical school curricula may also embrace these principles. Community-based curricula in medical schools offer students new perspectives and insights; these curricula not only afford students the opportunity to view the individuals they serve in a holistic manner but also emphasize the effects of social and environmental determinants on health. Furthermore, establishing long-term collaborations between communities and academic institutions enables medical students to work with community members during all developmental phases of health programs, interventions, and initiatives, including instrument development, implementation, data analysis, evaluation, and dissemination.

Currently, few medical schools provide community-based education that spans all four years.[4–17] Among these, the majority focus on serving underserved *rural* communities[5,8,9,12,16] and increasing the number of *primary care* physicians in underserved areas.[11–14,16] We identified only two schools that require community-based education for all medical students.[7,15] Most of the four-year community-based programs incorporated didactic and experiential learning, whereas a few required students to develop and implement community projects.[4,10,12,13,16] Further, few required students to evaluate the outcomes and impact of their projects on the community served.[10,12,14,17] The purpose of this study was to evaluate the effectiveness of the Urban Medicine Program (UMed), which incorporates all of these elements—a four-year, longitudinal, experiential curriculum; community-based projects; and evaluations of these projects—and to assess early student outcomes.

Background

The University of Illinois College of Medicine is the largest medical school in the United States, graduating an average of 300 medical doctors per year from its four campuses (Chicago, Peoria, Rockford, and Urbana-Champaign). Of these, about 35% consistently choose primary care fields; one-fourth self-identify as members of ethnic/racial groups underrepresented in medicine (URM), and one-third locate their practices in rural and urban underserved communities.[18] The University of Illinois College of Medicine at Chicago (UI-COMC) is among a limited number of MD-granting medical schools that has created an experiential, community-situated longitudinal curriculum that focuses on educating physician–leaders to work with underserved populations located in urban centers. UMed at UI-COMC was launched in 2005 with a mission *to prepare physician–leaders to serve underserved urban communities*. UMed takes advantage of UI-COMC's diverse student population and its location in inner-city Chicago to address not only the challenges of practicing in an urban setting but also the larger issues of community disparities.

Program Description

UMed provides a nonclinical, urban population health focus that spans all four years of medical school and is supplementary to the regular curriculum experienced by all UI-COMC students. The principal long-term objective of UMed is to graduate physicians equipped with the knowledge, skills, and attitudes to fulfill the roles of advocate, researcher, policy maker, and culturally competent practitioner. Notably, UMed does not focus on any particular specialty pathway. The premise is that physicians of all specialties can positively contribute to the health and well-being of people living in underserved, urban communities. To be effective leaders, UMed graduates need to understand the social determinants of health and how they contribute to health disparities. They require specific skills including those related to community-based collaborative program planning and evaluation, multidisciplinary teamwork, culturally appropriate communication, and conducting research. Furthermore, they must develop cross-cultural skills pertinent to conditions in the urban environment that adversely affect health (e.g., affordable, accessible pharmaceuticals and medical care, healthy foods, transportation, exposure to environmental toxins). The curriculum meets these educational objectives through time and instruction devoted to four themes: (1) diversity in the community and intercultural communication, (2) disparities in health care access and outcomes, (3) community-based participatory research (CBPR), and (4) advocacy and policy.

Student selection and admission process

Each year, UMed accepts 24 students from a pool of 100 to 110 students admitted to UI-COMC who also choose to apply to UMed. Admission into UMed is based not only on academic promise but also on the applicant's track record of service in urban settings and applied leadership skills. Fluency in a second language is given some preference. Successful candidates combine unique personal experiences and interests related to the practice of urban medicine.

Curriculum design

Theoretical framework. The UMed curriculum is informed by the experiential learning theory (ELT), which emphasizes experience as the central component in the learning process.[19–21] According to ELT, four iterative stages constitute the learning cycle. First, learners grasp information through real, tangible experiences (*concrete experience*). Learners then observe and reflect on this new knowledge or experience (*reflective observation*) and form *abstract conceptualizations* which they can use to create new ideas and implications for action. Next, learners act on and test the ideas and implications (*active experimentation*), which leads to creating or perfecting new knowledge and skills.[20,21]

This cycle of experiencing, reflecting, thinking, and acting is synonymous with action learning.[22] Experiential or action learning makes knowledge more explicit and encourages creative, innovative thinking[22] to be applied to new situations and complex problems. UMed students learn, develop, and apply new concepts to challenges in designing, implementing, and evaluating their longitudinal work. We have noted components of this process in our logic model (Figure 1).

Curriculum components. The curriculum comprises the following distinct components that together facilitate the achievement of intended program outcomes: (1) a seminar series, (2) a Web-based learning curriculum, (3) a longitudinal community project (LCP), and (4) a Policy and Advocacy Forum.

Seminar series. The seminar series addresses the four curricular themes and enables students to engage in all stages of the learning cycle. Students attend eight 2-hour seminars over the course of their first and second years of medical school (M1 and M2 years). The seminars are student centered: approximately 40 minutes of didactic learning followed by breakout sessions during which the students, in their LCP teams, look at the practical applications of the didactic information as it relates to their community site. The 24 students constitute a learning community; they participate in UMed together and share with one another their community rotation experiences as well as their progress on the LCPs. A multidisciplinary faculty, including faculty members from the College of Medicine, the College of Nursing, the College of Social Work, and the School of Public Health, among others, facilitate the seminars.

Web-based curriculum. UMed, in collaboration with the Department of Medical Education (DME), has developed an online curriculum that requires participating students to complete, during their M3 and M4 years, three modules that cover cultural competency, leadership, and communication skills. DME faculty review student responses to online assignments and are available to provide one-on-one feedback. Consistent with ELT, the students complete the modules during their clerkship years, when patient experiences and team-based learning predominate, so that they may reflect and apply what they are learning in their daily interactions in a variety of environments and with patients of varying cultural backgrounds.

The LCP. The LCP provides direct, long-term, team-based collaborative engagement with community agencies in underserved urban neighborhoods. The LCP employs the educational principles of experiential, self-directed learning and naturally integrates all ELT stages. Each fall, UMed holds a Community Partner Fair during which participating community agencies meet M1 students. After the fair, students individually rank their top three choices, and we match as many students as possible to their first choice. Agencies review the potential assignments before they are released to students so as to be involved in the decision-making process. After the teams form, the team members complete an asset mapping assignment, which includes a group observation of the community, interviewing members of the community, and assessing both strengths and weaknesses of their community of focus. Community agency mentors, students, and community members identify projects that are of greatest need to the community,

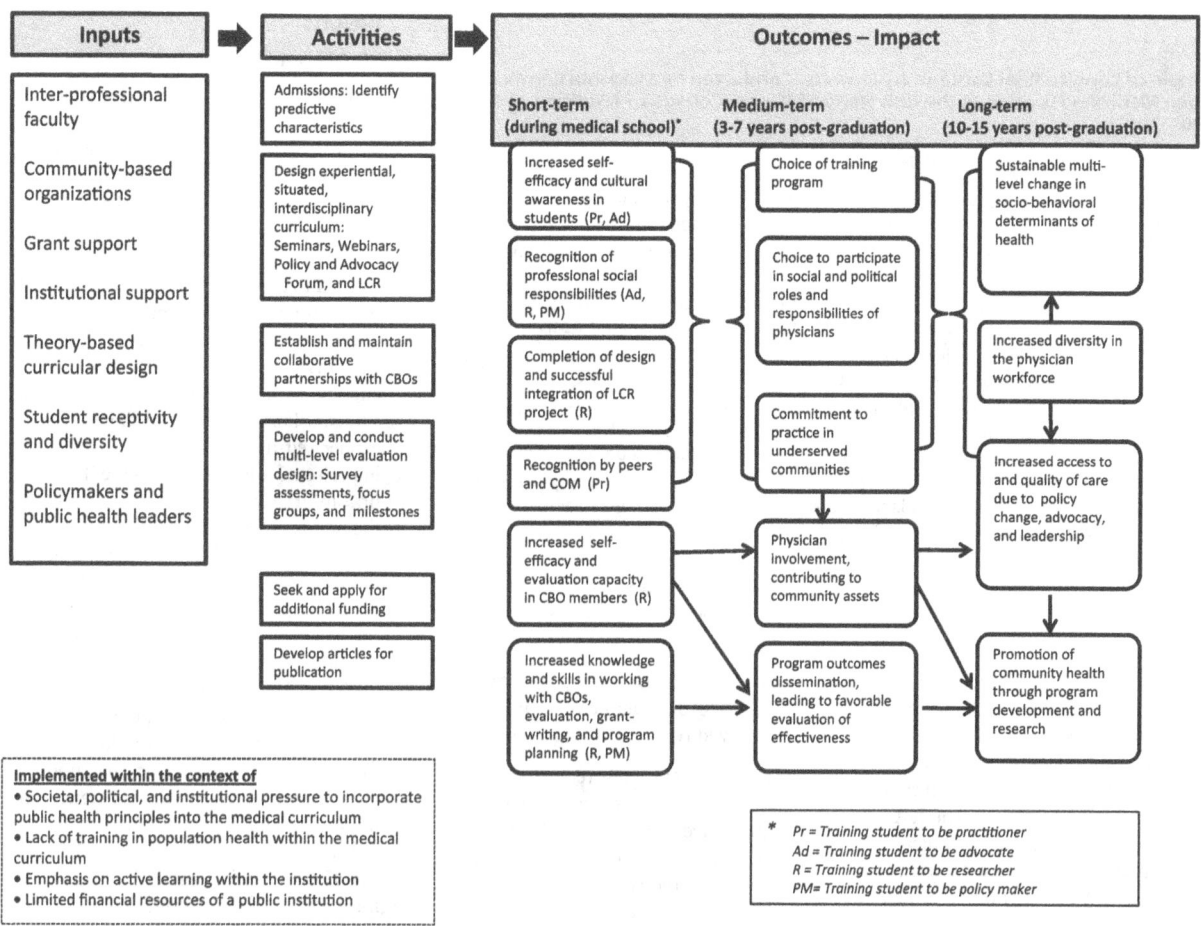

Figure 1 Logic model for the Urban Medicine Program at the University of Illinois College of Medicine. LCR indicates longitudinal community rotation; CBO, community-based organization; COM, college of medicine.

and—together with UMed faculty—agency mentors evaluate student progress through quarterly updates. We make an effort to involve the community in all aspects, and during all stages, of education and training. Upper-class students become mentors as other UMed students join the community partner in related projects. Projects continue through the M4 year and culminate in a final project evaluation paper, a CBPR grant application, or a program proposal. Agency mentors may be physicians, social workers, community organizers, community health workers, public health administrators, or program directors, and this diversity enhances the interprofessional experience of the UMed students.[23] Table 1 presents sample projects.

Policy and Advocacy Forum. During the M4 year, UMed students participate in a two-week Policy and Advocacy Forum, during which local health care leaders, physician activists, faculty, and community activists make didactic presentations and invite students to discuss emergent issues openly. Additionally, the forum gives students the opportunity to present their own projects or a policy tool (legislative testimony, letter to editor, fact sheet, etc.) that they have developed, which others can, in turn, use in their own advocacy efforts. The forum requires students to reflect on the knowledge they have gained, to discover how current policies affect community partners, and to cultivate new ideas for policy reform.

Credit for participation in UMed

At the end of the four years, students who have completed all elements of the program receive six credit hours and a certificate for their participation in UMed.

Method

The UMed curriculum was launched in fall 2005, and from that point until academic year 2012–2013, 180 students enrolled in the program. In 2011, to evaluate program effectiveness as accurately as possible, we began both to develop de novo surveys and to use instruments validated in previous studies, the results of which we report here.

The present study covers the UI-COMC entering classes of 2005–2009. We obtained institutional review board approval (protocols #2008-1037 and 2014-0530) to use the surveys and assessments described here. All students gave informed consent, and we offered no incentives for participation. To assess the effectiveness of the program on the development of student attitudes, knowledge, skills, and behaviors, we used the following instruments:

1. The Medical Students' Attitudes Toward the Underserved (MSATU) survey and the Intercultural and Professional Assessment (IPA) survey.

Table 1
Sample of Longitudinal Community Projects, Conducted by Students Enrolled in the Urban Medicine Program at the University of Illinois College of Medicine at Chicago (2009–2013)

Organization focus	Urban Medicine–Longitudinal Community Project
At-risk high school youth health and education	A wellness course for high school students covering mental health, sexual and reproductive health, and domestic violence
Diabetes	A four-week nutrition and wellness program for diabetic and prediabetic women
Domestic violence	A course in Spanish offered to local hairstylists to identify domestic violence in their clients and connect them with local services
HIV/AIDS	An education program for youth in the juvenile system on healthy decision making including prevention of HIV/AIDS
Homeless women	A peer nutrition educator program that brings together students, researchers, and community activists to discuss issues of food access, healthy food choices, and advocacy around food systems in Chicago
Pipeline to health careers	An after-school program at a Chicago high school to support and inspire students who are interested in pursuing a health career
Refugee women's health	A health care information library for Somali women that includes a resource manual for culturally aware health services in the area
Sickle cell disease	A mentorship and support program for adolescent sickle cell patients as they transition from pediatric to adult care

The MSATU is a validated survey[24] that assesses student attitudes related to the perceived roles of medical students, physicians, charitable organizations, and the government in providing health care. The IPA survey, developed by UMed faculty, is a method to compare differences between UMed and non-UMed UI-COMC medical students. The IPA asks students to self-assess, using Likert-type scales, their level of comfort when interacting with patients of various cultural and social backgrounds. Between August and November 2012, we invited all (M1–M4) UI-COMC medical students—both UMed and non-UMed (n = 819)—to participate in an intercultural and professionalism assessment (using the MSATU and IPA). We analyzed categorical variables using Pearson chi-square tests.

2. UMed pre/post assessments. We developed these assessments for M1 and M2 students completing UMed. They are based on seminar learning objectives and developed in collaboration with each seminar speaker. Each survey includes four to six multiple-choice direct knowledge questions (e.g., "What is the purpose of a program theory?") and three to four self-efficacy questions (e.g., "How confident are you in identifying a high-quality interview guide?"), which students respond to using a Likert-type scale. We invited UMed students (n = 48) to participate during the 2012–2013 academic year, and we analyzed responses using a paired t test.

3. UMed LCP progress report. This team-based report includes both qualitative data (not reported here) and quantitative data to assess program objectives, measurable outcomes, evaluation tools, and stage of project evaluation. Each student team completes a report four times each year. UMed faculty use the reports to track students' acquisition of UMed competencies and LCP progress. We invited all UMed students during academic year 2012–2013 (n = 96) to participate as teams.

Finally, to examine early program outcomes, we compared UMed and non-UMed students from the graduating classes of 2009–2013 (n = 887) using data obtained for all UI-COMC students. We analyzed the following characteristics of each graduating student: gender, original state of residency, age at matriculation, self-reported URM status, graduation outcomes (i.e., graduation with honors, Gold Humanism Honor Society, Alpha Omega Alpha Honor Society, and joint degrees), state of residency placement, and residency type (primary care, including family medicine or nonprimary care). We used Pearson chi-square tests to analyze categorical variables, using SAS Version 9.3 (SAS Institute, Cary, North Carolina).

We set significance at $P < .05$.

Results

MSATU and IPA surveys

Of the 819 M1–M4 students invited to complete the IPA/MSATU surveys (in the autumn of 2012), 297 students completed both IPA/MSATU (a response rate of 36%). Of these, 64 (22%) were completed by UMed students and 233 (78%) by non-UMed students. Analysis of MSATU data showed that overall, the UI-COMC student body strongly endorsed the four predictors of care to the indigent; however, UMed students were significantly more likely to endorse all four constructs than non-UMed students. Further, after adjusting for age, gender, self-reported ethnicity, involvement in projects for the needy, and the IPA uncomfortableness ranking assigned in the multivariate model, UMed students remained significantly more likely to adhere to three constructs: "Universal medical care is a right" ($P = .01$), "Access to basic medical care is a right" ($P = .03$), and "Access is influenced by social determinants" ($P = .03$). The fourth—"Students/physicians have a social responsibility to serve the needy"—was also endorsed more frequently by UMed students than non-UMed students, though this difference did not reach significance ($P = .16$).

The IPA survey indicated that the vast majority of students do not report feeling uncomfortable interacting with various types of patients, and we noted little difference between UMed and non-UMed students. When program year was included in the multivariable analyses, first year students had significantly higher levels of discomfort than other students ($P = .04$), and in the final multivariable model, Asian/Pacific Islander students showed higher levels of discomfort ($P = .05$). According to our multivariable analyses, no other characteristics were associated with significant levels of discomfort in dealing with patients of different backgrounds.

Pre/post seminar assessment

For the 2012–2013 academic year, there was a 96% response rate from both the M1 and M2 UMed students (n = 23/24 for both cohorts) on the six pre- and postseminar assessments. M1 students showed a gain in knowledge and confidence in implementing skills and information learned in the seminars. They seemed to especially learn from the Community Partner Fair and the seminars focused on evaluation, determinants of health, qualitative assessment, and CBPR. M2 students showed a gain in knowledge and confidence related to evaluation, qualitative assessment, community epidemiology, and community disparities. The M1 class showed greater gains overall for all seminars. We noted a statistically significant difference in levels of confidence between overall pre- and overall postseminar participation ($P < .001$; not shown).

LCP progress report

In academic year 2012–2013, a total of 96 UMed students (M2–M4) were working with 19 separate organizations on 22 individual LCP projects (see Table 1 for examples). On average, these organizations had worked with UMed students for 2.5 years, and 8 (42%) had worked with UMed students for 3.5 years or more. Student projects took place in 12 underserved neighborhoods throughout the city of Chicago. According to their most recent quarterly progress reports, M2 students spent an average of 40 hours at their site over three months, whereas M3 and M4 students spent, respectively, 20 and 22 hours over three months at their community sites. Five of the 22 teams (23%) changed the objectives of their projects. All but 1 of the teams (95%) had developed evaluation measures to assess the impact of their project on community recipients. The most common evaluation tools used by all student teams were surveys (n = 16; 73%), focus groups (n = 11; 50%), activity logs (n = 8; 36%), and organizational records (n = 8; 36%).

Early program outcomes

The first five graduating cohorts of UMed (2009–2013) totaled 99 graduates and represented 11% of all UI-COMC graduates for those years (n = 887). We compared the UMed graduates and the non-UMed graduates (n = 788) to evaluate the outcomes of the program at graduation, using the following variables: graduation with honors, Gold Humanism Honor Society membership, Alpha Omega Alpha Honor Society membership, conferral of joint degrees, state of residency placement, and residency type (primary care, nonprimary care). We also compared other characteristics of the two groups: gender, Illinois residence at entry, age at matriculation, race/ethnicity, and self-designated URM status.

We found significant differences in gender and Illinois residence at entry between UMed and non-UMed students. More females participated in UMed than males (UMed: n = 67 [68%]; non-UMed: n = 389 [49%]; $P = .0006$). A significantly greater number of non-Illinois residents were in the UMed group (UMed: n = 29 [29%]; non UMed: n = 148 [19%]; $P = .01$). We observed no significant differences between the two groups in age at matriculation, race/ethnicity, or URM status. Slightly over one-third of UMed students (36%, n = 36) self-identified as URM students compared with 27% (n = 213) of non-UMed students ($P = .0711$). In both groups, the majority of students identified as white (UMed: n = 27 [27%]; non-UMed: n = 300 [38%]), and for both the second largest ethnicity group was Hispanic (UMed: n = 22 [22%]; non-UMed: n = 123 [16%]).

In terms of graduation outcomes, we noted significant differences in several measures. Nearly one-third (31%, n = 31) of UMed students were inducted into the Gold Humanism Honor Society compared with 7% (n = 57) of non-UMed students ($P \leq .0001$). In addition, 12% (n = 12) of UMed students graduated with a joint degree (i.e., MD/MPH, MD/MBA) compared with approximately 2% (n = 14) of non-UMed students ($P \leq .0001$). A greater proportion of UMed students chose residencies in primary care (UMed: n = 54 [54%]; non-UMed: n = 319 [41%]; $P = .02$), in particular family medicine (UMed: n = 19 [19%]; non-UMed: n = 68 [9%]; $P = .002$). Although more UMed students were from out of state, the proportion that remained in Illinois for residency was similar (UMed: n = 43 [43%]; non-UMed: n = 355 [45%]; $P = .61$). Table 2 shows the complete results.

Table 2
Comparison of Educational Outcomes, Urban Medicine (UMed) Versus Non–Urban Medicine (non-UMed) Graduates[a]

Characteristic	UMed graduates, no. (% of 99)	Non-UMed graduates, no. (% of 788)	Chi-square value[b]	P value[c]
Sex			11.81	.0006
Male	32 (32.3)	399 (50.6)		
Female	67 (67.7)	389 (49.4)		
Legal state at entry			6.08	.0136
Illinois	70 (70.7)	640 (81.2)		
Other	29 (29.3)	148 (18.8)		
Age at matriculation			0.4462	.8000
23 and under	71 (71.7)	565 (71.7)		
24 to 27	22 (22.2)	162 (20.6)		
28 and over	6 (6.1)	61 (7.8)		
Race/ethnicity			6.73	.2415
Asian[d]	17 (17.2)	107 (13.6)		
Asian Indian[e]	13 (13.1)	111 (14.1)		
Black or African American	14 (14.1)	90 (11.4)		
Hispanic	22 (22.2)	123 (15.6)		
White	27 (27.3)	300 (38.1)		
Other[f]	6 (6.1)	57 (7.2)		
Self-designated underrepresented minority			3.26	.0711
Yes	36 (36.4)	213 (27.0)		
No	63 (63.6)	575 (72.9)		
Graduated with honors			2.48	.1151
Yes	4 (4.0)	68 (8.6)		
No	95 (96.0)	720 (91.4)		
Inducted into Gold Humanism Honor Society			57.06	< .0001
Yes	31 (31.3)	57 (7.2)		
No	68 (68.7)	731 (92.8)		

(Table continues)

Table 2
(Continued)

Characteristic	UMed graduates, no. (% of 99)	Non-UMed graduates, no. (% of 788)	Chi-square value[b]	P value[c]
Inducted into Alpha Omega Alpha Honor Society			0.34	.5578
Yes	15 (15.2)	138 (17.5)		
No	84 (84.9)	650 (82.5)		
Graduated with joint degree			33.08	*< .0001*
Yes	12 (12.1)	14 (1.8)		
No	87 (87.9)	774 (98.2)		
Remained in Illinois for residency			0.26	.6079
Yes	43 (43.4)	355 (45.1)		
No	56 (56.6)	414 (52.5)		
Missing	0	19 (2.4)		
Residency program type			27.43	*.0169*
Anesthesiology	4 (4.0)	58 (7.4)		
Emergency medicine	9 (9.1)	78 (9.9)		
Family medicine	19 (19.2)	68 (8.6)		
Surgery	9 (9.1)	57 (7.2)		
Internal medicine	20 (20.2)	140 (17.8)		
Neurology	0	31 (3.9)		
Medicine–pediatrics	4 (4.0)	15 (1.9)		
Pediatrics	3 (3.0)	53 (6.7)		
Psychiatry	6 (6.1)	38 (4.8)		
Obstetrics–gynecology	8 (8.1)	43 (5.5)		
Ophthalmology	5 (5.1)	16 (2.0)		
Orthopedic surgery	3 (3.0)	28 (3.5)		
Pathology	1 (1.0)	23 (2.9)		
Radiation/radiation–oncology	4 (4.0)	64 (8.1)		
Other[g]	4 (4.0)	48 (6.1)		
Missing	0	28 (3.6)		
Primary care[h]			5.63	*.0176*
Yes	54 (54.5)	319 (40.5)		
No	45 (45.5)	441 (56.0)		
Missing	0	28 (3.6)		
Family medicine			10.10	*.0015*
Yes	19 (19.2)	68 (8.6)		
No	80 (80.8)	692 (87.8)		
Missing	0	28 (3.6)		

[a]These data cover the 887 graduates from the University of Illinois College of Medicine at Chicago who graduated between 2009 and 2013, inclusive. Of these 887 graduates, 99 (11.2%) are UMed graduates and 788 (88.8%) are non-UMED graduates. Percentages may not equal 100 because of rounding.
[b]The chi-square calculations exclude the missing values (i.e., the data missing for non-UMed students in "Remained in Illinois for Residency," "Residency program type," "Primary care," and "Family medicine").
[c]The italicized P values are significantly different at $P < .05$.
[d]Individuals were categorized into the "Asian" race/ethnicity category if they self-identified as "Chinese," "Filipino," "Japanese," "Korean," "Other Asian," "Other Pacific Islander," or "Vietnamese."
[e]Individuals were categorized into the "Asian Indian" race/ethnicity category if they self-identified as "Asian Indian," "Indian," or "Pakistani."
[f]Individuals were categorized into the "Other" race/ethnicity category if they self-identified as "American Indian," "Alaska Native," "Multiple races/ethnicities," "No response," or "Unknown."
[g]Program types with fewer than 20 total students were placed in the "Other" category. Those programs include urology, physical medicine/rehab, dermatology, and otolaryngology.
[h]"Primary care" is defined as students who matched into residencies in family medicine, internal medicine, pediatrics, or obstetrics–gynecology.

Discussion

The purpose of this study was to evaluate the effectiveness of UMed in achieving program outcomes—namely, increasing student understanding of issues in urban, underserved communities and acquiring skills and knowledge to address these issues as practicing physicians. Further, we aimed to evaluate early outcomes of the first five program cohorts. We used several instruments to evaluate outcomes and to compare the social values and level of comfort with working with diverse populations of UMed and non-UMed students. We developed surveys and progress reports to assess gains of UMed students in knowledge, attitudes, and behaviors from the didactic seminars and the LCPs. We also compared outcomes at graduation for UMed versus non-UMed students to better understand early career choices.

Our findings validate the results of studies such as those by Ko and colleagues[8,9] that indicate that medical education can play a positive role in nurturing and enhancing the skills of students already predisposed to serving underserved communities. Our results show that the general UI-COMC student body is open and receptive to working with diverse communities, yet UMed students express even greater cultural understanding and acceptance than their non-UMed UI-COMC peers. Our results align with those found by Stearns and colleagues[12] that indicate that outcomes improve when predisposition for service in underserved communities is paired with appropriate content during medical school.

We also found—as did Haq and colleagues[13]—that, on the basis of mission and goals, programs such as UMed are more difficult to evaluate because the attitudes and behaviors they are designed to instill within students may take time to manifest; however, interestingly, notable early trends in UMed graduates' residency choices suggest that UMed students from states other than Illinois are proportionally more likely than non-UMed students from states other than Illinois to stay in Chicago. Further, although UMed does not select for students who want to go into primary care, a significant number of UMed graduates choose primary care residencies.

Findings related to the acquisition of skills and behaviors that align with leadership roles in underserved urban communities are difficult to contextualize to previous work because most studies evaluate outcomes at the point of graduation—rather than later, during graduates' careers, when leadership roles would be more likely.[6,8,9,13] On the basis of the results of the pre/post assessments, we found that programmatic content in the seminars resulted in significant improvements in knowledge and self-efficacy by UMed students. On the basis of students' LCP progress reports, we believe that the LCPs have become the cornerstone of our program. Community collaboration can be challenging, demanding that students be flexible and continually examine context for their projects to remain relevant. UMed faculty feel that these are necessary skills, as they reflect the general principles of CBPR (i.e., centrality of community partnerships, community building)[25,26] and require students to use systems-level thinking to develop solutions to dynamic, complex, population-level problems. Regular communication between students and UMed faculty has been critical to the success of the LCPs, as are regular meetings between UMed faculty and community partner mentors. Our findings confirm the assertion made by Meyer and colleagues[23]: Partnerships between community organizations and academic health centers are not only feasible but also sustainable—if based on mutual respect and understanding.

This study adds to the knowledge base regarding the importance of student selection, nurturing predisposition, and educational content as means to increase interest in and to provide preparation for leadership roles in urban underserved communities. The low dropout rate (2 out of 180 students) and the number of hours dedicated to UMed outside of the basic curriculum show that students respond positively to a program based on experiential learning, and that they willingly accept the challenge of taking on the additional responsibilities required to work in underserved communities. Overall, the results reported here show that well-designed, longitudinal programs linking medical students and underserved urban communities hold promise; the academic medicine community may be hopeful as we grapple with the burden of continuing disparities that afflict urban communities across the United States.

Although our results are robust, we acknowledge some limitations. Our competitive, nonrandom selection process is part of our strategy to support preexisting student interest in helping underserved populations while capitalizing on academic talent and a social justice mindset; however, this preexisting interest confounds our ability to measure the influence of the UMed curriculum on student attitudes and motivations. We have no information on the students who apply but are not chosen. UMed acceptances are communicated to accepted students, who may or may not attend UI-COMC. Limitations related to the interpretation of the MSATU results include low response rate and the possibility that students with greater cultural awareness and positive attitudes may be more motivated to complete these surveys. This preexisting difference would make the difference between UMed students and the general UI-COMC medical student group smaller.

The major limitation to scaling up the program is the nature of the seminar sessions, which are intentionally interactive, experiential, and in the style of a workshop. Small groups work actively to solve problems during the sessions. The current number of students (24) allows six to eight small groups to work together, to receive input from the instructor, and to share conclusions and discuss topics as a larger group. Two-hour seminars barely allow time for such a format, and adding more seminars to adequately accommodate more students may be a burden on faculty.

Scheduled UMed sessions do not replace any core teaching time; rather, UMed students complete the required activities and projects as they go through the regular medical school curriculum. The six credits they receive for the course appear as "a longitudinally structured self-designed elective." The three course collaborators (J.A.G., G.L.L., J.L.M.) have broad public health and medical backgrounds, and all serve as instructors in seminar sessions as needed. We have been fortunate to consistently secure donated time from faculty members—many from other schools and departments—who appreciate the opportunity to educate medical students on population health issues. A limitation of the program is the lack of consistent funding for the faculty and staff, given the time needed for teaching, advising, evaluating, and administrating UMed. Small grants and teaching assistantships have been the main support mechanisms.

At this point, we cannot determine with certainty whether graduate outcomes are a result of the selection process into UMed or a direct consequence of taking part in UMed. Furthermore, a rigorous medical school curriculum requires that the UMed curriculum be front loaded in the M1 and M2 years; thus, we are not sure whether UMed students sustain their reported increases in knowledge and confidence throughout their medical school training and beyond.

Current data reflect early programmatic outcomes and residency choices. To assess long-term outcomes of UMed, we will be conducting research with UMed graduates to gain a retrospective look at the impact UMed has had on how and where they practice medicine. In our continued effort to compare UMed and non-UMed students, we have also added three Likert-style questions and one qualitative question to the college-wide Graduate Outcomes Survey used for longitudinal tracking and evaluation of UI-COMC graduates. The additional quantitative questions assess how alumni feel the medical school curriculum prepared them for the following: to work with and advocate for underserved communities; to evaluate the effects and impact of public health programs in a community setting; and to provide sensitive and empathetic care to patients of varying cultural, racial, and socioeconomic backgrounds. The additional qualitative question asks alumni to comment on any learning experiences at UI-COMC that gave them skills to address health disparities.

With regard to the LCP component, the UMed approach to community engagement continues to evolve. Program evaluation to date has focused mainly on the effect UMed has made on students. We have developed tools to measure the effect the LCP component has had on the agency and community partners, which we will present in future reports. We have also invited partner agencies to become more involved by providing case studies, facilitating seminar discussions, and serving as consultants to identify topic areas and speakers for the Policy and Advocacy Forum.

Within a true CBPR paradigm, community members are an integral part of the partnership.[25,26] Two challenges of UMed have been (1) to capture long-term behavior change among the community participants in the LCP projects and (2) to include community stakeholders in LCP evaluation efforts. Consequently, a recent addition to our curriculum is the "Self Efficacy and Stage of Change Interview" assignment, which requires each student to use a template to develop and conduct an interview with a community member who has participated in his or her team's intervention. Evaluations of these interviews can serve as a proxy to measure UMed's overall impact on community members in Chicago. Community site mentors have also begun to complete yearly evaluations of their UMed students; these evaluations include a reflection on how their participation has affected the community as a whole, as well as information on if/how UMed has influenced agency program development and evaluation efforts.

Conclusions

Since its inception, UMed has consistently drawn on over 100 applicants for each entering class of 24 students, and it has developed a solid cadre of local community organizations that are willing and able to host student teams and create true partnerships. Through this four-year experience, UMed students learn the importance of continually reassessing community needs through evaluation and interaction with community members and mentors. Finally, students enjoy mentorship and the opportunity to develop leadership skills as subsequent cohorts work on projects developed by earlier students. Our hope is that UMed will serve as a model for medical school leaders who wish to implement community-based programs that prepare medical students to serve underserved populations.

Acknowledgments: The authors wish to thank the following individuals for their contributions to this manuscript: Lee Friedman for his analysis of the Medical Students' Attitudes Toward the Underserved and the Intercultural/Professional Assessment survey data, Katrina Stumbras for her analysis of graduation outcome data, and Judith Sayad for her helpful review of an early version of this report.

Funding/Support: Support for this work was received from the following: the Chicago Community Trust (grant #C2011-00454); the Portes Foundation; the University of Illinois at Chicago Office of the Vice Chancellor for Research—Areas of Excellence award; and the Centers of Excellence Program, Health Resources and Services Administration, U.S. Department of Health and Human Services (grant #D34HP24461).

Other disclosures: None reported.

Ethical approval: The work described here was approved by the University of Illinois at Chicago institutional review board on December 8, 2008 (protocol #2008-1037) and August 14, 2014 (protocol 2014-0530).

Previous presentations: This research has been presented in part at the Association of American Medical Colleges: Public Health in Medical Education Meeting; September 14–15, 2010; Cleveland, Ohio; the 139th American Public Health Association Annual Meeting; October 29–November 2, 2011; Washington, DC; and the 141st American Public Health Association Annual Meeting; November 2–6, 2013; Boston, Massachusetts.

J.A. Girotti is assistant professor, Department of Medical Education, and associate dean, Admissions and Special Curricular Programs, University of Illinois College of Medicine at Chicago, Chicago, Illinois.

G.L. Loy is professor, Department of Obstetrics and Gynecology, Rush Medical College, Chicago, Illinois.

J.L. Michel is adjunct assistant professor of medical education and associate director, Urban Medicine Program, University of Illinois College of Medicine at Chicago, Chicago, Illinois.

V.A. Henderson is a doctoral student, Division of Community Health Sciences, School of Public Health, University of Illinois, Chicago, Illinois.

References

1 Institute of Medicine. Primary care and public health: Exploring integration to improve population health. Released March 28, 2012. http://www.iom.edu/Reports/2012/Primary-Care-and-Public-Health.aspx. Accessed August 19, 2015.
2 Centers for Disease Control and Prevention. Public health and health care collaboration: The workforce perspective. Updated August 30, 2013. http://www.cdc.gov/ophss/csels/dsepd/strategic-workforce-activities/ph-healthcare-collaboration.html. Accessed August 19, 2015.
3 Maeshiro R, Koo D, Keck CW. Integration of public health into medical education: An introduction to the supplement. Am J Prev Med. 2011;41(4 suppl 3):S145–S148.
4 Godkin M, Weinreb L. A pathway on serving multicultural and underserved populations. Acad Med. 2001;76:513–514.
5 Rabinowitz HK, Diamond JJ, Markham FW, Hazelwood CE. A program to increase the number of family physicians in rural and underserved areas: Impact after 22 years. JAMA. 1999;281:255–260.
6 Manetta A, Stephens F, Rea J, Vega C. Addressing health care needs of the Latino community: One medical school's approach. Acad Med. 2007;82:1145–1151.
7 Doran KM, Kirley K, Barnosky AR, Williams JC, Cheng JE. Developing a novel Poverty in Healthcare curriculum for medical students at the University of Michigan Medical School. Acad Med. 2008;83:5–13.
8 Ko M, Edelstein RA, Heslin KC, et al. Impact of the University of California, Los Angeles/Charles R. Drew University Medical Education Program on medical students' intentions to practice in underserved areas. Acad Med. 2005;80:803–808.
9 Ko M, Heslin KC, Edelstein RA, Grumbach K. The role of medical education in reducing health care disparities: The first ten years of the UCLA/Drew Medical Education Program. J Gen Intern Med. 2007;22:625–631.
10 Lewis J. University of Connecticut School of Medicine: An urban partnership. In: Seifer SD, Hermanns K, Lewis J, eds. Creating Community-Responsive Physicians: Concepts and Models for Service–Learning in Medical Education. Washington, DC: American Association for Higher Education; 2000:78–90. http://files.eric.ed.gov/fulltext/ED449734.pdf. Accessed August 31, 2015.
11 Ramsey PG, Coombs JB, Hunt DD, Marshall SG, Wenrich MD. From concept to culture: The WWAMI program at the University of Washington School of Medicine. Acad Med. 2001;76:765–775.
12 Stearns JA, Stearns MA, Glasser M, Londo RA. Illinois RMED: A comprehensive program to improve the supply of rural family physicians. Fam Med. 2000;32:17–21.
13 Haq C, Stearns M, Brill J, et al. Training in urban medicine and public health: TRIUMPH. Acad Med. 2013;88:352–363.
14 Reuland DS, Frasier PY, Slatt LM, Alemán MA. A longitudinal medical Spanish program at one US medical school. J Gen Intern Med. 2008;23:1033–1037.
15 Carney PA, Schifferdecker KE, Pipas CF, et al. A collaborative model for supporting community-based interdisciplinary education. Acad Med. 2002;77:610–620.
16 Cosgrove EM, Harrison GL, Kalishman S, et al. Addressing physician shortages in New Mexico through a combined BA/MD program. Acad Med. 2007;82:1152–1157.
17 Rickards E, Borkan J, Gruppuso PA. Educating the next generation of leaders in medicine: The Scholarly Concentrations Program at the Warren Alpert Medical School of Brown University. Med Health R I. 2007;90:275–276, 280.
18 Mullan F, Chen C, Petterson S, Kolsky G, Spagnola M. The social mission of medical education: Ranking the schools. Ann Intern Med. 2010;152:804–811.
19 Kolb DA. Experiential Learning: Experience as the Source of Learning and Development. Vol 1. Englewood Cliffs, NJ: Prentice-Hall; 1984.
20 Kolb DA, Boyatzis RE, Mainemelis C. Experiential learning theory: Previous research and new directions. In: Sternberg RJ, Zhang L, eds. Perspectives on Thinking, Learning, and Cognitive Styles. Mahwah, NJ: Lawrence Erlbaum Associates; 2001.

21 Kolb AY, Kolb DA. Learning styles and learning spaces: Enhancing experiential learning in higher education. Acad Manag Learn Educ. 2005;4:193–212.
22 Zuber-Skerritt O. The concept of action learning. Learn Organ. 2002;9:114–124.
23 Meyer D, Armstrong-Coben A, Batista M. How a community-based organization and an academic health center are creating an effective partnership for training and service. Acad Med. 2005;80:327–333.
24 Crandall SJ, Volk RJ, Loemker V. Medical students' attitudes toward providing care for the underserved. Are we training socially responsible physicians? JAMA. 1993;269:2519–2523.
25 Israel BA, Schulz AJ, Parker EA, Becker AB. Review of community-based research: Assessing partnership approaches to improve public health. Annu Rev Public Health. 1998;19:173–202.
26 Israel BA, Eng E, Schulz AJ, Parker EA. Introduction to methods in community-based participatory research for health. In: Israel BA, Eng E, Schulz AJ, Parker EA, eds. Methods in Community-Based Participatory Research for Health. San Francisco, Calif: Jossey-Bass; 2005.

Invited Commentary

Spanish Language Concordance in U.S. Medical Care: A Multifaceted Challenge and Call to Action

Pilar Ortega, MD

Abstract

Patient–physician language discordance within the growing Spanish-speaking patient population in the United States presents a significant challenge for health systems. The Civil Rights Act, an Executive Order, and federal standards establish legal requirements regarding patients' legal right to access medical care in their language of origin and to culturally and linguistically appropriate services, and national competency standards for undergraduate and graduate medical education and licensing examinations support the importance of patient–physician communication. However, no requirements or guidelines currently exist for medical Spanish educational resources, and there is no standardized process to assess the competency of medical students and physicians who use Spanish in patient care. Relatedly, existing data regarding current medical Spanish educational resources are limited, and Spanish proficiency evaluations are often based on self-assessments. Future efforts should use a multifaceted approach to address this complex challenge. A standardized process for Spanish-language-concordant medical care education and quality assurance should incorporate the validation of medical Spanish educational resources, competency requirements for medical usage of Spanish, an incentivized certification process for physicians who achieve medical Spanish competency, and health system updates that include routine collection of language concordance data and designation of Hispanic-serving health centers.

Editor's Note: This New Conversations contribution is part of the journal's ongoing conversation on social justice, health disparities, and meeting the needs of our most vulnerable and underserved populations.

The 16.2 million and growing Spanish-speaking limited English-proficient (LEP) population of the United States, which makes up 64% of the country's LEP population,[1] presents a significant challenge for health systems lacking in language concordance resources and quality assurance strategies. With a majority of hospitals and providers encountering Spanish-speaking LEP patients on a regular basis,[2] patient–physician language concordance, defined as the ability of the patient and doctor to directly communicate with each other in the same language, becomes a recurrent public health issue, as well as an individual challenge for both the patient and the provider. Further, patients' language needs with respect to health communication may not be fully characterized by their general LEP status due to the added complexities involved in patient–physician interactions and health care decision making.

The Current State of Medical Language Concordance

All dimensions of health care system performance, including quality, cost, access, equity, patient experience, and patient safety,[3] are challenged by language discordance. Language discordance results in increased costs for medical interpretation, presents increased opportunities for medical errors, and is cited as a reason for patient dissatisfaction and inability to access services.[4] Patient outcome metrics, such as glycemic control for those with diabetes, may be diminished in language-discordant patient–physician relationships.[5] Further, even professional medical interpreting, which is appropriately considered to represent best practice and a federal requirement when language barriers are present, is inferior to language-concordant medical care with regard to the patient–physician relationship and patient satisfaction.[6] These factors suggest that strategies to improve language concordance could improve health system performance.

Data that directly link health system performance metrics—such as patient outcomes; patient satisfaction; costs; hospital length-of-stay; readmission rates; and quality measures for standard-of-care treatment of stroke, sepsis, or other time-sensitive conditions—to language concordance or discordance are rarely published. Data regarding patient language preference may not be appropriately captured despite state and federal mandates for collection of race, ethnicity, ancestry, and language preference (R/E/A/L) information.[7] Even when this collection does occur, providers' language abilities or use of trained interpreters are not consistently evaluated, certified, or documented. Studying language concordance variables requires collection of data pertaining not only to the patient's language preference but also the language proficiency of the provider, which is not routinely captured at U.S. medical centers.

Please see the end of this article for information about the author.

Correspondence should be addressed to Pilar Ortega, University of Illinois at Chicago, College of Medicine, 808 S. Wood St., Suite 990, Chicago, IL 60612; e-mail: POrtega1@uic.edu; Twitter: @pilarortegamd.

To read other New Conversations pieces and to contribute, browse the New Conversations collection on the journal's website (http://journals.lww.com/academicmedicine/pages/collectiondetails.aspx?TopicalCollectionId=61), follow the discussion on AM Rounds (academicmedicineblog.org) and Twitter (@AcadMedJournal using #AcMedConversations), and submit manuscripts using the article type "New Conversations" (see Dr. Sklar's announcement of the current topic in the November 2017 issue for submission instructions and for more information about this feature).

Acad Med. 2018;90:1276–1280.
First published online June 5, 2018
doi: 10.1097/ACM.0000000000002307
Copyright © 2018 by the Association of American Medical Colleges

In addition, despite patients' legal right to access medical care in their language of origin—as established by the Civil Rights Act of 1964 and further defined by an Executive Order in 2000[8] as well as existing federal standards for culturally and linguistically appropriate services (CLAS)[9]—there are no established competencies in the education, practice, or usage of a second language in medical care, although some have been proposed.[10] As a result, many self-identified but noncertified bilingual medical students, physicians, and other medical staff regularly use Spanish and other languages in patient care or as ad hoc interpreters without regulation or quality control.[11] This is problematic as even heritage language speakers vary in proficiency level and may lack the skills needed to provide competent medical care in their heritage language.[12] Proper practice would require language competency and proficiency evaluation[13] as is done in other industries, such as other customer-service-focused professions, including law enforcement, hospitality, or interpretation for medical or legal settings.

Schools of medicine tasked with the education of competent medical providers are challenged to address the communication issues that their students will face both in medical school and later in residency and independent practice. Interpersonal and communication skills are recognized as one of the six core graduate medical education competencies by the Accreditation Council for Graduate Medical Education (ACGME),[14] and the Liaison Committee on Medical Education (LCME) defines communication skills and cultural competence and health care disparities as two of the nine curriculum content standards for undergraduate medical education.[15] However, communication with non-English-speaking patients is not directly addressed by existing competencies or standards. When the language of a considerable percentage of the patient population is different from that of the English-speaking providers, achieving medical communication competency with that subset of the population takes on additional layers of complexity. The existing leading evaluation tool for physician communication, the United States Medical Licensing Examination (USMLE) Step 2 Clinical Skills (CS), "is intended to determine whether physicians seeking an initial license to practice medicine in the United States ... can communicate effectively with patients"[16] but is conducted with English-speaking standardized patients only and as such may not sufficiently address the communication needs for current U.S. medical providers given LEP population trends.

Additionally, although some literature mentions the importance of language concordance from the perspective of the patient, there is little focus on the effects that systematic improvements to LEP patient communication may have on the provider's job satisfaction, wellness, and productivity. Student demand is one of the primary factors cited for initiating language concordance tools, such as educational initiatives,[17] suggesting that medical Spanish is considered a desired skill from the provider's perspective, and acquisition of medical Spanish competencies may improve provider job satisfaction.

The Current State of Medical Spanish Education

Patient–physician language concordance can be addressed in a systematic way for the large U.S. population of Spanish-speaking patients by improving medical Spanish education for medical students on a national scale.[18] However, there is a paucity of resources for medical students to acquire competency in practicing medicine in Spanish and no requirements or guidelines as to what should be included in medical Spanish curricular content. Of the 147 U.S. allopathic medical schools, 131 participated in the Association of American Medical Colleges Curriculum Inventory in 2016–2017, and of those participants, only 10 (8% of participants, 7% of all medical schools) documented medical Spanish curricular content.[19] By contrast, a prior 2012 medical school survey identified that 73 out of 110 respondents (66% of respondents; 55% of the 132 total U.S. allopathic medical schools at the time) reported having a medical Spanish educational offering for medical students.[17] The discrepancy may be partly because some of the medical Spanish offerings from the 2012 survey consist of student-led extracurricular activities and thus may not meet criteria for curricular content and also because the Curriculum Inventory questionnaire did not specifically inquire about medical Spanish content.

A few studies have described medical Spanish educational programs that could be replicated at other institutions,[20] and *MedEdPORTAL* has published several curricular approaches to medical Spanish education, including two web-based modules or vignettes,[21,22] a student-run Spanish program,[23] and a proposed method for certifying medical students as trained interpreters.[24] Furthermore, some for-profit companies produce medical Spanish online, mobile, or audio podcast products that students sometimes use on their own time to improve their skills, though these educational resources have not been validated via academic peer review.

Compounding the paucity of resources is the fact that no standardized process exists to assess and certify bilingual qualifications of medical students or physicians prior to the provider initiating medical care in Spanish. Elements that may need to be tested or verified include general Spanish language proficiency, specific competency with medical Spanish, cultural health knowledge, and ability to use the language in patient interactions and at varied patient health literacy levels. Potential assessment methods have been proposed to address some of these components.[25,26] However, even institutions with medical Spanish educational programs vary in their processes for evaluating learner language proficiency, with many using self-assessment tools.[27,28] For providers who self-rate at the high or low ends of self-assessment scales, such tools have demonstrated reasonable accuracy,[27,29] but medical Spanish educational programs, which mainly target intermediate Spanish speakers, should be coupled with more substantive standardized feedback methods for learners to better recognize their limitations and minimize potential miscommunication that could result from a provider having an increased comfort level with—but not yet being competent in—medical Spanish usage.

Further, although prior work has demonstrated that underrepresented minority physicians are more likely to want to practice in areas with underrepresented minority patients,[30] this work has not evaluated the effect of language concordance on physician practice location preference. It is plausible that some physicians may choose to work with populations with which they share linguistic and cultural knowledge. Conversely, physicians who are not fluent in a second language may be understandably reticent to practice in an area with a large volume of LEP patients. Even though the presence of language barriers has been cited as a source of frustration and additional workload for physicians,[31] and the lack of organizational resources and support has been cited as a significant source of physician burnout,[32,33] few studies have specifically examined the direct link between language discordance and physician burnout, productivity, or practice location decisions.[34]

Recommendations

Though the literature to date demonstrates that patient–physician language discordance presents obstacles to health system metrics[2,4–6] and medical education,[10–12] and a few isolated solutions have been proposed,[18,21–27,31] future efforts should use a multifaceted approach to address this complex health challenge. A standardization process for Spanish-language-concordant medical care education and quality assurance should incorporate the following four elements: (1) medical Spanish educational resource validation, (2) competency requirements for medical usage of Spanish, (3) an incentivized certification process for physicians who achieve medical Spanish competency, and (4) health system updates that include routine collection of language concordance data and designation of Hispanic-serving health centers.

Medical Spanish educational resource validation

The multitude of available medical Spanish educational resources and the varied teaching techniques, educator qualifications, and student proficiency levels make the creation of new medical Spanish educational programs a daunting task for any institution without an existing one. In addition, the United States contains a unique subset of Spanish speakers from around the world, so the language each individual uses is influenced by the dialectical variations, pronunciation, and cultural nuances of many nationalities, including the significant influence of the English language and U.S. culture. Educational resources for the usage of medical Spanish in U.S. medicine should therefore be evaluated differently than those prepared for usage abroad and should be assessed with input from multiple disciplines and sources, including linguistic, community, and medical expertise.

Competency requirements for medical usage of Spanish

Although nationally accepted undergraduate and graduate medical core competencies already recognize the importance of communication skills for graduates, specific attention to the skills needed to communicate with LEP patients is needed, including standardized competencies that are expected of individuals who wish to practice medicine in a second language. National academic organizations should recognize medical Spanish as an important corollary, if not required, component of U.S. medical education. This would facilitate the recognition that medical Spanish educational programs require rigorous academic investment by medical schools that goes beyond student-led extracurricular activities or workshops. Having ACGME- and LCME-based competencies and standards that address second-language acquisition for medical usage would provide a framework to facilitate the establishment of medical Spanish educational programs and clarify core learning and performance objectives.

Additionally, curriculum surveys conducted by national academic organizations should include "communication with LEP patients" as a required component, of which two elements should be specifically evaluated: (1) the content of medical Spanish educational programs, if offered; and (2) students' general competency in LEP patient communication skills. The second element would include students' ability to recognize their own limitations in a second language, to identify appropriate language assistance resources, and specifically to work with medical interpreters. The use of increasingly available medical interpretation tools, including remote and on-site professional interpreters, should be paired with training and evaluating medical staff in their appropriate usage to maximize effectiveness, increase physician usage and satisfaction,[31] and reduce the common but high-risk practice of using family members or untrained staff as ad hoc interpreters in health settings. It is also critical to ensure that the language interpreter services hired are certified professionals; that they are readily available; and that staff are trained both in how to use the interpreters and, in the case of remote interpreters, how to use the applicable technology, such as telephone or video conferencing, and to troubleshoot.

An incentivized certification process for physicians who achieve medical Spanish competency

Existing processes for language certification in other industries or ancillary fields, such as professional medical interpretation, can be used as example processes for certifying medical providers in the use of medical Spanish. Unique to medical practice, Spanish proficiency for physicians may not be sufficiently evaluated by written or oral examinations of basic Spanish and may also need to incorporate aspects of patient interaction, cultural knowledge, and medical terminology.[18] The USMLE Step 2 CS, which assesses competency in English language communication for all U.S. residency applicants via standardized patient encounters, provides an existing framework for examining clinical skills competence that could be used to create a similar Spanish language communication examination for physicians.

Effectively implementing this type of certification program would require buy-in from accrediting organizations, such as the ACGME and LCME, who establish standards and competencies for undergraduate and graduate medical education, as well as organizations that monitor health system quality metrics, measure satisfaction scores, and accredit health systems. Methods for implementation on a health system level would include increasing recruitment of and providing rewards, such as financial incentives, for certified bilingual physicians and physicians who achieve validated language competency certifications. In the long term, these individuals present significant cost savings and quality metrics improvements for health systems by providing quality medical care in more than one language and obviating, in many cases, the need for medical interpretation services.

Health system updates that include routine collection of language concordance data and designation of Hispanic-serving health centers

Government guidelines, such as CLAS standards, that support nondiscrimination with regard to patient language preference should also be more prescriptive about the expected requirements for physicians who practice medicine in languages other than English. Guideline compliance and enforcement would be easier and more standardized if the expectations were clearly defined. For example, language proficiency documentation should be required for all physicians intending to use a language other than English in patient care.

Furthermore, medical centers and research studies receiving federal funding should be expected to comply with the collection of basic information regarding language concordance. R/E/A/L data alone are insufficient to study language concordance; improved implementation of R/E/A/L data collection needs to be coupled with the collection of data on physicians' language proficiency so that the data can be analyzed not only with regard to patient language but also to the concordance or discordance between patient and physician.

Increased data collection regarding the language skills of medical students, physicians, and other medical staff can be used to evaluate the accuracy of self-reported language skills in an objective fashion and be coupled with measures related not only to patient outcomes or satisfaction but also to physician job satisfaction and productivity. Future research should also investigate whether bilingual physicians feel a responsibility or a desire to use their bilingual skills in the practice of medicine and evaluate how this may be a factor in their practice location decisions. Understanding this may have further implications for how increasing the number of physicians competent in medical Spanish may increase the number of physicians interested in providing care to this underserved population. Improving data collection will also be critical to verifying that safety, quality, satisfaction, and cost metrics are being positively affected by any intervention to enhance language-concordant medical care.

Finally, incentives (e.g., special grant funding eligibility) for medical schools and medical centers meeting specific criteria as Hispanic-serving health centers ought to be considered. These criteria should require medical schools and centers to not only provide services to a minimum percentage of Hispanic patients but also to have a minimum percentage of documented Spanish-language-proficient providers to meet language concordance standards. A similar long-established system that has been used to designate Hispanic-serving institutions in higher education could be used as a framework for this[35] and could offer long-term recruitment and retention benefits to medical schools' and centers' diversity and inclusion efforts.

Conclusions

Language-related challenges to the practice of medicine are a reality in an increasingly global environment. It is an issue that can no longer be ignored by medical schools and centers and that requires multidisciplinary partnerships and standardized processes that can be provided on a national scale and adapted to the needs and curricular structures of individual medical schools.

Without a cohesive approach to this complex issue, current efforts will remain disparate and potentially redundant but will not produce the needed national impact. As such, the development and sustainment of the four elements of providing quality language-concordant care to the Spanish-speaking U.S. population—resource validation, competency requirements, an incentivized certification process, and health system updates that include routine collection of language concordance data and designation of Hispanic-serving health centers—may benefit from the establishment of an overseeing academy of Spanish language medicine. Such an academy would be tasked with the role of increasing access to high-quality medical Spanish education, defining competency goals, developing certification processes that acknowledge and reward providers with bilingual competencies, and promoting language concordance data collection strategies to understand the scope of current problems and measure the impact of potential solutions.

Attending to language concordance is an important step in achieving health equity for the growing Spanish language patient population, the wellness and productivity of the physicians who serve them, and the overall quality of care provided by the U.S. health system.

Funding/Support: None reported.

Other disclosures: P. Ortega receives author royalties from Saunders Elsevier.

Ethical approval: Reported as not applicable.

P. Ortega is assistant professor, Departments of Emergency Medicine and Medical Education, College of Medicine, University of Illinois at Chicago, Chicago, Illinois; ORCID: http://orcid.org/0000-0002-5136-1805.

References

1 U.S. Census Bureau. American FactFinder. Language spoken at home by ability to speak English for the population 5 years and over (Hispanic or Latino). https://factfinder.census.gov/faces/tableservices/jsf/pages/productview.xhtml?pid=ACS_16_5YR_B16006&prodType=table. Published 2016. Accessed May 15, 2018.
2 Huang J, Ramos C, Jones K, Regenstein M. Talking With Patients: How Hospitals Use Bilingual Clinicians and Staff to Care for Patients With Language Needs. Washington, DC: George Washington University; 2009. http://www.pacificinterpreters.com/docs/resources/talking-with-patients_how-hospitals-use-bilingual-clinicians-and-staff-to-care-for-patients-with-language-needs_california-endowment.pdf. Accessed May 15, 2018.
3 Ahluwalia SC, Damberg CL, Silverman M, Motala A, Shekelle PG. What defines a high-performing health care delivery system: A systematic review. Jt Comm J Qual Patient Saf. 2017;43:450–459.
4 Schenker Y, Karter AJ, Schillinger D, et al. The impact of limited English proficiency and physician language concordance on reports of clinical interactions among patients with diabetes: The DISTANCE study. Patient Educ Couns. 2010;81:222–228.
5 Fernández A, Schillinger D, Warton EM, et al. Language barriers, physician–patient language concordance, and glycemic control among insured Latinos with diabetes: The Diabetes Study of Northern California (DISTANCE). J Gen Intern Med. 2011;26:170–176.
6 Ngo-Metzger Q, Sorkin DH, Phillips RS, et al. Providing high-quality care for limited English proficient patients: The importance of language concordance and interpreter use. J Gen Intern Med. 2007;22(suppl 2):324–330.
7 Azar KM, Moreno MR, Wong EC, Shin JJ, Soto C, Palaniappan LP. Accuracy of data entry of patient race/ethnicity/ancestry and

preferred spoken language in an ambulatory care setting. Health Serv Res. 2012;47(1 pt 1):228–240.
8 Improving access to services for persons with limited English proficiency. Executive Order 13166. Fed Regist. 2000;65:50119–50122.
9 Office of Minority Health, U.S. Department of Health and Human Services. National standards for culturally and linguistically appropriate services in health and health care: A blueprint for advancing and sustaining CLAS—Policy and practice. https://www.thinkculturalhealth.hhs.gov/pdfs/EnhancedCLASStandardsBlueprint.pdf. Published April 2013. Accessed May 15, 2018.
10 Fernández A, Pérez-Stable EJ. ¿Doctor, habla español? Increasing the supply and quality of language-concordant physicians for Spanish-speaking patients. J Gen Intern Med. 2015;30:1394–1396.
11 Vela MB, Fritz C, Press VG, Girotti J. Medical students' experiences and perspectives on interpreting for LEP patients at two US medical schools. J Racial Ethn Health Disparities. 2016;3:245–249.
12 Martínez G, Rivera-Mills S, Trujillo JA. Medical Spanish for heritage learners: A prescription to improve the health of Spanish speaking communities. In: Rivera-Mills SV, Trujillo JA, eds. Building Communities and Making Connections. Newcastle upon Tyne, UK: Cambridge Scholars Publishing; 2010:2–15.
13 Andres E, Wynia M, Regenstein M, Maul L. Should I call an interpreter?—How do physicians with second language skills decide? J Health Care Poor Underserved. 2013;24:525–539.
14 Accreditation Council for Graduate Medical Education. ACGME core competencies. https://www.ecfmg.org/echo/acgme-core-competencies.html. Updated 2007. Accessed May 15, 2018.
15 Liaison Committee on Medical Education. Functions and structure of a medical school: Standards for accreditation of medical education programs leading to the MD degree. Effective academic year: 2019–20. http://lcme.org/publications. Published March 2018. Accessed May 15, 2018.
16 Federation of State Medical Boards, National Board of Medical Examiners. Content description and general information: Step 2 Clinical Skills (CS). http://www.usmle.org/pdfs/step-2-cs/cs-info-manual.pdf. Updated 2017. Accessed May 15, 2018.
17 Morales R, Rodríguez L, Singh A, et al. National survey of medical Spanish curriculum in U.S. medical schools. J Gen Intern Med. 2015;30:1434–1439.
18 Ortega P, Park YS, Girotti JA. Evaluation of a medical Spanish elective for senior medical students: Improving outcomes through OSCE assessments. Med Sci Educ. 2017;27:329–337.
19 Association of American Medical Colleges. Curriculum Inventory: Coverage of Medical Spanish Education Content 2016–2017. Washington, DC: Association of American Medical Colleges; December 5, 2017.
20 Hardin KJ, Hardin DM. Medical Spanish programs in the United States: A critical review of published studies and a proposal of best practices. Teach Learn Med. 2013;25:306–311.
21 Cesari WA, Brescia WF, Harricharan Singh K, et al. Medical Spanish. MedEdPORTAL. https://www.mededportal.org/publication/9171. Published May 8, 2012. Accessed May 15, 2018.
22 Rampal A, Wang C, Kalisvaart J. Pediatric medical Spanish vignettes. MedEdPORTAL. https://www.mededportal.org/publication/5110. Published July 29, 2009. Accessed May 15, 2018.
23 Dawson AL, Patti B. Spanish Acquisition Begets Enhanced Service (S.A.B.E.S.): A beginning-level medical Spanish curriculum. MedEdPORTAL. https://www.mededportal.org/publication/9057. Published December 7, 2011. Accessed May 15, 2018.
24 O'Rourke K, Gruener G, Quinones D, Stratta E, Howell J. Spanish bilingual medical student certification. MedEdPORTAL. https://www.mededportal.org/publication/9400. Published April 24, 2013. Accessed May 15, 2018.
25 Tucker JD, Chen AH, Glass RI. Foreign language assessment and training in U.S. medical education is a must. Acad Med. 2012;87:257.
26 O'Rourke KM, Gruener G. A standard for medical Spanish credentialing. Acad Med. 2014;89:531–532.
27 Diamond L, Chung S, Ferguson W, González J, Jacobs EA, Gany F. Relationship between self-assessed and tested non-English-language proficiency among primary care providers. Med Care. 2014;52:435–438.
28 Lion KC, Thompson DA, Cowden JD, et al. Clinical Spanish use and language proficiency testing among pediatric residents. Acad Med. 2013;88:1478–1484.
29 Chaufan C, Karter AJ, Moffet HH, et al. Identifying Spanish language competent physicians: The Diabetes Study of Northern California (DISTANCE). Ethn Dis. 2016;26:537–544.
30 Rodríguez JE, Campbell KM, Pololi LH. Addressing disparities in academic medicine: What of the minority tax? BMC Med Educ. 2015;15:6.
31 Karliner LS, Pérez-Stable EJ, Gildengorin G. The language divide. The importance of training in the use of interpreters for outpatient practice. J Gen Intern Med. 2004;19:175–183.
32 Azam K, Khan A, Alam MT. Causes and adverse impact of physician burnout: A systematic review. J Coll Physicians Surg Pak. 2017;27:495–501.
33 Aronsson G, Theorell T, Grape T, et al. A systematic review including meta-analysis of work environment and burnout symptoms. BMC Public Health. 2017;17:264.
34 Neill T, Irwin G, Owings CS, Cathcart-Rake W. Rural Kansas family physician satisfaction with caring for Spanish-speaking only patients. Kans J Med. 2017;10:1–15.
35 U.S. Department of Education. Definition of Hispanic-serving institutions. https://www2.ed.gov/programs/idueshsi/definition.html. Accessed May 15, 2018.

RESEARCH ARTICLE

Open Access

A longitudinal study of the characteristics and performances of medical students and graduates from the Arab countries

Ara Tekian[1*] and John Boulet[2]

Abstract

Background: While international physician migration has been studied extensively, more focused and regional explorations are not commonplace. In many Arab countries, medical education is conducted in English and students/graduates seek postgraduate opportunities in other countries such as the United States (US). Eligibility for residency training in the US requires certification by the Educational Commission for Foreign Medical Graduates (ECFMG). This study investigates ECFMG application trends, examination performance, and US physician practice data to quantify the abilities and examine the career pathways of Arab-trained physicians.

Methods: Medical students and graduates from 15 Arab countries where English is the language of medical school instruction were studied. The performances (1st attempt pass rates) of individuals on the United States Medical Licensing Examination Step 1, Step 2CK (clinical knowledge), and and a combination of Step 2CS (clinical skills) and ECFMG CSA (clinical skills assessment) were tallied and contrasted by country. Based on physician practice data, the contribution of Arab-trained physicians to the US healthcare workforce was explored. Descriptive statistics (means, frequencies) were used to summarize the collected data.

Results: Between 1998 and 2012, there has been an increase in the number of Arab trained students/graduates seeking ECFMG certification. Examination performance varied considerably across countries, suggesting differences in the quality of medical education programs in the Eastern Mediterranean Region. Based on current US practice data, physicians from some Arab countries who seek postgraduate opportunities in the US are less likely to stay in the US following specialty training.

Conclusion: Countries, or regions, with concerns about physician migration, physican performance, or the pedagogical quality of their training programs should conduct longitudinal research studies to help inform medical education policies.

Keywords: International medical graduates, Career pathways, International physician migration

Background

The migration of physicians is a worldwide phenomenon [1]. Medical professionals emigrate for a number of reasons including lack of local resources, insufficient opportunities for graduate training, and a desire to improve their lives financially [2]. While the flow of physicans from one country to another is often characterized as "brain drain", the lack of advanced practice training programs in some areas can induce individuals to seek opportunities elsewhere. While this travel can exacerbate workforce shortages in some areas, it may also foster educational and social improvements, provided that the emigrating physicians eventually return to their home country or provide some sort of reciprocal financial support.

Currently, approximately 25 % of the practicing physicians in the United States did not attend medical school in the the United States [3, 4]. These physicians, referred to as international medical graduates (IMGs), originate from many countries, including many Arab

* Correspondence: tekian@uic.edu
[1]Department of Medical Education, College of Medicine, University of Illinois at Chicago, 808 South Wood Street (MC 591), Chicago, IL 60612-7309, USA
Full list of author information is available at the end of the article

© 2015 Tekian and Boulet. **Open Access** This article is distributed under the terms of the Creative Commons Attribution 4.0 International License (http://creativecommons.org/licenses/by/4.0/), which permits unrestricted use, distribution, and reproduction in any medium, provided you give appropriate credit to the original author(s) and the source, provide a link to the Creative Commons license, and indicate if changes were made. The Creative Commons Public Domain Dedication waiver (http://creativecommons.org/publicdomain/zero/1.0/) applies to the data made available in this article, unless otherwise stated.

countries. While the contribution of IMGs to the US healthcare system has been documented in a number of studies, and it is clear that some regions (e.g., Caribbean) provide a large number of physicians to the US, more focused investigations of the contributions and characteristics of medical students and graduates from specific countries/medical schools are lacking [5–8].

To obtain a license to practice in the United States, IMGs must complete some postgraduate training (residency), normally at least 3 years. To enter a residency program, IMGs must be certified by the Educational Commission for Foreign Medical Graduates (ECFMG). The current requirements for ECFMG certification are listed elsewhere but include, amongst other criteria, primary source verification of the medical school diploma and successful performance on the United States Medical Licensing Examination (USMLE), which includes the Step 1 (Basic Science), Step 2CK (Clinical Knowledge) and Step 2CS (Clinical Skills) components [9]. For the most part, individuals who start the ECFMG certification process do so with the intent of obtaining residency training positions in the US, an essential requirement to obtain an unrestricted license to practice medicine in all US jurisdictions.

To better understand the various driving forces and possible reasons for seeking higher education and training in the US, it is important to study specific regions of the world, especially those where language issues are unlikely to hinder migration. Arab countries have interesting characteristics and conditions; medical education is conducted primarily in English, there is extreme wealth and poverty, government systems vary from dictatorship to full democracy, and there can be everything from political instability to relatively desirable living conditions. These qualities can certainly have some impact on immigration patterns, the quality of educational programs as measured through standardized examinations, and the individual motivation of international graduates to seek practice opportunities outside their home countries, particularly in the US. By exploring ECFMG application trends and certification examination performance, one can untangle some of the complexities of international medical education and provide a better description and understanding of the contribution of Arab-trained physicians to the US healthcare system. Such regional analytic studies will help policy makers, both in the US and abroad, to make informed policy decisions concerning medical education and immigration.

The certification process for IMGs can be quite challenging. Individuals must pay for and pass all examinations, one of which is only offered in the United States. It is not surprising that the performance of IMGs on these certification examinations has been quite varied, both over time and by country. Previous investigations indicate that, at least based on US medical licensing examination scores and outcomes, some countries, or medical schools within countries, produce more knowledgeable and skilled physicians [10, 11]. While individual performance on the examinations may fluctuate due to a number of factors (e.g., motivation, English language proficiency), aggregate performance (e.g., by medical school, country) may be more directly related to the quality of the educational and oversight (i.e., accreditation) program(s) [12]. It should be noted, however, that even in aggregate, performance on the ECFMG certification examinations is an imperfect marker of the quality of educational programs. The medical students and graduates who seek ECFMG certification may, or may not, be representative of all students/graduates from a particular program.

The purpose of this investigation is threefold: 1) to explore physician emigration trends from Arab countries to the United States; 2) to analyze and contrast examination performance for students/graduates who attended medical schools in Arab countries; and 3) to document the contribution of Arab-trained physicians to the US healthcare system.

Methods
Description of study population
For analysis of ECFMG application trends, the sample included all medical students and graduates from Arab countries where English is the language of instruction who applied for ECFMG certification in the period 1998-2012 (15 years). These countries include Bahrain, Egypt, Iraq, Jordan, Kuwait, Lebanon, Libya, Palestinian Territory, Oman, Qatar, Saudi Arabia, Sudan, Syria, United Arab Emirates, and Yemen. For the analysis of performance, 1st attempt pass rates for all examinations (described below) for the 1998-2012 cohort were aggregated and compared. For the analysis of Arab contribution to the US workforce, the sample included all physicians who attended medical school in the countries noted above and were active in the US healthcare system (Administration, Full-time Hopital Staff, Residents, Locum Tenens, Medical Teaching, Office-Based Practice, Other and Research). It should be noted that Arab physicians who currently practice medicine in the US may not necessarily have applied for, or achieved, ECFMG certification between 1998 and 2012. This analysis of this data yields the current status of Arab-trained workforce in the United States, reflecting the emigration of Arab-trained physicians to the US over a much longer ECFMG certification window.

Data sources
The number of medical schools in the study cohort of Arab countries was tallied from the International Medical

Education (IMED) and Avicenna Directories [13, 14]. Although there are a number of Arab countries, such as Saudi Arabia, that may have more medical schools than the number reported in this manuscript, only the ones that were included in the IMED or Avicenna directories at the time of this investigation are part of this study; these medical schools are recognized by the World Health Organization (WHO) and/or are formally accepted by the Ministries of Higher Education and/or Health in the country where they are located.

ECFMG records were accessed to gather demographic information on the study cohort. The "application date" was coded at the date when the student/graduate first registered for an examination required for ECFMG certification. The year of this initial examination registration yielded the applicant year.

For the initial study period (1998-2012), examination performance data for all applicants was obtained from the National Board of Medical Examiners (NBME) via the ECFMG Master Database. The examination performance data included first-time pass rates for USMLE Step 1 (Basic Science), Step 2CK (Clinical Knowledge) and a combination of the ECFMG Clinical Skills Assessment (CSA) and USMLE Step 2CS (Clinical Skills). USMLE Step 1 (Basic Science) assesses whether the candidate can understand and can apply important concepts of sciences basic to the practice of medicine, with special emphasis on principles and mechanisms underlying health, disease, and modes of therapy. USMLE Step 2 CK (Clinical Knowledge) assesses whether the candidate can apply medical knowledge, skills, and understanding of clinical science essential for the provision of patient care under supervision and includes emphasis on health promotion and disease prevention. Both the ECFMG Clinical Skills Assessment (CSA), administered from 1998-2004, and USMLE Step 2 CS (Clinical Skills), administered from 2004 to the present, use standardized patients to evaluate medical students and graduates on their ability to gather information from patients, perform physical examinations, and communicate their findings to patients and colleagues.

The 2013 American Medical Association (AMA) Physician Masterfile was accessed to quantify the contribution of physicians trained in Arab countries to the US physician workforce. The AMA Masterfile lists all physicians practicing in the United States. As previously noted, these practicing physicians will not necessarily have applied for ECFMG certfication between 1998 and 2012; many would have applied before 1998.

To (1) study trends in physician emigration patterns, (2) document performance on national examinations of students who attended medical schools in Arab countries, and (3) quantify the contribution of Arab-trained physicians to the US health care system, we examined the following data from each Arab country: number of medical schools, population size, trends in ECFMG applicants, pass rates from US national licensure examinations (USMLE Steps 1 and 2), number of Arab-educated physicians practicing in the US physician workforce.

Analysis

Descriptive statistics (means, frequencies) were used to summarize medical school numbers, ECFMG applications, certifications, ultimate certification rates, USMLE/CSA performance and number of practicing physicians in the United States.

Applicant data was based on all students/graduates who registered for an examination leading to ECFMG certification between 1998 and 2012 (15 year cohort). Since it can take a few years to achieve ECFMG certification (meet all the examination requirements), ultimate certification (meeting all the requirements for ECFMG certification, including passing all examinations) was only based on applicants in the 1998-2007 period. Ultimate certification was calculated as the percentage of 1998-2007 initial applicants who achieved ECFMG certification by September, 2013. For this analysis, individual applicants were tracked through the certification process.

To allow for valid comparisons between countries, performance data was based on first attempt pass rates. For clinical skills, both the ECFMG Clinical Skills Assessment and USMLE Step 2CS were combined.

The AMA Masterfile data (for those attending medical schools in Arab countries where the language of instruction was English) was summarized via frequencies and descriptive statistics. This study was approved by the Institutional Review Board of the University of Illinois at Chicago.

Results

Medical schools

The numbers of medical schools and population of the 15 Arab countries are presented in Table 1. Saudi Arabia (n = 34) has the greatest number of medical schools, followed by Sudan (n = 29). Overall, across all 15 countries, there is approximately 1 medical school for every 2 million inhabitants. While there are 19 medical schools in Egypt, this represents less than 1 medical school per 4 million inhabitants. The highest medical school density is located in Bahrain (3 medical schools for a population of 1.3 million).

Emigration trends from the Arab countires

Table 2 shows the total number of initial applicants for ECFMG certification for the past 15 years by country of medical school and gender. Of the Arab countries included in this investigation, Egypt, Syria and Lebanon

Table 1 Number of medical schools and population size in 15 Arab countries

Medical School Country	Population (millions)	Number of medical schools	Medical schools/ population (millions)
Bahrain	1.3	3	2.31
Egypt	82.6	19	0.23
Iraq	32.7	18	0.55
Jordan	6.6	4	0.91
Kuwait	2.8	1	0.36
Lebanon	4.3	7	1.63
Libya	6.4	11	1.72
Palestinian territory	4.2	3	0.71
Oman	3.0	2	0.67
Qatar	1.7	1	0.59
Saudi Arabia	27.9	34	1.22
Sudan	44.6	29	0.65
Syria	22.5	7	0.31
United Arab Emirates	7.9	5	0.63
Yemen	23.8	6	0.25
Total	272.3	150	0.55

have had the most applicants, representing over 50 % of the total (n = 9093). Over all countries and the 15 year time period, 72.8 percent of the applicants were male.

Over the past 15 years (1998-2012) there has been some variability over time in the number of applicants from the Arab countries (Table 3). Beginning in 2000 (n = 527), there has been a relatively steady increase in the number of initial applicants, with a maximum being reached in 2011 (n = 2015). For some countries (data not shown), the growth in applicants has been quite remarkable. In the 5 years between 1998 and 2002 there were 144 applicants from Saudi Arabia. More recently (2008-2012), the number of initial applicants was 1194, an over 7-fold increase. The number fo female applicants has also been growing, going from a low of 121 in 2000 to a more recent high of 637 in 2012. In 2012, $1/3^{rd}$ of the initial applicants from this region were female.

While initial applicants in this time period have come from a total of 117 (of 150) different medical schools in the 15 selected Arab countries, many were educated in just 5 institutions: University of Damascus Faculty of Medicine, Syria (n = 1543, 9.1 %); University of Cairo Faculty of Medicine, Egypt (n = 1184, 7.0 %); Ain Shams University Faculty of Medicine, Egypt (n = 1024, 6.0 %); Jordan University of Science and Technology Faculty of Medicine, Jordan (n = 992, 5.8 %); and American University of Beirut Faculty of Medicine, Lebanon (n = 896, 5.3 %).

Performance
Ultimate certification
Of the 8248 students/ graduates who applied for ECFMG certification between 1998 and 2007 (inclusive), 5480 (66.4 %) achieved certification. Ultimate certification did, however, vary by country. Although

Table 2 ECFMG applicants from 15 Arab countries with medical education taught in English, by gender (1998-2012)

Medical School Country	Male	Female	Total	Percent (of total applicants)
Bahrain	100	95	195	1.15
Egypt	3155	973	4128	24.29
Iraq	936	408	1344	7.90
Jordan	1476	437	1913	11.25
Kuwait	89	55	144	0.85
Lebanon	1603	790	2393	14.07
Libya	500	160	660	3.88
Palestinian Territory	84	27	111	0.65
Oman	67	52	119	0.70
Qatar	99	93	192	1.13
Saudi Arabia	1136	477	1613	9.48
Sudan	743	459	1202	7.14
Syria	2209	223	2572	15.12
United Arab Emirates	94	223	317	1.86
Yemen	76	11	87	0.51
Total	4623	12367	16990	100

Table 3 ECFMG applicants from 15 Arab countries with medical education in English, by application year and gender (1998-2012)

Application year	Male	Female	Total	% Female	Percent (of total applicants)
1998	791	253	1044	24.2	6.14
1999	419	135	554	24.4	3.26
2000	406	121	527	23.0	3.10
2001	475	119	594	20.0	3.49
2002	516	146	662	22.1	3.89
2003	469	166	635	26.1	3.73
2004	541	189	730	25.9	4.30
2005	667	248	915	27.1	5.39
2006	940	283	1223	23.1	7.20
2007	1001	356	1357	26.2	7.99
2008	963	356	1319	27.0	7.77
2009	1173	466	1639	28.4	9.65
2010	1292	551	1843	29.9	10.85
2011	1418	597	2015	29.6	11.84
2012	1296	637	1933	33.0	11.38
Total	12367	4623	16990	27.2	100

based on only 33 people (registered for an initial examination between 1998 and 2007), 93.9 % of Qatari applicants achieved certification (as of September 2013). For the countries with the most applicants (Egypt, Syria, Lebanon) the ultimate certification rates were 54.7 %, 75.3 %, and 80.8 %, respectively. For all IMG applicants between 1998-2007 (n = 121,980), 65 % achieved ECFMG certification.

Examination performance

Examination performance of the study cohort is presented in Table 4. The data for each examination is based on first attempts taken between 1998 and 2012. For the Clinical Skills certification requirement, the first examination attempt may have been for the CSA (offered from 1998-2004) or USMLE Step 2CS (offered from 2004-2012).

Based on 1st attempt pass rates for USMLE Step 1 (Basic Science), there was considerable variability in performance by country. Averaged over all schools within the country, both Oman and Kuwait had 1st attempt pass rates of less than 50 %. On average, students educated in Jordan had the highest 1st attempt pass rates (91 %). For all IMGs taking USMLE Step 1 for the first time between 1998 and 2012, the overall pass rate was 68.9 % (range by country: 47.4 % to 94.7 %). Eight of the 15 Arab countries studied had higher pass rates.

There was also country-based variability in 1st attempt pass rates for Step 2CK. Here, on average, medical students and graduates from Qatar performed best (95 % 1st attempt pass rate). Only the UAE and Yemen had 1st attempt pass rates that were less than 60 %. For all IMGs taking USMLE Step 2CK for the first time between 1998 and 2012, the overall pass rate was 76.7 % (range by country: 58.2 % to 95.3 %). Seven of the 15 countries studied had higher pass rates.

There was somewhat less variability, across countries, on 1st time performance on CSA/USMLE Step 2CS. Here, medical students and graduates from Qatar (94.6 % pass), the United Arab Emirates (85.5 % pass), Bahrain (85.6 % pass), and Lebanon (84.2 % pass) performed the best. For all IMGs taking CSA or USMLE Step 2CS for the first time between 1998 and 2012, the overall pass rate was 80.1 % (range by country: 62.5 % to 94.6 %). Four of the 15 countries studied had higher pass rates.

Arab-trained physicians in the US workforce

Based on the 2013 AMA Masterfile, there are 891,413 active physicians (Administration, Full-time Hopital Staff, Residents, Locum Tenens, Medical Teaching, Office-Based Practice, Research, other) in the United States. Of these, nearly 1/3rd (n = 291,759) were female. Only 1.6 % (n = 14,496) of the active physicians were educated in an Arab country where medical school instruction was in English. Within this Arab cohort, only 18.6 percent (n = 2702) were female.

Table 5 shows, by country, the total number of certificates issued by ECFMG from 1958 to 2012, the number of individuals in residency training, the total number of active physicians in the US and the approximate retention rate of Arab-trained physicians.

Table 4 First attempt pass rates for USMLE Step 1, USMLE Step 2CK and CSA/USMLE Step 2CS

Medical School Country	USMLE Step 1-1st attempt pass rate			USMLE Step 2CK-1st attempt pass rate			USMLE Step 2CS/CSA – 1st attempt pass rate		
	PASS	FAIL	%	PASS	FAIL	%	PASS	FAIL	P%
Bahrain	93	50	65.04	106	37	74.13	89	15	85.58
Egypt	2305	1103	67.64	2289	1365	62.64	1835	960	65.65
Iraq	917	300	75.35	866	242	78.15	782	229	77.35
Jordan	1388	138	90.96	1483	180	89.18	1243	317	79.68
Kuwait	54	60	47.37	66	43	60.55	48	13	78.69
Lebanon	2000	200	90.91	2018	145	93.30	1595	300	84.17
Libya	480	110	81.33	463	63	88.02	390	156	71.43
Palestinian Territory	71	4	94.67	94	6	94.00	52	26	66.67
Oman	34	37	47.89	60	22	73.17	15	9	62.50
Qatar	167	22	88.36	142	7	95.30	140	8	94.59
Saudi Arabia	863	403	68.17	844	280	75.09	814	264	75.51
Sudan	603	226	72.74	654	293	69.06	435	207	67.76
Syria	1938	316	85.98	1995	416	82.75	1507	582	72.14
United Arab Emirates	120	114	51.28	133	94	58.59	109	17	86.51
Yemen	37	21	63.79	39	28	58.21	28	13	68.30

Table 5 Contribution of Arab-educated physicians to the US workforce

Arab country	ECFMG Certficates Awarded (1958-2012)	Residents (Graduate Medical Education)	Number of active physicians in the US (includes residents)	Approximate US workforce retention rate (%)
Bahrain	108	29	50	46.3
Egypt	8138	528	4517	55.5
Iraq	2034	254	1171	57.6
Jordan	1892	424	1081	57.1
Kuwait	149	14	68	45.6
Lebanon	4329	551	2781	64.2
Libya	545	136	245	45.0
Palestinian Territory	56	20	27	48.2
Oman	26	1	2	7.7
Qatar	106	68	72	67.9
Saudi Arabia	959	199	307	32.0
Sudan	688	117	345	50.1
Syria	5121	565	3769	73.6
United Arab Emirates	103	28	45	43.7
Yemen	34	8	15	44.1
Total	24288	2942	14496	59.7

Note: Active physicans include administrators, full-time hopital staff, residents, locum tenens, medical teachers, office-based practitioners, other and clinical researchers

The retention rate is approximate because a) not all ECFMG certficate holders obtain residency positions, b) some physicians entered the system before ECFMG certification requirements were manadatory, and c) some physicians, after residency training, will eventually return to their country of origin. For countries where at least 100 graduates obtained ECFMG certification, the approximate retention rates were highest for Syria (73.6 %) and lowest for Saudi Arabia (32.0 %).

Based on Table 5, over 75 % of the Arab-trained physicians in the US were educated one of three countries: Egypt (n = 4517, 31.2 %); Syria (n = 3769, 26.0 %); Lebanon (n = 2781, 19.2 %). While all 15 countries provided physicians to the US workforce, over 50 % were educated in 1 of 5 medical schools: University of Damascus Faculty of Medicine (n = 2572, 17.8 %); American University of Beirut Faculty of Medicine (n = 1764, 12.2 %); University of Cairo Faculty of Medicine (n = 1617, 11.2 %); Ain Shams University Faulty of Medicine (n = 1349, 9.3 %); University of Alexandia Faculty of Medicine (n = 1008, 7.0 %).

Discussion

While physicians trained in Arab countries do not represent a large percentage of ECFMG initial applicants, and currently make up a fairly small percentage of US physician workforce, they are a heterogenous group, both in terms of educational attainment and motivation to emigrate. Unlike other groups of physicians who seek educational opportunities outside of their country of medical school training, their characteristics and qualities have not been specifically studied [15, 16]. The motivation to emigrate is influenced by a number of factors such as higher income opportunities, the desire for greater stability and security, the perceived educational benefit from being able to access enhanced technology, and the lack of advanced graduate training locally [17, 18]. Given the sizeable growth of medical schools in this region, spurred by the demand for highly trained healthcare workers, it is important to know more about the educational programs in these countries and the relative abilities of the graduates.

Like many other parts of the world, there has been a growth in the number of medical education programs in the Arab countries. However, while the number of medical schools per given population is only a proxy for the adequacy of physician workforce supply, there is still great variability in the number of institutions per given population. Of particular note is Egypt where there are relatively few medical schools for the given population and a large number of physicians emigrating to the United States. The large physician density in Egypt (2.83 physicians/1000 inhabitants) would suggest sizeable medical school class sizes [19]. Given the challenges of education large classes, especially the provision of adequate clinical experiences, this may explain, at least partically, the moderate performance of this group on the examinations required for ECFMG certification, most notably the clinical skills component. Even if medical school class size does not have a major impact on the quality of instruction, the rapid expansion of medical schools, especially if trained faculty are scarce, is certain to put strains on some educational programs [20].

The number of IMGs taking the USMLE steps 1 and 2 exams has increased over the years. This trend, which is undoubtedly linked to the inherent motives of the test takers, is particularly important for IMGs coming from Arab countries. Globally, there is an international recognition of the USMLE step 1 and 2 examinations as markers of achievement or competence. For many medical school graduates, ECFMG certification provides the opportunity to apply to international residency training programs and eventually to practice in any part of the world. Successful candidates who get matched into US residency training programs benefit from the reputation and the prestige of being a graduate from a North American graduate medical education (GME) program, and consequently are highly regarded when they return back to their home countries and institutions. Most important, they can become the core faculty for expanding medical education programs.

In the Arab countries within the Eastern Mediterrenean Region, the quality of the undergraduate medical education training varies from one institution to another both within a country, and from one country to another. Our data, while based on a select cohort of individuals who take the examinations required for ECFMG certification, would suggest that quality of medical education (likely reflected in the curriculum, class size, length of training, clinical experience, etc.), and/or the selection of medical students, is superior in some Arab countries. For example, Lebanese medical students/graduates outperform Egyptian medical students/ graduates by at least 20 % (1st time pass rates) on both Step 1 and Step 2CK. Although there are a number of explanations for the variability in performance across countries, the educational environment, financial resources, and the motivation of the individual to succeed cannot be discounted. A large number of medical graduates from Arab countries spend up to 18 months in the US preparing for the USMLE Step 1 and Step 2 examination [21]. There are many programs to prepare these Arab students to pass the USMLE exams [22]. While these programs can be costly, many countries from where the students originate provide financial aid to help these individuals pass these exams with the hope that they get admitted to US residency training programs. Although this information is not publicly available, some countries such as Saudi Arabia advertise the financial aid program through appropriate channels [23]. Success is important for the respective countries; they believe that such accredited programs produce high caliber graduates who in turn could specialize in any medical field and thus contribute to the improvement of the health care delivery system within their own countries. At a personal level, individuals are also quite motivated to complete US residency programs because, if they return to their home country, they are usually provided excellent positions with high paying salaries [24].

Medical students coming from well-resourced nations, such as the Gulf countries (Saudi Arabia, United Arab Emirates, Bahrain, and Oman), with the exception of Qatar, which caters to US citizens, have a great desire to return back home for the reasons mentioned above. Based on our longitudinal look at US workforce retention, albeit based on overlapping cross-sectional cohorts, only 32 % Saudi Arabian physicans who were certified between 1958 and 2012 were active in the US. This is likely an overestimate in that some of the active US physicians, namely residents and fellows, would eventually return to their home country. Medical students from relatively less well-resourced countries who complete their residency program in the US either attempt to stay in the US, or return to a richer Arab country to practice medicine. For example, nearly 75 % of Syrian physicians certified by ECFMG between 1958 and 2012 are currently active in the United States. It is clear that the migration of the physicians has political, economical and social implications [20]. While not specific to the Eastern Mediteranean Region, or the Arab world, physicians "brain drain" is characterized by emigration from poorer to richer nations, potentially exacerbating disparities in health care access.

Our investigation of the emigration and performance of medical students and graduates from Arab countries is not without limitations. First, the adequacy of the healthcare workforce, at least in terms of physicians, is only partially related to the number of educational institutions. Unfortunately, accurate longitudinal data concerning medical school graduation rates is difficult to obtain. Second, performance on ECFMG certification examinations (USMLE/ CSA) is an imperfect marker of the quality of medical education programs. Our data was based on all medical students/graduates who took examinations required for ECFMG certification. This cohort may or may not represent all students/ graduates from a given country. Finally, with respect to emigration, we only looked at inflow to the United States. Other countries such as Canada, the United Kingdom and Australia also provide training and practice opportunities for international medical graduates. A more complete picture of emigration from the Arab countries would necessarily demand data from other sources.

Conclusion

The desire to improve the medical education system in the Arab countries is very high, and in some countries is the top priority for the Ministry of Higher Education and/or Health. One way to achieve that goal is to send graduates for advanced training to other countries such as the United States. While the value of this strategy depends on individuals returning to their home country, we do not know if this is an efficient way to improving the quality of medical education within a country. Moreover, findings from this study do not provide any information on how internationally-trained physicians practice in the United States or, for those who return, how they augment the local workforce and/or improve international medical education programs. As such, longitudinal research focusing on faculty development and healthcare outcomes, combined with a more detailed exploration of the determinants of performance on certification and licensing examinations, are topics for future study. Our data analyses, while specific to physicans educated in Arab countries, could easily be replicated for other countries, yielding multi-regional migration trends and more systematic, and standardized, comparisons of physician performance.

Competing interests
The authors declare that they have no competing interests.

Authors' contributions
AT initiated the research project and articulated the research question. Both AT and JB designed the methodology, analyzed the data and prepared the manuscript. JB extracted the data. Both authors read and approved the final manuscript.

Authors' information
AT is Professor, Department of Medical Education, and Associate Dean, Office of International Education, College of Medicine, University of Illinois at Chicago, Chicago, Illinois.
JB is Vice President, Research and Data Resources, Foundation for Advancement of International Medical Education and Research, Philadelphia, Pennsylvania.

Author details
[1]Department of Medical Education, College of Medicine, University of Illinois at Chicago, 808 South Wood Street (MC 591), Chicago, IL 60612-7309, USA. [2]Foundation for Advancement of International Medical Education and Research, 3624 Market Street, Philadelphia, PA 19104, USA.

Received: 6 February 2015 Accepted: 30 October 2015
Published online: 05 November 2015

References

1. Mullan F. The metrics of the physician brain drain. N Engl J Med. 2005;353(17):1810–8.
2. Okeke EN. Brain drain: do economic conditions "push" doctors out of developing countries? Soc Sci Med. 2013;98:169–78.
3. Brotherton SE, Etzel SI. Graduate medical education, 2012-2013. JAMA. 2013;310(21):2328–46.
4. Hing E, Lin S. Role of international medical graduates providing office-based medical care: United States, 2005-2006. NCHS Data Brief. 2009;13:1–8.
5. van Zanten M, Boulet JR. Medical education in the Caribbean: quantifying the contribution of Caribbean-educated physicians to the primary care workforce in the United States. Acad Med. 2013;88(2):276–81.
6. Boulet JR, Norcini JJ, Whelan GP, Hallock JA, Seeling SS. The international medical graduate pipeline: recent trends in certification and residency training. Health Aff. 2006;25(2):469–77.
7. Norcini JJ, van Zanten M, Boulet JR. The contribution of international medical graduates to diversity in the U.S. physician workforce: graduate medical education. J Health Care Poor Underserved. 2008;19(2):493–9.
8. Adams O, Kinnon C. A Public Health Perspective. International Trade in Health Services: A Developmental Perspective. Geneva: World Health Organization; 1998.
9. Educational Commission for Foreign Medical Graduates. ECFMG Certification Fact Sheet. 2013. http://www.ecfmg.org/certification/index.html. Accessed January 28, 2015.
10. van Zanten M, Boulet JR. Medical education in the Caribbean: a longitudinal study of United States medical licensing examination performance, 2000-2009. Acad Med. 2011;86(2):231–8.
11. van Zanten M, Boulet JR. Medical education in the Caribbean: variability in medical school programs and performance of students. Acad Med. 2008;83(10):S33–6.
12. van Zanten M, Boulet JR. The association between medical education accreditation and examination performance of internationally educated physicians seeking certification in the United States. Qual High Educ. 2013;19(3): 283-299.
13. International Medical Education Directory. Foundation for Advancement of International Medical Education and Research. https://imed.faimer.org/. Accessed January 28, 2015.
14. Avicenna Directories. World Ferderation for Medical Education & World Health Organization. http://avicenna.ku.dk/database/medicine/. Accessed January 28, 2015.
15. Tankwanchi ABS, Özden C, Vermund SH. Physician emigration from Sub-Saharan Africa to the United States: analysis of the 2011 AMA Physician Masterfile. PLoS Med. 2011;2013:10(9).
16. Hallock JA, McKinley DW, Boulet JR. Migration of doctors for undergraduate medical education. Med Teach. 2007;29(2-3):98–105.
17. Astor A, Akhtat T, Matallana MA, Muthuswamy V, Olowu FA, Tallo V, et al. Physician migration: views from professionals in Colombia, Nigeria, India, Pakistan and the Philippines. Soc Sci Med. 2005;61(12):2492–500.
18. Syed NA, Khimani F, Andrades M, Ali SK, Paul R. Reasons for migration among medical students from Karachi. Med Educ. 2008;42(1):61–1.
19. Global Health Observatory (WHO). Physician Density. http://www.who.int/gho/health_workforce/physicians_density/en/index.html. Accessed January 28, 2015.
20. Snadden D, Bates J, Burns P, Casiro O, Hays R, Hunt D, et al. Developing a medical school: expansion of medical student capacity in new locations: AMEE Guide No. 55. Med Teach. 2011;33(7):518–29.
21. Kaplan preparation training options for USMLE. http://www.sacm.org/MedicalUnit/Kaplan_1.aspx. Accessed September 30, 2014.
22. Kaplan Medical. http://www.kaptest.com/Medical-Licensing/index.html. Accessed January 28, 2015.
23. Saudi Arabian Cultural Mission. http://www.sacm.org/AboutSACM/Mission.aspx. Accessed January 28, 2015.
24. Arah OA, Ogbu UC, Okeke CE. Too poor to leave, too rich to stay: developmental and global health correlates of physician migration to the United States, Canada, Australia, and the United Kingdom. Am J Public Health. 2008;98(1):148–54.

Yingling S, Park Y, Curry R, Monson V, Girotti J
MedEdPublish
https://doi.org/10.15694/mep.2018.0000274.1

Research article   Open Access

Beyond cognitive measures: Empirical evidence supporting holistic medical school admissions practices and professional identity formation

Sandra Yingling[1], Yoon Soo Park[1], Raymond H. Curry[1], Verna Monson[1], Jorge Girotti[1]

Corresponding author: Dr Sandra Yingling sying@uic.edu
Institution: 1. University of Illinois College of Medicine
Categories: Selection, Undergraduate/Graduate

Received: 30/11/2018
Published: 05/12/2018

Abstract

Background: Medical schools seek admissions methods that identify applicants who hold promise to become physicians who will navigate and shape the future medical landscape. The focus on traditional cognitive measures for admission has prompted calls for holistic admissions review during the past five years. Yet, empirical evidence linking selection measures to holistic admissions practices has not been fully established, including their relationship with professional identity formation over time. A non-cognitive admissions situational judgment screening test (CASPer) measuring personal and professional characteristics was added to the University of Illinois College of Medicine admissions process two years ago, as we implemented a new curriculum that emphasizes professional identity development.

Purpose: This study examined associations among admissions measures (Medical College Admission Test [MCAT], grade point average [GPA], interview, and CASPer), and their predictive relationships with curricular measures of professional identity formation (Professional Identity Essay [PIE]) and moral reasoning (Defining Issues Test [DIT2]).

Methods: Data were taken from two entering cohorts ($n = 596$; entering class of 2017 and 2018 across 3 regional sites). Correlations and regression analyses were used to examine associations between admissions and professional identity measures.

Results: CASPer and in-person admissions interview ratings had significant positive correlations, suggesting that CASPer can contribute to effective screening processes. In addition, CASPer demonstrated statistically significant positive relationships with professional identity (CASPer and PIE, $r=.10$, $p<.05$) and a measure of moral reasoning (CASPer and DIT2 type indicator, $r=.09$, $p<.05$). Association between CASPer and PIE remained consistent, even after controlling for MCAT, interview, and GPA.

Conclusion: Our institutional focus on professional identity formation has provided new ways to conceptualize students' readiness for medical school – demonstrated academic rigor as well as signs of professionalism, ethics, and motivation. Non-academic factors measured in situational judgment tests may promote better alignment of admissions practices and desired educational outcomes.

Keywords: situational judgment; assessment; admissions; CASPer; professional identity; Professional Identity Essay; PIE; Defining Issues Test; DIT2; non-cognitive; selection; holistic admission

Introduction

Historically, medical schools have relied on quantitative, cognitively-based measures like national standardized test scores and grade point averages as the central criteria for medical school admission. However, given the need for physicians to be leaders in addressing complex ethical and moral dilemmas, and in being champions of the health of the communities they serve, medical schools are broadening the scope of their admissions processes. This approach is often referred to as "holistic review," defined as "a flexible, individualized way of assessing an applicant's capabilities by which balanced consideration is given to experiences, attributes, and academic metrics... and, when considered in combination, how the individual might contribute value as a medical student and future physician" (AAMC, 2013).

Concurrent with the implementation of a newly integrated undergraduate curriculum in 2017, the University of Illinois College of Medicine [hereinafter "the College"] introduced an early and consistent emphasis on professional identity (Irby and Hamstra, 2016) as the cornerstone of resilience in the face of challenges to professional and ethical behavior. Students complete two measures at the beginning of medical school: the Professional Identity Essay (PIE, Bebeau and Monson, 2012) and a moral reasoning assignment (Defining Issues Test, or DIT2, Rest, 1999; Bebeau, 2002). Individualized written feedback reports and subsequent discussions highlight ways in which students can influence their professional identity formation and increase their capacity for effective, real-time moral reasoning in the clinical workplace.

The College admits approximately 300 students per year and has humanism as its focus: the whole physician serving the whole patient. We thus had a compelling need to respond to the national call for admissions practices that will support our goal of developing physicians who are ready to face complex challenges, to form effective teams, and to turn experiences into knowledge and knowledge into wisdom. We sought evidence-based "non-cognitive" factors in the admissions process that would help to identify strong candidates; this required using selection methods that go beyond standardized testing. The factors that currently determine admissions decisions include academic credentials such as MCAT score and grade-point average; other academic and non-academic experiences in research, clinical settings, campus and community; and personal attributes of the applicant. Those who meet preset criteria are invited to a personal interview, which is added to the previous criteria. The College added an application requirement in 2017: completion of the online Computer-based Assessment for Sampling Personal Characteristics (CASPer). The CASPer data has not been used in admissions decisions to date.

CASPer is an online situational judgment screening test that has demonstrated predictive validity for personal and professional characteristics as many as six years after medical school admission (Dore, 2017). CASPer was introduced at our College as an additional dimension of non-cognitive characteristics, to supplement the in-person admissions interviews conducted by our administrators, faculty, staff, and students. Admissions interviewers provide ratings that address the professionalism, motivation, and other attributes that each interviewee demonstrates during a

45-minute interview; the ratings are then compiled into a composite interview score for each interviewee.

The College has a commitment to nurture students' professional identity formation that is reflected in our curriculum. From their first days in medical school, students participate in a structured, longitudinal curriculum of professional identity formation that includes reflective writing and small group discussions led by faculty facilitators. Early in their training, students receive a detailed, personalized feedback report on two measures, the Professional Identity Essay and the Defining Issues Test (DIT2). The feedback report gives students a framework for thinking about how professional identity develops: from first being focused on individual achievement as it is externally defined, to then discerning how to be a contributing member of a clinical team, to then defining for oneself how to take responsibility for complex clinical challenges that have no roadmap and creating one's own definition of what the community of practice will be.

This study provides empirical support for the inclusion of non-cognitive elements in the admissions process. CASPer is a systematic, efficient, and standardized method of incorporating important evidence of applicants' orientation toward professionalism, ethics, and motivation that can support and supplement our existing in-person admissions interviews.

Methods

Admissions Process

CASPer as part of admissions process: CASPer is a situational judgment test that comprises 12 sections, requiring eight responses to video and four responses to written scenarios. CASPer requires applicants to provide open-ended responses rather than choosing from a list of response options. An application is not considered complete without a CASPer score on record. Only those applicants who take the test and submit their score can be considered for potential in-person interviews. This data set is of matriculants whose offer of matriculation was not based on CASPer.

Interview as part of admissions process: In-person interviews, average of multiple interviewers including administrators, faculty, staff and students. Results are aggregated into a single 5-point scale.

MCAT, Science GPA, Cumulative GPA: All academic data are verified by AMCAS before an application arrives at the college. By July 1st (just before enrolling in the college), an admitted student must provide an official transcript that must show that they were awarded a baccalaureate degree.

Professional Identity Formation in the Curriculum

The College curriculum provides longitudinal integration of themes such as Professional Development, which addresses professional identity formation (PIF) through focused reflective writing and recurring small group discussions with faculty. Professional identity formation is emphasized as a key to understanding and addressing challenges to professionalism and ethical behavior, and is explained within the frameworks proposed by Bebeau and Faber-Langendoen (2014) and Cruess et al. (2014). During medical school orientation, students attend a 90-minute large group introducton to the developmental nature of professionalism, our institution's role in guiding and supporting the formation of students' professional identity formation, and each student's opportunities to prepare and practice and therefore exert influence on their own development. Students receive an assignment to complete both the Professional Identity Essay (PIE) and a moral reasoning measure (Defining Issues Test, DIT2).

At the time the assignment is given, students are provided with the following context: each student will receive a written report that includes individualized feedback, the PIE stage that best reflects their writing, and DIT2 category that best reflects their responses to a set of hypothetical moral dilemmas. The individual written reports are for the students' use and can be shared or not shared based on the students' preference; individual reports are not provided to faculty who facilitate PIF small groups. Students are asked to engage fully in the assignment by being thoughtful, by providing complete elaborated responses to prompts, and by being aware that these conceptual frameworks and this report will be referenced throughout the curriculum.

The Professional Identity Formation Report

Deidentified PIE narrative responses were scored by Dr. Verna Monson and Dr. Aja King. DIT2 responses were scored by the Center for Ethical Development at the University of Alabama. Feedback reports were generated for each student that included a description of professional identity formation stages, the prompts, and the student's responses, along with individualized narrative feedback with observations and developmental suggestions.

About eight weeks into the curriculum, students receive their PIF reports, gather for a plenary on professional identity formation, and meet with their faculty-facilitated PIF small groups. Students then complete a reflective and analytic writing assignment about their understanding of the PIF report data they received; they are asked to write a note to themselves in the future ("Write to your future self... What do you want to remind yourself about - your concerns and aspirations as a beginning medical student? What challenges do you anticipate as you begin to act and feel like a physician?"). Their note to themselves is then revisited a year later before they begin clerkships.

Professional Identity Essay

The Professional Identity Essay (PIE) elicits respondents' conceptualization of their professional role in society and measures stages of mental complexity (i.e., psycho-social-emotional capacities). PIF stages for individual respondents are assigned based on narrative responses to nine prompts. Previously reported PIE inter-rater ICC: .83, 95% CI [.57 - .96], and intra-rater ICC .85, 95% CI [.50 - .93] (Kalet et al., 2016). The nine prompts to which students are asked to provide thoughtful and fully elaborated responses are:

1. What does being a member of the medical profession mean to you? How did you come to this understanding?
2. What do you expect of yourself as you work towards becoming a full-fledged physician?
3. What will the profession expect of you?
4. What conflicts do you experience or expect to experience between your responsibility to yourself and others—patients, family, and profession? How do you resolve them?
5. What would be the worst thing for you if you failed to live up to the expectations you have set for yourself?
6. What would be the worst thing for you if you failed to live up to the expectations of your patients?
7. What would be the worst thing for you if you failed to live up to what society expects of physicians? How did you come to this understanding?
8. Think of a physician you consider an exemplar of professionalism. Describe why you chose this person, illustrating with an incident or pattern of decisions or actions that supports your choice.
9. Reflect on your experiences in medical school or in the community that have been critical in fostering change in your understanding of what it means to be a professional – to be a physician.

Students' narrative responses are coded, resulting in descriptions of professional identity that range along a continuum of mental complexity from identity that is primarily externally defined (independent operator and team-oriented idealist) to identity that is increasingly self-defined (self-authoring integrated professional and self-transformational). Four descriptive categories mirror Kegan's model of developmental stages relevant to adults,

Stages 2-5 (Kegan, 1994). The independent operator roughly equates to Kegan's instrumental mind (Stage 2), the team oriented idealist to the socialized mind (Stage 3), the self-authoring integrated professional to the self-authoring mind (Stage 4), and self-transformational (Stage 5).

Defining Issues Test (DIT2)

Multiple studies indicate that medical training itself may decrease sensitivity to moral dilemmas and also may slow growth in moral reasoning (Patenaude et al, 2003; Murrell, 2014). The defining issues test (DIT2) identifies the types of moral arguments an individual finds persuasive when confronted with a moral problem and therefore is a measure of moral judgment, one central component of moral behavior (Bebeau 2002). The DIT2 presents a series of written cases of moral dilemmas and asks respondents to choose an action from a list, and then to rank a set of justification statements as to how important each statement was in their choice. The resulting DIT2 score reflects the proportion of the time students use universal ethical principles, or defined rules, or personal interest to justify a response to six moral dilemma cases. The DIT2 has been extensively validated and is highly resistant to social desirability bias (Rest et al, 1999).

An overall score ranging from 1 to 7 is calculated, reflecting the relative proportion of personal interest, maintaining norms, or postconventional thinking that was in evidence (DIT "type" indicator). Separate scores for each of the three categories are also calculated.

Scoring and Data Analysis

Data: We used retrospective data from 596 students collected across two cohorts of the College's students (cohort 2017: $n = 286$; cohort 2018: $n = 310$). Admissions data collected prior to matriculation (standardized global MCAT scores, undergraduate science and cumulative GPAs, interview scores, and standardized CASPer scores) were merged with professional identity and development data collected during first year of medical school (PIE, DIT: Personal Interest, DIT: Maintain Norms, DIT: Post Conventional, and DIT: Type Indicator).

Analysis: Descriptive statistics were used to examine trends across measures and between years. Pearson correlations were used to examine associations. Multiple regression analyses were used to evaluate the predictive relationship between admissions data and professional identity and development data. Data compilation and analyses were conducted using Stata 14 (College Station, TX, USA). The institutional review board at the University of Illinois at Chicago approved this study (Protocol #2012-0783).

Results/Analysis

Descriptive Statistics (See Table 1):

Admissions measures (MCAT, Science GPA, Cumulative GPA, interview score, and CASPer) and professional identity and development measures (PIE and DIT measures) were not significantly different between the 2017 and 2018 cohorts. Descriptive statistics pertaining to these measures are presented in Table 1.

Table 1. Descriptive Statistics

Factors	Measures	Cohort 2017 ($n = 286$)	Cohort 2018 ($n = 310$)	Overall ($n = 596$)

Admissions Measures	MCAT	510.17	(7.31)	512.02	(6.13)	511.20	(6.73)
	Science GPA	3.56	(0.33)	3.63	(0.33)	3.60	(0.34)
	Cumulative GPA	3.66	(0.25)	3.72	(0.24)	3.69	(0.25)
	Interview Score	4.26	(0.50)	4.31	(0.44)	4.28	(0.47)
	CASPer	0.12	(0.92)	0.18	(0.91)	0.15	(0.91)
Professional Identity and Development	Professional Identity Essay (PIE)	3.14	(0.42)	3.18	(0.35)	3.16	(0.38)
	DIT: Personal Interest	19.60	(11.26)	18.64	(11.29)	19.10	(11.28)
	DIT: Maintain Norms	25.50	(12.46)	26.69	(13.60)	26.13	(13.07)
	DIT: Post Conventional	50.78	(14.37)	50.48	(14.33)	50.62	(14.33)
	DIT: Type Indicator	6.13	(1.51)	6.10	(1.55)	6.11	(1.53)

Note: Values in parentheses are standard deviations.

Relationships among Admissions variables (See Table 2):

Cognitive admissions measures (MCAT, Science GPA and cumulative GPA): **Positive linear relationships were found** between MCAT and Science GPA (moderate correlation: r=.36, p<.001), MCAT and cumulative GPA (moderate correlation: r=.32, p<.001), Science GPA and cumulative GPA (strong correlation: r=.94, p<.001).

MCAT and Admissions interview ratings: **No relationship** between standardized admissions test (MCAT) and ratings provided by College admissions interviewers was found (r=-.01, p=.862 NS).

MCAT, Admissions interview ratings and Non-cognitive admissions measure (CASPer): **Positive linear relationships** were found between CASPer and MCAT (modest correlation: r=.12, p<.01) and between CASPer and ratings provided by College admission interviewers (modest correlation: r=.13, p<.01).

Relationships among Non-Cognitive variables (See Table 2):

Admissions non-cognitive elements (CASPer and Interview) and measure of professional identity (PIE): Positive relationships between PIE and CASPer (modest correlation: r=.10, p<.05) and between PIE and Interview (modest correlation: r=.13, p=.002) were found.

Admissions non-cognitive element (CASPer) and measure of moral reasoning (DIT2): A positive relationship between DIT2 Type Indicator and CASPer (modest correlation: r=.09, p<.05) was found. **A negative relationship** between DIT2: Personal Interest and CASPer (modest correlation: r=-.09, p<.05) was found.

Measures of Professional identity formation (PIE) and moral reasoning (DIT2): Positive relationships between the Professional Identity Essay (PIE) and a measure of moral reasoning (Defining Issues Test, DIT2) were found. PIE and DIT Type Indicator show modest associations: r=.11, p<.05; PIE and DIT Post-Conventional Thinking show a modest correlation: r=.12, p<.01. However, PIE and DIT Personal Interest show a small negative correlation: r=-.13, p<01.

Table 2. Associations between Measures: Pearson Correlation

Measure	Statistic	PIE	DIT: Personal Interest	DIT: Maintains Norms	DIT: Post Conventional	DIT: Type Indicator	Casper	MCAT	Science GPA	Cumulative GPA
DIT: Personal Interest	Correlation	-.13								
	p-value	.002								
DIT: Maintains Norms	Correlation	-.05	-.31							
	p-value	.276	.000							
DIT: Post Conventional	Correlation	.12	-.48	-.63						
	p-value	.004	.000	.000						
DIT: Type Indicator	Correlation	.11	-.46	-.38	.72					
	p-value	.013	.000	.000	.000					
Casper	Correlation	.10	-.09	.03	.06	.09				
	p-value	.017	.034	.508	.176	.043				
MCAT	Correlation	.00	-.12	-.09	.19	.11	.12			
	p-value	.943	.005	.039	.000	.008	.004			
Science GPA	Correlation	-.07	-.06	.02	.03	.01	.05	.36		
	p-value	.078	.159	.589	.537	.802	.276	.000		
Cumulative GPA	Correlation	-.09	-.05	.00	.05	.03	.07	.32	.94	
	p-value	.040	.224	.950	.268	.528	.086	.000	.000	
Interview	Correlation	.13	-.06	-.01	.07	.08	.13	-.01	-.03	-.01
	p-value	.002	.119	.777	.100	.057	.002	.862	.466	.870

Relationships between Admissions variables and Professional Identity Formation variables (See Table 3):

Predicting PIE: In a linear regression model, CASPer is consistently a significant predictor variable for PIE scores (p<.05). Admissions interview ratings are also a significant predictor variable for PIE scores (p<.01), but MCAT, science GPA, and cumulative GPA are not.

Predicting moral reasoning: In linear regression models predicting various aspects of moral reasoning (DIT2), CASPer is not a significant predictor variable. However, both the MCAT and Admissions Interview ratings are highly significant positive predictors of one of the three moral reasoning schemas: the application of principles, also called "postconventional thinking" (MCAT p<.001 and Interview rating p<.05). MCAT is also a highly significant *negative* predictor of one of the other moral reasoning schemas, maintaining norms (p<.001).

Table 3. Relationship between Admissions Measures and Professional Identity Formation: Linear Regression

Measures	Professional Identity Essay		Defining Issues (DIT2)						Type Indicator	
			Personal Interest		Maintains Norms		Post Conventional			
	β	p-value	β	p-value	β	p-value	β	p-value	β	p-value
Casper	.09	.041*	−.07	.104	.07	.129	.00	.927	.05	.249
MCAT	−.01	.791	−.08	.091	−.16	.001**	.22	<.001***	.12	.008**
Science GPA	.09	.534	−.09	.498	.21	.130	−.14	.304	−.13	.328
Cumulative GPA	−.19	.180	.12	.393	−.18	.175	.10	.464	.12	.377
Interview	.13	.003**	−.07	.101	−.04	.388	.09	.034*	.08	.056

Note: * $p < .05$, ** $p < .01$, *** $p < .001$. Effect sizes represent standardized beta coefficients.

Discussion

As anticipated, the Admissions cognitive measures tended to be highly correlated with each other: MCAT, science GPA, and cumulative GPA all showed significant positive relationships. The MCAT and Admissions Interview ratings displayed no relationship. However, CASPer demonstrated significant positive relationships with both a traditional cognitive measure (MCAT) and with a non-cognitive measure (Admissions interview ratings) as well. Additional sub-analyses of CASPer data will be conducted to determine how CASPer relates conceptually to both the cognitive and non-cognitive measure.

Our newly integrated curriculum incorporates two measures of professional identity formation into our orientation to medical school: the Professional Identity Essay and the Defining Issues Test. We note with interest that CASPer displayed statistically significant positive relationships with both of these PIF measures. Changes in medical students' professional identity as measured by PIE have been documented during the first 15 months of medical school (Kalet et al, 2018). Since PIE is based on well-established constructive-developmental theories, further examination of this measure may contribute to the evidence base to guide medical education practice and policy (Cook, Bordage, & Schmidt, 2008; Rabow et al., 2010).

This study provides empirical support for the inclusion of CASPer in a holistic approach to medical school admissions. CASPer may be a feasible alternative to the more intensive structured in-person admissions interviews, the Multiple Mini-Interviews (MMI; Reiter et al, 2007). The physicians we train need to be context-builders for their community of practice, so we must continue to look beyond standardized test scores and GPA to identify applicants who will grow to become great physicians. Based on two years of data (almost 600 students), CASPer demonstrates significant positive relationships with other admissions measures - and importantly, with some measures used in the curriculum (e.g., stage of professional identity formation). The College curriculum explicitly teaches professional identity formation as a) our institutional responsibility and b) something on which students have more influence if they understand why professional identity formation is important, how it is formed, and how moral reasoning develops through deliberate practice. CASPer is a step toward better alignment of our admissions practices with our educational practices and desired outcomes.

Conclusion

This study supports the inclusion of CASPer as a contributing non-cognitive element in making holistic admissions decisions. Our institutional focus on professional identity formation has given us new ways to conceptualize individual student differences in readiness for medical school - not just for the academic rigors, but for the life experiences that form the core of the perspective and ethical decision-making required of a professional. These are differences in readiness that, once apparent and explicit, can be embraced as another dimension of our student body's diversity and strength.

Take Home Messages

- Applying holistic admissions practices for selecting and recruiting students can contribute to shaping the professional identity of learners.
- Standardized tests of admissions and GPAs are not sensitive to detecting professional identity development.
- Situational judgment tests can be a useful indicator that bridges traditional cognitive measures and non-cognitive measures to form robust admissions signals.
- Measure and monitor professional identity development from early stages of medical education training.

Notes On Contributors

Sandra Yingling, PhD is the Associate Dean for Educational Planning at the University of Illinois College of Medicine, and Assistant Professor in the Department of Medical Education at the University of Illinois at Chicago. She focuses on curricular innovation, self-regulated learning among medical students, and professional identity formation.

Yoon Soo Park, PhD is Associate Professor in the Department of Medical Education at the University of Illinois at Chicago. His research interests extend across multiple disciplines in psychometrics, biostatistics, educational psychology, and medicine.

Raymond H. Curry, MD is the Senior Associate Dean for Educational Affairs at the University of Illinois College of Medicine, and Professor of Medicine and Medical Education, University of Illinois at Chicago.

Verna Monson, PhD is a consultant to the University of Illinois College of Medicine on the assessment of professional identity formation for medical education. Her research interests include professional education curriculum development and evaluation, and holistic approaches to remediating professionalism lapses.

Jorge Girotti, PhD is the Associate Dean for Admissions and Special Curricular Programs for the University of Illinois College of Medicine, and Assistant Professor in the Department of Medical Education at the University of Illinois at Chicago.

Acknowledgements

We thank Muriel J. Bebeau, PhD, Professor in the Department of Primary Dental Care, School of Dentistry, University of Minnesota and former Director of the Center for the Study of Ethical Development for her inspiring contributions to the field and Adina Kalet, MD, MPH, Professor in the Department of Internal Medicine and Director of the Research on Medical Education Outcomes unit at the New York University School of Medicine for her leadership in scholarship focused on professional identity formation.

We also thank Michelle Tichy, Ph.D. and Aja King, Ed.D., LPCC, for their support in data analysis and establishing scoring reliability of the Professional Identity Formation Essay. Our work is supported by the Office of Educational Affairs of the University of Illinois College of Medicine and the Department of Medical Education of the University of Illinois at Chicago.

Bibliography/References

Association of American Medical Colleges (2013). *Roadmap to excellence: Key concepts for evaluating the impact of medical school holistic admissions.* Washington, D.C.

Bebeau, M. J. (2002). 'The defining issues test and the four component model: contributions to professional education'. *J Moral Educ*, 31(3), 271-295. https://doi.org/10.1080/0305724022000008115

Bebeau, M. J., & Faber-Langendoen, K. (2014). 'Remediating lapses in professionalism'. *Remediation in medical education* (pp. 103-127): Springer. https://doi.org/10.1007/978-1-4614-9025-8_7

Bebeau, M. J., & Monson, V. E. (2012). 'Professional identity formation and transformation across the life span'. *Learning trajectories, innovation and identity for professional development* (pp. 135-162). London: Springer. https://doi.org/10.1007/978-94-007-1724-4_7

Cook, D. A., Bordage, G., & Schmidt, H. G. (2008). 'Description, justification and clarification: a framework for classifying the purposes of research in medical education'. *Medical Education*, 42(2), 128-133. https://doi.org/10.1111/j.1365-2923.2007.02974.x

Cruess, R. L., Cruess, S. R., Boudreau, J. D., Snell, L., & Steinert, Y. (2014). 'Reframing medical education to support professional identity formation'. *Academic Medicine*, 89(11), 1446-1451. https://doi.org/10.1097/ACM.0000000000000427

Dore, K. L. (2017). CASPer, an online pre-interview screen for personal/professional characteristics: prediction of national licensure scores|SpringerLink. *Advances in Health Sciences Education.* 22: 327–336. https://doi.org/10.1007/s10459-016-9739-9

Irby, D. M., & Hamstra, S. J. (2016). 'Parting the Clouds: Three Professionalism Frameworks in Medical Education'. *Academic Medicine*, 91(12). https://doi.org/10.1097/ACM.0000000000001190

Kalet, A., Buckvar-Keltz, L., Monson, V., Harnik, V., Hubbard, S., *et al.* (2018). 'Professional Identity Formation in medical school: One measure reflects changes during pre-clerkship training'. *MedEdPublish*

Kalet, A., Buckvar-Keltz, L., Harnik, V., Monson, V., Hubbard, S., *et al.* (2017). 'Measuring professional identity formation early in medical school'. *Medical Teacher*, 39(3), 255-261. https://doi.org/10.1080/0142159X.2017.1270437

Kegan, R. (1994). *In over our heads: The mental demands of modern life*. Harvard University Press.

Patterson, F., Roberts, C., Hanson, M.D., Hampe, W., Eva, K., *et.al.* (2018). '2018 Ottawa consensus statement: Selection and recruitment to the healthcare professions'. *Medical Teacher*, Sep 25, 1-11. https://doi.org/10.1080/0142159X.2018.1498589

Rabow, M. W., Remen, R. N., Parmelee, D. X., Inui, T. S. (2010). 'Professional formation: extending medicine's lineage of service into the next century'. *Academic Medicine*, 85(2), 310-317. https://doi.org/10.1097/ACM.0b013e3181c887f7

Reiter, H. I., Eva, K. W., Rosenfeld, J., Norman, G. R. (2007). 'Multiple mini-interviews predict clerkship and licensing examination performance'. *Medical Education*, 41: 378–384. https://doi.org/10.1111/j.1365-2929.2007.02709.x

Rest, J., Narvaez, D., Bebeau, M. J., & Thoma, S. J. (1999). 'Postconventional moral thinking: A neo-Kohlbergian approach'. Mahwah, NJ, US: Lawrence Erlbaum Associates Publishers.

Appendices

None.

Declarations

The author has declared that there are no conflicts of interest.

This has been published under Creative Commons "CC BY 4.0" (https://creativecommons.org/licenses/by-sa/4.0/)

Ethics Statement

The institutional review board of the University of Illinois at Chicago reviewed and approved this study (protocol # 2012-0783).

External Funding

This paper has not had any External Funding

AMEE MedEdPublish: rapid, post-publication, peer-reviewed papers on healthcare professions' education. For more information please visit www.mededpublish.org or contact mededpublish@dundee.ac.uk.

Part IV: Bias Issues

Overview

Michael Blackie
Associate Professor, Department of Medical Education

The forms bias takes in this section's three articles vary considerably. Bias starts as a prejudice against racial, cultural, and physical differences, becomes an example of favoring one kind of student over another, and ends as a problem of cognition. Despite these differences, the authors of these articles believe the surest way to address bias is through education. In the following, I provide a synopsis of each article and conclude with a forecast of future work in the Department of Medical Education.

In "Narrative intersectionality in caring for marginalized or disadvantaged patients: thinking beyond categories in medical education and care," Blackie and colleagues, Wear and Zarconi, propose a critical framework of "narrative intersectionality" to oppose bias in health care. Although they recognize the essential role that categories play in health care, they also identify a problematic reliance on broad categorizations that divide patients in "two systems of social classification – the interesting/uninteresting patient as relates to his or her illness, and the ideal/despised patient marked by their personal characteristics and social status outside of the hospital". The educational approach they develop to combat this biased sorting of patients combines narrative approaches to medical practice with the theoretical term "intersectionality". At its core, intersectionality is the belief that "individual lives cannot be fully understood by attending simply to narrow bands or categories of identity – gender, race, age, class, sexual identity, disability, immigration status, and so forth – in isolation". To demonstrate how educators can incorporate this framework in their teaching, the authors use it to examine two films, *Precious* (2009) and *Dirty Pretty Things* (2003), that present characters whose lives comprise numerous and often-contradictory identities. Blackie and colleagues conclude by proposing that narrative intersectionality provides medical educators with a valuable tool for teaching future physicians to appreciate the complexities of patients' lives.

Hirshfield, Yudkowsky, and Park examine another kind of bias, that which assumes students who majored in science before coming to medical school are more successful than their peers who did not. Their article, "Pre-medical majors in the humanities and social sciences: impact on communication skills and specialty choice", looks specifically at effective communication and interpersonal skills (CIS), skills the Accreditation Council for Graduate Medical Education define as one of the six core competencies. Citing scholars who have long argued "that a student's academic success may have little bearing on his or her later medical skill and that achievement in scientific courses may be less important than aptitude related to human interaction", Hirshfield and colleagues draw attention to how admissions committees continue to view students whose pre-medical education emphasized the humanities or social sciences as less prepared for the rigors of medical school. With data collected from 465 students, Hirshfield used correlation and regression analyses "to examine relationships between pre-medical background, performance on graduation competency examination standardized patient encounters CIS scores" and Step 2 and Step 2 Clinical Knowledge scores. The results counter the bias that pre-medical science majors score higher on these exams and show that graduating medical students who majored in the humanities or social sciences "performed significantly better in terms of CIS than those with natural science majors". Ultimately, this study suggests that recruiting students with a broad mix of pre-medical backgrounds may actually improve their learning experiences in medical school and postgraduate training.

In "Training induces cognitive bias: the case of a simulation emergency airway curriculum," Park and colleagues, Stojiljkovic, Milicic, Lin, and Dror, chart the effects on 23 novice anesthesiology residents of changing the order of techniques for addressing a cannot-ventilate, cannot-intubate simulation scenario. Motivating this study was the hunch that cognitive bias influences decision making and may in turn compromise performance. Park and colleagues define cognitive bias as "an inclination in judgement based on incomplete perspective and preformed patterns of thought". Because this inclination may hold constant "at the expense of other valid, potentially better, alternatives" when decisions must be made quickly and under stress, individuals are prone to bias. To test their hypothesis, Park and colleagues designed two different training sessions in which the sequences of information, techniques, and practical training presented to the residents differed. After dividing the residents into two groups – those initially trained in cricothyroidotomy (CRIC group) and those trained in supraglottic airway (SGA group) – and taking them through the sessions, the authors found that "practical training in only one technique caused bias in both groups". Residents in both groups favored the first technique they learned regardless of its appropriateness. But what stood out most between the groups was "an asymmetrical effect": the group who received training in cricothyroidotomy first remained biased toward it despite receiving subsequent training in the other procedure. In the words of Park and colleagues, the important take-home is: "By deciphering the underpinnings of cognitive bias in education, educators will be able to tailor strategies to minimize bias and improve patient safety".

Each of these articles identifies a particular form of bias in medical education and draws attention to the formal and informal means that cause or perpetuate them. Each set of authors also provides strategies and recommendations for correcting or preventing these biases. Looking forward, the Department of Medical Education will continue to invest in and support the kind of research and scholarship represented by these articles, which attest to the Department's commitment to intellectual diversity and multidisciplinary training.

Article

Narrative Intersectionality in Caring for Marginalized or Disadvantaged Patients: Thinking Beyond Categories in Medical Education and Care

Michael Blackie, PhD, Delese Wear, PhD, and Joseph Zarconi, MD

Abstract

Categories are essential to doctors' thinking and reasoning about their patients. Much of the clinical categorization learned in medical school serves useful purposes, but an extensive literature exists on students' reliance on broad systems of *social* categorization. In this article, the authors challenge some of the orthodoxies of categorization by combining narrative approaches to medical practice with the theoretical term "intersectionality" to draw students' attention to the important intersecting, but often overlooked, identities of their patients. Although intersectionality applies for all patients, the focus here is on its importance in understanding and caring for marginalized or disadvantaged persons.

Intersectionality posits that understanding individual lives requires looking beyond categories of identity in isolation and instead considering them at their intersection, where interrelated systems of power and oppression, advantage and discrimination are at play and determine access to social and material necessities of life. Combined with narrative approaches that emphasize the singularity of a person's story, narrative intersectionality can enable a more robust understanding of how injustice and inequality interrelate multidimensionally to produce social disadvantage.

The authors apply this framework to two films that present characters whose lives are made up of numerous and often-contradictory identities to highlight what physicians may be overlooking in the care of patients. If the education of physicians encourages synthesis and categorization aimed at the critically useful process of making clinical "assessments" and "plans," then there must also be emphasis in their education on what might be missing from that process.

Social life is considered too irreducibly complex ... to make fixed categories anything but simplifying social fictions.
—McCall, 2005[1]

Medical education depends on categories. From the first day of medical school, students are trained to see, hear, and think in categories. In the preclinical curriculum, a great deal of this thinking is binary: healthy versus diseased, normal versus abnormal, typical versus atypical.

M. Blackie is associate professor of health humanities, Department of Medical Education, College of Medicine, University of Illinois at Chicago, Chicago, Illinois.

D. Wear is professor of family and community medicine, Northeast Ohio Medical University, Rootstown, Ohio.

J. Zarconi is professor and chair of internal medicine and senior associate dean for health affairs, Northeast Ohio Medical University, Rootstown, Ohio.

Correspondence should be addressed to Michael Blackie, Department of Medical Education, University of Illinois at Chicago, 808 S. Wood St., CME 986, Chicago, IL 60612; e-mail: blackie@uic.edu.

Acad Med. 2019;94:59–63.
First published online August 21, 2018
doi: 10.1097/ACM.0000000000002425
Copyright © 2018 by the Association of American Medical Colleges

In the clinical environment, much of this thinking involves "preset algorithms and practice guidelines in the form of decision trees."[2] Does it look normal/feel normal/sound normal, or not? Do the numbers/counts/values fall within a range called "normal," or outside that range? Such categories, then, are essential to doctors' thinking and reasoning about their patients' health and illnesses. Indeed, much of the clinical categorization that is learned serves useful purposes. For instance, identifying a person within one of the body-mass-index-based categories of obesity (underweight, normal weight, overweight, overweight obesity I, overweight obesity II, overweight obesity III) offers the benefits of understanding differences in risk factors, responsiveness to treatments, and prognosis.

The categorizing work of medicine isn't, however, limited to the purely clinical. Even though the *social* categorization of patients is generally not part of the formal curriculum, such categorization is unequivocally taught or modeled, or both, explicitly and implicitly throughout students' clinical education. A wide literature exists on the *social* categorization of patients, beginning over a half century ago with Howard Becker and colleagues'[3] classic study of medical education, *Boys in White*. This study found that students engage in continuous categorizing of patients into two major systems of social classification—the interesting/uninteresting patient as relates to his or her illness, and the ideal/despised patient marked by their personal characteristics and social status outside of the hospital. Such sorting patients into groups or types was elaborated further a quarter century later in Terry Mizrah's[4] *Getting Rid of Patients*, and 20 years later by several of us in "Making Fun of Patients,"[5] both of which detailed the often-subtle and complex categorization of patients. Importantly, all of this categorization—whether clinical or social—is purposeful, meant to frame how physicians might approach those so categorized in their efforts to "help them."

Here we attempt to challenge the orthodoxies of categorization using an educational approach we call narrative intersectionality. This approach draws from narrative medicine and the concept of intersectionality, which holds that we are all made up of many different, intersecting identities. In what follows, we introduce intersectionality and then link it to narrative approaches within medicine. From there, we demonstrate how we use two films to explore the insights about social categories that narrative intersectionality makes available to learners. By linking narrative to the concept of intersectionality, we make a case for blending the two orientations as a means of offering future physicians a richer, and thus more beneficial, understanding of the patients for whom they will provide care. And although the concept of intersectionality can be applied to all patients, albeit differently depending on their intersecting traits and the interplay of advantage and disadvantage, we focus specifically on how the approach we outline here can lead to a greater understanding of disadvantaged people, and greater appreciation of the complexities of health disparities.

Intersectionality

Intersectionality is a concept and methodology used widely in many academic disciplines outside of medicine. It is most often traced to scholar Kimberlé Crenshaw,[6] who works in the field of law, and who describes intersectionality as "an analytic sensibility, a way of thinking about identity and its relationship to power." At its core is the belief that individual lives cannot be fully understood by attending simply to narrow bands or categories of identity—gender, race, age, class, sexual identity, disability, immigration status, and so forth—in isolation. Rather, individuals must be considered at the intersection of their identity categories, where interrelated systems of oppression and discrimination, advantage and disadvantage are at play and determine access to the social and material necessities of life. Thus, intersectionality offers a framework that "captures the complexity of lived experiences and concomitant, interacting factors of social inequity, which in turn are key to understanding health inequities."[7] Here such a framework can enable a more robust understanding of how injustice and inequality occur on a multidimensional basis, and in fact interrelate, producing a "complex synergy" of social disadvantage, "the parts interacting to form a complex whole that cannot be disentangled into any single phenomenon."[8] Using an intersectionality framework, one begins to pay attention, for example, to how different types of discrimination intersect to oppress people in multiple and simultaneous ways, contributing to social inequality and systemic injustice. For example, knowing that a woman lives in a sexist society is not enough to understand her experience of that sexism: one must also know her race, sexuality, age, and class [among other factors] to begin to understand her unique experience of discrimination.[9]

In other words, "a real life person is not, for example, a woman on Monday, a member of the working class on Tuesday, and a woman of African descent on Wednesday."[10] She is already and always all of these identities. It is equally important to dispel the notion that these identities are hierarchically situated, or that singly each has an equivalent effect on her life; these identifications are continually overlapping and intersecting in *this* particular person. Thus, when seeking to understand the life experiences of any one person, any stand-alone category of identity falls short of broadening such understanding when treated as a discrete entity.[11]

Although the concept of intersectionality is seldom discussed in the actual practice of health care, it often informs the literature of medical education,[12–14] medical sociology, and public health,[15,16] as well as any number of disciplines focusing on women's health.[1,8,10] Because it focuses on power, privilege, and discriminating social practices,

> Intersectionality embraces rather than avoids the complexities that are essential to understanding social inequities, which in turn manifest in health inequities. It therefore has the potential to create more accurate and inclusive knowledge of human lives and health needs.[7]

In addition, the concept of intersectionality lends itself to narrative traditions involving case studies, which we discuss below.

Narrative Intersectionality

Narrative medicine, as Rita Charon[17] contends, is an approach that recognizes that the "care of the sick unfolds in stories" and that "the effective practice of health care requires the ability to recognize, absorb, interpret, and act on the stories and plights of others." The kind of knowledge one gains from stories of all kinds—novels, poems, film, newspaper and magazine articles—provides a "rich, resonant comprehension of a singular person's situation as it unfolds in time."[17] This *singularity* is key to the link between narrative and intersectionality, for this link emphasizes the singular person who, in her singularity, may embody many categories of identity. It highlights her uniqueness, her particularity, as she presents to the health care provider in the variegated aspects of her life that are present in no one else's. Intersectionality, then, "can be considered an intellectual descendent of narrative studies."[1]

Sayantani DasGupta[18] has written eloquently about narrative medicine, adding the critical element of humility to this inquiry. Doctors and other caregivers do not ever fully "get" their patients' lived experiences, and the efforts of medical educators and evaluators to move medical students and residents toward "competency" in such understanding are, at best, mythical thinking. Rather, she contends, they must enter such relationships with humility about their ability to understand, acknowledging that when patients walk into health care settings, there is a

> parallel sociopolitical narrative that enable[s] the telling of certain sorts of stories and silence[s] other stories. Narrative humility allows clinicians to recognise that each story we hear holds elements that are unfamiliar—be they cultural, socioeconomic, sexual, religious, or idiosyncratically personal. Assuming that our reading of any patient's story is the definitive interpretation of that story is to risk closing ourselves off to its most valuable nuances and particularities.[18]

Such is the link between narrative and intersectionality for clinicians, bringing together two analytic sensibilities that rest on the "multiple, intersecting, and complex social relations"[1] always present in patients' lives and the stories they bring to health care settings. In the next section, we offer examples of how to illustrate this link for students in discussions of two films.

Narrative Intersectionality in Two Films

In what follows, we examine two films, *Precious*[19] and *Dirty Pretty Things*,[20] that present characters whose lives comprise numerous and often-contradictory identities. The objective of this exercise is not to deny the power and influence of categories—either on individuals thus labeled, or by viewers who apply those same labels—but, rather, to invite interpretations that acknowledge the limitations of such efforts to categorize. As Leslie McCall[1] argues, categories are often inescapable, but developing a critical stance toward their application is a worthwhile endeavor that fosters a greater appreciation of the complexities of intersecting identities.

Precious

Precious depicts the story of Claireece Precious Jones, a 16-year-old African American woman living in Harlem during the late 1980s. When the film begins, she is pregnant with her second child, who, like her first, is a product of incest perpetrated by her father, Carl. Precious lives in squalid public housing with her mother, Mary, who is verbally, physically, and sexually abusive. Precious's first child, Mongo, a daughter born with Down syndrome, lives with Precious's grandmother.

Precious is a difficult film to watch and can be seen as trafficking in stereotypes—what has been called "poverty porn" by more than one reviewer[21,22]—but perhaps the film's problematic aspects make it especially useful for discussions of narrative intersectionality. Just as a reliance on single categories in the practice of medicine may lead to an oversimplification of patients' lives, so too does a focus on the character Precious as only female, only illiterate, or only poor reduce the complexities engendered when those identities intersect in a single individual. Narrative intersectionality recognizes that more is going on than any single category or identity can explain. With such recognition comes the possibility for greater appreciation of patients' complex and particular lived experiences beyond the exam room.

One particular scene in *Precious*, titled "For the Social Worker," offers medical educators a rich depiction of how these complexities play out. In this scene, Precious and her mother are at home, where Precious's grandmother has arrived with Precious's daughter Mongo for a staged "performance" for the social worker, who believes Mongo belongs to Mary, not her teenage daughter, Precious. Once the social worker arrives, Precious assists in her mother's performance, clearly understanding how to play her part in her mother's deception. Only once during the social worker's visit does Precious speak; she answers "I'm doing good" when asked about her own well-being. Staring coolly at the social worker, Precious inhabits intersecting identities: a teenage mother, victimized by incestuous rape and an abusive mother; a young woman living in poverty; an illiterate high school student wronged by dysfunctional public schools; and a morbidly obese teenager force-fed by her mother.

To further explore the powerful nature of these intersecting identities, we suggest introducing into the discussion the following description of Precious by Sapphire, the author of the novel on which the film is based, who writes: "I wanted to show that this girl is locked out through literacy. She's locked out by her physical appearance. She's locked out by her class, and she's locked out by her color."[23] We would add that she is also locked out by her limited education, and as a victim of abuse. As Sapphire makes clear, no single factor or characteristic explains Precious's situation. To simply focus on one of them is to oversimplify the complexities of her lived experience.

While the social worker in the scene never recognizes these complexities, and seems to function as an example of the institutions that fail to assist Precious, the film offers examples of individuals within those same institutions who do not fail her: Ms. Rain, a teacher at an alternative school Precious ultimately attends; and Ms. Weiss, another social worker, who works with Precious directly. In both instances, these individuals invite Precious to tell her story, a strategy that assists her efforts to speak authoritatively about herself as she is able to name and ultimately resist the forces that have formed her.

Just as *Precious* is a difficult film to watch, discussions of it can be equally tough, especially given the complexities of Precious's intersecting identities. Asking students to imagine a patient like Precious seeking their care offers them an opportunity to focus their attention on those complexities, rather than on a single category such as obesity, and then to describe how her obesity intersects with sexual abuse, illiteracy, and poverty. Through this exercise, students begin to realize that to focus entirely on Precious's obesity in a health care setting dooms the care she receives.

Dirty Pretty Things

Dirty Pretty Things offers a darkly layered, disturbing portrait of characters whose lives are lived on the margins of British society, all who find themselves for one reason or another at West London's Baltic Hotel. Okwe was a doctor in his native Nigeria but is now a political exile who works by day as a cab driver, by night as a desk attendant at the Baltic Hotel. He rents a couch at the apartment of Senay, who fled Turkey and is now working as a maid at the hotel—illegal work because of her immigration status. One evening when Okwe is managing the front desk, he is called upstairs to check a clogged toilet, and the first thread of the plot begins: A human heart is the source of the blockage. When he reports this to the hotel night manager Juan, himself an immigrant, he is told to mind his own business, but ultimately uncovers the cruel activity taking place there. In makeshift surgical suites, desperate people—here, undocumented persons—are having their kidneys extracted in exchange for fake passports, the flushed heart resulting from a procedure gone awry.

In the meantime, Senay is having her own problems with immigration officials who are on to her illegal employment at the Baltic. Forced to take a job at a sweatshop, she and dozens of women, most of them undocumented, work under a similar threat of being discovered. The following scene at the sweatshop illuminates the intersectionality Senay embodies, which goes to the heart of this film about the human lives found in the hidden world of undocumented workers. The manager of the sweatshop preys on their vulnerability and targets Senay with demands for sexual acts. Claiming that he wants to be "respectful" of the religious code of chastity for Muslim women, he forces her to engage in oral sex as payment for his silence to immigration authorities. Her humiliation is immense, and ongoing, until she can no longer yield to his demands and, quite simply, "bites" and flees the sweatshop. At the close of this scene, Senay's plight becomes more desperate as she lives her life as a woman, a Muslim, an undocumented immigrant without employment and family support, and now a person without a place to live. The remainder of the film's action links back to the earlier scene involving organ trafficking which increasingly involves Senay and Okwe as they work to avoid deportation and build lives with some semblance of hope.

Discussion of this scene is fraught with complexity. Where, one might ask learners, would a health care provider even *begin* when Senay appears in the exam room, disclosing, perhaps, sleeplessness and anxiety? As Zowie Davy[24] points out, immigrant women are usually in lower-paid, "part-time, precariously safeguarded work, often a great distance away from friendship and kin networks; this, joined with racism and poor housing, results in unfavorable social conditions, all of which can add associated bodily stresses that may exacerbate ill health." Senay's story is variegated with issues that are folded together, intersecting, not layered one on top of the other in discrete categories of identity. Moreover, choosing to focus on only one identity obscures the others, and to prevent that, a caregiver would have to begin at the beginning to address who she is, how she arrived in London, what her life has been like, and what she currently faces. Attempting to understand the intersections that define who and where Senay is, is thus a move toward patient-centered care.

Narrative Intersectionality, Film, and Medical Education

Given how often time constraints and curricular demands limit the space available for humanities courses in medical education, we find that using film provides educators with a means of introducing humanities concepts and tools for analyzing complex narratives with students in an efficient but valuable manner. If possible, we recommend requiring students to watch a film in advance, so class time can be devoted to discussing specific scenes that can be watched and rewatched collectively.

Rewatching a scene is especially valuable for introducing students to a concept such as narrative intersectionality because it offers them opportunities to practice its application. The following is a description of how the scene from *Precious*, where the social worker visits Precious's home, can be used in the classroom for this purpose. Begin by providing students with a brief setup for the first viewing of it as a class. After watching the scene, ask students to identify what they see as most important about it. The point here is to encourage open dialogue, while taking notice of what students do and do not discuss. Before the second viewing, introduce the concept of narrative intersectionality and ask students to name Precious's various identities, prompting them when necessary to think beyond obese or pregnant to include others that are less obvious medical concerns. Then return to the scene and ask students to look for instances where these identities become apparent and when and how they intersect. The objective for the discussion following the second viewing is to guide students toward a recognition of factors, such as illiteracy and poverty, that influence health outcomes of patients. Although this overview focuses on *Precious*, the approach can also be applied to the scene from *Dirty Pretty Things* discussed previously, as well as to other films.

Insights and Implications

We have drawn attention to the commonalities between narrative and intersectionality. The development of Precious into a literate and self-possessed person, along with her eventual decision to care for her two children and distance herself from her family, comes as a result of her learning to tell her story, and meeting a teacher and a social worker who have the skills necessary to recognize the many intersecting identities that constitute it. Similarly, our understanding of Senay does not rest on any one aspect of the multiple identities that converge into her particular life story. Such understandings involve what Charon[17] calls narrative competence—that is, the ability to "absorb, interpret, and respond to stories." Such competence is, however, not to be mistaken for mastery of another's story,[25] a process that can lead to a reliance on the same systems of categorization we have cautioned against. As a strategy for the practice of medicine, narrative intersectionality recognizes that any given patient's life comprises many different identities, the telling of which may never occur completely in the health care setting. Herein lies the importance of DasGupta's[18] concept of narrative humility, which acknowledges that "patients' stories are not objects that we can comprehend or master, but rather dynamic entities that we can approach and engage with, while simultaneously remaining open to their ambiguity and contradiction."

If the nature of the clinical education of physicians moves them toward synthesis and categorization aimed at the critically useful process of making clinical "assessments" and "plans," then there must also be emphasis in that education on what might be missing to inform such assessments and plans. Students are taught to gather a detailed history and conduct a thorough examination, all the while progressively focusing more and more on the disease dimensions of that history and exam, and then to synthesize all the gathered data into a cogent unifying summarization—an aim Robert Coles[26] describes as getting "to the concise, penetrating heart of things." Coles, reflecting on his own training, refers to this process as learning to construct a concise but all-encompassing "theory," an abstraction that results from "how we shape what we have heard into our own version of someone's troubles."[26] Describing his own "acquiring facility with abstractions," Coles goes on to confess that despite being chided by a mentor for "more stories, less theory," he often remained "in pursuit of *le mot juste*,"[26] a way of turning all of a particular patient's experiences and identities into a single, often one-sentence characterization: a 58-year-old black male who presents with chest pain likely cardiac in origin. Coles discovers, with the help of his more narratively focused mentor, the cautionary flag that needs to be waved here, that "in our self-consciousness as … theorists, we lose sight of human particularity."[26]

Traditional efforts to move clinicians toward tying all of what is known about a suffering person into a tidy little bow risk enforcing a system of categorization that ignores elements of such a person's multiple and complex life experiences, identities, and life worlds. Clinical scenarios unfold each day in which physicians encounter patients at the intersection of their complex and varied identities, and in which physicians overlook important identities and oppressive experiences in ways that lead to substandard care, and even to patient harm. Consider a patient who presents, for example, to a local free clinic—a place where many assumptions are made about patients, where "single story thinking"[27] is prevalent, and where patients often have multiple overlapping identities and life circumstances, many of which they may seek to hide from their caregivers. In the initial interview, the patient ultimately discloses that she is a retired college professor who has fallen on hard times financially since her university employer terminated her pension benefits. Such a person must be approached with every attempt to understand her lived experiences as having been shaped in the contexts of the identities not only of an older person, a woman, an African American, a patient at a free clinic, and a person of limited financial means but also a highly educated scholar and professor. Absent a fuller understanding, the disconnects that can develop between such a patient and her physician can only be overcome by greater self-knowledge on the part of the physician, a fuller understanding of the person standing before them, and a greater humility regarding physicians' always-incomplete knowledge of others. A narrative intersectionality framework for relationships with patients offers some hope that medical education can do better.

Over a century ago, William James wrote that "we carve out order by leaving the disorderly parts out."[28] At the heart of any one person's "intersectional self" is disorder—the disorder of multiple, interweaving identities that converge uniquely in the story of a solitary life. In the training of physicians and other health care professionals who are invited into just such a solitary life to engage with a particular person possessing many intersected identities, it is clearly not enough to simply strive toward checking all of the competency boxes in their "learned" understanding of such others. As medical education has begun to move away from learning pedagogies aimed solely at achieving *competency* toward more complex assessments aimed at *mastery*, a focus on intersectionality offers students a broader appreciation of the always-incomplete understanding of others. In all such efforts, health care professionals and health professions educators are better served to surface the discomfort, the disorder, the complexity, and the oppression that reside within the intersectionality of each particular patient's lived experiences. Only then can we offer hope that patients whom we always thought we would come to understand fully might be invited into humble and healing relationships with those whose care they seek.

Funding/Support: None reported.

Other disclosures: None reported.

Ethical approval: Reported as not applicable.

References

1 McCall L. The complexity of intersectionality. Signs. 2005;30:1771–1794.
2 Groopman J. How Doctors Think. New York, NY: Houghton Mifflin; 2007.
3 Becker HS, Geer B, Hughes ED, Strauss AL. Boys in White: Student Culture in Medical School. Chicago, IL: University of Chicago Press; 1961.
4 Mizrahi T. Getting Rid of Patients: Contradictions in the Socialization of Physicians. New Brunswick, NJ: Rutgers University Press; 1985.
5 Wear D, Aultman JM, Varley JD, Zarconi J. Making fun of patients: Medical students' perceptions and use of derogatory and cynical humor in clinical settings. Acad Med. 2006;81:454–462.
6 Crenshaw K. Why intersectionality can't wait. Washington Post. September 24, 2015. www.washingtonpost.com/news/in-theory/wp/2015/09/24/why-intersectionality-cant-wait. Accessed July 27, 2018.
7 Hankivsky O, Christoffersen A. Intersectionality and the determinants of health: A Canadian perspective. Crit Public Health. 2009;18:271–283.
8 McGibbon E, McPherson C. Applying intersectionality and complexity theory to address the social determinants of women's health. Womens Health Urban Life. 2011;10:59–86.
9 Butler C. Intersectionality in family therapy training: Inviting students to embrace the complexities of lived experience. J Fam Ther. 2015;37:583–589.
10 Russell K. Feminist dialectics and Marxist theory. Radic Philos Rev. 2007;10:33–54.
11 Crenshaw K. Mapping the margins: Intersectionality, identity politics, and violence against women of color. Stanford Law Rev. 1991;43:1241–1271.
12 Sears KP. Improving cultural competence education: The utility of an intersectional framework. Med Educ. 2012;46:545–551.
13 Eckstrand KL, Eliason J, St Cloud T, Potter J. The priority of intersectionality in academic medicine. Acad Med. 2016;91:904–907.
14 Tsouroufli M, Rees CE, Monrouxe LV, Sundaram V. Gender identities and intersectionality in medical education research. Med Educ. 2011;43:213–216.
15 Walby S, Armstrong J, Strid S. Intersectionality: Multiple inequalities in social theory. Sociology. 2012;46:224–240.
16 Bauer GR. Incorporating intersectionality theory into population health research methodology: Challenges and the potential to advance health equity. Soc Sci Med. 2014;110:10–17.
17 Charon R. Narrative medicine: A model for empathy, reflection, profession, and trust. JAMA. 2001;286:1897–1902.
18 DasGupta S. The art of medicine: Narrative humility. Lancet. 2008;371:980–981.
19 Daniels L. Precious [DVD]. Santa Monica, CA: Lionsgate; 2009.
20 Frears S. Dirty Pretty Things [DVD]. La Crosse, WI: Echo Bridge Home Entertainment; 2011.
21 Durham AS. Precious in the classroom. New Black Mag. December 12, 2009. www.thenewblackmagazine.com/view.aspx?index=2185. Accessed July 27, 2018.
22 Downs J. Are we all Precious? Chron High Educ. December 13, 2009. http://chronicle.com/article/Are-We-All-Precious-/49458. Accessed July 27, 2018.
23 Sapphire's story: How Push became Precious. NPR's All Things Considered. November 6, 2009. http://www.npr.org/templates/story/story.php?storyId=120176695. Accessed July 27, 2018.
24 Davy Z. The promise of intersectionality theory in primary care. Qual Prim Care. 2011;19:279–281.
25 Garden R. The problem of empathy: Medicine and the humanities. New Lit Hist. 2007;38:551–568.
26 Coles R. The Call of Stories: Teaching and the Moral Imagination. Boston, MA: Houghton Mifflin; 1989.
27 Zarconi J. Commentary: Narrative lessons from a Nigerian novelist: Implications for medical education and care. Acad Med. 2012;87:1005–1007.
28 Myers GE. William James: His Life and Thought. New Haven, CT: Yale University Press; 1986.

Pre-medical majors in the humanities and social sciences: impact on communication skills and specialty choice

Laura E Hirshfield,[1,2] Rachel Yudkowsky[1] & Yoon Soo Park[1]

CONTEXT Medical school admissions committees use a variety of criteria to determine which candidates to admit to their programmes. Effective communication is increasingly considered a key requisite to the practice of effective medicine. Medical students with pre-medical backgrounds in the humanities and social sciences may be more likely to acquire skills relevant to patient-centred communication, either prior to or during medical school.

OBJECTIVES The purpose of this study was to investigate the relationship between pre-medical backgrounds in the humanities and social sciences and outcomes in medical school, including in communication and interpersonal skills (CIS), licensure examination results and postgraduate specialty choice (primary care versus non-primary care specialties).

METHODS The American Medical College Application Service database was used to identify pre-medical college majors, demographic characteristics, Medical College Admission Test scores and college grade point averages for medical students at a large, midwestern medical school. Data were obtained for 465 medical students across three cohorts (classes of 2014–2016). Correlation and regression analyses were used to examine relationships between pre-medical background, performance on graduation competency examination standardised patient encounter CIS scores and on United States Medical Licensing Examination (USMLE) Step 1 and Step 2 Clinical Knowledge scores, and postgraduate specialty choice.

RESULTS Graduating medical students with pre-medical humanities or social sciences majors performed significantly better in terms of CIS than those with natural science majors (Cohen's $d = 0.28$, $p = 0.011$). There were no significant associations between pre-medical majors and USMLE Step 1 and Step 2 Clinical Knowledge scores or postgraduate specialty choice.

CONCLUSIONS These results suggest that considering humanistic factors as part of admissions criteria may promote the selection and training of physicians with good communication skills.

Medical Education 2018
doi: 10.1111/medu.13774

[1]Department of Medical Education, College of Medicine, University of Illinois at Chicago, Chicago, Illinois, USA
[2]Department of Sociology, College of Liberal Arts & Sciences, University of Illinois at Chicago, Chicago, Illinois, USA

Correspondence: Laura E Hirshfield, Department of Medical Education, College of Medicine, University of Illinois at Chicago, 808 South Wood Street, 963 CMET (MC 591), Chicago, Illinois 60612-7309, USA. Tel: 00 1 312 996 5448; E-mail: lhirshf@uic.edu

INTRODUCTION

Medical school admissions committees use a variety of criteria to select trainees, the majority of which are considered demonstrations of 'academic excellence' through aptitude test scores or college grade point averages (GPAs).[1,2] In the USA, scientific knowledge is clearly valued by the medical profession and is measured using the Medical College Admission Test (MCAT) and the United States Medical Licensing Examination (USMLE) Step 1 and Step 2 Clinical Knowledge (CK) tests.[3–5] Studying science or mathematics is considered as preparation for studying the material that must be mastered in medical school. Scientific courses are believed to be 'the foundations upon which success in medicine is based' and are used, in some ways, to help predict students' potential future success in medical school coursework (which relies heavily on scientific models of knowledge production).[1]

Nonetheless, scholars have long argued that a student's academic success may have little bearing on his or her later medical skill and that achievement in scientific courses may be less important than aptitude related to human interaction.[1,2] This view has been slow to translate to the context of medical school admissions committees, however. For example, although some admissions committee members believe that a liberal arts background can be advantageous,[6] in many international settings, students who study the humanities or social sciences as part of pre-medical education tend to be viewed as less prepared for medical education than students with pre-medical science majors.[7]

The context for examining pre-medical background is relevant as many countries require applicants to have obtained post-secondary education degrees prior to beginning medical training. Prior studies examining the relationship between pre-medical backgrounds and medical school performance have generally focused on assessments of medical knowledge and have demonstrated little to no effect on medical school academic performance,[8,9] national medical licensure examinations,[9,10] and commencement distinctions or honours.[7] Although medical knowledge is indeed critical for success in medical education, medical students are also expected to demonstrate excellent communication and interpersonal skills (CIS) and professionalism.

Pre-medical programmes in the humanities and social sciences focus on the accumulation of 'cultural capital' that may later translate to greater skills in other aspects of patient care, such as physician–patient interactions and cultural competency.[11,12] Specifically, students with these backgrounds are more likely to have a 'sophisticated use of verbal and written language and confidence in their broad knowledge of history, culture, and politics' that may benefit their patient care.[11] The possible benefits of humanities and social sciences courses for physicians in training have also motivated the proliferation of medical humanities programmes in medical schools nationwide, with the often explicitly stated expectation of improving physician communication and the provision of patient-centred care.[13] Yet no study to date has empirically investigated the relationship between a humanities or social sciences pre-medical background and communication skills.

However, communication skills are considered so central to the necessary training for medical students that they represent one of the six core competencies defined by the Accreditation Council for Graduate Medical Education.[14] This focus on communication stems, in part, from extensive research that demonstrates a correlation between effective physician–patient communication and improvements in patient health outcomes.[15]

Humanities and social sciences backgrounds may also be related to medical students' postgraduate specialty choice. Whereas some scholars have found no relationship between undergraduate major and postgraduate specialty choice,[16,17] others have found that medical students with humanities or social sciences backgrounds are more likely to choose specialties that emphasise patient–physician interaction and communication, such as primary care specialties and psychiatry.[7,18]

The purpose of this study was to investigate the relationship between a humanities or social sciences pre-medical college major and: (i) performance in CIS in medical school, and (ii) selection of medical specialty for postgraduate training. Based on previous findings, we developed the following hypotheses (Fig. 1):

> Hypothesis 1: medical students with pre-medical undergraduate college majors in the humanities or social sciences will have better communication skills than their peers with majors in the natural sciences;

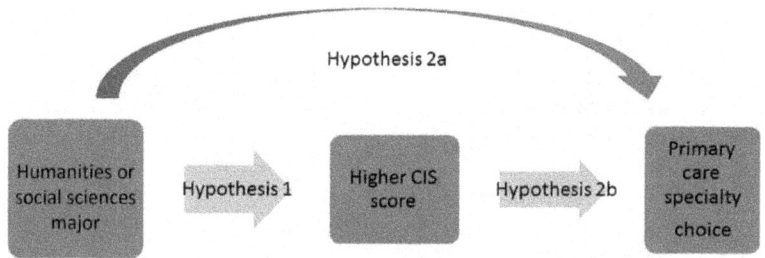

Figure 1 Study hypotheses. CIS = communication and interpersonal skills

Hypothesis 2a: medical students with undergraduate college majors in the humanities and social sciences will be more likely than their peers to choose primary care specialties that emphasise patient–physician interaction, and

Hypothesis 2b: medical students with better communication skills will be more likely than their peers to choose primary care specialties that emphasise patient–physician interaction.

METHODS

We merged student records for three graduating student cohorts and from four data sources at a large, midwestern medical school. These data included: (i) medical school admissions data, including undergraduate major, mean MCAT score, undergraduate science GPA, and undergraduate cumulative GPA; (ii) USMLE scores, including Step 1 (Basic Sciences) and Step 2 CK scores; (iii) medical school graduation competency examination (GCE) data, including CIS scores and patient note (PN) clinical reasoning scores, and (iv) postgraduate training placement data (specialty choice) obtained from the school registrar's office.

Data

Data for three medical school cohorts were used, for a total of 465 students (class of 2014, $n = 170$; class of 2015, $n = 119$; class of 2016, $n = 176$).

Pre-medical college majors

Undergraduate college majors (obtained prior to medical school) were identified using applicants' self-reported fields of study from the American Medical College Application Service (AMCAS) database. The AMCAS system provides a drop-down menu from which applicants select their undergraduate major; in addition, they can write in their major or principal subject if it is not available in the menu (i.e. they can select 'Other Major' and enter their major as an open-ended response). Students with multiple majors were able to add all of their majors.[19] We first classified college undergraduate majors into four groupings (humanities, social sciences, biological sciences and physical sciences) based on previous research on science, technology, engineering and mathematics majors, which often describes qualitative differences in climate, gender demographics or research focus between the biological sciences and the physical sciences.[20] However, given our research question, these distinctions are less likely to be relevant. For this reason, as well as to increase statistical power, a second grouping of variables was created: (i) humanities and social sciences, and (ii) all other majors. We included any student who had majored in a humanities or social sciences subject in the former category, including those who selected multiple undergraduate majors.

Admissions data

Using AMCAS, we identified and merged applicant information for the 465 students who matriculated at the medical school. Data included student gender, race and ethnicity, under-represented minority (URM) status, undergraduate college, undergraduate college major, degree type, degree date, MCAT score and GPAs (cumulative and science).

Graduation competency examination

The medical school administers GCEs to rising Year-4 students. The GCE replicates the format used in the USMLE Step 2 Clinical Skills (CS) examination[21] by integrating standardised patient (SP) encounters that measure physical examination skills and CIS and a written component of the USMLE-style PN.[22] In this study, we used data from three administrations of the GCE (2013, 2014 and 2015), corresponding to the graduating class years of the study sample. Each GCE included five SP cases (2013 GCE: trouble sleeping, shortness of breath, wrist pain, vomiting, dead arm; 2014 GCE: chest pain, weight loss, shortness of breath, abdominal pain, dizziness; 2015 GCE: paediatrics telephone call, headache, joint pain, fatigue, coughing up blood). Each SP encounter was limited to 15 minutes and was followed by 10 minutes in which the student was expected to write the PN. Validity studies of the GCE using Messick's unified validity framework have been reported previously,[23–25] indicating consistency in scores and validity evidence with regard to content, response process, internal structure, relationships to other variables, and consequences.

The CIS component of the GCE is measured using a 4-point behaviourally anchored rating scale composed of 14 items (see Table 2 for a full list of these items), rated by the SP directly after each encounter.[24] The PN is scored by trained physician raters using a scoring rubric that refers to four tasks; a prior study of this rubric showed high inter-rater reliability (weighted $\kappa = 0.79$) and validity evidence supporting its use.[26]

Scores on the USMLE®

We obtained first-attempt USMLE scores and pass or fail status for the Step 1 and Step 2 CK examinations from the medical school's registrar's office. Scores on the Step 2 CS examination were not included in the analysis because Step 2 CS scores are provided only in pass or fail format and nearly all students passed the examination, which resulted in a lack of variability.

Postgraduate specialty choice

Data on students' choices of specialty for postgraduate training were obtained from the school registrar's office and merged with pre-medical data, and GCE and USMLE scores. Postgraduate specialty choice was classified into the primary care specialties (internal medicine, paediatrics, family medicine, and obstetrics and gynaecology) versus the non-primary care specialties.

Analysis

We analysed our data by first examining trends using descriptive statistics by major fields (humanities and social sciences versus all other majors). Next, we compared means and proportions by major fields using *t*-tests and chi-squared tests, respectively. Finally, we investigated whether differences in major fields hold after controlling for confounding factors (Step 1, Step 2 CK and GCE PN scores) using multiple logistic and multiple linear regression models.

Data compilation and analyses were conducted using STATA Version 14.0 (StataCorp LLC, College Station, Texas, USA). The study was approved by the Institutional Review Board at the University of Illinois at Chicago.

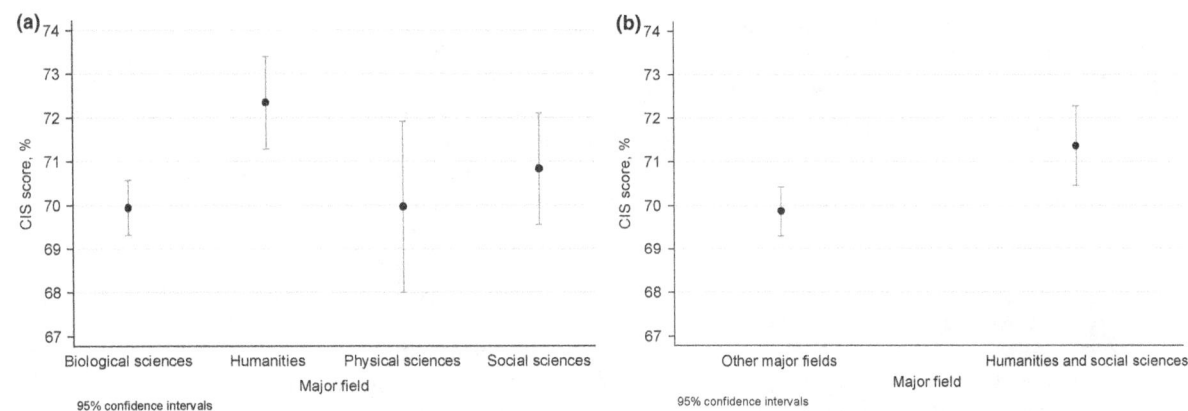

Figure 2 Comparison of communication and interpersonal skills (CIS) scores by undergraduate major field, with 95% confidence intervals, using: (a) four, and (b) two categories of field. There were significant differences in CIS scores between students with humanities or social sciences backgrounds and those with other pre-medical backgrounds (p = 0.011, Cohen's $d = 0.28$)

Table 1 Comparison of means between major fields: descriptive statistics and t-test

Factor	Mean difference (Cohen's d)	Humanities and social sciences (n = 103)		Other majors (n = 362)		p-value	All (n = 465)	
		Mean	SD	Mean	SD		Mean	SD
MCAT®†	− 0.53 (0.37)	9.93	1.51	10.47	1.37	< 0.001	10.35	1.42
Science GPA†	− 0.18 (0.45)	3.34	0.41	3.52	0.38	< 0.001	3.48	0.40
Cumulative GPA†	− 0.11 (0.38)	3.51	0.29	3.62	0.28	< 0.001	3.59	0.29
Step 1 scores*	− 6.03 (0.29)	223.75	21.45	229.78	20.51	0.010	228.44	20.85
Step 2 CK scores	− 5.35 (0.29)	236.06	18.92	241.41	17.92	0.062	240.31	18.22
GCE CIS*	1.50 (0.28)	71.36	4.65	69.86	5.44	0.011	70.19	5.31
GCE PN scores	− 1.64 (0.21)	60.51	7.32	62.15	8.13	0.065	61.79	7.98

* $p < 0.05$.
† $p < 0.001$.
CIS = communication and interpersonal skills; CK = Clinical Knowledge; GCE = graduation competency examination; GPA = grade point average; MCAT = Medical College Admission Test; PN = patient note; SD = standard deviation.

RESULTS

Descriptive statistics

Based on our initial classification, we found the following distribution of undergraduate college majors across the study cohort ($n = 465$): (i) biological sciences majors: 67%; (ii) humanities majors: 9%; (iii) physical sciences majors: 8%, and (iv) social sciences majors: 16%. As we had expected, given the small number of humanities and social sciences majors and the similarities between the biological and physical sciences, we found only marginally significant differences between groups when four major field groupings were used to examine differences in CIS scores ($p = 0.051$) (Fig. 2a). We thus restricted our subsequent analyses to the comparison between students with humanities or social sciences majors, and all others. There were no significant differences in the proportions of students with humanities and social sciences majors and other majors by demographic characteristics, such as state residence, gender and graduation year. Students who had majored in sciences were younger by 1.3 years ($p < 0.001$). Table 1 shows the descriptive statistics for admissions data (MCAT score and GPA), USMLE scores (Step 1 and Step 2 CK), and GCE performance (CIS and PN scores).

Comparison between majors (humanities and social sciences and others)

With respect to MCAT score, science GPA, cumulative GPA and USMLE Step 1 scores, students with non-humanities and social sciences majors (i.e. those with physical and biological sciences majors) showed significantly higher performance ($p < 0.05$ for all) (Table 1). However, there were no significant differences in Step 2 CK performance and PN scores between students with the respective categories of majors ($p = 0.062$ and 0.065, respectively). By contrast, with respect to CIS, students with humanities and social sciences majors gained significantly higher scores ($p = 0.011$). The difference in CIS scores between students with humanities and social sciences majors and those with other majors translated to a Cohen's d of 0.28, representing a moderate difference in effect size (Fig. 2b).

Factors affecting differences in CIS performance

When examined more closely, there were also some specific CIS items on which students with humanities and social sciences majors scored significantly better than did their peers with science majors (Table 2). Specifically, these included 'Friendly communication' (Cohen's $d = 0.36$, $p = 0.001$); 'Physical examination' (Cohen's

d = 0.28, p = 0.010); 'Sensitive subject matters' (Cohen's d = 0.28, p = 0.010), and 'See again as personal physician?' (Cohen's d = 0.37, p = 0.002). Notably, this final item is the most global measure of patient satisfaction in the scale and, as such, suggests that SPs are more likely to feel satisfied with the communication and interpersonal interaction they experience with students with humanities and social sciences majors than they are with those with biological sciences and physical sciences majors.

Comparison of differences in medical school outcomes

We used linear regression to explore whether the relationship we observed between college major and communication skills could be explained by demographic or educational factors (Table 3). We also examined the relationship for Step 1 and Step 2 CK scores. We found that the positive relationship between communication skills scores and having a humanities and social sciences major remained even after controlling for gender, residence (i.e. in-state versus out-of-state), URM status, MCAT score, science GPA and cumulative GPA (standardised β = 0.11, p = 0.025).

Postgraduate specialty choice

Overall, 51% of students were matched into primary care specialties. There were no significant differences in postgraduate specialty placement (primary care versus non-primary care specialties) based on pre-medical college major (p = 0.229). Moreover, students' CIS performance did not significantly predict their likelihood of choosing a primary care specialty in postgraduate training (p = 0.595).

DISCUSSION

This study aimed to explore the impact of pre-medical college major on outcomes of undergraduate medical education, including communication skills and specialty choice. Using our unique dataset and by linking CIS scores with medical students' undergraduate majors (as well as with several other key demographic and education-

Table 2 Comparison of mean communication and interpersonal skills item rating by major fields: descriptive statistics and t-test

CIS item	Cohen's d	Humanities and social sciences		Other majors		p-value
		Mean	SD	Mean	SD	
1 Friendly communication[†]	0.36	3.08	0.31	2.95	0.37	0.001
2 Respectful treatment	0.18	3.09	0.20	3.05	0.23	0.082
3 Listening to my story	0.16	2.79	0.34	2.74	0.31	0.162
4 Honest communication	0.14	2.91	0.27	2.87	0.30	0.272
5 Interest in me as a person	0.14	2.23	0.42	2.17	0.43	0.235
6 Discussion of options/plans	0.15	2.73	0.30	2.69	0.35	0.230
7 Encouraging my questions	0.06	2.80	0.34	2.79	0.36	0.648
8 Providing clear explanation	0.15	2.94	0.20	2.90	0.28	0.218
9 Physical examination*	0.28	2.89	0.35	2.79	0.35	0.010
10 Appropriate vocabulary	0.04	2.98	0.26	2.98	0.26	0.787
11 Sensitive subject matters*	0.28	2.91	0.33	2.81	0.36	0.010
12 Closing the encounter	0.13	2.81	0.25	2.77	0.31	0.275
13 Receptive to SP feedback	0.13	3.33	0.35	3.28	0.39	0.201
14 See again as personal physician?[†]	0.37	2.72	0.34	2.59	0.39	0.002

* $p < 0.05$.
[†] $p < 0.01$.
CIS = communication and interpersonal skills; SD = standard deviation; SP = standardised patient.
CIS items were scored on a 4-point scale by an SP; values above reflect averages across five SP encounters.

Table 3 Comparison of differences in medical school outcomes (communication and interpersonal skills, US Medical Licensing Examination® Step 1, Step 2 Clinical Knowledge: linear regression)

Factor	GCE CIS scores			Step 1 scores			Step 2 CK scores		
	Coefficient	SE	p-value	Coefficient	SE	p-value	Coefficient	SE	p-value
Major field (humanities and social sciences = 1; other = 0)	1.35	0.60	0.025	0.00	1.96	0.999	1.68	2.35	0.474
Gender (male = 1, female = 0)	−0.36	0.51	0.488	3.60	1.68	0.033	−3.72	1.90	0.051
Residence (IL = 1, non-IL = 0)	0.41	0.70	0.558	−2.79	2.29	0.223	−0.89	3.13	0.776
URM status (URM = 1, non-URM = 0)	−2.14	0.83	0.010	−1.43	2.72	0.600	3.95	3.08	0.201
Average MCAT®	−0.56	0.25	0.024	5.29	0.81	< 0.001	6.59	0.91	< 0.001
Science GPA	−3.35	1.56	0.032	8.50	5.10	0.097	−2.26	5.58	0.686
Cumulative GPA	4.20	2.09	0.045	4.13	6.83	0.546	16.95	7.48	0.024
GCE PN scores	0.04	0.03	0.181	0.46	0.10	< 0.001	0.63	0.13	< 0.001
Intercept	70.07	4.87	< 0.001	101.64	15.94	< 0.001	79.19	17.82	< 0.001
R^2	0.05			0.34			0.41		
F-test	$F_{(8,456)}$ = 3.03, p = 0.003			$F_{(8,456)}$ = 29.56, p < 0.001			$F_{(8,239)}$ = 20.62, p < 0.001		

CIS = communication and interpersonal skills; CK = Clinical Knowledge; GCE = graduation competency examination; GPA = grade point average; IL = Illinois; MCAT® = Medical College Admission Test; PN = patient note; SE = standard error; URM = under-represented minority.

related variables), we found that students with humanities and social sciences majors do perform significantly better than their science major peers on the communication section of the GCE. In particular, for the CIS items 'Friendly communication' and 'See again as personal physician?', Cohen's *d* effect sizes were 0.36 and 0.37, respectively, indicating a small, yet significant impact. Humanities and social sciences majors also perform slightly better than their science major peers on communication related to sensitive subject matters and during the physical examination. Finally, though our overall results for CIS show that students with humanities and social sciences majors and their science major peers performed similarly on the majority of CIS items, the last item on the CIS list ('See again as personal physician?') functions as a sort of global measure of patient satisfaction and hence it is especially noteworthy that humanities and social sciences majors received significantly higher marks on this item. Although these effects are relatively small, we argue that they should be taken into account when evaluating potential medical school applicants, particularly given the ongoing calls for increased proficiency in physician–patient communication[14] and doubts about the usefulness of scientific ability as a predictor for medical school success.[2]

By contrast, we found that humanities and social sciences majors fared slightly worse than their science major peers on the USMLE Step 1 (Cohen's *d* = 0.29). However, there were no significant differences between the groups in Step 2 CK performance, or in PN performance on the GCE. As such, our findings align with previous research suggesting that humanities and social sciences majors do just as well as science majors on Step 2 CK examinations.[8,10] Moreover, with respect to the Step 1 and 2 CK examinations, our results suggest that the gap in test scores between humanities and social sciences majors and science majors may narrow and that this difference may weaken over time, which echoes the findings of Ellaway et al.[27]

Consistent with earlier studies by Koenig[16] and Dickman et al.,[17] and contrary to Hypothesis 2a, we found no relationship between having a humanities and social sciences major and the trainee's subsequent choice of primary care specialty. Further, counter to Hypothesis 2b, we found no clear relationship between communication skills and choice of specialty. In other words, students with pre-medical backgrounds in the humanities and social sciences select a wide range of specialties, beyond choosing only primary care specialties;

moreover, students with higher CIS performance are also distributed across specialties.

Our results demonstrating the empirical association between a pre-medical background in the humanities and social sciences and CIS can have important consequences for student selection and admission processes, as well as implications for creating a student cohort of a type that will facilitate the acquisition of communication skills. Currently, most schools base admissions decisions primarily on academic performance and on science background. Our results underscore the need to consider other factors (such as college major) that may be related to physician empathy and communication skills. These findings mirror trends promoting a 'holistic admissions' review, which is a 'flexible, individualised way for schools to consider an applicant's capabilities, providing balanced consideration to experiences, attributes, and academic metrics'.[28] Competitive applicants in holistic admissions formats include those with 'exceptional CIS'. Our results suggest that students with pre-medical backgrounds in humanities and social sciences may be more likely to have such skills, and that any disadvantage they may have in their test scores is likely to recede by the time they take the USMLE® Step 2 CK examination. Recently, the use of core entrustable professional activities (EPAs) has been promoted in medical school as a way to enhance the transition to postgraduate medical training. At the core of these EPAs are CIS and, as such, advancing our understanding of which students enter medical school with greater communication skills or how students acquire them may require continued empirical studies and discussion.

This study has several key limitations. Firstly, our sample was drawn from a single institution, which may affect our ability to generalise our findings. Secondly, the small numbers of humanities and social sciences majors at our institution required us to collapse these majors into one large group. However, there may be important distinctions between majors that focus more fully on social interaction (such as psychology or sociology) and those that do not (such as economics or studio art) that we were not able to identify or explore. Future studies should explore these issues using national samples, such as results on the Step 2 CS examination, to enhance generalisability and to allow for such disaggregation of college majors.

In summary, our results suggest that there may be value in admitting medical students from humanistic backgrounds (e.g. humanities and social sciences majors). They may be better communicators and thereby possess skills the USMLE® increasingly values and which may be difficult to teach.[11] Moreover, students with pre-medical backgrounds in the humanities and social sciences were not disadvantaged on the USMLE® Step 2 CK and were successfully matched to a wide range of primary care and non-primary care specialties. Selecting students with a broad mix of pre-medical backgrounds may result in a more diverse cohort of learners, which may facilitate their learning experiences and transition to postgraduate training.

Contributors: LEH conceived the original research study design. RY and YSP were involved in gathering the data used for the analyses. YSP performed the computations. LEH and YSP drafted the manuscript with significant input and feedback from RY. All three authors approved the final manuscript and are accountable for the accuracy of the findings.
Acknowledgements: the authors would like to thank Georges Bordage, Department of Medical Education, College of Medicine, University of Illinois at Chicago, Chicago, Illinois, USA, for his extensive and insightful comments on this paper.
Funding: none.
Conflicts of interest: none.
Ethical approval: this study was approved by the Institutional Review Board of the University of Illinois at Chicago.

REFERENCES

1. Glick SM. Selection for entry to medicine and specialist training. *Med Teach* 2000;**22** (5):443–7.
2. McGaghie WC. Perspectives on medical school admission. *Acad Med* 1990;**65** (3):136–9.
3. Federation of State Medical Boards of the United States, Inc. and National Board of Medical Examiners®. United States Medical Licensing Examination® (USMLE®) Step 1. 1996–2018. http://www.usmle.org/step-1/ [Accessed 7 July 2016.]
4. Federation of State Medical Boards of the United States, Inc. and National Board of Medical Examiners®. United States Medical Licensing Examination® (USMLE®) Step 2 CK. 1996–2018. http://www.usmle.org/step-2-ck/ [Accessed 7 July 2016.]
5. Association of American Medical Colleges (AAMC). Taking the MCAT® Exam. 1995–2018. https://www.aamc.org/students/applying/mcat/ [Accessed 7 July 2016.]
6. Stratton TD, Elam CL, McGrath MG. A liberal arts education as preparation for medical school: how is it valued? How do graduates perform? *Acad Med* 2003;**78** (10 Suppl): S59–61.

7 Muller D, Kase N. Challenging traditional premedical requirements as predictors of success in medical school: the Mount Sinai School of Medicine Humanities and Medicine Program. *Acad Med* 2010;**85** (8):1378–83.

8 Smith SR. Effect of undergraduate college major on performance in medical school. *Acad Med* 1998;**73** (9):1006–8.

9 Hall JN, Woods N, Hanson MD. Is social sciences and humanities (SSH) premedical education marginalized in the medical school admission process? A review and contextualization of the literature. *Acad Med* 2014;**89** (7):1075–86.

10 Kleshinski J, Khuder SA, Shapiro JI, Gold JP. Impact of preadmission variables on USMLE Step 1 and Step 2 performance. *Adv Health Sci Educ Theory Pract* 2009;**14** (1):69–78.

11 Goyette KA, Mullen AL. Who studies the arts and sciences? Social background and the choice and consequences of undergraduate field of study. *J Higher Educ* 2006;**77** (3):497–538.

12 Satterfield JM, Mitteness LS, Tervalon M, Adler N. Integrating the social and behavioral sciences in an undergraduate medical curriculum: the UCSF essential core. *Acad Med* 2004;**79** (1):6–15.

13 Bleakley A, Marshall R. Can the science of communication inform the art of the medical humanities? *Med Educ* 2013;**47** (2):126–33.

14 Rider EA, Keefer CH. Communication skills competencies: definitions and a teaching toolbox. *Med Educ* 2006;**40** (7):624–9.

15 Stewart MA. Effective physician-patient communication and health outcomes: a review. *CMAJ* 1995;**152** (9):1423–33.

16 Koenig JA. Comparison of medical school performances and career plans of students with broad and with science-focused premedical preparation. *Acad Med* 1992;**67** (3):191–6.

17 Dickman RL, Sarnacki RE, Schimpfhauser FT, Katz LA. Medical students from natural science and nonscience undergraduate backgrounds: similar academic performance and residency selection. *JAMA* 1980;**243** (24):2506–9.

18 Zeleznik C, Hojat M, Veloski J. Baccalaureat preparation for medical school: does type of degree make a difference? *J Med Educ* 1983;**58**:26–33.

19 Association of American Medical Colleges (AAMC). *2019 AMCAS Applicant Guide*. Washington, DC: AAMC 2019.

20 Committee on Maximizing the Potential of Women in Academic Science and Engineering. *Beyond Bias and Barriers: Fulfilling the Potential of Women in Academic Science and Engineering*. Washington, DC: National Academies Press 2007.

21 Federation of State Medical Boards of the United States, Inc. and National Board of Medical Examiners®. USMLE® Step 2 Clinical Skills (CS) content description and general information. 2015. http://www.usmle.org/pdfs/step-2-cs/cs-info-manual.pdf [Accessed 25 January 2017.]

22 Federation of State Medical Boards of the United States, Inc. and National Board of Medical Examiners®, United States Medical Licensing Examination®. Step 2 CS Patient Note Entry Form. 2017. http://www.usmle.org/practice-materials/step-2-cs/patient-note-practice2.html [Accessed 25 January 2017.]

23 Yudkowsky R, Park YS, Hyderi A, Bordage G. Characteristics and implications of diagnostic justification scores based on the new patient note format of the USMLE Step 2 CS exam. *Acad Med* 2015;**90** (11 Suppl):S56–62.

24 Iramaneerat C, Myford CM, Yudkowsky R, Lowenstein T. Evaluating the effectiveness of rating instruments for a communication skills assessment of medical residents. *Adv Health Sci Educ Theory Pract* 2009;**14** (4):575–94.

25 Park YS, Lineberry M, Hyderi A, Bordage G, Xing K, Yudkowsky R. Differential weighting for subcomponent measures of integrated clinical encounter scores based on the USMLE Step 2 CS examination. *Acad Med* 2016;**91** (11 Suppl):S24–30.

26 Park YS, Hyderi A, Bordage G, Xing K, Yudkowsky R. Inter-rater reliability and generalizability of patient note scores using a scoring rubric based on the USMLE Step 2 CS format. *Adv Health Sci Educ Theory Pract* 2016;**21** (4):761–73.

27 Ellaway RH, Bates A, Girard S, Buitenhuis D, Lee K, Warton A, Russell S, Caines J, Traficante E, Graves L. Exploring the consequences of combining medical students with and without a background in biomedical sciences. *Med Educ* 2014;**48** (7):674–86.

28 Association of American Medical Colleges (AAMC). Holistic review in medical school admissions 2016. https://students-residents.aamc.org/choosing-medical-career/article/holistic-review-medical-school-admissions/ [Accessed 11 September 2017.]

Received 28 June 2018; editorial comments to authors 13 September 2018; accepted for publication 16 October 2018

Training Induces Cognitive Bias
The Case of a Simulation-Based Emergency Airway Curriculum

Christine S. Park, MD;

Ljuba Stojiljkovic, MD, PhD;

Biljana Milicic, MD, PhD;

Brian F. Lin, BS;

Itiel E. Dror, PhD

Introduction: Training-induced cognitive bias may affect performance. Using a simulation-based emergency airway curriculum, we tested the hypothesis that curriculum design would induce bias and affect decision making.
Methods: Twenty-three novice anesthesiology residents were randomized into 2 groups. The primary outcome measure was the initiation of supraglottic airway and cricothyroidotomy techniques in a simulated cannot-ventilate, cannot-intubate scenario during 3 evaluation sessions. Secondary outcomes were response times for device initiation. After a baseline evaluation and didactic lecture, residents received an initial practical training in either surgical cricothyroidotomy (CRIC group) or supraglottic airway (SGA group). After the midtest, the groups switched to receive the alternate training.
Results: From baseline to midtest, the SGA group increased initiation of supraglottic airway but not cricothyroidotomy. The CRIC group increased initiation of cricothyroidotomy but not supraglottic airway. After completion of training in both techniques, the SGA group increased initiation of both supraglottic airway and cricothyroidotomy. In contrast, the CRIC group increased initiation of cricothyroidotomy but failed to change practice in supraglottic airway. Final test response times showed that the CRIC group was slower to initiate supraglottic airway and faster to initiate cricothyroidotomy.
Discussion: Practical training in only 1 technique caused bias in both groups despite a preceding didactic lecture. The chief finding was an asymmetrical effect of training sequence even after training in both techniques. Initial training in cricothyroidotomy caused bias that did not correct despite subsequent supraglottic airway training. Educators must be alert to the risk of inducing cognitive bias when designing curricula.
(*Sim Healthcare* 9:85–93, 2014)

Key Words: Cognitive bias, Cognitive error, Simulation, Difficult airway, Emergency airway, Cricothyroidotomy.

Performance may be compromised when cognitive bias influences decision making. Cognitive bias is an inclination in judgment based on incomplete perspective and preformed patterns of thought. This inclination is held at the expense of other valid, potentially better, alternatives. Especially when decisions have to be made and executed quickly, individuals may be even more prone to bias, which leads to cognitive error.[1] Decision-making biases are systematic errors rather than random ones[2] and represent failures to make optimal decisions.[3] Because cognitive bias may result in exclusion of appropriate actions or deviation from an algorithm, patient care and safety may be threatened.

All training may be vulnerable to induction of bias. As training methods grow in effectiveness, a potential trade-off exists whereby the development of skills entails an increase in vulnerability to problems such as bias.[1] Technology-enhanced learning has increased impact on the cognitive representations that are acquired, but training-based bias may also be more likely to emerge.[4] For example, in cognitive science, it has been demonstrated that the order of presentation biases what and how information is recalled.[5] The relationship between training and bias has not been well established in the medical domain. Effective learning outcomes in simulation-based training have been well described,[6–11] and it is important to also explore the potential development of associated biases.

To test this concept, we used a simulation-based curriculum for training novice residents in the management of the unanticipated emergency airway. An unanticipated, cannot-ventilate, cannot-intubate airway is an emergent and potentially fatal event requiring swift intervention,[12] and training for this event is essential. Airway complications are a leading cause of morbidity and mortality in the American Society of Anesthesiologists Closed Claims Database, with 67% of difficult airways occurring during the induction of anesthesia.[13] The American Society of Anesthesiologists has

---

From the Department of Anesthesiology (C.S.P., L.S., B.F.L.), and Simulation Technology and Immersive Learning (C.S.P., L.S.), Center for Education in Medicine, Northwestern University–Feinberg School of Medicine, Chicago, IL; Department of Statistics (B.M.), School of Dentistry, University of Belgrade; and Department of Anesthesiology Clinical Center of Serbia (B.M.), Belgrade, Serbia; and Institute of Cognitive Neuroscience (I.E.D.), University College London (UCL), and Cognitive Consultants International (CCI), London, UK.

Reprints: Christine S. Park, MD, Department of Anesthesiology, Northwestern University–Feinberg School of Medicine, 251 E. Huron St, Feinberg 5-704, Chicago, IL 60611 (e-mail: christinepark@northwestern.edu).

The authors declare no conflict of interest.

Copyright © 2014 Society for Simulation in Healthcare
DOI: 10.1097/SIH.0b013e3182a90304

developed an algorithm for difficult airway management, including the emergent cannot-ventilate, cannot-intubate event.[14] The sequence of action begins with less invasive techniques (mask ventilation, direct laryngoscopy, and other devices). This is followed by attempted rescue with a supraglottic airway and culminates in a final invasive step of emergency cricothyroidotomy. However, especially when performed in an emergency, surgical cricothyroidotomy is associated with severe, life-threatening complications, and it should be used only after noninvasive alternatives fail.[15] Simulation is well suited for training skills in such low-frequency high-consequence events.

We investigated whether curriculum design, specifically training sequence, could influence bias in the setting of simulation-based medical education. We hypothesized that initial training in only 1 technique would result in a bias for that technique in a simulated cannot-ventilate, cannot-intubate scenario and that completion of training in both techniques would correct this bias regardless of the training sequence.

MATERIALS AND METHODS

The study, using a randomized, prospective crossover design (Fig. 1), was approved by the institutional review board of Northwestern University (Chicago, IL). All incoming postgraduate year 2 (PGY-2) residents to the Northwestern University anesthesiology residency program were considered for inclusion. The exclusion criterion was previous postgraduate training in anesthesiology. Written informed consent was obtained from the participants before enrollment. No resident was excluded, and all agreed to participate. Training was conducted in the Simulation Technology and Immersive Learning laboratory in the Center for Education in Medicine. Evaluations were conducted in the Northwestern Center for Clinical Simulation in the Department of Anesthesiology, using a full-body mannequin simulator (HPS; Medical Education Technologies, Inc, Sarasota, FL).

The primary outcome measure was the use of supraglottic airway and surgical cricothyroidotomy techniques (initiated or not initiated) in a simulated, emergency cannot-ventilate, cannot-intubate scenario for residents during 3 evaluation sessions: baseline, mid (3 weeks), and final evaluation (6 weeks). In the primary analysis, we documented initiation of supraglottic airway and cricothyroidotomy for all residents enrolled in the study. In a subanalysis, we considered the subset of residents who did not attempt either cricothyroidotomy or supraglottic airway at the baseline evaluation.

The secondary outcome measure was response time: we measured airway takeover time, time to initiation of supraglottic airway, time to initiation of surgical cricothyroidotomy, and interval time. Times were measured in seconds from a running time counter on the video. Airway takeover time was defined as length of time from the entry of the resident into the scenario to take over the airway from the medical student. Time to supraglottic airway was defined as the interval from airway takeover to initiation of supraglottic airway and time to cricothyroidotomy as interval from airway takeover to initiation of cricothyroidotomy. Interval time was defined as time elapsed between initiation of supraglottic airway and initiation of cricothyroidotomy.

Airway management maneuvers used during each scenario were documented by post hoc video review by a single rater who was blinded to subject identity, group assignments, and test date. The expected sequence of airway maneuvers was mask ventilation, direct laryngoscopy, supraglottic airway placement, and cricothyroidotomy. All 4 airway maneuvers were rated as initiated or not initiated. A maneuver was documented and timed when the resident physically initiated the technique. For supraglottic airway, this was defined as introduction of the device into the mouth. For surgical cricothyroidotomy, this was defined as initiation of a skin incision, which also ended the scenario. All noninvasive airway maneuvers were designed to be ineffective.

Procedure

Twenty-three clinical anesthesiology residents during their first 6 weeks of anesthesiology training following an internship (PGY-1) year were eligible and elected to participate in the study. During the initial 6-week period, residents received operating room training with supervision

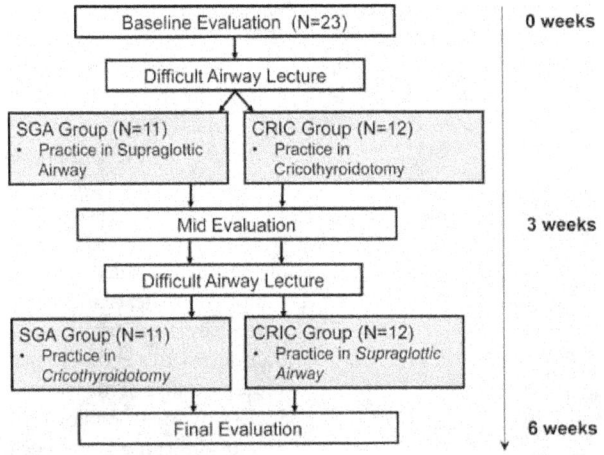

FIGURE 1. Study design of parallel groups with crossover to training in alternate method after 3 weeks.

at a 1:1 faculty-to-resident ratio, daily 1-hour didactic lectures covering basic concepts of anesthesia, and simulation-based training in a variety of critical events, including intraoperative hypotension, intraoperative hypoxemia, intraoperative cardiac arrest, postanesthesia care unit events, handoffs, teamwork, and emergency airway management (supraglottic airway and surgical cricothyroidotomy), during eight 3-hour sessions in the simulation laboratory during routine work hours.

Before the baseline test, residents were randomly divided into 2 groups using a computer-generated random numbers table. All residents were familiarized with the simulator environment and mannequin during a general orientation. At the baseline evaluation session before the educational intervention, all residents underwent individual testing in the unanticipated emergency airway scenario as part of a set of other intraoperative critical event scenarios as described in a previous article, including hypoxemia caused by bronchospasm, hypoxemia caused by endobronchial intubation and circuit leak, hypotension caused by hypovolemia, and hypotension caused by myocardial ischemia.[16] No debriefing took place following the test scenarios. Evaluation sessions were videotaped for post hoc evaluation of performance only by the rater.

Approximately 1.5 weeks after the baseline evaluation, residents participated in a 3-hour emergency airway module. Each group received a standardized lecture covering the American Society of Anesthesiologists Difficult Airway Algorithm in detail. The PowerPoint based lecture was a step-by-step description of the algorithm. It included photographs and descriptions of equipment pertinent to difficult airway management, including pharyngeal airways, supraglottic airways, equipment for direct and video laryngoscopy, intubating stylets, fiber-optic intubation, and emergency surgical cricothyroidotomy. All residents received a copy of the algorithm for reference. There were 3 total instructors blinded to group assignment, a single instructor for the supraglottic airway training sessions, and 2 instructors for the cricothyroidotomy training sessions. Instructors agreed upon the lecture content and agreed to adhere to the PowerPoint material. Because the goal was to investigate the effect of technical skills training and training sequence on decision making, we standardized the instruction for both supraglottic airway and cricothyroidotomy to restrict variables in training and sources of bias across experimental conditions. Instruction was limited to technical direction only during the training sessions. Other than reading the American Society of Anesthesiologists Difficult Airway Algorithm, instructors did not provide case studies, anecdotes, or further comment on decision making. Instructors did not discuss risks and benefits, including acute and chronic morbidity and mortality, because of its potential to introduce bias beyond that of the technical training. After the lecture, 1 group (SGA group) received initial standardized practical training in supraglottic devices and practiced placement of a variety of supraglottic airway devices on partial task trainers. The other group (CRIC group) received initial standardized practical training in emergency surgical cricothyroidotomy. They practiced 3 different emergency surgical cricothyroidotomy techniques, 3-step, 4-step, and Seldinger techniques,[17–19] on partial-task trainers using sheep tracheas covered with artificial skin. Equipment consisted of a Melker cricothyroidotomy kit[20] (Cook Medical, Inc, Bloomington, IN) and an Eschmann stylet (Bell Medical, Inc, St. Louis, MO).

A midtest was performed at 3 weeks of training. The evaluation was conducted in the same manner as the baseline evaluation. The groups were then crossed over, receiving the identical lecture given at the previous training session accompanied by practical training in the other technique (ie, the SGA group now practiced cricothyroidotomy, and the CRIC group now practiced supraglottic airway). This session occurred approximately 1.5 weeks after the midtest. A final evaluation, again in the same manner as the baseline evaluation, was conducted at the conclusion of week 6. Residents also completed a survey at the final evaluation, indicating their difficult airway experience during their PGY-1 year and first 6 weeks of training.

Emergency Airway Scenario

An unanticipated cannot-ventilate, cannot-intubate scenario was developed for use at all 3 evaluation sessions. The simulated patient histories varied slightly at baseline, mid, and final evaluations, but each simulated patient history was a healthy adult, without known airway pathology, predictors of difficult airway, or previous anesthetics. Each patient was presenting for elective ambulatory surgery (orthopedic, aesthetic plastic, and gynecologic), requiring general endotracheal anesthesia. Before each testing session, the resident received general prebriefing instructions as follows: (1) he/she is assuming care of a patient in the operating room under anesthesia, (2) think out loud, and (3) ask at any time for anything, or anyone, needed. The scenario began with the resident being asked for assistance with airway management by a confederate acting as a medical student. The medical student informed the resident that he was a medical student and that after he and the attending anesthesiologist had induced anesthesia with propofol 200 mg and rocuronium 50 mg, the attending anesthesiologist had to emergently leave and was unavailable.

We used this opening of the scenario to obligate the resident to assume management of the airway. When a resident called for help from an anesthesiologist, he/she was informed that help had been urgently called but was not immediately available. If a resident called for help from a surgeon, he/she was informed that the surgeon did not feel comfortable with invasive airway management and that an otolaryngology surgeon was not immediately available. Simulating the typical setup in the operating room, an anesthesia cart contained supplies such as induction and resuscitation medications and intravenous catheters of various sizes, a styletted 7.5-mm endotracheal tube and laryngoscope fitted with a #3 Macintosh blade were on the anesthesia machine, and supraglottic airways (sizes 3 and 4 LMA) were available in the top drawer of the anesthesia machine. If the resident verbalized a request for a supraglottic airway, the medical student immediately provided the supraglottic airways. Information regarding fiber-optic bronchoscope, video laryngoscope, and other airway equipment availability was not provided before the scenario and would not have been readily available if requested. The cricothyroidotomy kit was not in the room. If the resident verbalized a request for a cricothyroidotomy kit, the medical student immediately provided the kit.

The vital sign sequence was identical at all testing sessions. Time zero for the scenario was the entry of the resident into the scenario. The initial vital signs remained unchanged for 15 seconds, followed by 2 phases of progressive oxygen desaturation and sympathetic stimulation and two phases of profound oxygen desaturation and development of bradycardia and relative hypotension (Fig. 2). The scenario ended at 5 minutes or when the resident initiated the cricothyroidotomy procedure, whichever came first. The termination time of the scenario was selected because cerebral hypoxia lasting longer than 3 to 5 minutes is associated with permanent brain injury.[21] The medical student confederate remained in the room throughout the scenario and was knowledgeable about the patient history upon inquiry. The medical student was able to assist with patient monitoring as requested and obtaining and preparing, but not using, any requested equipment. The medical student did not prompt the resident, ask questions, make unsolicited observations, or suggest any course of action.

Statistical Analysis

The number of participants was a convenience sample determined by the number of incoming residents (n = 23) to the anesthesiology residency program. There were 11 residents assigned to the SGA group and 12 residents assigned to the CRIC group (Fig. 1). In a post hoc power analysis, the sample size of 11 in the SGA group achieves 98% power to detect the difference in supraglottic airway placements between the baseline and midtests using McNemar test for categorical variables with binomial attributes with $\alpha = 0.05$ (DSS Statistical Power Calculator, Fort Worth, TX). The sample size of 12 in the CRIC group achieves 87% power to detect the difference in cricothyroidotomy placement between the baseline and midtest using McNemar statistics ($\alpha = 0.05$). A $P < 0.05$ was required to reject the null hypothesis. Descriptive data for both groups were expressed as mean (SD) for continuous measures or percentage of a group for discrete measures. Numeric data were tested for normal distribution using the Kolmogorov-Smirnov test. Independent samples t test and repeated-measures analysis of variance were used to assess differences in response times. Categorical data were analyzed using the McNemar and Fisher exact tests. Statistical analyses were performed using SPSS software version 20 (Chicago, IL).

RESULTS

There was no difference between groups with regard to sex or type of internship. There was no difference with respect to previous exposure to difficult airway management techniques. Previous exposure was defined as either observation of or participation in the use of a technique. None of the residents who reported previous exposure to either supraglottic airway or cricothyroidotomy initiated the respective technique at the baseline test. There was no difference with respect to difficult airway experience during the first 6 weeks. Finally, there was no difference with respect to elective clinical airway experience throughout the study period (Table 1).

We compared the initiation of supraglottic airway and cricothyroidotomy techniques within each group (within group analysis) and also assessed differences based on group assignment (between-group analysis).

Within-Group Analysis

Within-group analysis of supraglottic airway and cricothyroidotomy initiation is presented in Table 2. The SGA group significantly increased initiation of supraglottic airway from baseline to midtest, and performance was maintained from midtest to final evaluation. With regard to cricothyroidotomy, the SGA group did not change initiation of cricothyroidotomy from baseline to midtest. After the cricothyroidotomy training in the second 3-week period, the SGA group significantly increased initiation of cricothyroidotomy from midtest to final evaluation.

The CRIC group significantly increased initiation of cricothyroidotomy from baseline to midtest, and performance

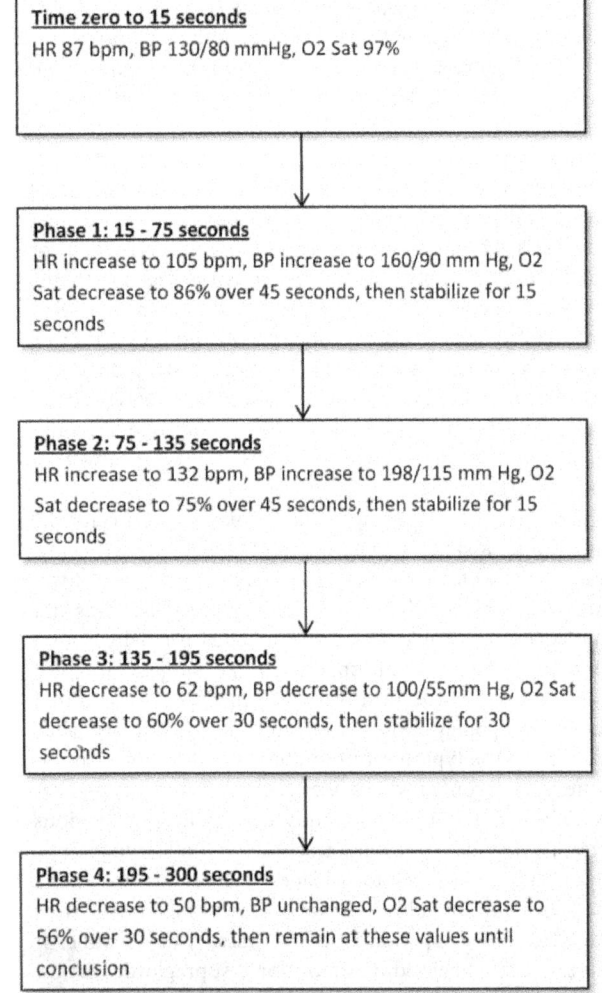

FIGURE 2. Scenario progression.

TABLE 1. Demographics and Airway Experience

	SGA Group		CRIC Group		P*
Sex	Female	Male	Female	Male	0.371
n (%)	4 (36)	7 (64)	2 (17)	10 (83)	
Internship	Medical	Surgical	Medical	Surgical	0.590
n (%)	9 (82)	2 (18)	11 (92)	1 (8)	
Previous difficult airway exposure, n (%)					
SGA		3 (27)		1 (8)	0.317
CRIC		0 (0)		1 (8)	1.000
Difficult airway experience (6 wk), n (%)					
SGA		2 (18)		1 (8)	0.590
CRIC		0 (0)		0 (0)	N/A
Elective airway experience (6 wk)					
SGA	No. elective SGA performed				0.371
	1–10	11–20	1–10	11–20	
n (%)	7 (64)	4 (36)	10 (83)	2 (17)	
DL	No. elective DL performed				0.217
	11–20	>20	11–20	>20	
n (%)	0 (0)	11 (100)	3 (25)	9 (75)	

*Fisher exact test.
DL indicates direct laryngoscopy; N/A indicates not applicable.

was maintained from midtest to final evaluation. With regard to supraglottic airway, the CRIC group did not change initiation of supraglottic airway from baseline to midtest. Even after receiving training the supraglottic airway in the second 3-week period, the CRIC group demonstrated no significant change in initiation of supraglottic airway technique at the final evaluation.

Between-Group Analysis

Between-group analysis of initiation of supraglottic airway and cricothyroidotomy techniques is presented in the upper panel of Table 3. Significantly more residents in the CRIC group than in the SGA group attempted supraglottic airway at the baseline test. However, there was no significant association between previous exposure to SGA for difficult airway management and SGA initiation during the baseline test (McNemar, $P = 1.000$). No baseline difference was observed between groups for initiation of cricothyroidotomy.

Only 9% of the residents in the SGA group and 17% of residents in the CRIC group attempted all 4 airway maneuvers (mask ventilation, direct laryngoscopy, supraglottic airway, and cricothyroidotomy) at the midtest ($P = 1.000$). Sixty-four percent of residents in the SGA group and 42% of residents in the CRIC group attempted all 4 airway maneuvers at the final evaluation ($P = 0.29$).

Subgroup Analysis

Further analysis focused on the performance of residents who did not attempt either technique at the baseline test. Therefore, 5 residents who attempted supraglottic airway and 3 residents who initiated cricothyroidotomy at baseline test were excluded. The subgroup analysis is presented in the bottom panel of Table 3.

After completion of training in both techniques, there were no differences in initiation of cricothyroidotomy: in both subgroups, 80% of the residents initiated cricothyroidotomy. However, with regard to supraglottic airway, although 80% of residents from the SGA subgroup attempted supraglottic airway, none of the residents from the CRIC subgroup attempted supraglottic airway.

With regard to overall performance, 70% of the residents in the SGA subgroup attempted all 4 airway maneuvers. By contrast, none of the residents from the CRIC subgroup attempted all 4 airway maneuvers ($P = 0.03$).

Use of Other Airway Techniques and Calling for Help

Although mask ventilation and direct laryngoscopy were not part of the practical training curriculum, all residents performed mask ventilation as a first maneuver at mid and final evaluations. Ninety-two percent of the residents performed direct laryngoscopy at the midtest, and 100% performed direct laryngoscopy at the final evaluation.

No resident requested fiber-optic bronchoscope, video laryngoscope, or any other airway equipment at baseline, mid, or final evaluations. No resident attempted needle cricothyroidotomy at baseline, mid, or final evaluations.

Despite having been informed that the attending anesthesiologist was unavailable, all residents at baseline, mid, and final evaluations still correctly called for help during the first desaturation phase of the scenario.

Response Times

In addition to maneuvers attempted, response times were measured. These data were normally distributed.

Airway Takeover Time

Airway takeover times are presented in Table 4. Both groups significantly decreased takeover time among evaluation sessions. However, there was no significant difference among groups at any evaluation session.

Final Evaluation: Time to Supraglottic Airway and Cricothyroidotomy

The times to initiation of supraglottic airway and cricothyroidotomy maneuvers in those residents who performed both supraglottic airway and cricothyroidotomy

TABLE 2. Within-Group Analysis

		Evaluation Session			P*	
	Technique	Base	Mid	Final	Base to Mid	Mid to Final
SGA group (n = 11)	Supraglottic airway, n (%)	0 (0)	8 (73)	8 (73)	0.008	1.000
	Cricothyroidotomy, n (%)	1 (9)	1 (9)	9 (82)	1.000	0.008
CRIC group (n = 12)	Supraglottic airway, n (%)	5 (42)	5 (42)	6 (50)	1.000	1.000
	Cricothyroidotomy, n (%)	2 (17)	9 (75)	10 (83)	0.016	1.000

*McNemar test.

TABLE 3. Between-Group Analysis

Evaluation Session		Supraglottic Airway Initiated		P*	Cricothyroidotomy Initiated		P*
		All Participants					
		SGA Group (n = 11), n (%)	CRIC Group (n = 12), n (%)		SGA Group (n = 11), n (%)	CRIC Group (n = 12), n (%)	
	Base	0 (0)	5 (42)	0.04	1 (9)	2 (17)	1.000
	Mid	8 (73)	5 (42)	0.21	1 (9)	9 (75)	0.003
	Final	8 (73)	6 (50)	0.40	9 (82)	10 (83)	1.000
		Subgroup					
		SGA Subgroup (n = 10) n (%)	CRIC Subgroup (n = 5) n (%)		SGA Subgroup (n = 10) n (%)	CRIC Subgroup (n = 5) n (%)	
	Base	0 (0)	0 (0)	N/A	0 (0)	0 (0)	N/A
	Mid	7 (70)	1 (20)	0.12	0 (0)	4 (80)	0.004
	Final	8 (80)	0 (0)	0.007	8 (80)	4 (80)	1.000

*Fisher exact test.

after training in both techniques are presented in Figure 3. The mean time to supraglottic airway initiation was longer in the CRIC group compared with the SGA group. The time to cricothyroidotomy incision was significantly faster in the CRIC group than in the SGA group. In addition, the interval between initiation of supraglottic airway and cricothyroidotomy in those residents who performed both supraglottic airway and cricothyroidotomy was significantly shorter in the CRIC group than in the SGA group.

DISCUSSION

After initial training in only 1 technique, both groups demonstrated bias for their respective technique. This was as expected. Despite a detailed presentation of the difficult airway algorithm, a didactic lecture did not prevent bias in either group after training in only 1 device.

The chief finding of this study was the appearance of an unexpected asymmetrical effect of training sequence after the conclusion of emergency airway training in both supraglottic airway and cricothyroidotomy. Beginning with training in cricothyroidotomy, the CRIC group demonstrated persistent bias for cricothyroidotomy and did not increase initiation of supraglottic airway despite subsequent supraglottic airway training and routine experience with supraglottic airway during clinical duties. By contrast, beginning with practical training in supraglottic airway resulted in increased initiation of both devices during simulated emergency airway management. To our knowledge, this is the first report of such a finding in medical education.

The analysis of final test response times offers further insight regarding the difference in behavior. Although all residents began with efforts at mask ventilation and direct laryngoscopy, the CRIC group was slower to initiate supraglottic airway and initiated cricothyroidotomy sooner than the SGA group. By contrast, the SGA group was faster to initiate supraglottic airway and initiated cricothyroidotomy later. There are no definitive standards for timing of supraglottic airway and cricothyroidotomy initiation because a number of additional clinical variables must be considered. Nevertheless, for the identical conditions presented to all participants in this study, the asymmetry of the groups based on training sequence is notable. For the CRIC group, the short interval time between supraglottic airway and cricothyroidotomy may represent a reduction of window of opportunity to rescue and pose a greater risk for bypassing supraglottic airway.

Furthermore, we analyzed the use of techniques in the subgroups including only residents who performed neither supraglottic airway nor cricothyroidotomy at baseline. Although group sizes are small, the convergent data from the subgroups complement the overall finding of a bias effect.

Cognitive error, such as those resulting from cognitive bias, is a thought process error distinct from knowledge or technical deficits. The types of cognitive error and predisposing biases are many, but they are all low-visibility, latent failures.[22-25] Latent failure is a precondition that remains hidden until a triggering event exposes the potential harm to patients. Simulation has been used as a method to investigate latent errors.[26] In this study, simulation served a dual purpose as a training methodology and strategy to uncover latent conditions.

Cognitive error seems to be a prevalent latent problem in anesthesiology.[24] Indeed, the phenomenon of bypassing supraglottic airway for cricothyroidotomy has been observed in other studies. In a study of practicing anesthesiologists, subjects participated in a session reviewing difficult airway guidelines and hands-on cricothyroidotomy teaching. In cannot-ventilate, cannot-intubate scenarios after the session, the number of participants bypassing supraglottic airway was nearly doubled, and the time to cricothyroidotomy

TABLE 4. Airway Takeover Time

Evaluation Session	SGA Group, Mean (SD), s	CRIC Group, Mean (SD), s	P*	
			Among Evaluation Sessions	Among Groups
Baseline	91 (62)	64 (35)	0.02	0.08
Mid	46 (13)	52 (13)		
Final	50 (12)	42 (9)		

*Repeated-measures analysis of variance. s indicates seconds.

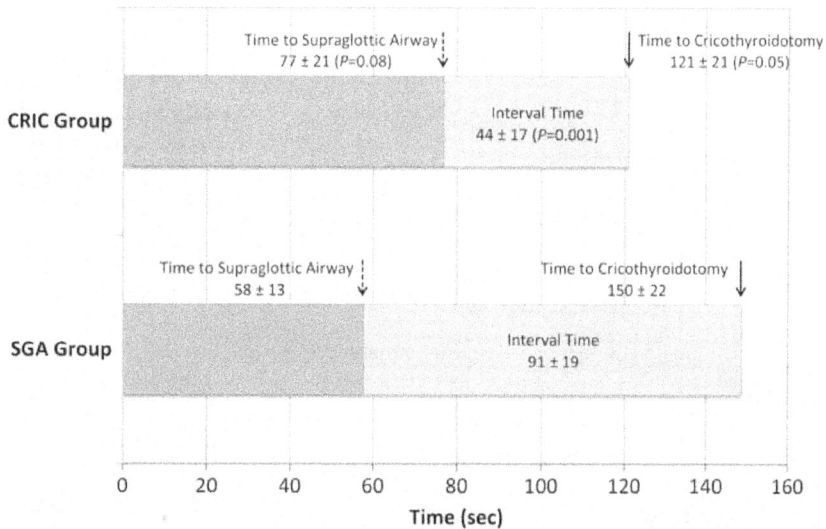

FIGURE 3. Response times. Times to supraglottic airway placement and cricothyroidotomy were measured in those residents who performed both supraglottic airway and cricothyroidotomy at the final test (SGA group, n = 7; CRIC group, n = 5). SGA Time: Time in seconds from takeover to initiation of supraglottic airway placement; CRIC time, time in seconds from takeover to initiation of cricothyroidotomy incision; interval time, interval in seconds between SGA time and CRIC time. The mean SGA time was not significantly different between the SGA group (58 [13] seconds) and CRIC group (77 [21] seconds) P = 0.076. On the contrary, CRIC time was shorter in CRIC group (121 [21] seconds), as compared with SGA group (150 [22] seconds) P = 0.048. The interval between SGA time and CRIC time in those residents who performed both supraglottic airway and cricothyroidotomy was significantly shorter in the CRIC group (44 [17] seconds) than in the SGA group (91 [19] seconds) P = 0.001. Statistical test, independent samples t test.

was significantly decreased.[27] In another study, 54% of senior anesthesiology residents bypassed supraglottic airway in an obstetric cannot-ventilate, cannot-intubate scenario, whereas 94% performed cricothyroidotomy.[28] The observations of these studies support our data and highlight the importance of cognitively informed curriculum design and delivery.

Supraglottic airway devices are used every day for routine elective airway management during surgical anesthesia as well as for airway rescue. In contrast, cricothyroidotomy is a rarely necessary, and always emergent, procedure. Knowing that trainees use supraglottic airways in routine practice, educators may prefer to focus on the high-stakes skill of cricothyroidotomy. In 2 studies assessing practicing anesthesiologists in a cannot-ventilate, cannot-intubate scenario, cricothyroidotomy was a training goal and outcome measure, but supraglottic airway placement was not.[29,30] This may be educationally and clinically justified, but such training may induce cognitive bias. In this study, all residents had clinical experience with elective supraglottic airways for routine airway management during surgical anesthesia. However, for the CRIC group, additional experience with this device in one cognitive frame (routine/elective) did not result in application of that skill in another cognitive frame (simulated emergency airway).

The persistent bias for cricothyroidotomy may have partly been an effect of primacy, in which learning or memory is biased toward the first stimulus presented.[5] Primacy has been observed in a variety of settings.[31,32] However, a corresponding primacy effect in the SGA group was not observed, arguing against primacy as a dominant effect. Cricothyroidotomy may also have a more salient, or memorable, mental representation because its nature as a rare and invasive technique draws more attention than frequently used, noninvasive techniques. Furthermore, as a stimulus becomes routine, such as elective experience with the supraglottic airway, the amount of attention to and additional learning about the routine stimulus may be impaired.[33] The ongoing elective experience in supraglottic airway might therefore have contributed to an even weaker learning outcome when supraglottic airway training followed cricothyroidotomy training.

The SGA group received training in the expected order of actions (ie, supraglottic airway as rescue attempt, followed by cricothyroidotomy as a final intervention), but the CRIC group received training in a scrambled order. The chunking[34] and scrambling of clinical actions during training may also have contributed to the group differences.

Metacognition, processing by the learner about when and how to use particular strategies for problem solving, is an important component of decision making. Dual process theory is a metacognitive model that provides insight into cognition. According to this theory, 2 cognitive systems are used to reason and make decisions. System I, the "intuitive" system, is a fast and automated response system best used for routine decisions. System II, the "analytical" system, is slower and cognitively demanding, using conscious application of learned rules.[35,36] Individuals default to a state requiring low cognitive effort without checking,[37] even during urgent situations.[38] System I thinking is therefore prone to bias and judgment error. For the CRIC group, a default to system I thinking may have contributed to the persistent bias. It seems that both reasoning strategies are important in avoiding error,[39] and because system I is always active, its bias can only be mitigated by the enhanced monitoring and vigilance of system II.[40] In addition to teaching skills and knowledge, educators may consider strategies to teach learners to engage both systems of thinking, especially in high-stakes situations, to minimize bias.

Limitations

Because of scheduling limitations, the didactic lecture could not be given to all residents simultaneously, and a single instructor could not teach all sessions. Therefore, the lecture was standardized for content and delivery, and efforts were made to limit the number and to maximize consistency of instructors. We cannot tell whether residents would have identified a correct sequence of maneuvers in a written test. We considered assessing knowledge via a written test, but whether a test either preceded or followed the scenario, one could have significantly influenced the other. In addition, our primary outcome measure was not knowledge, but deployment of decisions; therefore, we did not administer a written test.

We did not obtain qualitative measures such as structured interviewing partly because doing so at the baseline or midtest could have had significant influence on the subsequent evaluations, and partly because we did not expect to observe a bias effect after completion of training in both techniques. We therefore do not know the participants' assumptions and thoughts about the decisions they made or what was expected of them. For example, we cannot rule out the possibility of experimenter bias, in which subjects, consciously or unconsciously, attempt to predict what might be the desired answer. This may have influenced the timed measures in the simulation test.

We assessed a single variable of training sequence. Although we have discussed several potential contributing sources of bias, this data set does not allow the specific delineation of the types of bias, a topic for further investigation.

Not all residents achieved 100% initiation of all 4 airway maneuvers. We would expect 100% achievement only with a mastery-training design, where the amount of training may vary for each subject until the set goal of 100% is achieved. Standardization of the amount and type of training for each participant was an essential study design element to study the effect of training sequence. Bias relating to mastery-training experimental design is another variable worthy of investigation.

Finally, this study assessed initiation of airway management techniques in one type of simulated scenario, with limited time and opportunities for choice of action, in a relatively small sample of novice residents from 1 institution during 6 weeks. We do not know how performance in a simulated event would correspond with real clinical behaviors, and interpretation of the data should be undertaken with caution. Data from longer-term follow-up are necessary, and additional data from subjects with more clinical experience, over a range of scenarios, and additional variables in training strategy, will further enhance understanding of the complex relationships between training and bias.

CONCLUSIONS

More than 75% of US and Canadian anesthesiology residency programs use simulation for airway management training.[41] Simulation is used for training supraglottic airway placement[42] and cricothyroidotomy skills.[43,44] As the goal of transferring skills to the clinical environment is progressively achieved,[45,46] understanding the cognitive underpinnings of medical education in general and simulation-based training in particular is an opportunity to guide educators how best to train medical professionals.[47]

Selection and order of presentation of examples and stimuli is likely to play a role in determining the outcome and effectiveness of training. The examples, order, and manipulation of saliency have been shown to play a critical role in training US Air Force pilots.[48,49] In the case of emergency airway training, it seems that similar elements affected decision making and vulnerability to cognitive bias.

Our study showed that the sequence of training in a simulation-based emergency airway curriculum contributed to the formation of cognitive bias. Therefore, curricular design should consider potential effects of cognitive bias and error. Additional studies can further characterize the causes of and corrections for training-based biases and errors. By deciphering the underpinnings of cognitive bias in education, educators will be able to tailor strategies to minimize bias to improve patient safety.

REFERENCES

1. Dror IE. The paradox of human expertise: why experts get it wrong. In: Kapur N, ed. *The Paradoxical Brain*. Cambridge, UK: Cambridge University Press; 2011:177–188.
2. Gilovich T, Griffin D, Kahneman D. *Heuristics and Biases: The Psychology of Intuitive Judgment*. Cambridge, UK: Cambridge University Press; 2002.
3. Rehak LA, Adams B, Belanger M. Mapping biases to the components of rationalistic and naturalistic decision making. *Proc Hum Factors Ergonomics Soc* 2010;54:324–328.
4. Dror I. Technology enhanced learning: the good, the bad, and the ugly. *Pragmatics Cogn* 2008;16:215–223.
5. DiGirolamo G, Hintzman D. First impressions are lasting impressions: a primacy effect in memory for repetitions. *Psychon Bull Rev* 1997;4:121–124.
6. Bruppacher HR, Alam SK, LeBlanc VR, et al. Simulation-based training improves physicians' performance in patient care in high-stakes clinical setting of cardiac surgery. *Anesthesiology* 2010;112:985–992.
7. Daniels K, Arafeh J, Clark A, Waller S, Druzin M, Chueh J. Prospective randomized trial of simulation versus didactic teaching for obstetrical emergencies. *Simul Healthc* 2010;5:40–45.
8. McCoy CE, Menchine M, Anderson C, Kollen R, Langdorf MI, Lotfipour S. Prospective randomized crossover study of simulation vs. didactics for teaching medical students the assessment and management of critically ill patients. *J Emerg Med* 2011;40:448–455.
9. Niazi AU, Haldipur N, Prasad AG, Chan VW. Ultrasound-guided regional anesthesia performance in the early learning period: effect of simulation training. *Reg Anesth Pain Med* 2012;37:51–54.
10. Wang CL, Schopp JG, Petscavage JM, Paladin AM, Richardson ML, Bush WH. Prospective randomized comparison of standard didactic lecture versus high-fidelity simulation for radiology resident contrast reaction management training. *AJR Am J Roentgenol* 2011;196:1288–1295.
11. Park CS. Simulation and quality improvement in anesthesiology. *Anesthesiol Clin* 2011;29:13–28.
12. Benumof JL. Management of the difficult adult airway. With special emphasis on awake tracheal intubation. *Anesthesiology* 1991;75:1087–1110.
13. Peterson GN, Domino KB, Caplan RA, Posner KL, Lee LA, Cheney FW. Management of the difficult airway: a closed claims analysis. *Anesthesiology* 2005;103:33–39.

14. American Society of Anesthesiologists Task Force on Management of the Difficult Airway. Practice guidelines for management of the difficult airway: an updated report by the American Society of Anesthesiologists Task Force on Management of the Difficult Airway. *Anesthesiology* 2003;98:1269–1277.
15. Isaacs JH Jr, Pedersen AD. Emergency cricothyroidotomy. *Am Surg* 1997;63:346–349.
16. Park CS, Rochlen LR, Yaghmour E, et al. Acquisition of critical intraoperative event management skills in novice anesthesiology residents by using high-fidelity simulation-based training. *Anesthesiology* 2010;112:202–211.
17. Holmes JF, Panacek EA, Sakles JC, Brofeldt BT. Comparison of 2 cricothyrotomy techniques: standard method versus rapid 4-step technique. *Ann Emerg Med* 1998;32:442–446.
18. Schaumann N, Lorenz V, Schellongowski P, et al. Evaluation of Seldinger technique emergency cricothyroidotomy versus standard surgical cricothyroidotomy in 200 cadavers. *Anesthesiology* 2005;102:7–11.
19. MacIntyre A, Markarian MK, Carrison D, Coates J, Kuhls D, Fildes JJ. Three-step emergency cricothyroidotomy. *Mil Med* 2007;172:1228–1230.
20. Melker JS, Gabrielli A. Melker cricothyrotomy kit: an alternative to the surgical technique. *Ann Otol Rhinol Laryngol* 2005;114:525–528.
21. Hemphill JC III, Smith WS, Gress DR. Neurologic Critical Care, Including Hypoxic-Ischemic Encephalopathy and Subarachnoid Hemorrhage, Harrison's Principles of Internal Medicine, 18th edition. Edited by Longo DL, Fauci AS, Kasper DL, Hauser SL, Jameson JL, Loscalzo J. New York, McGraw-Hill, 2012. Available at: http://www.accessmedicine.com.ezproxy.galter.northwestern.edu/content.aspx?aID=9111325. Accessed June 5, 2013.
22. Arnstein F. Catalogue of human error. *Br J Anaesth* 1997;79:645–656.
23. Croskerry P. The importance of cognitive errors in diagnosis and strategies to minimize them. *Acad Med* 2003;78:775–780.
24. Stiegler MP, Neelankavil JP, Canales C, Dhillon A. Cognitive errors detected in anaesthesiology: a literature review and pilot study. *Br J Anaesth* 2012;108:229–235.
25. Graber M, Gordon R, Franklin N. Reducing diagnostic errors in medicine: what's the goal? *Acad Med* 2002;77:981–992.
26. Blike GT, Christoffersen K, Cravero JP, Andeweg SK, Jensen J. A method for measuring system safety and latent errors associated with pediatric procedural sedation. *Anesth Analg* 2005;101:48–58.
27. Borges BC, Boet S, Siu LW, et al. Incomplete adherence to the ASA difficult airway algorithm is unchanged after a high-fidelity simulation session. *Can J Anaesth* 2010;57:644–649.
28. Balki M, Cooke ME, Dunington S, Salman A, Goldszmidt E. Unanticipated difficult airway in obstetric patients: development of a new algorithm for formative assessment in high-fidelity simulation. *Anesthesiology* 2012;117:883–897.
29. Kuduvalli PM, Jervis A, Tighe SQ, Robin NM. Unanticipated difficult airway management in anaesthetised patients: a prospective study of the effect of mannequin training on management strategies and skill retention. *Anaesthesia* 2008;63:364–369.
30. Siu LW, Boet S, Borges BC, et al. High-fidelity simulation demonstrates the influence of anesthesiologists' age and years from residency on emergency cricothyroidotomy skills. *Anesth Analg* 2010;111:955–960.
31. Mantonakis A, Rodero P, Lesschaeve I, Hastie R. Order in choice: effects of serial position on preferences. *Psychol Sci* 2009;20:1309–1312.
32. Carney D, Banaji M. First is best. *J Behav Decis Mak* 2012;22:378–389.
33. Hintzman D, Curran T, Oppy B. Effects of similarity and repetition on memory: registration without learning? *J Exp Psychol Learn Mem Cogn* 1992;14:240–247.
34. Ruitenberg MF, De Kleine E, Van der Lubbe RH, Verwey WB, Abrahamse EL. Context-dependent motor skill and the role of practice. *Psychol Res* 2012;76:812–820.
35. Pelaccia T, Tardif J, Triby E, Charlin B. An analysis of clinical reasoning through a recent and comprehensive approach: the dual-process theory. *Med Educ Online* 2011;16. Available at: http://med-ed-online.net/index.php/mep/article/view/5890. Accessed November 6, 2013.
36. Thompson VA, Prowse Turner JA, Pennycook G. Intuition, reason, and metacognition. *Cogn Psychol* 2011;63:107–140.
37. Kahneman D, Klein G. Conditions for intuitive expertise: a failure to disagree. *Am Psychol* 2009;64:515–526.
38. Croskerry P. Clinical cognition and diagnostic error: applications of a dual process model of reasoning. *Adv Health Sci Educ Theory Pract* 2009;14(Suppl 1):27–35.
39. Eva KW, Hatala RM, Leblanc VR, Brooks LR. Teaching from the clinical reasoning literature: combined reasoning strategies help novice diagnosticians overcome misleading information. *Med Educ* 2007;41:1152–1158.
40. Kahneman D. *Thinking Fast and Slow.* New York, NY: Farrar, Straus and Giroux; 2011:28.
41. Pott LM, Randel GI, Straker T, Becker KD, Cooper RM. A survey of airway training among U.S. and Canadian anesthesiology residency programs. *J Clin Anesth* 2011;23:15–26.
42. Laiou E, Clutton-Brock TH, Lilford RJ, Taylor CA. The effects of laryngeal mask airway passage simulation training on the acquisition of undergraduate clinical skills: a randomised controlled trial. *BMC Med Educ* 2011;11:57.
43. Wong DT, Prabhu AJ, Coloma M, Imasogie N, Chung FF. What is the minimum training required for successful cricothyroidotomy?: a study in mannequins. *Anesthesiology* 2003;98:349–353.
44. Friedman Z, You-Ten KE, Bould MD, Naik V. Teaching lifesaving procedures: the impact of model fidelity on acquisition and transfer of cricothyrotomy skills to performance on cadavers. *Anesth Analg* 2008;107:1663–1669.
45. Ross AJ, Kodate N, Anderson JE, Thomas L, Jaye P. Review of simulation studies in anaesthesia journals, 2001–2010: mapping and content analysis. *Br J Anaesth* 2012;109:99–109.
46. Nestel D, Groom J, Eikeland-Husebo S, O'Donnell JM. Simulation for learning and teaching procedural skills: the state of the science. *Simul Healthc* 2011;6(Suppl):S10–S13.
47. Dror I, Schmidt P, O'Connor L. A cognitive perspective on technology enhanced learning in medical training: great opportunities, pitfalls and challenges. *Med Teach* 2011;33:291–296.
48. Dror IE, Stevenage SV, Ashworth ARS. Helping the cognitive system learn: exaggerating distinctiveness and uniqueness. *Appl Cogn Psychol* 2008;22:573–584.
49. Ashworth ARS, Dror IE. Objective identification as a function of discriminability and learning presentations: the effect of stimulus similarity and canonical frame alignment on aircraft identification. *J Exp Psychol* 2001;6:148–157.

Part V: Accommodation and Ethics

Overview

Kristi Kirschner
Clinical Professor, Department of Medical Education

The papers you will read in this section on accommodation and ethics reflect the disciplinary expertise and interdisciplinary work of DME faculty whose work touches upon themes of social justice, disability studies, and ethical questions raised medical advances, changing social mores, and new technologies.

The first paper, "Leading practices and future directions for technical standards in medical education" is a white paper and work product of the Association of Academic Physiatrists (AAP). Led by Kezar (physiatrist and former student affairs dean at University of Alabama School of Medicine), two of the six authors are DME faculty: Curry and Kirschner. Curry and I have worked together on this topic for years, influencing each other's thoughts – through my lens of disability studies and rehabilitation, and his medical educator lens. The charge to the group was to update the 1993 AAP white paper on technical standards, informed by the changing practices of medicine and law, technology, and social and cultural mores. Defined as "the nonacademic requirements deemed essential for participation in an educational program", technical standards had largely remained unchanged since the guidelines were published by the Association of American Medical Colleges in 1979, and have served as barriers to the profession for people with disabilities (a notably underrepresented group in medical schools). In the movement toward competency-based curriculum, we challenge the notion that perfect bodies and senses are required to practice medicine and discuss what might be alternative ways to view and frame technical standards and reasonable accommodations. We also raise questions about how the inclusion of doctors with disabilities in the profession might benefit the culture of medicine. This conversation is far from over, but we hope this white paper provides rich food for thought, and that it augments the frameworks medical educators can use to include students with disabilities in medical schools.

The second paper in this series is by Sufian, who draws upon both her medical history and disability studies expertise in her manuscript "Engaging in productive conversation: writing histories of medicine and disability in the Middle East and North Africa". This work is both timely and urgent. She notes that "since this academic dialogue began five years ago, scholars and students from both fields have asked: How can we write histories that maintain the respective concerns and emphases of each field [disability history and history of medicine] but that also reflect a more serious engagement of one with the other? How can such mutuality generate new insights into a multitude of societal dynamics and hierarchies? ... One of the main questions shared by both disability history and history of medicine is how notions of capacity, fitness, perfection, and normality operate conceptually and practically in nationalist movements. To be sure, within the colonial context, Western medical notions of what constituted the modern body and its symbolic meanings seeped into the ways in which non-Western (but perhaps Western-educated) leaders framed their nationalist projects". If you anticipate that there might be practical lessons for today's divisive political climate, you will not be disappointed.

Last but not least, the third paper in this section is by philosopher and bioethicist Murphy, "The ethics of helping transgender men and women have children." Murphy, as one of the foremost philosophers on assisted reproductive technologies (ART), sex and gender also tackles questions about social justice and inclusion in analyzing the stigma and bias a transgender man experienced when seeking ART, especially from the medical profession and psychiatry in particular. Is gender identity disorder a pathological condition? Should ART be available to transgender men, and are children who are the product of such ART "at risk"? Dr Murphy concludes that "the normalization of transgender identities by the law and professional organizations contributes, moreover, to the need to reassess pathological interpretations of cross-sex identities, and trans-parenthood puts those interpretations into sharp relief".

For those who are not aware, the University of Illinois College of Medicine, has been in the midst of a major curriculum transformation, implemented in August 2017 (for a curricular map, see: https://chicago.medicine.uic.edu/education/md-curriculum/curriculum-overview/phase-1-curriculum-map/). In preparing to build the new curriculum from the ground up, the Health Humanities Program (housed in DME) has had to grow. I joined UICOM four years ago and have contributed to scholarship on access to care, disability, ethics, and education. I am also the subtheme leader for the health humanities curriculum. We have added one new faculty member, a literature and medicine scholar (Blackie) who joined our team of philosopher and bioethicist (Murphy), sociologist (Hirshfield), and medical historian and disability studies scholar (Sufian). We have also cultivated a number of partners both within the medical school campuses and our local communities.

Our program defines health humanities as *describing and interpreting* "the theory and practice of medicine through works of philosophy, ethics, history, literature, sociology and anthropology". (see: https://healthhumanities.red.uic.edu/about/history/). We have added a rich arts initiative to this programming as well (e.g., graphic medicine, medical improvisation, art, and observation). DME faculty members have contributed to the development and growth in the health humanities curriculum at UICOM and also the scholarship, as exemplified in this section.

Leading Practices and Future Directions for Technical Standards in Medical Education

Laura B. Kezar, MD, Kristi L. Kirschner, MD, Daniel M. Clinchot, MD, Elisa Laird-Metke, JD, Philip Zazove, MD, and Raymond H. Curry, MD

Abstract

The medical profession first addressed the need for technical standards (TS), defining the nonacademic requirements deemed essential for participation in an educational program, in guidelines published by the Association of American Medical Colleges in 1979. Despite many changes in the practice of medicine and legal, cultural, and technological advances that afford greater opportunities for people with disabilities, the profession's approach to TS largely has not changed over the ensuing four decades. Although physicians with disabilities bring unique perspectives to medicine and contribute to a diverse physician workforce of culturally competent practitioners, they remain underrepresented in the profession.

As part of an initiative sponsored by the Association of Academic Physiatrists, the authors describe the need for an updated TS framework, outlining interval changes in the legal and regulatory climate, medical practice, and medical education since the initial TS guidelines were put forth. They conclude by offering eight recommendations and two functional approaches to TS that are consistent with now-prevalent competency-based medical education constructs.

The profession's commitment to diversity and inclusion should extend explicitly to people with disabilities, and this stance should be clearly communicated through medical schools' TS and procedures for requesting accommodations. To this end, schools should consider the principles of universal design to create policies and assessments that work for all learners, to the greatest extent possible, without the need for after-the-fact accommodations. A thoughtful and concerted effort along these lines is long overdue in medical education.

The term *technical standards* (TS) comes from the Rehabilitation Act of 1973 (Section 504), which defined a qualified individual as someone "who meets the academic and technical standards requisite to admission or participation in the [school's] education program or activity...."[1] Guidance from the federal government regarding this regulation states, "The term 'technical standards' refers to all nonacademic admissions criteria that are essential to participation in the program in question."[2] For example, TS include interpersonal skills and professional attitudes and behaviors. TS are distinct from essential functions, which are the job duties that employed individuals must be able to perform, and from learning outcomes, which are the information and skills that students should learn during their education.

The Association of American Medical Colleges (AAMC) first issued TS guidelines in 1979.[3] A white paper, sponsored by the Association of Academic Physiatrists (AAP) in 1993, updated the AAMC's guidelines and provided additional recommendations regarding their implementation.[4] More than 25 years later, though, the AAMC TS guidelines remain the primary point of reference for most related policies. Although subsequent AAMC publications[5–8] have provided additional guidance for medical schools to comply with evolving legal and regulatory expectations, the underlying principles guiding schools in the construction of their TS have not been revisited. The Liaison Committee on Medical Education (LCME) and the American Osteopathic Association (AOA) require medical schools both to create TS that are consistent with their mission and to publicize those TS in accordance with applicable law. The LCME's TS definition[9] is based on the 1979 AAMC guidelines, whereas the AOA does not specify the content required in TS.[10] As a result, TS language and implementation vary considerably among schools.[11] Many TS may not be compliant with Americans with Disabilities Act (ADA) standards because they are vaguely articulated, rely on outdated language and concepts, and/or are not clearly presented in the schools' admissions materials or websites.[12]

Given this history, along with the many changes in medical education, medical practice, and the medico-legal landscape in the last quarter century, the AAP commissioned one of us (L.B.K.) to convene an expert task force to revisit their 1993 consensus recommendations. The task force consisted of disability experts, medical education leaders, and disability service professionals who have been engaged in responding to these changes. In this article, we, as members of the task force, propose substantive updates to the 1979 AAMC and 1993 AAP TS guidelines for medical education. Our proposed updates take into account the many legal, cultural, and technological advances that have afforded greater opportunities for people with disabilities and highlight recent changes in some schools' TS to facilitate the inclusion of students with disabilities.

The Need for Updated TS

Despite some progress in the integration of people with disabilities into

---

Please see the end of this article for information about the authors.

Correspondence should be addressed to Laura B. Kezar, Spain Rehabilitation Center, 1717 6th Ave. South, Birmingham, AL 35294-0019; telephone: (205) 934-2785; e-mail: kezar@uab.edu.

Acad Med. 2019;94:520–527.
First published online November 5, 2018
doi: 10.1097/ACM.0000000000002517
Copyright © 2018 by the Association of American Medical Colleges

Supplemental digital content for this article is available at http://links.lww.com/ACADMED/A612.

professional employment settings since the implementation of the ADA and Section 504 of the Rehabilitation Act, people with disabilities remain substantially underrepresented in medicine. Of the noninstitutionalized U.S. population aged 18 to 24, approximately 3.5% have a physical or sensory disability,[13] and up to 10% have some type of disability.[14] Estimates of the prevalence of disabilities among medical students are much lower, ranging from 0.6%, an estimate that includes students with physical or sensory disabilities,[15] to 2.7%, an estimate that also includes students with learning and psychological disabilities.[16] Internal and external factors may contribute to the underrepresentation of these students in medical education, including lack of access to appropriate accommodation at any point in the educational pipeline; lack of knowledge about accommodation strategies; concerns about the cost of accommodations to the institution; stigma, particularly surrounding physical and mental health disabilities[17]; bias and discrimination in the admissions process and the medical community at large[18]; and other barriers, real or imagined, regarding the ability of people with disabilities to function as physicians.[19] Most likely, a combination of these factors is at play.

The ADA transformed many areas of society; curb cuts, ramps, designated parking spaces, and closed captioning are now accepted parts of American culture.[20] Universal design is more commonplace as well (i.e., "the design of products and environments to be usable by all people, to the greatest extent possible, without the need for adaptation or specialized design"[21]). Despite these changes, health care institutions still have unacceptably high rates of inaccessible environments and discriminatory practices, as reports of significant ongoing health care barriers show even long after the passage of the ADA.[22–24]

Revising TS, in and of itself, will not remove these barriers to inclusion, but inattention to how TS play out in practice has clearly impeded progress. Outdated TS can, paradoxically, serve as a barrier to entry to the medical profession for people with disabilities. On reviewing these standards, potential applicants may incorrectly assume that their disabilities preclude them from matriculating, which may inhibit their desire to apply at all. Further, many current TS do not support reasonable accommodations as intended by the ADA,[12] and students with disabilities have had to resort to the courts to require compliance from schools, as we describe below. In addition to improving equity and inclusion, updating TS to reflect the current climate would keep schools aligned with evolving social constructs and bring their TS in line with actual practice.

Some health professions schools have adopted a "functional" approach to TS, promoting inclusivity by emphasizing candidates' abilities rather than their limitations.[25,26] (We use the term *candidates* to refer to applicants to medical school as well as current medical students who are candidates for the MD degree.) Functional TS focus on what needs to be accomplished rather than how it must be done. These standards allow students to use accommodations and permit the ongoing incorporation of technological and medical advances as they become available. Functional TS describe the skills that students must master (e.g., assessment of patients' functioning, effective communication with patients and the care team) but not the manner in which students must achieve them (e.g., using vision, hearing, speech). In contrast, many traditional TS (termed "organic" TS) are informed by the 1979 AAMC standards and focus on candidates' innate sensory, physical, and mental abilities instead of their ability to achieve the tasks at hand. Of note, the potential use of intermediaries to accomplish tasks is difficult to address using organic TS. In the most restrictive cases, organic TS require students with disabilities to demonstrate specific physical or mental capabilities without technology (i.e., to hear and communicate orally without the use of hearing aids).[27]

Changes in the Legal and Regulatory Climate

Although federal civil rights laws mandating equal access for people with disabilities have existed since 1973 with the passage of the Rehabilitation Act, in 1990 the ADA expanded schools' obligations to provide access and accommodations to people with disabilities. In response to years of court decisions that gradually narrowed the scope of the law, the ADA was amended in 2008 to specify and expand on who is considered "disabled."[28] As disability rights statutes and regulations have steadily progressed, so have the courts' interpretations of those laws.

In 1979, the first legal challenge regarding disability accommodations, *Southeastern Community College v. Davis*, reached the U.S. Supreme Court.[29] The court upheld a nursing school's decision to refuse admission to a student with significant hearing loss, deferring to the school's TS that a student must be able to hear to qualify for enrollment. In its decision, however, the court explicitly acknowledged a future where technological advances could trigger greater obligations for institutions of higher education to admit students with disabilities. This future envisioned by the Supreme Court nearly four decades ago has indeed come to pass. For example, individuals with hearing disabilities now have instant access to auditory information not only in the classroom but also in clinical and surgical settings.[30,31] Real-time captioning, smartphones and tablets, remote interpreters through video relay services, and digital stethoscopes can access and monitor data previously accessible only via hearing. Today, subspecialist interpreters are trained to support both providers and patients in the health care environment.[27] New tools and technological innovations similarly have opened doors for those with limited vision and other types of disabilities.

This new reality is reflected in recent court decisions. In direct contrast to the 1979 *Southeastern Community College v. Davis* case, the majority of decisions since 2013 have mandated that schools admit and provide accommodations for students with disabilities, particularly for students with sensory disabilities. There has not been complete uniformity, however, as at least one case, *McCulley v. University of Kansas School of Medicine*, held that a school did not need to admit a student with physical disabilities.[32] Although cost is sometimes cited by schools as a limitation to providing disability accommodations, a university's entire budget must be considered, which usually renders the concern moot.[33]

In light of the numerous cases that found rigid, organic TS discriminatory, we believe that schools that rely on the *McCulley v. University of Kansas* decision to defend their use of organic TS do so at their peril. Alternatively, schools that create functional TS are more closely aligned with the intent of federal disability rights laws.

Table 1 provides a summary of the key legal decisions that informed our task force's work.

Changes in Medical Practice

Twenty-first century medicine employs far fewer solo practitioners and places greater emphasis on team-based care, interprofessional practice, information and health care systems, and quality and safety practices. Physician assistants and nurse practitioners are increasingly partnering with physicians to gather and interpret data.[34] A wide range of technological advances have armed clinicians with new tools for diagnosis and treatment; some, like telehealth applications, may obviate the need for the physical presence of a clinician. Specialties and subspecialties are becoming more clearly divided between those that are "cognitive" and those that are "procedural"; many physicians' routine work involves little or no need to perform procedures or even physical examinations.

Moreover, studies demonstrate that proficiency is tied to the frequency with which a procedure is performed. In addition, many practicing physicians are performing fewer types of procedures, while those who do perform procedures acquired their skills during specialty training rather than in medical school. In a 2004 American College of Physicians survey, general internists reported routinely performing only half as many types of procedures as they did in 1986 (from 16 to 7).[35] In addition, the increasing use of "procedure teams" in hospitals and advances in interventional radiology have been shown to improve the safety and quality of care.[36]

Changes in Medical Education

Just as medical practice is embracing the concepts of team-based care and information management skills, medical educators are focusing more on students' ability to function effectively as part of a team, and they are becoming more interested in students' problem-solving skills than their factual memory or procedural skills. The rise of competency-based medical education[37,38] has helped drive these changes, broadening the aims of medical education to include teaching professionalism, practice-based learning and improvement, and systems-based practice, and shifting the focus of assessment to measuring performance rather than knowledge alone. The AAMC's Admissions Initiative applied this concept to premedical education as well.[39] With this approach, schools can assess the performance of students with disabilities using reasonable accommodations, allowing students to demonstrate their mastery of skills through alternative methods. Some schools have integrated their TS into their competencies, a process that highlights the outcomes themselves rather than the method for achieving them.[40]

Even new competency-based approaches, however, do not fully integrate disability accommodations. One of the AAMC's 13 Core Entrustable Professional Activities (EPAs) for Entering Residency focuses on a procedural competency: "All physicians need to demonstrate competency in *performing* (emphasis added) a few core procedures ... basic cardiopulmonary resuscitation (CPR),

Table 1
Summary of Recent U.S. Case Law Regarding Technical Standards (TS) and Accommodations for People With Disabilities

Year	Case	Summary
1979	Southeastern Community College v. Davis[29]	The U.S. Supreme Court upheld the school's TS requiring students to be able to hear, supporting the rejection of a deaf nursing applicant. But the court explicitly acknowledged that future technological advances could trigger greater obligations for schools to admit students with disabilities.
2014	Palmer College of Chiropractic v. Davenport Civil Rights Commission[56]	The Supreme Court of Iowa considered whether a student with limited vision could complete a chiropractic training program with the following TS: "Sufficient use of vision, hearing, and somatic sensation necessary to perform chiropractic and general physical examination, including the procedures of inspection, palpation, auscultation, and the review of radiographs as taught in the curriculum." The court held that the school's rigid adherence to its TS as a threshold for participation in the program constituted a violation of the student's Americans with Disabilities Act rights.
2014	Featherstone v. Pacific Northwest University of Health Sciences[57]	A federal district court ordered a medical school to immediately admit a deaf student who requested sign language interpreters and real-time captioning to access instruction, saying that the school's "concerns that the requested accommodations would amount to a fundamental modification of its program not only lacks merit but is wholly speculative."
2013	Argenyi v. Creighton University[58]	A federal court of appeal held that a medical school that refused to provide real-time captioning or interpreters for a matriculated student with a significant hearing disability must provide him with such accommodations as would allow him equal access to his medical education under federal law.
2014	McCulley v. University of Kansas School of Medicine[32]	A federal court of appeal considered the TS of a medical school that required students to perform certain manual tasks, such as lifting patients and performing CPR. A student whose disability caused her to have limited upper body strength requested a surrogate to perform these tasks for her while she directed the surrogate's actions. The school refused her request, saying that such physical tasks must be completed by the student herself for the completion of an undifferentiated degree, even though the student did not intend to pursue a medical career that would require such physical exertion. The court upheld the school's decision; however, it acknowledged that another school with different TS may have admitted her, saying: "Our disposition should not be read as holding that medical schools cannot reasonably admit McCulley or other students with similar disabilities."

bag and mask ventilation, venipuncture, inserting an intravenous line" (EPA 12).[41] The need to perform these procedures even in residency is questionable, as specialty boards do allow programs to waive the requirement for proficiency in performing specific procedures as a reasonable accommodation for residents with disabilities.[42] In addition, one of the AAMC's proposed admissions competencies champions applicants' ability to recognize barriers to communication and to adjust their approach, but it also requires applicants to use "spoken words and sentences," effectively excluding users of American Sign Language or those with other speech-related disabilities who do not rely on their voices. Just as assistive technologies have become increasingly available[43] and TS have evolved, so too should the scope of skills that learners must demonstrate as EPAs.

Approaches to Revising TS

The 1979 AAMC TS guidelines require that candidates demonstrate skills including observation; communication; motor function; conceptual, integrative, and quantitative thinking; and appropriate behavioral and social attributes. They also require that medical students be able to perform these actions independently. The LCME uses this TS construct in the glossary of terms that accompanies its current accreditation standards.[9] The LCME's glossary is, however, meant as a guideline; schools already have the flexibility to vary their approach, within the bounds of applicable law.[44]

The original AAMC TS guidelines accepted technological compensation for disabilities but not human assistance, stating that an intermediary might impose "someone else's power of selection and observation" on a student's judgment.[3] Many education leaders, including many from the AAP, disagree with this argument and believe that the ADA mandates a rethinking of this position.[45–48] Michael Reichgott,[46] in a published adaptation of his 1995 AAP-sponsored address at the AAMC annual meeting, asked, "Is the hands-on, personal touching experience ... necessary for the effective integration of basic science knowledge and the understanding of pathophysiology?" He noted, "If a trained assistant does the physical examination and provides data to the student (or resident), does this really impose a negative 'interpreter' effect?" The 2010 AAMC publication *Medical Students With Disabilities: Resources to Enhance Accessibility* included a specific discussion of intermediaries playing a role in data gathering:

> Certain parts of the exam may not be physically possible for the student and may require the use of peers or physician extenders.... It may be necessary to modify the requirement for manual tasks, to emphasize cognitive aspects (recognition of abnormal findings and development of differential diagnosis and treatment plan) rather than the ability to perform the task itself.[8]

Although many schools were already permitting language intermediaries (interpreters) for students with hearing or speech disabilities, this language from the AAMC signaled a new opportunity to explore the use of *physical* intermediaries for data collection. A number of medical schools now provide a paid staff intermediary who can assist students with physical disabilities.[49,50] Of note, functional TS allow a student to "direct" another individual, while organic TS do not.

Recommendations

To allow for accommodations like those we discussed above, we propose two functional approaches to revising TS that schools may adopt, depending on which best meets their needs. In the first model, shown in Appendix 1, we propose new language for TS using the five functional categories initially proposed by Reichgott.[46] Changing the TS categories allows for a sharper focus on "what" students must demonstrate rather than on "how" they must demonstrate it. Many of the skills in Appendix 1 are essentially the same as those in the AAMC groupings. The second model, shown in Appendix 2, retains the TS categories originally set forth by the AAMC,[3] which defined some skills based on the physical attributes of candidates, but it updates the content to promote a functional, rather than organic, approach. By allowing candidates to "provide or direct" medical care, both models allow for the use of intermediaries when appropriate.

We also offer the following recommendations, intended as an update of the 1993 AAP guidelines. The goal of these recommendations is to address the call to action, from a number of groups including the AAMC, for enhanced accessibility for students with disabilities and for the further promotion of a diverse physician workforce.[8,13,17,51–54]

We recommend that medical schools:

1. Include students with disabilities as part of their commitment to diversity and inclusion and monitor admission and retention data in a manner that is sensitive to the privacy and preferences of these students.

2. Critically review and update their TS, taking into account the substantial evolution of the role of the physician in clinical care, the potential for new technologies to provide reasonable accommodation for an increasingly broad range of disabling conditions, and recent changes in legal and regulatory expectations for schools to be more accommodating.

3. Use a functional rather than organic approach to writing TS. See Appendix 1 and 2 for two approaches that meet current legal standards and allow schools and students appropriate flexibility.

4. Correlate or integrate the expectations of their TS with the core competencies and/or EPAs expected of all students.

5. Review and ensure the accessibility of their TS to applicants, students, and the public via their website. These communications should both clearly state that the school accepts qualified students with disabilities and delineate the criteria all students must meet to be admitted and continue in the school.

6. Clearly define procedures for requesting accommodations, which must be appropriately confidential and individualized, and readily available on websites and in admissions materials, student handbooks, syllabi, and other resources routinely used by students. See Supplemental Digital Appendix 1 (available at http://links.lww.com/ACADMED/A612) for detailed recommendations about the accommodations process.

7. Ensure that the process of making decisions about accommodations is interactive and actively includes the student with the disability and

an individual with expertise in disability accommodations and ADA requirements who is not in a position to evaluate the student. This process should be ongoing to address evolving needs throughout the student's education.

8. Implement the principles of universal design in education[55] by creating instructional goals, methods, materials, and assessments that work for all learners, to the greatest extent possible, without the need for after-the-fact disability accommodations to make them accessible to students with disabilities.

Future Directions

As medical education leaders have articulated for more than two decades, people with disabilities bring unique perspectives to medicine and help create a diverse physician workforce made up of culturally competent practitioners who can meet the needs of their patients and educate their peers. Sponsoring and accrediting agencies must expand their review of and heighten expectations for medical education programs with respect to the inclusion of people with disabilities and programs' adherence to the ADA and Section 504 of the Rehabilitation Act. Doing so will require modifications to current data tracking systems to include questions about disability status on standard surveys and questionnaires. Additionally, for students with disabilities who are unable to do the physical work of medicine themselves, the profession should address the appropriate use of intermediaries in collecting data and performing elements of the physical examination. We also advocate for further research into the barriers that impede people with disabilities in the medical education pipeline, patient perceptions and outcomes when they receive care from students and physicians with disabilities, and the use of both human and technological intermediaries to advance the inclusion of people with disabilities in medical education. We anticipate that the emerging focus on universal design and competency-based medical education will eventually render TS obsolete. In the meantime, the prevailing approach to TS must be revised.

Acknowledgments: The authors thank Danielle Powell, MD, MSPH, and Joan Bisagno, PhD, for their contributions to the task force.

Funding/Support: None reported.

Other disclosures: This article represents the conclusions of the Task Force on Technical Standards for Medical Students established by the Association of Academic Physiatrists and was reviewed and approved by the Board of Trustees of the Association of Academic Physiatrists.

Ethical approval: Reported as not applicable.

L.B. Kezar is professor, Departments of Physical Medicine & Rehabilitation and Medical Education, University of Alabama School of Medicine, Birmingham, Alabama.

K.L. Kirschner is clinical professor, Department of Medical Education, University of Illinois College of Medicine, adjunct professor of disability and human development, College of Applied Health Sciences, University of Illinois at Chicago, and attending physician, Schwab Rehabilitation Hospital, Chicago, Illinois.

D.M. Clinchot is vice dean for education, associate vice president for health sciences, professor of physical medicine and rehabilitation, Ohio State University College of Medicine, Columbus, Ohio.

E. Laird-Metke is director, Disability Resource Center, Samuel Merritt University, Oakland, California.

P. Zazove is George A. Dean, M.D. Chair and professor, Department of Family Medicine, University of Michigan Medical Center, Ann Arbor, Michigan.

R.H. Curry is senior associate dean for educational affairs, University of Illinois College of Medicine, and professor of medicine and medical education, University of Illinois at Chicago, Chicago, Illinois.

References

1 HHS Regulations, Section 504 of the Rehabilitation Act of 1973, 45 C.F.R. § 84.3(k)(3) (1978).
2 Section 504 Federal Guidance, 45 C.F.R. pt. 84, App. A, p. 405 (1978).
3 Association of American Medical Colleges. Special Advisory Panel on Technical Standards for Medical School Admission. Washington, DC: Association of American Medical Colleges; 1979.
4 Association of Academic Physiatrists. Recommended guidelines for admission of candidates with disabilities to medical school. Am J Phys Med Rehabil. 1993;72:45–47.
5 Association of American Medical Colleges. The Americans with Disabilities Act (ADA) and the Disabled Student in Medical School: Guidelines for Medical Schools. Washington, DC: Association of American Medical Colleges; 1993.
6 Medical School Objectives Writing Group. Learning objectives for medical student education: Guidelines for medical schools. Report I of the Medical School Objectives Project. Acad Med. 1999;74:13–18.
7 Watson JE, Hutchens SH. Medical Students With Disabilities: A Generation of Practice. Washington, DC: Association of American Medical Colleges; 2005.
8 Hosterman JA, Shannon DP, Sondheimer HM, eds. Medical Students With Disabilities: Resources to Enhance Accessibility. Washington, DC: Association of American Medical Colleges; 2010.
9 Liaison Committee on Medical Education. LCME standards, publications, and notification forms. http://lcme.org/wp-content/uploads/filebase/standards/2018-19_Functions-and-Structure_2017-08-02.docx. Accessed October 30, 2018.
10 American Osteopathic Association. COM accreditation. http://www.osteopathic.org/accreditation. Accessed October 17, 2018.
11 Sandhouse M. Technical requirements to become an osteopathic physician. Intl J Osteopath Med. 2014;17:43–47.
12 Zazove P, Case B, Moreland C, et al. U.S. medical schools' compliance with the Americans with Disabilities Act: Findings from a national study. Acad Med. 2016;91:979–986.
13 DeLisa JA, Lindenthal JJ. Commentary: Reflections on diversity and inclusion in medical education. Acad Med. 2012;87:1461–1463.
14 National Center for Education Statistics. U.S. Department of Education. Fast facts: Students with disabilities. https://nces.ed.gov/fastfacts/display.asp?id=64. Accessed October 17, 2018.
15 Eickmeyer SM, Do KD, Kirschner KL, Curry RH. North American medical schools' experience with and approaches to the needs of students with physical and sensory disabilities. Acad Med. 2012;87:567–573.
16 Meeks LM, Herzer KR. Prevalence of self-disclosed disability among medical students in US allopathic medical schools. JAMA. 2016;316:2271–2272.
17 Meeks LM, Jain NR. Accessibility, Action, and Inclusion in Medical Education: Lived Experiences of Learners and Physicians With Disabilities. Washington, DC: Association of American Medical Colleges; 2017.
18 Mehta L, Clifford G. Admissions as a facilitator of inclusion—Not a gatekeeper. Disabil Compliance Higher Educ. 2016;22:7.
19 Neal-Boylan L, Hopkins A, Skeete R, Hartmann SB, Iezzoni LI, Nunez-Smith M. The career trajectories of health care professionals practicing with permanent disabilities. Acad Med. 2012;87:172–178.
20 Americans with Disabilities Act, 42 U.S.C. § 12101 (1990).
21 NC State University College of Design. The Center for Universal Design. https://projects.ncsu.edu/ncsu/design/cud/about_ud/about_ud.htm. Accessed October 17, 2018.
22 Peacock G, Iezzoni LI, Harkin TR. Health care for americans with disabilities—25 years after the ADA. N Engl J Med. 2015;373:892–893.
23 United States Department of Justice, Civil Rights Division. Barrier-Free Health Care Initiative. https://www.ada.gov/usao-agreements.htm. Accessed October 17, 2018.
24 National Council on Disability. The current state of healthcare for people with disabilities. https://ncd.gov/publications/2009/Sept302009. Accessed October 17, 2018.
25 Marks B, Ailey S. White Paper on Inclusion of Students With Disabilities in Nursing Educational Programs for the California Committee on the Employment of People With Disabilities. Chicago, IL: American Association of Colleges of Nursing; 2014.
26 University of Minnesota Medical School. Essential capacities for matriculation, promotion, & graduation.

https://www.med.umn.edu/md-students/policies-governance/academic-progression/essential-capacities-matriculation-promotion-graduation. Accessed October 17, 2018.
27 McKee M, Case B, Fausone M, Zazove P, Ouellette A, Fetters MD. Medical schools' willingness to accommodate medical students with sensory and physical disabilities: Ethical foundations of a functional challenge to "organic" technical standards. AMA J Ethics. 2016;18:993–1002.
28 ADA Amendments Act, Public Law 110-325, sec. 8, 122 Stat. 3553, 3559 (2008).
29 Southeastern Community College v. Davis, 442 U.S. 397 (1979).
30 UC Davis Health. Technology assures deaf student learns surgery at UC Davis School of Medicine [video file]. https://www.youtube.com/watch?v=AwDvgFrbY5w. Published November 30, 2011. Accessed October 17, 2018.
31 Meeks LM, Laird-Metke E, Rollins M, Gandhi S, Stechert M, Jain NR. Practice brief: Accommodating deaf and hard of hearing students in operating room environments—A case study. J Postsecond Educ Disabil. 2015;28:383–388.
32 McCulley v. University of Kansas School of Medicine, 591 F. App'x. 648 (10th Cir. 2014).
33 Searls v. Johns Hopkins Hospital, 158 F. Supp3d 427 (D.Md. 2016).
34 Cooke M, Irby DM, O'Brien BC. Part I: Today's practice, yesterday's legacy, tomorrow's challenges. In: Educating Physicians: A Call for Reform of Medical School and Residency. Stanford, CA: Jossey-Bass; 2010:11–71.
35 Wigton RS, Alguire P; American College of Physicians. The declining number and variety of procedures done by general internists: A resurvey of members of the American College of Physicians. Ann Intern Med. 2007;146:355–360.
36 McCormack J. The new proceduralists: Have they found their niche? AMedNews. September 17, 2007.
37 Batalden P, Leach D, Swing S, Dreyfus H, Dreyfus S. General competencies and accreditation in graduate medical education. Health Aff (Millwood). 2002;21:103–111.
38 Carraccio C, Englander R, Van Melle E, et al; International Competency-Based Medical Education Collaborators. Advancing competency-based medical education: A charter for clinician–educators. Acad Med. 2016;91:645–649.
39 Association of American Medical Colleges. AAMC Admissions Initiative: A pathway to competency-based admissions. https://www.aamc.org/download/308462/data/admissionsinitiativesummary.pdf. Published 2012. Accessed October 17, 2018.
40 Ohio State University College of Medicine. Core educational objectives of the medical curriculum. https://medicine.osu.edu/students/life/resources/core_objectives/pages/index.aspx. Published 2008. Accessed October 17, 2018.
41 Flynn TF, Call S, Carraccio C, et al. Core Entrustable Professional Activities for Entering Residency. Washington, DC: Association of American Medical Colleges; 2014.
42 Aboff B, Burday M, Salam T. Residents with disabilities. In: Williams F, Winiger D, eds. A Textbook for Internal Medicine Education Programs. 12th ed. Alexandria, VA: Alliance for Academic Internal Medicine; 2017.
43 Atcherson SR, Moreland C, Zazove P, McKee MM. Hearing loss: Hearing augmentation. FP Essent. 2015;434:18–23.
44 Barzansky B, Catanese VM. Co-secretaries, Liaison Committee on Medical Education. Personal communication with R. Curry, April 10, 2017.
45 Meier RH 3rd. Issues concerning medical school admission for students with disabilities. Am J Phys Med Rehabil. 1993;72:341–342.
46 Reichgott MJ. "Without handicap": Issues of medical schools and physically disabled students. Acad Med. 1996;71:724–729.
47 Reichgott MJ. The disabled student as undifferentiated graduate: A medical school challenge. JAMA. 1998;279:79.
48 VanMatre RM, Nampiaparampil DE, Curry RH, Kirschner KL. Technical standards for the education of physicians with physical disabilities: Perspectives of medical students, residents, and attending physicians. Am J Phys Med Rehabil. 2004;83:54–60.
49 Callahan B. University of Washington. Personal communication with E. Laird-Metke, September 11, 2017.
50 Blacklock B. University of Minnesota. Personal communication with E. Laird-Metke, September 11, 2017.
51 Cohen J. A word from the president. Reconsidering disabled applicants. AAMC Reporter. 2004;13(9):2.
52 DeLisa JA, Thomas P. Physicians with disabilities and the physician workforce: A need to reassess our policies. Am J Phys Med Rehabil. 2005;84:5–11.
53 Shakespeare T, Iezzoni LI, Groce NE. Disability and the training of health professionals. Lancet. 2009;374:1815–1816.
54 Addams AN, Bletzinger RB, Sondheimer HM, White SE, Johnson LM. Roadmap to Diversity: Integrating Holistic Review Practices Into Medical School Admissions Processes. Washington, DC: Association of American Medical Colleges; 2010.
55 Burgstahler S. An approach to ensure that educational programs serve all students. Universal Design in Education: Principles and Applications. 2012. https://www.washington.edu/doit/sites/default/files/atoms/files/Universal-Design-Education-Principles-Applications.pdf. Accessed October 30, 2018.

References cited in Table 1 only

56 Palmer College of Chiropractic v. Davenport Civil Rights Commission, 850 NW2d 326 (2014).
57 Featherstone v. Pacific Northwest University of Health Sciences, No. 1:CV-14-3084-SMJ (E.D. Wash. 2014).
58 Argenyi v. Creighton University, 703 F. 3d 441 (8th Cir. 2013).

Appendix 1

A Functional Model for Revised Technical Standards (TS) for MD and DO Medical Education Programs, Using Michael Reichgott's Categories[46]

[School name] seeks to produce highly skilled and compassionate doctors. Students are expected to develop a robust medical knowledge base and the requisite clinical skills, with the ability to appropriately apply their knowledge and skills, effectively interpret information, and contribute to patient-centered decisions across a broad spectrum of medical situations and settings. The following technical standards, in conjunction with the academic standards, are requirements for admission, promotion, and graduation. The term "candidate" refers to candidates for admission to medical school as well as current medical students who are candidates for retention, promotion, or graduation. These requirements may be achieved with or without reasonable accommodations. Candidates with disabilities are encouraged to contact [disability office or position] early in the application process to begin a confidential conversation about what accommodations they may need to meet these standards. Fulfillment of the technical standards for graduation from medical school does not guarantee that a graduate will be able to fulfill the technical requirements of any specific residency program.

Category	Technical standard
Acquiring fundamental knowledge	Candidates must be able to learn through a variety of modalities, including, but not limited to, classroom instruction; laboratory instruction, including cadaver lab; physical demonstrations, small-group, team, and collaborative activities; individual study; preparation and presentation of reports; and use of computer technology.
Developing communication skills	Candidates must exhibit interpersonal skills to accurately evaluate patient conditions and responses and enable effective caregiving of patients. Candidates must be able to clearly and accurately record information and accurately interpret patients' verbal and nonverbal communication. Candidates must demonstrate effective communication, participation, and collaboration with all members of a multidisciplinary health care team, patients, and those supporting patients, in person and in writing.
Interpreting data	Candidates must effectively interpret, assimilate, and understand the complex information required to function within the medical school curriculum, including, but not limited to, the ability to comprehend three-dimensional relationships and understand the spatial relationships of structures; synthesize information both in person and via remote technology; interpret causal connections and make accurate, fact-based conclusions based on available data and information; formulate a hypothesis and investigate the potential answers and outcomes; and reach appropriate and accurate conclusions. Candidates must be able to correctly interpret diagnostic representations of patients' physiologic data.
Integrating knowledge to establish clinical judgment	Candidates must conduct routine physical examinations and diagnostic maneuvers to form an accurate and comprehensive assessment of relevant patient health, behavioral, and medical information. Candidates must be able to provide or direct general care and emergency treatment for patients and respond to emergency situations in a timely manner. Candidates must meet applicable safety standards for the environment and follow universal precaution procedures.
Developing appropriate professional attitudes and behaviors	Candidates must exercise good judgment; promptly complete all responsibilities attendant to the diagnosis and care of patients; and develop mature, sensitive, and effective relationships with patients. The skills required to do so include the ability to effectively handle and manage heavy workloads, function effectively under stress, adapt to changing environments, display flexibility, and learn to function in the face of uncertainties inherent in the clinical problems of patients. Candidates are expected to exhibit professionalism, personal accountability, compassion, integrity, concern for others, and interpersonal skills including the ability to accept and apply feedback and to respect boundaries and care for all individuals in a respectful and effective manner regardless of gender identity, age, race, sexual orientation, religion, disability, or any other protected status. Candidates should understand, and function within, the legal and ethical aspects of the practice of medicine and maintain and display ethical and moral behaviors commensurate with the role of a physician in all interactions with patients, faculty, staff, students, and the public. Interest and motivation throughout the educational processes are expected of all candidates.

Appendix 2
A Functional Model for Revised Technical Standards (TS) for MD and DO Medical Education Programs, Using the Association of American Medical Colleges' Categories[3]

[School name] seeks to produce highly skilled and compassionate doctors. Students are expected to develop a robust medical knowledge base and the requisite clinical skills, with the ability to appropriately apply their knowledge and skills, effectively interpret information, and contribute to patient-centered decisions across a broad spectrum of medical situations and settings. The following technical standards, in conjunction with the academic standards, are requirements for admission, promotion, and graduation. The term "candidate" refers to candidates for admission to medical school as well as current medical students who are candidates for retention, promotion, or graduation. These requirements may be achieved with or without reasonable accommodations. Candidates with disabilities are encouraged to contact [disability office or position] early in the application process to begin a confidential conversation about what accommodations they may need to meet these standards. Fulfillment of the technical standards for graduation from medical school does not guarantee that a graduate will be able to fulfill the technical requirements of any specific residency program.

Category	Technical standard
Observational skills	Candidates must acquire information as presented through demonstrations and experiences in the foundational sciences. In addition, candidates must be able to evaluate patients accurately and assess their relevant health, behavioral, and medical information. Candidates must be able to obtain and interpret information through a comprehensive assessment of patients, correctly interpret diagnostic representations of patients' physiologic data, and accurately evaluate patients' conditions and responses.
Communication skills	Candidates must exhibit interpersonal skills to enable effective caregiving of patients, including the ability to communicate effectively, with all members of a multidisciplinary health care team, patients, and those supporting patients, in person and in writing. Candidates must be able to clearly and accurately record information and accurately interpret verbal and nonverbal communication.
Clinical skills	Candidates must perform routine physical examination and diagnostic maneuvers. Candidates must be able to provide or direct general care and emergency treatment for patients and respond to emergency situations in a timely manner. Candidates must meet applicable safety standards for the environment and follow universal precaution procedures.
Intellectual-conceptual, integrative, and cognitive skills	Candidates must effectively interpret, assimilate, and understand the complex information required to function within the medical school curriculum, including, but not limited to, the ability to comprehend three-dimensional relationships and understand the spatial relationships of structures; effectively participate in individual, small-group, and lecture learning modalities in the classroom, clinical, and community settings; learn, participate, collaborate, and contribute as a part of a team; synthesize information both in person and via remote technology; interpret causal connections and make accurate, fact-based conclusions based on available data and information; formulate a hypothesis and investigate potential answers and outcomes; and reach appropriate and accurate conclusions.
Behavioral attributes, social skills, and professional expectations	Candidates must exercise good judgment; promptly complete all responsibilities attendant to the diagnosis and care of patients; and develop mature, sensitive, and effective relationships with patients. The skills required to do so include the ability to effectively handle and manage heavy workloads, function effectively under stress, adapt to changing environments, display flexibility, and learn to function in the face of the uncertainties inherent in the clinical problems of patients. Candidates are expected to exhibit professionalism, personal accountability, compassion, integrity, concern for others, and interpersonal skills including the ability to accept and apply feedback and to respect boundaries and care for all individuals in a respectful and effective manner regardless of gender identity, age, race, sexual orientation, religion, disability, or any other protected status. Candidates should understand, and function within, the legal and ethical aspects of the practice of medicine and maintain and display ethical and moral behaviors commensurate with the role of a physician in all interactions with patients, faculty, staff, students, and the public. Interest and motivation throughout the educational processes are expected of all candidates.

The Ethics of Helping Transgender Men and Women Have Children

Timothy F. Murphy

ABSTRACT A transgender man legally married to a woman has given birth to two children, raising questions about the ethics of assisted reproductive treatments (ARTs) for people with cross-sex identities. Psychiatry treats cross-sex identities as a disorder, but key medical organizations and the law in some jurisdictions have taken steps to protect people with these identities from discrimination in health care, housing, and employment. In fact, many people with cross-sex identities bypass psychiatric treatment altogether in order to pursue lives that are meaningful to them, lives that sometimes include children. Cross-sex identification does not render people unfit as parents, because transgender identities do not undercut the ability to understand the nature and consequences of pregnancy or necessarily interfere with the ability to raise children. Moreover, no evidence suggests that being born to and raised by transgender parents triggers the kind of harm that would justify exclusion of trans-identified men and women from ARTs as a class. The normalization of transgender identities by the law and professional organizations contributes, moreover, to the need to reassess pathological interpretations of cross-sex identities, and trans-parenthood puts those interpretations into sharp relief.

In the 1990s, Tracy Lagondino underwent certain treatments to conform her body to the male-typical appearance that reflected Langondino's gender identity. After those treatments and a change of name, the law recognized Lagondino—now Thomas Beatie—as male, but that legal reclassification did not

---

Department of Medical Education, m/c 591, University of Illinois College of Medicine, 808 S. Wood Street, Chicago IL 60612-7309.
Email: tmurphy@uic.edu.

Perspectives in Biology and Medicine, volume 53, number 1 (winter 2010):46–60
© 2010 by The Johns Hopkins University Press

require the alteration of ovaries, uterus, or vagina. Beatie subsequently married a woman who was unable to bear children. After stopping male hormone treatment, Beatie twice conceived by insemination with donor sperm, gestated the pregnancies, and had two children (Beatie 2008). Prior to these births, a transgender man did have a child, without a fraction of the media attention that followed Beatie's pregnancy, perhaps because that transman was not recognized as male by the law or married in a legal sense (Califia-Rice 2000). As these matters are not monitored, other transgender men may have borne children but not brought their choice to public attention. Even so, some transmen now use on-line networks to discuss options in having children, so more pregnancies in transgender men may be forthcoming.

Both medical ethics and the law have had searching debates about the ethics of helping men and women with nonstandard sexual identities and people in unconventional relationships become parents. Some critics maintain that the rights and welfare of children born to gay and lesbian parents are compromised in serious ways. Law professor Margaret Somerville (2003) makes this argument from a secular point of view, while others do so from religious perspectives (Congregation for the Doctrine of the Faith 1987). These views have not, however, proved an impediment to most lesbian and gay men who want help from fertility clinicians: Western societies have moved toward acceptance of homosexuality in significant ways. With some exceptions, U.S. courts generally have not found a parent's homosexuality to be an impediment to custody and visitation, even in earlier decades when homosexuality was far less accepted than today (Green 1992). In 2008, the California Supreme Court found that a fertility clinic that turned away a lesbian patient had acted in violation of the state's anti-discrimination law (North Coast v. San Diego County Superior Court, 2008). Professional groups in medicine have also moved toward nondiscrimination standards as well. For example, the American Society for Reproductive Medicine (2006) issued an ethics advisory that its members should not turn away men and women looking for help in having children because of their sexual orientation. That's remarkable for happening only 33 years after the American Psychiatric Association (APA) walked away from its judgment that homosexuality is a mental disorder (Bayer 1987).

The debate about homosexuality is, of course, far more settled than the debate about transgender identities. At present, the same psychiatric organization—the APA—that declassified homosexuality as a disorder continues to define "gender identity disorder'" (GID) as pathological. But the question about the nature of transgenderism—disease or not?—is not the only question at stake when it comes to health-care ethics. In light of the choices made by Thomas Beatie and his wife, it is well worth asking whether transgender people are entitled to the same access to assisted reproductive treatments (ARTs) as everyone else. In fact, one clinic turned Beatie and his wife away when they went looking for help in having children (Beatie 2008). Is that a defensible option? Should ARTs be withheld, either because people with the psychiatric disorder of GID are fundamentally compromised as parents, or because children face unacceptable risks by reason of having transgender parents?

The Medical Status of Cross-Sex Identification

According to reigning psychiatric views, people with GID are mentally disordered. The APA describes GID as strong and persistent cross-gender identification, involving persistent discomfort with one's sex or a sense of its inappropriateness and the experience of significant distress or impairment in social interactions, occupation, or other important areas of function so long as these disturbances are not concurrent with a physical intersex condition (APA 1994). Taking this diagnostic category at face value means, of course, that clinicians should work to prevent and treat the disorder where it occurs, whether in children, adolescents, or adults. Indeed, some clinicians work toward exactly that goal (Rekers and Kilgus 1995).

By contrast, some health-care professionals reject the view that transgender identities always represent a mental disorder (Bartlett, Vasey, and Bukowski 2000), as do many people with those identities. Some parties in this debate believe that human beings vary in how they sense themselves as male or female, and that these variations are not pathological in any meaningful sense (McCloskey 1999). Put another way, these commentators think there is no reason why male and female *gender identities* must appear only in male and female *bodies* respectively (Murphy 2004). These commentators find no pathology in cross-sex gender identification, only the variability characteristic of the human species, regardless of whether that variability is ultimately rooted in biology or in psychological development.

Even within psychiatry there is something of a paradox in the professional response to transgender people. Some health professionals are persuaded that there are no broadly validated therapies capable of bringing GID under control—that is, therapies that can restore a male gender identity to male bodies and a female gender identity to female bodies. On the contrary, they think that cross-sex identification can be intractable to treatment, or at least to treatment as it currently exists. Some clinicians therefore believe it is acceptable to offer people with GID the hormone treatments and surgeries they want, that allow them to live in the desired gender role. In this way, the symptoms of the disorder are managed, without directly treating the underlying condition, in much the same way that insulin treatments manage diabetes without altering the underlying disorder. Medical management of symptoms can be enough to give people with diabetes and GID an acceptable quality of life, even though their disorder is never "cured" properly speaking. For example, two leading commentators in this area have said: "When the patient's gender dysphoria is severe and intractable, sex reassignment may be the best solution" (Green and Blanchard 2000). It should be noted that this approach—compliance with requests for sex reassignment—does not by itself repudiate the view that GID is a psychiatric disorder. If a validated treatment for GID came along, I suspect some psychiatrists would withdraw their support for sex reassignment, but in the absence of effective treatments, some clinicians are willing to support gender interventions, even as early as puberty, if not before (à Campo et al. 2003). Their goal is to reduce psychic distress across a lifetime rather than insist on treatment that will not work. Of course, psychiatrists and psychologists who altogether reject the view that cross-sex identification is a disorder see hormonal and surgical body modifications as cosmetic treatments. From that perspective, sex reassignment is not morally problematic so long as clinicians observe professional standards in the treatments they offer: rigorous informed consent, scrupulous avoidance of risk not balanced by corresponding benefit, and humane behavior in the clinical relationship.

This ambiguity within the health-care profession—defining GID as pathological but also accommodating sex reassignment—sends mixed signals, and it is not surprising that some transgender men and women prefer to bypass psychiatric treatment for their "disorder." Some will seek a formal psychiatric diagnosis of GID, but only because some clinicians require as much before they will offer surgery and hormone treatment, not because they believe themselves psychiatrically disordered (Benjamin Gender Dysphoria Association 2001; McCloskey 1999). Paradoxically, a diagnosis under these circumstances liberates people to pursue the body traits and social roles they want without triggering treatment for the underlying disorder in question.

Changes in the social and political perception of transgenderism have also done their part to erode the desirability of psychiatric treatments for GID. For example, the American Medical Association (AMA) has adopted advisories that—if heeded—would effectively decrease the incentives for people to seek treatment for GID. The AMA has said that it is not its policy to discriminate on the basis of gender identity, for all matters falling under its jurisdiction (AMA 2007). The Association also opposes discrimination in society at large and has called on hospitals and health-care institutions to avoid discrimination on the basis of gender identity when assigning staff privileges to medical professionals. It has also called on medical educators to avoid discrimination in admissions to medical school and inappropriate behavior based on the gender identity of students, such as making demeaning or derogatory remarks. Furthermore, it has called for national surveys to address the specific health-care needs of transgender youth and called on youth organizations to reconsider exclusionary policies based on gender identity. The AMA has also pledged itself to work to discourage violence directed against youths because of their gender identity. The AMA also rejects health insurance discrimination based on gender identity and recommends that public and private health insurers cover the treatment of GID, as recommended by the patient's physician, including the cost of body modifications if they are in the patient's best interests (AMA 2008). Overall, the AMA asserts the right of transgender people—mentally ill or not—to have access to important social goods and to receive equitable treatment at the hands of social institutions.

In a sense, these kinds of recommendations treat people with cross-sex identities as a social minority denied access to civil rights, rather than as mentally ill people for whom access to psychiatric treatment is the foremost question, and some legal jurisdictions have taken steps to protect transgender people as a class from civil discrimination. According to the Transgender Law and Policy Institute (2007), as of 2007 13 U.S. states, the District of Columbia, and 93 cities or counties protect against employment and housing discrimination based on gender identity or gender expression. In 2009, a court ruled that transgender federal employees are protected as a matter of law from any wrongful discrimination based on their gender identity (Diamond 2009). To the extent existing law is effective, some jurisdictions afford transgender men and women the prospect of lives free from discrimination, which in turn decreases the incentive to look for any kind of GID cure.

To estimate the consequences of these ethical and legal standards, imagine the life of transgender men and women living under the full force of their protections. If these ethical and legal standards were heeded scrupulously, they would afford transgender youth the right to have their identities taken seriously by health professionals, to participate in youth organizations without ill effect, to enter medical school (or other professional schools) with no expectation of demeaning treatment, and to work at hospitals (or other institutions) of their choosing for the entirety of their careers. To the extent that someone with a cross-sex identity is able to mature, secure health care, secure an education, to find employment, and build relationships, precisely to this extent there is less incentive to secure treatment for GID. If transgender people can achieve rewarding and meaningful lives without treatment and cure of GID, such treatment would be almost beside the point. Where transgender men and women can lead their lives openly and in rewarding ways, they are not only likely to shun psychiatric treatment, and they are likely to explore options that might have been closed off previously. The pregnancy of transgender men has proved to be one of those surprising explorations.

THE ETHICS OF HAVING CHILDREN

There is generally nothing wrong with taking steps to have a child, unless there is some serious risk in doing so. For example, a girl might be too young to have a child, in the sense of being unprepared to cope with pregnancy, or a woman might have medical condition that pregnancy could aggravate, and both females and males of all ages can be wholly unprepared to shoulder parental responsibilities. People with severe, untreated psychoses or schizophrenia may not have the ability to understand the nature and consequences of pregnancy and may be in no position to care for children of any age. Does GID renders transgender men unfit as parents in any similar way? Is there something about the disorder that renders someone incapable of understanding the nature and consequences of pregnancy or carrying out the responsibilities of parenthood?

Strictly speaking, GID represents a very narrow disorder: males and females misapprehend their sex. This disorder does not necessarily involve gross incapacity or general cognitive deficits, though there can be certain co-morbidities. For example, children with GID may exhibit separation anxiety disorder, generalized anxiety disorder, and depression; adolescents may exhibit depression; and adults may exhibit depression or autogynephilia (APA 1994). Strictly speaking, however, there is nothing about cross-gender identification that undermines the ability to understand the nature of pregnancy and parenthood. Transgender people can fully appreciate what it is to conceive, gestate, and give birth to children. Furthermore, there is no reason to think that their desire for children is an artifact of GID, that cross-sex identification induces people to want children: most men and women want to have children. Neither is there anything about GID that necessarily undermines the ability of transgender men and women to understand the responsibilities of parenthood, in regard to feeding a baby, keeping the child warm and clean, playing with the baby, seeing that the child is schooled, or, indeed, any of the other activities that are important to children's welfare. GID does involve distress and discomfort at not having the desired body traits and at being excluded from a specific gender role. Could this distress stand in the way of a transgender man's ability to care for and raise children? If distress or depression were serious enough in a particular individual, they certainly could interfere with the ability to care for children, but that outcome would depend entirely on the extent of the distress and depression. Thomas Beatie seems content in his identity, work life, and relationships. It's not clear that he is disabled from parenthood because of whatever amount of distress, depression, and social stigma he has faced in his life.

By conceiving and gestating a child, Beatie disrupted received opinion about the role of males in having children, which is to provide sperm (at the very least) but not to gestate. From time to time, commentators have chattered about the prospect of pregnant men, thinking though the implications of a male giving birth, but that commentary has focused on gestation in non-transgender men. For example, the psychologist John Money (1988) was persuaded that male pregnancy was possible if an embryo attached to the lining of a male's intestine and if Cesarean section was carried out at the end of gestation, a process that has happened in fact to a few women. Some commentators point out that while this kind of pregnancy is possible in men, it would carry significant risks to the male carrying the pregnancy and to the developing child, if only because there is no prior experience of this kind of event in human history (Teresi 1996). (One Web site, allegedly from an institution called the RYT Hospital [2009] for advanced technologies, did describe a report of pregnancy in a male, but the entire site is a tongue-in-cheek satire.) Beatie's pregnancy short-circuited the established assumptions of this discussion, however, by introducing transgender identities into the mix. Beatie was in a position to bypass worries about unusual gestations, about embryos attached to intestinal walls, and about fetuses growing not within a uterus but amid the sprawl of the intestinal tract. Even so, there are risks in pregnancies like his.

Risks to the Pregnant Party

In his effort to become pregnant, Beatie faced the risks of artificial insemination by donor. Depending on the techniques used, these risks include infection, cramping, puncture wounds, ovarian hyperstimulation syndrome, and the risks of multiple conceptions. Transgender parents might also have an interest in ARTs other than insemination, which would expose them to the risks specific to each of those techniques (Hansen et al. 2005). Pregnant parties face risks of ectopic pregnancy, hypertension, hemorrhage, infection, among others, and pregnant transgender males would face those risks as well (Cunningham et al. 2001). These risks can be minimized and managed through skilled clinical care, and none is of an order that means the techniques should never be used. There is nothing about these risks, moreover, that emerges simply because the party in question is a transgender male rather than a conventional female.

Beatie's pregnancy focused attention on pregnancy in transgender men. Even so, research programs might create the opportunity for pregnancies in transgender women as well. For example, some researchers have carried out vaginal-ovarian-uterine transplants in rats, and they have speculated that these kinds of transplants could open the door to similar transplants in human beings (Lee et al. 1995). Some clinicians have carried out human uterus transplants, though there has not been a successful permanent transplantation, and none has involved a pregnancy (Gosden 2008). If clinicians do achieve uterus transplants that are routinely successful, they need not be permanent. That is, clinicians could transplant a uterus into a woman who has lost her own uterus through disease or injury, or into a transgender woman who never had a uterus to begin with. Techniques of embryo transfer (ET) could then be used to achieve a pregnancy, and at the end of gestation, both the child and the uterus could be removed from the woman's body. Indeed, the apparent objective of uterus transplants is to allow women the opportunity to gestate children, and that experience might be especially desirable for a transgender woman interested in consolidating a female identity that way. It is hard to know whether uterus transplants can become safe and effective, and the prospects for a successful uterus transplant and pregnancy might even be different for transgender women, compared to non-transgender women. However, what will not differ are the calculations that should be made before attempting any such venture: are there good scientific reasons for thinking that the transplant will work, and will the benefits outweigh the risks? At the moment, only speculative answers are available for these questions.

Medical Risks to the Fetus or Child

The pregnant party is not, of course, the only object of ethical concern. In all conceptions and pregnancies, embryos and fetuses face a variety of developmental and genetic disorders as well as risks of premature birth and overlong gestation. People who rely on ARTs may also face risks of multiple pregnancies, certain risks of developmental and genetic disorders in their children, and low birth weights (Cunningham et al. 2001). In transgender men, other risks come into play too: one possible source of risks to the fetus is exposure to the male hormones taken by transgender men to achieve male-typical body traits. To avoid this exposure, Beatie stopped taking testosterone for several months prior to insemination (Beatie 2008). The risks of hormone exposure diminish if a washout period is observed and the body is given time to metabolize and excrete the hormones. Even if some residual hormones remain, this kind of exposure is not unknown during the course of pregnancies in general (Ayeung et al. 2009). Judging from the numbers of babies born through ARTs, most people don't think the risks outweigh the benefits or that the ethical questions involved in those treatments require walking away from the treatments as immoral (Harris and Holm 2003). Most people who turn to ARTs seem to believe that the identifiable risks facing mothers, children, and fathers are outweighed by the benefit of having a child, and that the social implications of these choices can be managed through carefully crafted law and policy.

Psychological Risks to the Child and Family

What about the psychological effects of transgender parents on children and families? In fact, many transgender people already have children, though these children were usually born prior to their parents' shift in gender identity. The psychological well-being of these children is not well studied by any measure, and many questions are worth asking. Is there anything about transgender identity in a parent that harms the child's self-perception or its perception of its family? Does a parent's transgender identity lead children to be confused about their own gender? Does the transgender identity weaken family bonds—parent to child, child to parent, sibling to sibling—in any way? Is there anything about a transgender identity that leads to confusion about family roles on the part of parent or child alike? Is social perception of the child—by classmates as an outsider or freak—possible and likely to have damaging effects?

As I say, this is a poorly studied area, and there are only preliminary studies of these kinds of effects—but what evidence there is does not show meaningful harm. This may be due to the fact that children of transgender parents grow up not knowing any other life: they adapt to the lives they have and know. Children may also be protected from social stigma by the fact that their parents' gender identity need not be known by anyone outside the family. Family dynamics may be altered somewhat by transgendered parents, but family dynamics already vary in terms of how parents relate to their children and how children relate to their parents. In any case, it would be hard to see why transgender parents would have to be "better" than other parents when it comes to attachment to their children, modeling gender roles, and promoting ideal sibling relationships. One expert, Richard Green, looked at the issue in 1978 and concluded that "Available evidence does not support concerns that a parent's transsexualism directly adversely impacts on the children" (p. 697). Twenty years later, Green (1998) revisited the matter but found nothing that required him to change that judgment. Certainly, questions about the propriety of transgender parenthood should be revisited in the future, should evidence come to light that children were systematically harmed in some way, but in the absence of that evidence the welfare of children should not be used as a pretext for denying transmen and transwomen access to ARTs.

Wronged But Not Harmed

Some commentators condemn conception and gestation outside opposite-sex marriage and maintain that children have the right to be born via the sexual intercourse of their married, opposite-sex partners (Congregation for the Doctrine 2008). Many children are, in fact, born under other circumstances: countless babies have been born from IVF and ET, for example, and these children have lives that are virtually indistinguishable from the lives of children born via intercourse in opposite-sex marriage. Yet according to the philosophical perspective just mentioned, these children have been deprived of a right said to belong to children as such. This position creates the paradox that children may be wronged even if they show no signs of harm, ever.

The value of this position turns on how much weight should be given to the idea that children can be wronged even if they are not perceptibly harmed. Judging from effects, this alleged "wrong" does not interfere with the prospect for meaningful and happy lives. If the wrong involves a philosophical injury but does not manifest itself as harm, it seems to me that one can reasonably set this argument to the side when framing law and policy. The idea of a philosophical harm may function as a religious or spiritual ideal for some people, and they may want to take steps to avoid that harm to their children. In the absence of demonstrable harm to children, however, this ideal should not be treated as a convincing reason to exclude people from help in having children who are otherwise fit to do so.

The Significance of Risk for Clinical Practice

Under conditions of uncertainty, clinicians have two possible options when deciding whether to help transmen and transwomen have children. The professions could decline to assist on the grounds that evidence regarding the safety of pregnancy in transgendered men is lacking. This option has the disadvantage, of course, that it will leave unanswered the very question at issue. The other option is to help transgender men have children on the grounds that there is no evidence that doing so must necessarily cause harm to anyone. This option has its own disadvantage: the process might harm children and families before risks become evident.

It is obviously desirable to identify and bypass risks associated with conception and gestation for both the pregnant party and the child alike. However, the threshold for trying to have a child cannot be no risk whatsoever: women and men always face some risk when they act to have children. Responsible parenthood means that men and women should act prudently in decisions concerning whether and when to have children, but the very conditions of human existence mean that risk is an irreducible part of having children. Requiring risk-free conception, gestation, and childhood sets the bar for having children too high to be reasonable.

It is tempting to imagine lots of possible damaging social effects to children born of transgender men, just as earlier it was easy to imagine lots of possible damaging social effects to children born to surrogate mothers, by IVF and ET, children born to unmarried or unpartnered women, and children born to homosexual men and women (single or coupled). Nevertheless, while the risks of pregnancy in transgender men and the overall effects of transgender parents on children are not well studied, the knowable risks do not set this kind of parenting apart from all others. In the absence of risks sufficient to bar the practice altogether, why not set the presumption in favor of transgender men and women using ARTs to have children? After all, many of the dire outcomes predicted for children born in unconventional ways or born to unconventional parents have proved hollow, as shown by the satisfactory welfare of children born by donor insemination, by IVF, or born to gay and lesbian parents. The point that transmen and transwomen have the presumptive right to try and have children is not meant to condone the knowing exposure of pregnant parties and children to non-trivial risk. My point here is that as a matter of equity—treating people alike in relevant ways—it is unfair to require that transgender parents have children only under ideal circumstances, when parents elsewhere have and rear children in ways that involve risks and vagaries that emanate from disease and disorders, from unforeseeable changes in relationships, and from events beyond anyone's control. It would be unacceptable for transgender males to conceive and gestate children if doing so led routinely and predictably to harm, harm that interfered with a child's ability to form and pursue a good life for itself (Savulescu 2001). In the absence of outcomes like that, however, a presumption of liberty to try and have children should prevail for any adults capable of understanding the nature and consequences of pregnancy as well as the responsibilities of parenthood.

Should evidence emerge that parenting by transmen and women causes harms to children in identifiable ways, it does not follow that the clinical professions should cease all efforts to help transgender people have children. Evidence like this should lead clinicians to identify and control the specific cause of those harms. For example, more detailed screening of candidates for clinical services could identify people likely to have problematic pregnancies. Or more attentive medical monitoring during pregnancy might resolve those problems in a way that does not require closing the door to all transgender people wanting to have children.

Disclosure

Questions about helping transgender men and women have children are important, but they are not the only moral concerns associated with transgender parenthood. Like others who have children in unconventional ways, transgender parents will have to decide whether and when to disclose the circumstances of their children's conception and gestation. To some extent, models for disclosure of transgender parenthood exist in disclosures about the use of ARTs, and people who use ARTs have three options when it comes to disclosure. They can try to hide the use of ARTs altogether, they can never hide the circumstances, or they can delay disclosure about the ARTs until the child reaches a certain level of maturity.

Parents who have relied on ARTs do not share uniform opinions about how to make disclosures to their children about the use of donor gametes, donor embryos, intra-cytoplasmic sperm injection, or other ARTs (Peters et al. 2005). In their own family settings, individual parents are replaying questions that society at large is debating about what information should be given to children born via ARTs as a matter of law: what information, for example, are children entitled to in regard to the identity of donors who offered gametes or embryos? Are children entitled to know the identity of the donors, just their general characteristics, their medical history, or nothing at all?

These are broad questions, but this is not the place to settle them all in the detail they require. Let me say, though, that when it comes to transgender parenthood, several arguments converge in support a rule of disclosure by the parents to the child. First of all, secrets are hard to keep; they fall apart for all kinds of unforeseeable reasons. Sometimes death will undo a secret, as it did in 1989, when the three children of musician Billy Tipton learned after his death that the man they knew as their adoptive father was born female (Middlebrook 1998). In other cases, unexpected disclosures can be triggered by a medical evaluation that reveals nongenetic paternity or maternity. Moreover, there is no evidence that disclosures about ARTs necessarily disrupt the psychological well-being of the child or family bonds in general, something that Susan Golombok (2006) has studied extensively. We also know that children can and do accept their parents' transgender identities and thrive in their family relationships (White and Ettner 2007).

Lastly, disclosures about the use of ARTs—when they involve donor gametes or embryos—do make it possible to seek out medical information from donors that is sometimes important to the health care of children born through their use.

These concerns so far bear on the use of ARTs in general, but what about the matter of transgender gestation specifically? Gestation by a transgender man is unusual, but it is not clear that a disclosure of this origin must be disruptive or damaging to a child. Certainly, the circumstances of the child's birth are both intelligible and explicable. This kind of birth is intelligible in the sense that no mysteries or unknowable processes are involved; it is explicable in the sense that the causal chain of events can be identified—there is nothing here that defies understanding. Of course, disclosure must be made to a child on its own terms: perhaps literature written for children could help, just as books written for children help explain adoption and other kinds of family relationships. The actual impact of disclosing to children that they were gestated by the parent whom they know as their father is, of course, knowable only after the fact. For that reason, it will be important to pay close attention to the nature and timing of disclosure to children that they were gestated by a transgender man, just as researchers now study the effects of disclosure and nondisclosure across the range of ARTs (Lycett et al. 2005).

The Significance of Transgender Parenthood

More and more people who never would have had children in the past are now doing so: postmenopausal women who gestate children, infertile heterosexual couples relying on donor gametes and donor embryos, same-sex couples doing the same, single men and women of all sexual orientations turning to surrogate mothers, female same-sex couples sharing the biology of having a child by having one donate the ovum while the other gestates, and women conceiving children by sperm extracted from dead men (Murphy 1993, 1995). Clinicians have given some children the genetic endowment of three parents, through embryo nucleus transplantation into enucleated human ova (Barritt et al. 2001). Against this backdrop of parental practices, the choice by a transgender man to gestate children does not seem beyond the moral pale, especially when that choice is also made within the confines of a legally recognized marriage.

Beatie's choice to gestate is not available, of course, to all transgender men. Some transgender men have hysterectomies, perhaps because they want to leave female-typical traits behind as far as they can. It is unlikely, however, that Thomas Beatie has made a choice that no other transgender men will emulate. In fact, transgender people could even pursue other reproductive options: for example, they might ask to have their ovarian tissue or sperm preserved, so that they could serve as "mother" or "father" to a child even after gender transition to man and woman respectively. How should clinicians respond to requests for ARTs from transgender people looking for help in having children? In the absence of meaningful evidence that children born to transgender parents are injured in systematic or significant ways, fertility clinicians may defensibly help transgender people try to have children. In general, clinicians should rely on the standards that guide their decisions in regard to other prospective parents: whether their clients understand the nature and consequences of ARTs, whether they are healthy enough to bear children, whether they exhibit any psychological deficits that would pose dangers to themselves or their children. Fertility clinicians already evaluate women and men in order to protect them and their children from poor choices (Haseltine et al. 2006), and the same standards should apply transgender men and women. Should evidence come in that children of transgender parents are in fact systematically harmed, then certainly clinicians should reconsider their choices, but only future study will tell whether reconsideration is necessary.

In all of this we should not forget that Thomas Beatie and other transgender men and women are mentally disordered according to the standards of contemporary psychiatry. Whether the APA retains, modifies, or discards the diagnosis of GID depends, of course, on the decisions of its members, who are witness to broad social changes in the social perception of uncommon expressions of gender. No one has a crystal ball to discern how the future will unfold, but perhaps the APA will someday look back on GID as a mistake, in the way it looks back on pathological interpretations of homosexuality as a mistake. Psychiatrists themselves will have to debate this matter, paying attention to scientific studies and, hopefully, the voices of the people most affected by the decisions. In the meantime, the gulf between the psychiatric theory of people with GID (prevent and treat) and the growing social response to gender variation (accept and protect) is likely to widen, if only because these two approaches to transgender identities antagonize one another. Even as this debate about the meaning of cross-sex identities continues, fertility clinicians may offer their help to people wanting children so long as they are healthy enough and prepared for the work ahead, and this standard does not exclude men and women with unconventional gender identities.

References

à Campo, J., et al. 2003. Psychiatric comorbidity of gender identity disorders: A survey among Dutch psychiatrists. *Am J Psychol* 160:1332–36.

American Medical Association (AMA). 2007. Report of the Board of Trustees: Recommendations to modify AMA policy to ensure inclusion for transgender physicians, medical students and patients. http://www.ama-assn.org/ama1/pub/upload/mm/467/bot11a07.doc.

American Medical Association (AMA). 2008. Removing barriers to care for transgender patients (H-185.950). http://www.ama-assn.org/ama1/pub/upload/mm/471/115.doc.

American Psychiatric Association (APA). 1994. Gender identity disorder—302.85 (adult); 302.6 (child), *Diagnostic and statistical manual of mental disorders*, 4th ed. [DSM-IV], 576–82. Washington, DC: APA.

American Society for Reproductive Medicine. Ethics Committee. 2006. Access to fertility treatment by gays, lesbians, and unmarried persons. *Fertil Steril* 86(5):1333–35.

Ayeung, B., et al. 2009. Fetal testosterone and autistic traits. *Br J Psychol* 100(1):1–22.

Barritt, J. A., et al. 2001. Mitochondria in human offspring derived from ooplasmic transplantation. *Hum Reprod* 16(3):513–16.

Bartlett, N. H., P. L. Vasey, and W. M. Bukowski. 2000. Is gender identity disorder in children a mental disorder? *Sex Roles* 43(11–12):753–85.

Bayer, R. 1987. *Homosexuality and American psychiatry*, 2nd ed. Princeton: Princeton Univ. Press.

Beatie, T., 2008. *Labor of love: The story of one man's extraordinary pregnancy*. Berkeley: Seal Press.

Benjamin Gender Dysphoria Association. 2001. Harry Benjamin International Gender Dysphoria Association's standards of care for GID, 6th version, Feb. http://www.wpath.org/documents2/socv6.pdf.

Califia-Rice, P. 2000. Two dads with a difference: Neither of us was born male. *Village Voice*, June 20. http://www.villagevoice.com/2000-06-20/news/family-values/.

Congregation for the Doctrine of the Faith. 1987. *Donum vitae: Instruction on respect for human life in its origin and on the dignity of procreation*. Feb. 22. http://www.vatican.va/roman_curia/congregations/cfaith/documents/rc_con_cfaith_doc_19870222_respect-for-human-life_en.html.

Congregation for the Doctrine of the Faith. 2008. *Dignitas personae*. http://www.usccb.org/comm/Dignitaspersonae/Dignitas_Personae.pdf.

Cunningham, F. G., et al. 2001. *Williams obstetrics*, 21st ed. New York: McGraw-Hill.

Diamond, J. 2009. Transgendered woman wins sex discrimination case. Sept. 19. http://www.abc.news.go.com/TheLaw/Health/story?id=5843396.

Golombok, S. 2006. New family forms. In *Families count: Effects on child and adolescent development*, ed. A. Clarke-Stewart and J. Dunn, 273–98. Cambridge: Cambridge Univ. Press.

Gosden, R. G. 2008. Ovary and uterus transplantation. *Reproduction* 136(6):671–80.

Green, R. 1978. Sexual identity of thirty-seven children raised by homosexual or transsexual parents. *Am J Psychiatry* 135:692–97.

Green, R. 1992. *Sexual science and the law*. Cambridge: Harvard Univ. Press.

Green, R. 1998. Transsexuals' children. *Internat J Transgenderism* 2. http://www.symposion.wm/ijt/ijtc0601.htm.

Green, R., and R. Blanchard. 2000. Gender identity disorders. In *Kaplan and Sadock's comprehensive textbook of psychiatry*, ed. B. A. Sadock and V. A. Sadock, 1646–62. New York: Lippincott, Williams & Wilkins.

Hansen, M., et al. 2004. Assisted reproductive technologies and the risk of birth defects: A systematic review. *Hum Reprod* 20(2):328–38.

Harris, J., and S. Holm, eds. 2003. *The future of human reproduction: Ethics, choice, and regulation*. Oxford: Oxford Univ. Press.

Haseltine, F. P., et al. 2006. Psychological interviews in screening couples undergoing in vitro fertilization. *Ann NY Acad Sci* 442(1):504–16.

Lee, S., et al. 1995. Transplantation of reproductive organs. *Microsurgery* 16(4):191–98.

Lycett, E., et al. 2005. School-aged children of donor insemination: a study of parents' disclosure patterns. *Human Repro* 20(3)810–19.

McCloskey, D. 1999. *Crossing: A memoir*. Chicago: Univ. of Chicago Press.

Middlebrook, D.W. 1998. *Suits me: The double life of Billy Tipton*. Boston: Houghton Mifflin.

Money, J. 1988. *Gay, straight, and in-between: The sexology of erotic orientation*. New York: Oxford Univ. Press.

Murphy, T. F. 1993. Lesbian motherhood and genetic choices. *Ethics Behav* 3(2):211–22.

Murphy, T. F. 1995. Sperm harvesting and postmortem fatherhood. *Bioethics* 9(4):380–98.

Murphy, T. F. 2004. Gender identity and gender identity disorders. In *Encyclopedia of bioethics*, 3rd ed., ed. S. Post, 2:943–48. New York: Macmillan Thomson Gale.

North Coast Women's Care Medical Group, Inc. et al. v. San Diego County Superior Court, S 142892 Ct.App.4/1D045438, 2008.

Peters, C., et al. 2005. Parental attitudes toward disclosure of the mode of conception to their child conceived by in vitro fertilization. *Fertil Steril* 83(4):914–19.

Rekers, G. A., and M. D. Kilgus. 1995. Differential diagnosis and rationale for treatment of gender identity disorders and transvestism. In *Handbook of child and adolescent sexual problems*, ed. G. A. Rekers, 255–71. New York: Lexington Books.

RYT Hospital. 2009. Male pregnancy. http://www.malepregnancy.com.

Savulescu, J. 2001. Procreative beneficence: Why we should choose the best children. *Bioethics* 15(5–6):413–26

Somerville, M. 2003. A brief submitted to the standing committee on justice and human rights. April 29. http://www.marriageinstitute.ca/images/somerville.pdf.

Teresi, D. 1994. How to get a man pregnant. *NY Times*, Nov. 24.

Transgender Law and Policy Institute. 2007. Non-discrimination laws that include gender identity and expression. http://www.transgenderlaw.org/ndlaws/index.htm.

White, T., and R. Ettner. 2007. Adaptation and adjustment in children of transsexual patients. *Eur Child Adolesc Psychiatry* 16(4):215–21.

Engaging in Productive Conversation: Writing Histories of Medicine and Disability in the Middle East and North Africa

SANDY SUFIAN

Department of Medical Education, University of Illinois College of Medicine, Department of Disability and Human Development, University of Illinois-Chicago College of Applied Health Sciences, Chicago, Ill.;
e-mail: sufians@uic.edu
doi:10.1017/S002074381800123X

When I wrote "Mental Hygiene and Disability in the Zionist Project" in 2007, I could not have imagined that there would eventually be an *IJMES* special roundtable on disability and the Middle East. That article, featured in *Disability Studies Quarterly*, charts the place of disability as a historical category and the treatment of disabled people in the Zionist project in Mandate Palestine. In it, I suggest that "the concept of disability figures as a prominent cultural signifier that underscores many facets of the Zionist nationalist project."[1] To illustrate this contention, I specifically examine mental disability as a "marker of whether or not Jews could constitute a legitimate normalized nation" and people with mental illness as objects of selective immigration policy, ultimately translating into prioritized access of the able bodied to the *Yishuv* (Jewish community in Mandate Palestine). Indeed, barriers to immigration based upon disability debunked the movement's promise to welcome all Jews to create a resilient, ideal society.[2] This article was much more in line with the historical interventions of disability history than my book about malaria eradication in Mandate Palestine. Although I had already started to engage with disability history by the time the book was published, I mainly positioned the book within the history of medicine, particularly the subfield of colonial medicine.

Since then, a seminal set of essays featured in the *Bulletin of the History of Medicine* in Winter 2013, and a more recent elaboration on the subject by prominent disability historian Catherine Kudlick in 2018, highlight the distinctions between disability history and the history of medicine but also the potential for these two fields to engage in "productive conversation."[3] As I suggested as part of a 2014 conference panel on the subject, a main distinction between the fields is that a disability historian asks a research question that seeks, *first and foremost*, to understand the meanings of disability and the experiences of disabled people in any given society. According to theorist Aly Patsavas, this priority forms *the* key component of a disability analytic.[4] This analytic derives from the fact that, as Kudlick aptly notes, disability history as a field comes out of the work of the Western disability rights movement; it is fundamentally a project that considers the rich histories of disabled people but also how concepts surrounding disability (like normalcy, difference, marginality, able-bodiedness, deviance, or pathology) structure spatial, family, political, economic, ideological, and societal relations.[5]

In contrast to the history of medicine, which tends to represent people with impairments as patients, disability history also considers the actions and thoughts of people with impairments outside of the clinic, treating them as actors with a full range of interests, ambitions, and politics. Whereas disability historians acknowledge that not all disabled people are actually ill or even interface regularly with the medical establishment, historians of medicine primarily emphasize the workings of medicine, its stakeholders, and its impact upon patients.[6]

Since this academic dialogue began five years ago, scholars and students from both fields have asked: How can we write histories that maintain the respective concerns and emphases of each field but that also reflect a more serious engagement of one with the other? How can such mutuality generate new insights into a multitude of societal dynamics and hierarchies? By extension, I want to ask: what are some possibilities for ways MENA historians can advance this productive conversation, even finding ways to push boundaries and forge new understandings about disability and medicine/public health (or other domains) and how they intersect or diverge in particular localities? The thoughts that I will pose here reflect a partiality to engaging with disability history approaches—since that is where the lacuna in Middle East Studies mostly exists—but I also try to speculate what a history of medicine of the Middle East would look like that treats people with disabilities as historical actors in their own right, rather than as appendages to history.

One of the main questions shared by both disability history and history of medicine is how notions of capacity, fitness, perfection, and normality operate conceptually and practically in nationalist movements. To be sure, within the colonial context, Western medical notions of what constituted the modern body and its symbolic meanings seeped into the ways in which non-Western (but perhaps Western-educated) leaders framed their nationalist projects. Further, colonial medical discourses and those about disability often overlap, which makes sense given their shared foundations in late 19th- and early 20th-century, social Darwinist and eugenic thinking and practices. How do these themes manifest in the territories of British and French colonial rule in the Middle East?

The MENA region offers potentially numerous, intriguing cases to examine such ideas and their practical implications, not only during the period of colonialism but also in postcolonial contexts. First, the MENA scholar could ask: what constitutes these and related notions in Middle Eastern contexts and what cultural and political work do these concepts do at different moments in time? So, for instance, a scholar of Algeria might seek to understand how (or if) these ideas help structure the language and strategies of Algerian resistance to French rule. Other scholars might explore how Arab nationalist leaders refracted correlative concepts in various political texts and/or how (and why) different groups leveraged such ideas in, for example, the Egyptian, Libyan, or Iraqi movements. Using the insights of histories of medicine of Africa or South East Asia to inform a disability analysis of the MENA's case specificities, still others might look at how or if these discourses impacted family relations, debates about the nation's future, and the formulation and implementation of educational or social welfare programs. Scholars could consider more recent historical instantiations, asking how such threads operate(d) in specific antiautocratic Arab revolutionary movements.

Beyond discursive inquiries, explorations about the historical treatment of people with disabilities and how people with disabilities responded to and shaped their communities in MENA remains a relatively open field. Certainly such treatment by the medical and religious establishments, by governments, by political parties, by individual families, and by labor and educational systems, reflects broader societal orientations to vulnerability and fragility, empowerment and tenacity.

Charting the historical treatment of people with disabilities could certainly enhance medical histories that explore, for example, the politics of medical technology and medical care, health NGOs and development, and the impacts of migration, trauma, and war. MENA scholars working in any of those areas could begin to reconsider how the dynamics of medicine, development, and migration, respectively, *affect and are affected by* people with disabilities. A history that engages these concerns could trace the politics of medical care in contemporary Lebanon, for instance, while also giving weight and attention to the providers *and* recipients of medical care, their caregivers, and their interpretations of and engagement with those politics. Certainly thinking about the availability of medical interventions, pharmaceuticals, and networks of care can be part of this account, but a history that pushes the boundaries of disability and medical history would treat patients and healthcare professionals as *not only* inhabiting those roles but also others, like fathers, mothers, sisters, brothers, workers, activists, and public personas. Such a history would treat both types of actors as bringing equally valuable perspectives about Lebanese medical care and society.

For their part, instead of passive or ignored observers, people with disabilities in MENA societies—those interfacing with medical systems or not—have formed disability federations and close disability communities, worked toward greater access to clinical and public spaces, and created innovative tools and strategies to navigate their worlds. Outside of the clinic, they have forged relationships with teachers, siblings, caregivers, employers, and politicians, and have influenced social and cultural terrains. To be sure, people with disabilities embody other axes of identity—age, gender, race, religion, sexuality, and more—which together have produced varied, complicated historical experiences that scholars have yet to explore.

The stories of these people—and of marginalized populations more broadly—should not be written as an "add on" but rather as an integral part of the historical narrative. They can serve as a way to understand societal and political hierarchies, the mechanisms of and forms of resistance to structural violence, and a variety of other phenomena in this very complex region.[7]

I have offered more questions than answers in this short essay but have tried to give *IJMES* readers ways to imagine how to more deeply engage with notions and practices concerning disability in their historical work. I agree with Kudlick that the fields of history of medicine and disability history have distinct orientations that should be honored and preserved. But I have also found in my own research and teaching that when each field's scholarship deeply informs the other, new questions and critical perspectives emerge, leading to well-grounded insights and unexpected conclusions.

NOTES

[1]Sandy Sufian. "Mental Hygiene and Disability in the Zionist project," *Disability Studies Quarterly* 27 (2007): 1.

[2]Ibid., 2, 17.

[3]Catherine Kudlick, "Social History of Medicine and Disability History," in *Oxford Handbook of Disability History*, ed. Michael Rembis, Catherine Kudlick, and Kim E. Nielsen (Oxford: Oxford University Press, 2018), accessed 15 October 2018, http://www.oxfordhandbooks.com/view/10.1093/oxfordhb/9780190234959.001.

0001/oxfordhb-9780190234959-e-7, 3; Kudlick, "Comment: On the Borderland of Medical and Disability History: A Survey of the Fields," *Bulletin of the History of Medicine* 87 (2013): 540–59.

[4]Series of personal conversations between the author and Patsavas on the subject between 2004 and 2017.

[5]Kudlick, "Comment." 540–59. Recently, scholars have also highlighted disability as relational and have contemplated the potential for imagining disability futures; Alison Kafer, *Feminist, Queer, Crip* (Bloomington, Ind.: Indiana University Press, 2013).

[6]Kudlick, "Social History," 3.

[7]Paul Farmer, "On Suffering and Structural Violence: Social and Economic Rights in the Global Era," in *Pathologies of Power: Health, Human Rights and the New War on the Poor* (Berkeley, Calif.: University of California Press, 2004), 29–50.

Notes on DME Contributors

Michael Blackie, PhD
Michael Blackie is Associate Professor of Health Humanities in the Department of Medical Education in the College of Medicine at the University of Illinois at Chicago. He has published widely in health humanities pedagogy and medical education. His scholarly and teaching interests include health humanities, narrative medicine, death studies, and medical education. Before coming to UIC in 2017, Blackie co-directed the Center for Literature and Medicine and chaired the Department of Biomedical Humanities, both at Hiram College, and co-directed the humanities curriculum at Northeast Ohio Medical University. He received his doctorate in English from the University of Southern California, where he taught narrative medicine courses at the Keck School of Medicine. He is associate editor of *The Journal of Medical Humanities*, book review editor for *Literature and Medicine*, and editor of the *Literature and Medicine* book series published by Kent State University Press.

Georges Bordage, MD, MSc, PhD
Georges Bordage is Professor Emeritus in the Department of Medical Education in the College of Medicine at the University of Illinois at Chicago. He is the recipient of four honorary doctoral degrees (Sherbrooke, Moncton, Louvain, Laval), and a visiting professor at the universities of Bern (Switzerland) and Tokyo (Japan). He taught courses in Scholarship in Health Professions Education, Research Design and Grant Writing, and Scientific Writing. His research includes the study of clinical reasoning, the written and oral assessment of clinical decisions (including the "key features" approach first developed for the Medical Council of Canada in the early 90's and now used worldwide), the hypothesis-driven approach to teaching and assessing the physical exam, and scientific writing. He is the recipient of multiple awards, including the Abraham Flexner Award of the Association of American Medical Colleges for extraordinary contributions to the medical education community, the John P. Hubbard Award from the National Board of Medical Examiners for significant contributions to the pursuit of excellence in the field of evaluation in medicine, the American Education Research Association Distinguished Career Award, and the Dr. Louis Levasseur Distinguished Service Award for Outstanding Contributions to the Vision and Mission of the Medical Council of Canada.

Raymond H. Curry, MD
Raymond Curry is Senior Associate Dean for Educational Affairs at the University of Illinois College of Medicine, and Professor of Medicine and Medical Education at the University of Illinois at Chicago. As chief academic officer of the College, he oversees educational programs across the school's four campuses in Chicago, Peoria, Rockford, and Urbana. A native of Lexington, Kentucky, Dr. Curry is a graduate of the University of Kentucky and of the Washington University School of Medicine in St. Louis. He completed residency training in internal medicine at Northwestern University/McGaw Medical Center in 1985. From 1998 to 2014, Dr. Curry served as vice dean for education at Northwestern University Feinberg School of Medicine, and from 2004 to 2014 also served as president of the McGaw Medical Center of Northwestern University. Dr. Curry's academic interests

include the study and teaching of doctor-patient communication and the role of learner-centered educational methods in promoting patient-centered care. He also focuses on the enhancement of access to medical education for those under-represented in the profession, in particular students with disabilities, and has extensive experience in curriculum development and medical school accreditation.

Marcia Edison, PhD
Marcia Edison is Research Assistant Professor in the Department of Medical Education. She joined DME as a postdoctoral fellow in 1997 shortly after receiving her PhD in Higher Education Policy from UIC. She came late to the field of medical education, having served as a university administrator from 1979 until 1994 at Illinois Institute of Technology. Dr. Edison earned her MBA degree from the University of Chicago (Booth) Graduate School of Business in 1976, where she specialized in the management of not-for-profit enterprises. Since joining DME, she co-authored grant proposals that resulted in awards to the University of over $4 million. Currently, Dr. Edison works not only with DME but also with the UIC Center for Global Health and the UIC Department of Emergency Medicine.

Jorge Girotti, PhD
Jorge Girotti is Research Assistant Professor in the Department of Medical Education (DME). He is also Director of the Hispanic Center of Excellence, which aims to promote science and medical careers for Hispanic youth, expose undergraduate and medical students to biomedical and clinical research, and increase the representation of Latino faculty in our medical school. In addition to his DME faculty duties, he is the Associate Dean for Admissions and Special Curricular Programs for the College of Medicine. In this capacity he oversees the admissions process to the MD program, as well as Joint Degree programs (MD-MPH, MD-MBA, and MD-MS-CTS), the Guaranteed Professional Program Admissions (GPPA) in Medicine, and the Urban Medicine program. Dr. Girotti's research interests reflect his focus on the development of opportunities for students from minority and disadvantaged backgrounds. The design, implementation, and evaluation of educational programs to improve cultural competence among physicians and other health professionals, and programs to improve leadership skills in future physicians are his current priorities. Dr. Girotti's research and training work has been funded by Federal agencies (National Institutes of Health, Agency for Healthcare Research and Quality, Health Resources and Services Administration), by foundations (Chicago Community Trust, Portes Foundation), and by UIC (Vice Chancellor for Research, Council for Excellence in Teaching and Learning).

Ilene B. Harris, PhD
Ilene Harris is Professor, Departments of Medical Education (DME) and of Pathology, and Associate Dean of Strategic Communication for the College of Medicine (COM). She was Head of DME from 2008 to 2019, and Director of Graduate Studies and of the Masters in Health Professions Education (MHPE) program. Currently, she is Director of the collaborative PhD program, with the UIC College of Education (COE), in Curriculum Studies with a concentration in Health Professions Education. She completed her bachelor's, master's and doctoral degrees at the University of Chicago. She has had national leadership roles, serving as Chair for the Association of American Medical Colleges (AAMC)

Research in Medical Education (RIME) Steering Committee and AAMC Central Region RIME Section, as well as President of the Division of Education in the Professions (Division I) in the American Educational Research Association (AERA). Her research, reported in over 150 publications and 400 presentations, has focused on curriculum deliberation, qualitative methods, performance assessment, and program evaluation. Dr. Harris is on the editorial board of leading journals, among which are the *Archives of Pathology & Laboratory Medicine* and also *Evaluation and the Health Professions*. She has received prestigious awards, including: the AERA Division I Distinguished Career Award, given every two years for having a "significant impact on research in the Professions"; the CGEA Medical Education Laureate award for Leadership, Faculty Development, and Scholarly Standards; and UIC awards for excellence in teaching and exceptional contributions to UIC College of Medicine programs.

Laura E. Hirshfield, PhD

Laura Hirshfield is Assistant Professor in the Department of Medical Education and faculty affiliate in the Department of Sociology at the University of Illinois at Chicago. She received her Ph.D. in Sociology from the University of Michigan and her B.A. from Swarthmore College, where she studied Sociology/Anthropology and Education. In her work at UIC, Dr. Hirshfield works closely with a variety of trainees, including undergraduates, medical students, residents, faculty, and graduate students (both in Health Professions Education and in Sociology). A sociologist and ethnographer by training, Dr. Hirshfield is broadly interested in social interaction, identity, education, science, work/organizations, and medicine. Her research centers on gender and other forms of inequality in academic and clinical settings, particularly in the natural sciences and medicine. Her main research includes studies focusing on the "hidden labor" undertaken by and expected of members of marginalized groups in the workplace, cultural competence (broadly defined) in medical contexts (particularly related to trans patients), and socialization (especially regarding communication and emotions) in medical school.

Kristi L. Kirschner, MD

Kristi Kirschner is Clinical Professor in the Department of Medical Education. She is a physician in Physical Medicine and Rehabilitation with a certificate in Clinical Medical Ethics from the MacLean Center at the University of Chicago. Dr. Kirschner joined UIC four years ago. Much of her academic work over the past 25 years has focused on access to care, disability, and ethics, including developing and facilitating educational curriculum for medical students. She is currently serving on the College of Medicine's curricular transformation team as subtheme leader for the health humanities curriculum.

Timothy Murphy, PhD

Timothy Murphy is Professor of Philosophy in the Biomedical Sciences and holds a doctorate in philosophy from Boston College. He teaches and conducts research in the areas of professional ethics, assisted reproductive technologies, medicine and sexuality, and ethical aspects of genetic research. He is the author or editor of nine books, including *Justice and the Human Genome Project* (University of California Press), *Gay Science: The Ethics of Sexual Orientation Research* (Columbia University Press), and *Case Studies in*

Biomedical Research Ethics (The MIT Press). His most recent book is *Ethics, Sexual Orientation, and Choices about Children* (The MIT Press). He has published widely in professional journals such as the *Journal of Medical Ethics, American Journal of Bioethics, Bioethics, Cambridge Quarterly of Healthcare Ethics*, and *Reproductive Biomedicine Online*, among others. His work has been supported by grants from the U.S. Department of Defense and the National Institutes of Health. He has been a member of ethics committees for such groups as the American College of Surgeons Oncology Group, the American Academy of Pain Medicine. He has been a visiting scholar at the Institute for Ethics of the American Medical Association and is a member of the editorial board of the journal *Bioethics*.

Pilar Ortega, MD
Pilar Ortega is Clinical Assistant Professor and Medical Spanish Instructor. She is an emergency physician who completed her undergraduate work at Johns Hopkins University and her graduate and residency training at the University of Chicago. She has taught medical Spanish for over 15 years, authored a textbook for teaching medical Spanish, and is the founder and director of the Medical Spanish Taskforce (MST)—a collaborative interdisciplinary network, including physicians, medical educators, linguists, interpreters, and researchers across the country. Dr. Ortega is also the Co-Founder and President of the Medical Organization for Latino Advancement (MOLA), a Chicago-based non-profit association with goals to improve Latino health equity, diversity, and inclusion. She has received numerous awards on a local, national, and international setting, including Crain Magazine's 40 under 40 (2017), the National Hispanic Medical Association's Young Physician of the Year (2018), and Spain's Royal National Academy of Medicine Award for Health Information, Communication and Dissemination (2018) for her commitment to developing medical communication skills in Spanish to enhance care for Spanish-speaking patients on a global scale.

Christine Park, MD
Christine Park is Professor of Clinical Anesthesiology (Department of Anesthesiology) and Professor of Clinical Medicine (Department of Medical Education) at the University of Illinois at Chicago. She serves as Director of the Graham Clinical Performance Center, and as the Associate Head for Learning and Innovation in the Department of Anesthesiology. Dr. Park received her undergraduate degree in English Literature at Yale University, followed by her MD degree from Indiana University School of Medicine. She completed anesthesiology residency at the Brigham and Women's University. Dr. Park is Past-President of the Society for Simulation in Healthcare, a global non-profit organization comprising nearly 4000 members from more than 50 countries. She is also a member of the editorial board of its journal, *Simulation in Healthcare*. Her interests include leadership development, dynamic decision-making during critical events, maintenance of competence in practicing providers, and most importantly, finding and growing new applications for simulation across the health professions.

Yoon Soo Park, PhD
Yoon Soo Park is Associate Professor and Associate Head of the Department of Medical Education. He is also Director of Research for the Office of Educational Affairs at the

University of Illinois – College of Medicine. He holds a Ph.D. in Measurement, Evaluation, and Statistics from Columbia University. Dr. Park's experiences include both academic and industry settings, with research interests and experiences across multiple disciplines in psychometrics, biostatistics, educational psychology, and medicine. Dr. Park's research agendas have focused on psychometric methods, focusing on statistical modeling of educational and psychological processes using latent class models and item response theory models. Dr. Park serves and contributes to national and international professional organizations. He is Incoming Chair of the Association of American Medical Colleges (AAMC) Research in Medical Education (RIME) Committee and is currently Vice President of the American Educational Research Association (AERA), serving Division I: Education in the Professions.

Janet Riddle, MD
Janet Riddle is Research Assistant Professor and Director of Faculty Development in the Department of Medical Education. She has been involved in faculty development in the health professions since completing her Internal Medicine residency. While at Rush University Medical Center, she developed a residents-as-teachers program for the Department of Internal Medicine and co directed a HRSA-funded faculty development program for clinician-teachers at Cook County Hospital. Since joining the Department of Medical Education at UIC, she has directed teaching skills programs for medical students and resident physicians. She is the director of and primary instructor in a longitudinal faculty development program, the Scholars for Teaching Excellence Faculty Fellowship. Her research interests focus on longitudinal faculty development programs as communities of practice. Dr. Riddle is currently studying the processes that contribute to learning and uses qualitative approaches such as semi-structured interviews, focus groups, and analysis of reflective writing.

Leslie Sandlow, MD
Leslie Sandlow is former Head of the Department of Medical Education. He had been an adjunct member for many years and in 1993 was appointed Interim Head of the Department. In 1996, following a search, he became permanent Head. Prior to his retirement in 2010, he also served the College as Associate Dean for Graduate Medical Education and Continuing Medical Education; and as the Senior Associate Dean for Medical Education encompassing the continuum of education throughout the four program sites of the College. In addition to his academic appointment as Professor of Medical Education, he is Professor of Medicine in the Department of Medicine. Prior to coming to UIC, in 1989 he was Senior Vice President for Academic & Medical Affairs at Michael Reese Hospital & Medical Center. In his years at Michael Reese Hospital, he held numerous medical administrative positions as well as establishing the Educational Unit which flourished until the hospital was sold to a for-profit chain. He has been a surveyor for Liaison Committee on Medical Education & the Accreditation Council for Continuing Medical Education. His research interests include outcomes research and evidence-based medicine, program evaluation, curricular design and innovation, and use of new teaching modalities and media in education. Clinical teaching and innovation in Graduate Medical Education teaching and assessment.

Alan Schwartz, PhD
Alan Schwartz is Professor and Interim Head, The Michael Reese Endowed Professor of Medical Education, Department of Medical Education and Research Professor for the Department of Pediatrics. Dr. Schwartz joined DME in 1997 after receiving his PhD in Cognitive Psychology and MS in Organizational Behavior and Industrial Relations from the University of California, Berkeley. His research interests include the psychology of decision making among patients and physicians. Among patients, his work has focused on risk perception, patient-physician fit, and the impact of non-medical goals on the evaluation of health states. In physicians, his work has focused on contextual errors in decision making and updating beliefs when exposed to new evidence. Dr. Schwartz has received the John M. Eisenberg Award for Practical Application of Medical Decision Making Research, the Ray E. Helfer Award for Innovation in Pediatric Education, the UIC Distinguished Researcher of the Year award, the UIC Honors College Fellow of the Year award, and three UIC teaching awards, including the Excellence in Teaching award, UIC's highest recognition for teaching. He serves as Editor-in-Chief of the journals *Medical Decision Making* and *Medical Decision Making Policy & Practice*, and Director of the Association of Pediatric Program Directors Longitudinal Educational Assessment Research Network (APPD LEARN). His most recent books are *Listening for What Matters: Avoiding Contextual Errors in Health Care* (with Saul Weiner, Oxford University Press, 2015) and *Medical Decision Making: A Physician's Guide* (with George Bergus, Cambridge University Press, 2008).

Sandra Sufian, PhD, MPH
Sandra Sufian is Associate Professor of Health Humanities and History in the Department of Medical Education at UIC College of Medicine and Associate Professor of Disability Studies in the Department of Disability and Human Development. Sufian received her doctorate from New York University in Middle East History and her Masters of Public Health in Epidemiology and Biostatistics from Oregon Health Sciences University. Dr. Sufian specializes in the history of medicine and disability. She has published two books: *Healing the Land and the Nation: Malaria and the Zionist project in Mandatory Palestine, 1920-1947* (U Chicago Press, 2007) and *Reapproaching the Border: New Perspectives on the Study of Israel/Palestine* (Rowman Littlefield, 2007). Sufian is currently working on a book project about the history of disability and adoption in America in the twentieth century. She teaches courses on the history of disability and the modern history of medicine and public health to medical students, PhD students, and undergraduate students. She co-organizes the Health and Society working group of the Institute for the Humanities and is the founder of the Global Network of Researchers on HIV/AIDS in the Middle East and North Africa. Dr. Sufian is chair of the Disability History Association and serves on the editorial boards of *Disability Studies Quarterly* and the *International Journal of Middle East Studies*.

Ara Tekian, PhD, MHPE
Ara Tekian is Professor and Director of International Affairs at the Department of Medical Education (DME), and the Associate Dean for the Office of International Education at the College of Medicine, the University of Illinois at Chicago (UIC). He joined DME in 1992, and is involved in both teaching courses offered in the Master's of Health Professions

Education (MHPE) program and advising graduate students. He is the recipient of the 2012 ASME (Association for the Study of Medical Education) Gold Medal Award which is one of the most prestigious international awards in medical education. In 2014, he was honored by receiving the most revered Lifetime Achievement Award by the Armenian American Medical Society. He also received the "Faculty of the Year" award from DME in 2015. He has served as the President of the Division of Education in the Professions of the American Educational Research Association (AERA) from 2009 to 2012, which is a major venue for presentation of scholarship in health professions education. In 2017, Dr. Tekian received AERA's most prestigious Division I's Distinguished Career Award. He was also the 2017 recipient of the Ellis Island Medal of Honor, which recognizes individuals who have made their mission to share with those less fortunate their wealth of knowledge, courage, compassion, and unique talents, all while maintaining the traditions of their ethnic heritage as they uphold the vision and spirit of America.

Annette L. Valenta, DrPH
Annette Valenta is Professor and Academic Director of the Patient Safety Leadership (PSL) programs. She was a founding member of Institute for Patient Safety Excellence (IPSE) at UIC. With funding from the Agency for Healthcare Research & Quality (AHRQ), Health and Human Services, the Department of Defense, the National Patient Safety Foundation, and the National Institutes of Health, Dr. Valenta's research and teaching focus on social and organizational issues related to health technology, including the role information systems play in patient safety. She was a consulting faculty member for the AHRQ-funded grant entitled "The Seven Pillars: Crossing the Patient Safety-Medical Liability Chasm". Dr. Valenta's publications have appeared in major journals such as the *Journal of the American Medical Informatics Association, Academic Medicine, International Journal of Computational Models and Algorithms in Medicine, Aviation, Space and Environmental Medicine, Joint Commission Journal on Quality and Patient Safety,* and *International Journal of Health Policy and Management*. She has chaired two national committees leading to the establishment of content domains and core competencies in the fields of quality and safety as well as health informatics. In recognition of her work, she was awarded the 2016 Leadership Award by the American Medical Informatics Association.

Sandra L. Yingling, PhD
Sandra Yingling is Associate Dean of Educational Planning and Quality Improvement for all three of the College of Medicine's regional campuses. Dr. Yingling oversees the design and implementation of student assessment and curricular program evaluation systems. She identifies new technologies for collecting, analyzing, and visualizing medical education data, with an emphasis on creating self-regulated learning cycles for students and quality improvement cycles for leadership and teaching faculty.

Rachel Yudkowsky, MD, MHPE
Rachel Yudkowsky is Professor and Interim Director of Graduate Studies in the Department of Medical Education at the University of Illinois at Chicago College of Medicine. She served as Director of the Dr Allan L and Mary L Graham Clinical Performance Center

from 2000 to 2018, where she developed standardized patient and simulation-based programs for the instruction and assessment of students, residents, and staff. She also served as Director of the University of Illinois Health Sciences Simulation Consortium from 2009 to 2018. Dr. Yudkowsky received her MD from Northwestern University Medical School in 1979 and is Board Certified in Psychiatry. She obtained her Master in Health Professions Education (MHPE) degree from UIC in 2000. Dr. Yudkowsky served as Chair of the Research and Grants Committee of the Association of Standardized Patient Educators (ASPE) from 2007 to 2009. She was the founding Co-President of the Chicago Simulation Consortium (CSC) in 2013, and served as Chair of the CSC Professional Development Committee from 2015 to 2017. She was an Associate Editor of the journal *Simulation in Healthcare* from 2015 to 2017. She received the Outstanding Educator Award from ASPE in 2009, and the Society for Simulation in Healthcare SP SIG Award in 2016. Areas of research interest include performance assessment using standardized patients and other simulations, especially for physical exam skills, communication skills, clinical reasoning, and basic procedural skills; and setting passing standards for performance exams.

Past and Present DME Faculty

Over the years, many faculty have worked in the Department of Medical Education. Here we list all faculty appointed primarily in DME during its history. Unfortunately, Department and University records have not always survived UIC's many changes; the list below is necessarily incomplete. Our apologies to any faculty whose names we were unable to locate. Please contact us, as necessary, to help us correct our records.

Names of past and present Directors and Department Heads are underlined.

Alberti, Jean
Algina, James
Alschuler, Marjorie
Anderson, Max
Barzansky, Barbara
Bashook, Philip
Berner, Eta
Bernstein, Lionel
Bers, Howard
Blackie, Michael
Bladwin, Lisa
Bligh, Thomas
Bobula, James
Bordage, Georges
Brier, Ellen
Browdy, Marshall
Bussigel, Margaret
Campbell, M. Lory
Chan, Kee
Chapman, Gretchen
Christiansen, Caryn
Clemmons, James
Conley, Patrick
Connell, Karen
Crawford, William
Curry, Raymond
Diekma, Anthony
Douard, John
Downing, Steven
Edison, Marcia
Elstein, Arthur
Elster, Nanette
Engel, John
Filling, Constance
Fletcher, William
Foley, Richard
Ford, David
Forman, Philip
Fortna, Greg
Fox, Ellen
French, Ruth

Gaines, Ann
Gali, Kari
Gamble, Thomas
Garg, Mohan
Gelula, Mark
Getz, Howard
Gevitz, Norm
Gifford, Frederick
Gilman, Sander
Giordano, Fran
Girotti, Jorge
Goldberg, Julie
Gorr, Alan
Grenholm, Gary
Grobman, Hulda
Gross, Leon
Grove, William
Guerin, Robert
Gunderson, Anne
Halpern, Sydney
Harliss, William
Harris, Ilene
Hazelip, David
Heinemann, Ruth
Hemmelgarn, Carole
Hirshfield, Laura
Holzemer, William
Hynes, Kevin
Juul, Dorthea
Kamin, Carol
Keunstler, Amanda
Kirschner, Kristi
Kleinmuntz, Benjamin
Lackmann, John
LaDuca, Anthony
Lappe, Marc
Lee, Laura
Leonardi, Michael
Levine, Harold
Lineberry, Matthew
Lipetz, Marcia

Lipson, Laurette
Lochman, John
Loiacono, David
Madigan, Jeanne
Martin, Isabel
Mavrias, Sherri
McGaghie, William
McGuire, Christine
Melnik, Michael
Michaels, Robert
Michel, Joanna
Miller, George
Monahan, James
Moon, Margaret
Mrtek, Robert
Murphy, Timothy
Myers, Robert
Nerenberg, Renee
Noe, Michael
Nord, Lynn
Olson, Carl
Ortega, Pilar
Ozog, Gregory
Pach, Alfred
Page, Gordon
Park, Christine
Park, Yoon Soo
Pascarella, Ernest
Payne, Jobe
Penta, Frank
Perlmutter, Shirley
Perloff, Janet
Pinsker, Eva
Pochyly, Donald
Poirier, Suzanne
Popovich, Elizabeth
Pukala, Donald
Quinlan, Thomas
Razfar, Aria
Rezler, Agnes
Richards, Ronald

Riddle, Janet
Risley, Betty
Risley, Mary
Sajid, Abdul
Sandlow, Leslie
Schwartz, Alan
Seefeldt, Michael
Sharf, Barbara
Sheverbush, Robert
Shirkey, William
Simpson, Kenneth
Smilansky, Jonathan
Smith, Kelly
Sorlie, William
Sovine, Melanie
Stapleton, Gerald
Steinberg, Louis
Sufian, Sandra
Swerdlow, Martin
Tajeu, Kathleen
Tekian, Ara
Telder, Thomas
Trent, Pamela
Troy, Loreen
Tyska, Cynthia
Urogulo, Peggy
Valenta, Annette
Vaux, Kenneth
Vukotich, George
Ways, Peter
Weiner, Saul
Wezeman, Fredenida
Williams, Reed
Wolf, Charles
Yingling, Sandra
Yonke, Annette
York, Joseph
Yudkowsky, Rachel
Zimmerman, Thomas

Citations and Credits

Names of past and present Department of Medical Education faculty members are underlined.

Blackie M, Wear D, Zarconi J. Narrative intersectionality in caring for marginalized or disadvantaged patients: Thinking beyond categories in medical education and care. *Acad Med.* 2019;94(1):59-63. doi: 10.1097/ACM.0000000000002425. Reprinted with permission from Wolters Kluwer Health, Inc.

Blouin D, Tekian A, Kamin C, Harris IB. The impact of accreditation on medical schools' processes. *Med Educ.* 2018;52(2):182-191. doi:10.1111/medu.13461. Reprinted with permission from John Wiley and Sons.

Bordage G, Page G. The key-features approach to assess clinical decisions: validity evidence to date. *Adv Health Sci Educ.* 2018;23(5):1005-1036. doi:10.1007/s10459-018-9830-5. Reprinted with permission from Springer Nature.

Girotti JA, Loy GL, Michel JL, Henderson VA. The Urban Medicine Program: Developing physician–leaders to serve underserved urban communities. *Acad Med.* 2015;90(12):1658-1666. doi:10.1097/ACM.0000000000000970. Reprinted with permission from Wolters Kluwer Health, Inc.

Hirshfield LE, Yudkowsky R, Park YS. Pre-medical majors in the humanities and social sciences: impact on communication skills and specialty choice. *Med Educ.* 2019;53(4):408-416. doi:10.1111/medu.13774. Reprinted with permission from John Wiley and Sons.

Kezar LB, Kirschner KL, Clinchot DM, Laird-Metke E, Zazove P, Curry RH. Leading Practices and Future Directions for Technical Standards in Medical Education. *Acad Med.* 2019;94(4):520-527. doi:10.1097/ACM.0000000000002517. Reprinted with permission from Wolters Kluwer Health, Inc.

Murphy TF. The ethics of helping transgender men and women have children. *Perspect Biol Med.* 2010;53(1):46-60. doi:10.1353/pbm.0.0138. Reprinted with permission from The Johns Hopkins University Press.

Ortega P. Spanish language concordance in US medical care: A multifaceted challenge and call to action. *Acad Med.* 2018;93(9):1276-1280. doi:10.1097/ACM.0000000000002307. Reprinted with permission from Wolters Kluwer Health, Inc.

Park CS, Stojiljkovic L, Milicic B, Lin BF, Dror IE. Training induces cognitive bias: the case of a simulation-based emergency airway curriculum. *Simul Healthc.*

2014;9(2):85-93. doi: 10.1097/SIH.0b013e3182a90304. Reprinted with permission from Wolters Kluwer Health, Inc.

Park YS, Riddle J, Tekian A. Validity evidence of resident competency ratings and the identification of problem residents. *Med Educ.* 2014;48(6):614-622. doi: https://doi.org/10.1111/medu.12408. Reprinted with permission from John Wiley and Sons.

Ramesh A, LaBresh KA, Begeman R, Bobrow B, Campbell T, Chaudhury N, Edison M, et al. Implementing a STEMI system of care in urban Bangalore: Rationale and Study Design for heart rescue India. *Contemp Clin Trials Commun.* 2018;10:105-110. doi:10.1016/j.conctc.2018.04.002. Reprinted open access article under the CC BY-NC-ND license (http://creativecommons.org/licenses/BY-NC-ND/4.0/).

Riddle JM. Lessons from practice. *Inter J H Educ.* 2018;2(1):6-8. doi:10.17267/2594-7907ijhe.v2i1.2026. Reprinted open access article under a Creative Commons Attribution 4.0 International License (http://creativecommons.org/Licenses/by/4.0/).

Schoenbaum SC, Crome P, Curry RH, et al. Policy issues related to educating the future Israeli medical workforce: an international perspective. *Isr J Health Policy Res.* 2015;4(1):37. doi: 10.1186/s13584-015-0030-y. Reprinted open access article under a Creative Commons Attribution 4.0 International License (http://creativecommons.org/Licenses/by/4.0/).

Schwartz A, Young R, Hicks PJ, APPD LEARN F. Medical education practice-based research networks: facilitating collaborative research. *Med Teach.* 2016;38(1):64-74. doi:10.3109/0142159X.2014.970991. Reprinted open access article under the terms of the Creative Commons Attribution License (http://creativecommons.org/Licenses/by/4.0/).

Sufian S. Engaging in Productive Conversation: Writing Histories of Medicine and Disability in the Middle East and North Africa. *Int J Middle East Stud.* 2019;51(1):120-123. doi: 10.1017/S002074381800123X. Reprinted with permission from Cambridge University Press.

Tekian A, Boulet J. A longitudinal study of the characteristics and performances of medical students and graduates from the Arab countries. *BMC Med Educ.* 2015;15(1):200. doi:10.1186/s12909-015-0482-3. Reprinted open access article under a Creative Commons Attribution 4.0 International License (http://creativecommons.org/Licenses/by/4.0/).

Valenta AL, Berner ES, Boren SA, et al. AMIA Board White Paper: AMIA 2017 core competencies for applied health informatics education at the master's degree level. *J Am Med Inform Assoc.* 2018;25(12):1657-1668. doi:10.1093/jamia/ocy132. Reprinted with permission from Oxford University Press.

Yingling S, Park YS, Curry RH, Monson V, Girotti J. Beyond cognitive measures: Empirical evidence supporting holistic medical school admissions practices and professional identity formation. *MedEdPublish.* 2018;7. doi:10.15694/mep.2018.0000274.1. Reprinted open access article under Creative Commons "CC BY 4.0" (https://creativecommons.org/licenses/by-sa/4.0/).

Yudkowsky R, Downing SM, Sandlow LJ. Developing an institution-based assessment of resident communication and interpersonal skills. *Acad Med.* 2006;81(12):1115-1122. doi: 10.1097/01.ACM.0000246752.00689.bf. Reprinted with permission from Wolters Kluwer Health, Inc.

Yudkowsky R, Otaki J, Lowenstein T, Riddle J, Nishigori H, Bordage G. A hypothesis-driven physical examination learning and assessment procedure for medical students: initial validity evidence. *Med Educ.* 2009;43(8):729-740. doi:10.1111/j.1365-2923.2009.03379.x. Reprinted with permission from John Wiley and Sons.